THE PRINCIPLES OF NAVIGATION

The Principles of Navigation

E. W. ANDERSON

O.B.E. D.F.C., A.F.C., F.R.Met.S., F.R.I.N.

Royal Institute of Navigation
Gold Medallist, 1965

Foreword by
D. H. SADLER, O.B.E.

Superintendent of H.M.
Nautical Almanac Office

HOLLIS & CARTER

LONDON   SYDNEY

TORONTO

© E. W. Anderson 1966
ISBN 0-370-00311-X
Printed and bound in Great Britain for
Hollis & Carter
an associate company of
The Bodley Head Ltd
9 Bow Street, London WC2E 7AL
by Redwood Burn Ltd,
Trowbridge & Esher
Set in Monotype Imprint
First published 1966
Second impression 1970
Third impression 1979

To the Manx Shearwater
that, taken from his nest off the coast
of Wales and carried three thousand miles
across the Atlantic to Boston,
was back in twelve days.

Foreword

by D. H. SADLER, o.b.e.

Superintendent of H.M. Nautical Almanac Office,
former President of the Institute of Navigation

In 1939 E. W. Anderson was headmaster of a school. By 1945, in addition to being an outstandingly successful operational navigator, he had acquired within the Royal Air Force a reputation for brilliant unorthodoxy. He combined three rather unusual qualities: the ability to see straight through the conventional approach to a technical subject to the basic principles, and to understand them thoroughly; the imagination to visualize, in the broadest terms and unencumbered by orthodox treatments, the most direct application of those principles to practical navigation; and a flair for vivid presentation. Even before the end of the war he had made many significant contributions to navigational techniques, and had injected new thoughts into navigational philosophy. Many generations of school-boys have been the poorer for having lost the inspiration of his teaching as a result of his decision to remain in the R.A.F. after the war; but navigation, and all connected with navigation, have gained immeasurably.

Wing Commander Anderson has since devoted himself, almost entirely, to navigation; professionally in the Royal Air Force, and later in private industry, he has acquired a thorough appreciation of the operational and engineering aspects of navigation, to add to his already wide theoretical knowledge and practical experience. But it is through his many activities in the Institute of Navigation (he was President in 1959–1961, and Chairman of the Technical Committee for 1952–1957 and again for 1962–1964) that his special qualities have still further developed and have been fully exercised. It is no coincidence that, before the publication of this book, which will undoubtedly add much to his stature, the Council awarded him the Gold Medal of the Institute, 'in recognition of the leadership and inspiration that he has provided, throughout many years and in many distinct aspects on the subject, to all concerned with navigational matters; and in recognition of the importance and originality of his ideas and the stimulus of their graphic and brilliant presentation'.

Such a brief introduction to the author is necessary for an understanding of the philosophy underlying *The Principles of Navigation*. This is no ordinary text-book, and must not be confused with the many excellent treatises that spell out, in detail and usually for a limited field, the technicalities that necessarily arise from an application of the basic principles. The range of navigation, from under the sea to outer space, is now so great that, with the increasing number of both problems and methods of solution, the author must be one of the very few capable of bringing them all together within one book; and this is necessary to demonstrate clearly the essential unity of philosophy that underlies, for example, such widely differing techniques as astronomical navigation, air-traffic control and hyperbolic radio fixing systems. Apart, however, from any deeper philosophical questions there is one very practical consideration that permeates almost all navigational problems—namely, that of errors. Wing Commander Anderson has succeeded not only in making navigators 'error-conscious' but also in getting them to accept and use the basic principles of the theory of errors. Thoughout this book errors are treated realistically: for its main object discussion in full detail is unnecessary, and some treatments may appear rather superficial; but let the reader beware of too hasty a judgment, for he will find that the simplification is quite deliberate.

The broad theme, and general outline, of this book stems from Wing Commander Anderson's stimulating presidential address to the Institute of Navigation, 'A Philosophy of Navigation', on 26 October 1960. It has necessarily been greatly expanded to embrace the methods and techniques now used in all forms of navigation, and to include the mass of essential factual information; but in spite of this expansion the original stimulus has been preserved. This is a book that has been carefully and deliberately designed to encourage the reader to think for himself—which is most assuredly the great aim of the teacher. The author is still, at heart, the wise and kindly preceptor of a quarter of a century ago!

D. H. SADLER

Preface

Navigation was born of the homing instinct. It developed into an art that guided the Polynesians across the Pacific. Today it is being translated into a science for travel to the Moon and beyond.

The translation of an art into a science comes from a fusion of artists and scientists. In the last twenty years, Institutes of Navigation have appeared all over the world in order to foster this fusion. To these Institutes come seamen, airmen, submariners, glider-pilots, yachtsmen and explorers of land and space to join with the mathematicians, meteorologists, hydrographers, astronomers, oceanographers and, above all, the radio, electronic and mechanical engineers.

The object of this book is to contribute to the exchange of ideas between the navigator and the scientist and engineer in two ways. First, by painting a broad picture of navigation as a whole so that each problem may be seen against a wider background. Secondly, by attempting to suggest a common language appropriate to a study of navigation.

Because all fields of navigation stemmed from sea navigation, many of the words used are common. Unfortunately, a few key words have developed different meanings. For these, one of the meanings has had to be chosen for use throughout the book. Abbreviations have similarly had to be standardized and are given on page 623.

The language of navigation is not only a matter of precise terminology. In the past, arithmetic and spherical trigonometry have provided links between the navigator and the scientist. More recently, the language of probability has found a place. These essential elements are, unfortunately, static. To them must be added dynamic languages, such as servo-mechanics and calculus, appropriate to a science of motion.

The presentation of the book has been chosen for its appeal to the navigator. The scientist is trained to communicate but the navigator is not. The principles of navigation are therefore presented in an order that may be acceptable to the seaman and the airman. The scientist and the engineer will be able to apply the presentation to their own interests.

It would be quite impossible to give credit to all those who have contributed to this book. The navigator spreads his ideas about so freely that their origin is lost almost at once. However, certain parts of the book have been read by acknowledged experts, in particular by Mr J. K. Bannon, of the Meteorological Office; Mr H. J. Elwertowski, Chief Scientist of the Admiralty Compass Observatory and an authority on inertial navigation; Mr J. B. Parker of the Atomic Energy Authority, whose work on probability and statistics in navigation is well known; Mr C. Powell of the Decca Navigator Company, a frequent contributor to scientific journals; and Mr D. H. Sadler, Superintendent of H.M. Nautical Almanac Office, an ex-President of the Institute of Navigation, whose name will always be connected with the new outlook on astro-navigation tables.

The author is a member of the Aviation Division of Smith's Industries Limited. Although the book may in no way be taken to represent Company policy or views, it owes a great deal both directly and indirectly to associations with navigators and engineers within the Company. In particular, thanks are due to Mr R. W. Chandler for his comments on radio, and to Mr G. H. Burrows for his patient and painstaking checking of the details of the book. Mr K. Meredith has transformed rough sketches into drawings suitable for reproduction. Outside the Aviation Division, helpful advice on marine radar and sonar has come from Mr W. Halliday and Mr A. Harrison of the Kelvin Hughes Division, and, in particular, from Mr G. Wikkenhauser.

The book could not have been written without the permission of Mr K. Fearnside, Divisional Technical Director, whose stature in the field of flight control is widely recognized. Acknowledgment is also made to the kind encouragement by the late Divisional Managing Director, Mr A. M. A. Majendie, who was formerly Master of the Guild of Air Pilots and Navigators and President of the Institute of Navigation. The last chapter of the book is based on his original ideas.

Finally, a special word of thanks to Mr Michael Richey, the

Executive Secretary of the Institute of Navigation and internationally famed as an ocean racing navigator. Readers of the *Journal of the Institute of Navigation* will appreciate how valuable his over-all guidance has been. Not only has he assisted greatly with help and advice, but also it was he who started me working on the book in the first instance.

Bishops Cleeve,   E. W. Anderson
Cheltenham,   August 1965
Gloucestershire

This new impression has enabled me to correct a small handful of minor faults in the original edition.

E. W. Anderson
August 1970

Contents

The diagrams are lettered by M. A. Verity.

List of Tables

Introduction

The Introduction is an attempt to outline the field of navigation not in terms of type of craft nor in terms of phases of operations, such as terminal or en-route, but in a generalized form which may be applied to any craft and, in a greater or lesser degree, to any phase of operation of that craft. From this emerges the pattern of the rest of the book.

CONTENTS

1. *Definition.* Navigation is the business of conducting a craft as it moves about its ways.

THE SCOPE OF NAVIGATION

2. From the definition, it follows that navigation starts from the moment that a craft gets under way and ends only when the journey is completed. Navigation therefore includes not only the en-route phase of a journey but also the departure and the arrival phases. These two phases are sometimes referred to as terminal navigation and sometimes as pilotage.

3. When a new field of navigation is opened up, the problem is to find the way. As traffic increases, navigation aids are provided. Accordingly, the emphasis shifts from finding the way to avoiding collision. This gradual shift of emphasis is a feature of all forms of navigation.

4. Transport systems need to conform to time-tables, but adverse weather may cause delays, particularly in congested terminal areas. Delay in entering a seaport leads to a build-up of running costs without a corresponding increase in cargo dues. The threat of delay in entering an airport will compel aircraft to carry wasteful reserves of fuel. Hence the demand for all-weather navigation, particularly at terminals.

5. Wasteful reserves of fuel are a particular problem in the operation of high-speed craft because the fuel carried may be several times as great as the pay-load. A fractional reduction in fuel may greatly affect the carrying capacity. Navigation may therefore be involved with problems of fuel economy.

THE THREE STAGES OF NAVIGATION

6. The business of conducting a craft is inconsistent with aimless wandering. Navigation must therefore start with an aim. For example, an ocean liner may aim to carry passengers in perfect safety from Southampton to New York, or a guided missile may aim to carry a warhead with perfect certainty from launching pad to target. This aim is translated into the consequent progress of the craft through three stages which are illustrated in Fig. 1:

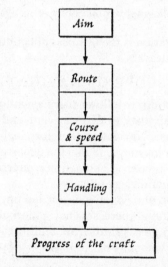

FIG. 1   The three stages of navigation

(a) *Distance.* A *route* is chosen that will achieve the aim. This route may be linked with a time schedule and, in high-speed craft, with fuel requirements. Except in the instance of craft operating on the surface of the sea, the route will involve three dimensions.

(b) *Velocity*. In order to follow the route and maintain the time schedule, the craft will have to be steered in a certain direction, known generally as a *course*, and at a certain *speed*. Direction and speed will often involve three dimensions.

(c) *Acceleration*. To achieve the required velocity, the craft has to be accelerated. Acceleration along the line of a craft generally results from the thrust of its power plant. Acceleration sideways may be initiated by a rudder, which changes the course of the craft, or by elevators which alter its angle of climb or dive. The control of these accelerations is often known as *handling* the craft.

7. It is evident that distance, velocity and accleration are linked by time. The conversion from one to the other involves the following processes:

(a) *Differentiation with respect to time*. This involves breaking down a *total* quantity over an infinitesimal difference of time to evolve a *rate*. Thus distance may be differentiated with respect to time to evolve a *rate* of change of distance or velocity, and velocity may be similarly differentiated to evolve a *rate* of change of velocity or an acceleration. Alternatively, distance may be differentiated twice with respect to time to evolve an acceleration.

(b) *Integration with respect to time*. Integration is the inverse of differentiation and involves the building up of a *total* quantity from a continuous measurement of *rate*. Thus a *total* velocity can be built up by integrating accelerations over a period of time and a *total* distance by integrating velocities over a period of time. By double integration over a period of time, distance can be built up from accelerations. This assumes that velocity and distance start at zero. If there is an initial velocity or distance, the integrated accelerations or velocities will have to be added to it.

THE VELOCITY DILEMMA

8. Distance can be measured directly and acceleration can be sensed according to the force that results from the inertia that opposes acceleration. Velocity, however, is less easily measured.

It may be derived from a changing distance and hence may involve an element of differentiation. Still more frequently it will be derived from acceleration and hence will involve an element of integration.

9. In practice, velocity is evolved from integration rather than by differentiation for reasons emphasized by Fig. 2, which shows graphs of distance, of velocity and of acceleration, each plotted against time and all three representing the same journey. The distance graph is smooth, the velocity graph is kinked, and the acceleration graph is extremely irregular.

10. All devices suffer from minor irregularities known as noise. Suppose that an irregularity in the measurement of distance should make it appear that distance has temporarily decreased by a very small amount. This will appear as a reversal of velocity and as an extraordinary deceleration. Thus the minor irregularities of distance measurement inevitable in any system will appear as large changes of velocity and as very large changes of acceleration. For this reason, differentiation of distance will not generally provide instantaneous indications of velocity and still less of acceleration.

11. A large acceleration, such as appears on the acceleration graph at $+20$ minutes, which is a jump from one extreme of the scale to the other, is reduced to a kink on the velocity graph and a mere change of curvature on the distance graph. Hence, integration of accelerations will provide a smooth measurement of velocity and an even smoother measurement of distance.

Example. Man measures distances with the eyes and acceleration by means of semicircular canals in the ears. He does not measure velocity directly. If he shuts his eyes, he can still walk and, in familiar surroundings, judge distances. This shows that he can integrate accelerations to provide velocity and distance. On the other hand, if his semicircular canals are deranged temporarily, he becomes giddy and cannot walk at all, even if he can see perfectly. This suggests that he cannot so readily differentiate distance to produce velocity and acceleration.

THE PROCESSES OF NAVIGATION

12. *Servo Loops.* The business of navigating has been likened to the way in which a stick is balanced on the palm of the hand.

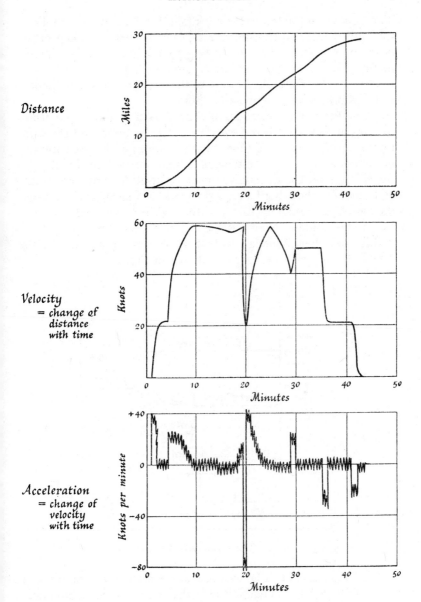

FIG. 2 Distance, velocity and acceleration

The light from the top of the stick falls on the eyes which follow the movements and transmit messages to the brain. This process is known as feed-back. According to the feed-back of information, the brain sends orders to the arm muscles which move the hand. This shifts the bottom of the stick so that the tendency of the top to move is opposed.

13. The continuous circulation of information and action from the top of the stick to the eyes, through the brain and the arm muscles to the hand and thence to the bottom of the stick and up to the top again is an example of a closed-loop system. Evidently, the closed loop has the ability to correct itself by a process of hit and miss. On the other hand, if the feed-back element is missing, the loop becomes an open loop with no ability to correct itself.

14. A closed-loop system often consists of a number of loops one within the other. This is a feature of navigation, which consists fundamentally of three loops as shown in Fig. 3:

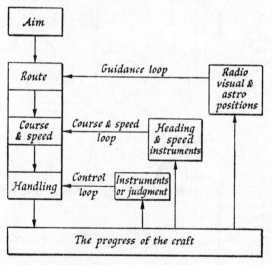

FIG. 3 The basic navigation loops

(a) *Guidance loop*. The progress of the craft along the route is followed by navigation aids that fix position at intervals, generally either radio aids, visual aids or astronomical aids. The route is accordingly amended and corrections are translated into amendments to the progress of the craft through the stages of course and speed and of handling.

(b) *Course and speed loop.* The progress of the craft in terms of course and speed is measured by navigational instruments. These record the direction in which the craft is heading and its speed. Corrections are made at frequent intervals and translated into amendments to the progress of the craft through the handling stage.

(c) *Control loop.* The acceleration of the craft is continuously measured by instruments in high-speed craft or estimated by human judgment in slower craft, and the craft is handled accordingly.

15. Engineers concerned with automatic systems, such as guided weapons, may recognize only two loops, guidance and control. Nevertheless, in most forms of navigation, the course and speed loop is fundamental. Guidance is a means of determining course and speed, and control is a means of achieving course and speed. Indeed, it is the element of course and speed that distinguishes navigation from survey, which is only concerned with position. It is the element of course and speed that distinguishes navigation from aimless sailing or flying, which is only concerned with handling the craft.

DEAD RECKONING

16. Fig. 4 is an amplification of Fig. 3 which acts as a reminder that equipments which measure accelerations tend also to be used to measure velocity. The figure also shows that course and speed instruments may produce an estimate of position derived from the progress of the craft. This form of integration is known as dead reckoning (D.R.).

17. Dead reckoning can be used to calculate a future as well as a present position. Planning a journey will therefore introduce an element of dead reckoning. Dead reckoning is also particularly valuable when the aids used to find position are such that time is consumed in reducing the incoming information into a form in which it may be used. With such aids, by the time that the navigator has discovered his position, he will have moved to a new position which will have to be calculated by dead reckoning.

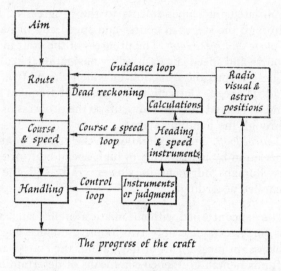

FIG. 4   Finding the way

18. Dead reckoning has been such a prominent feature of navigation that heading and speed instruments are sometimes known as dead-reckoning instruments. Nevertheless, dead reckoning is essentially an open-loop system (para 13) and not self-correcting. Any error in the measurement of course, speed or time will therefore be perpetuated in the calculation of the dead-reckoning position.

AVOIDING COLLISION

19. The requirement to avoid collision involves loops similar to the three fundamental loops shown in Fig. 3. However, these loops generally have special names as suggested in Fig. 5:

(a) *Separation loop.* Separation is generally achieved by traffic regulation either in the form of rules of the road, such as 'keep to starboard', or in the form of instructions sent to craft en-route by a traffic-control organization. This loop is particularly used for high-speed traffic since high-speed craft find last-minute avoiding action particularly difficult.

(b) *Avoidance loop.* The progress of the craft may be compared directly with the progress of other craft in the vicinity by some form of look-out. Avoiding action is translated through the steering and handling stages into corrections to the progress of the craft. This loop is a particular feature of marine navigation.

(c) *Handling.* At the last moment, it may be necessary to turn the bows of a craft towards danger in order to swing the stern away. This is a special instance of collision avoidance and therefore is shown in Fig. 5 as a minor loop dependent normally on human judgment.

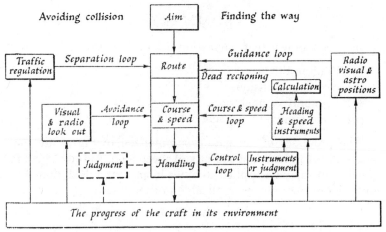

FIG. 5 The pattern of navigation

THE PATTERN OF STUDY

20. The study of navigation may be based on the various loops, starting with the control loop, because this can provide information for the outer loops. Before considering the loops, it will be advisable to examine the craft and the environment on which the loops depend. In order to provide a basis for these discussions, it will be necessary first to outline the language that has to be used. This language is mathematics.

21. The layout of a possible study of navigation now appears. It will begin with the background information, the language of mathematics and errors, the craft and its environment. Next the handling loop and the heading and speed instruments can be

described. This will lead naturally on to setting course, dead reckoning and routing and thence to position finding, visual aids, astro and radio aids, culminating in a consideration of navigation systems.

22. It would be possible to split the collision-avoidance techniques from the position-finding techniques. However, the same instruments are used and similar procedures. Therefore, at all stages, the requirements of collision avoidance will be treated in parallel with the problems of finding the way.

SUMMARY

It has been shown that navigation has to do with:

    (a) Finding the way.
    (b) Avoiding collision.
    (c) Economy of operation.
    (d) Maintaining a time schedule.

The processes of navigation summarized in Fig. 5 are built around the fundamental course and speed loop. Aids designed for inner loops may be applied to outer loops, but aids designed for outer loops may not be applicable to inner loops.

BIBLIOGRAPHY:
PHILOSOPHY OF NAVIGATION

The philosophy of navigation is concerned so intimately with methods of navigating that generally it will be found imbedded in books of navigation listed on page 613. As a result, few papers have been written directly concerned with philosophy as such:

Anderson, E. W., A philosophy of navigation (Presidential Address), *J. Inst. Navig.*, **14**, 1.

Majendie, A. M. A. The display and use of navigational intelligence (Presidential Address), *J. Inst. Navig.*, **11**, 1.

PART ONE

THE BACKGROUND

CHAPTER I. MATHEMATICS AND ERRORS. The short section on mathematics covers the background necessary for a study of navigation. The section on computers has been included because computing is today an essential feature of navigation. The parts of the chapter that deal with errors are slanted towards the navigation requirement and special consideration is given to faults and blunders. There is a section on two-dimensional errors which will be assumed as background throughout the book.

CHAPTER II. ENVIRONMENT. The world is touched on briefly, largely as an introduction to the weather and, for this reason, the effects of the rotation of the Earth have been examined. It has also been found convenient to fit altimeters into this section. The sections on weather have been drastically pruned to include only elements that are of direct interest to the navigator in the craft. For navigational planning, it is assumed that the navigator will have the assistance of a meteorologist.

CHAPTER III. THE CRAFT. In order to appreciate the problems of control and the factors that determine the tactics of navigation, it will be essential to have a working knowledge of certain aspects of the craft. In particular, stability, resistance to motion, method of propulsion, fuel economy and steering have important consequences.

CONTENTS

CHAPTER I

Mathematics and Errors

1. THE ELEMENTS

QUANTITIES

1. The units in which the three basic quantities of distance, velocity and acceleration are measured by engineers and scientists may vary throughout the world. In English-speaking countries, the quantities may be measured as follows:

  (a) *Distance*: measured in feet (ft).
  (b) *Velocity*: measured in feet per second (ft/s).
  (c) *Acceleration*: measured in ft/s per second (ft/s²).

2. When measuring height or changes of height, the navigator uses feet or feet per second, with the exception that the mariner records the depth of water in 6-foot intervals known as fathoms. For general operations, however, the navigator uses the following:

  (a) *Distance*. Measured in nautical miles (n. miles or n.m.). The International Nautical Mile is 6076·12 feet (1852 metres) but the nautical mile of 6080 feet is commonly used, the discrepancy seldom being significant in practical navigation. A tenth of a nautical mile is known as a cable. The statute or American mile of 1760 yards is not used except for certain land operations (76 statute miles = 66 nautical miles).
  (b) *Velocity*. Measured in knots. A knot is a nautical mile per hour. 60 knots is roughly 100 ft/s.
  (c) *Acceleration*. Often expressed as a multiple of the acceleration due to gravity at the surface of the Earth which is known as g. It is assumed generally that g is approximately 32 ft/s². The figure internationally agreed is 32·17 ft/s² (980·665 cm/s²).

3. *Distance and Speed in Minutes of Arc.* Position on the surface of the Earth is defined according to the direction of the vertical. Latitude (lat.) is the angle between the vertical and the plane of the equator measured at right angles to the equator. Longitude (long.) is the angle between the vertical and the vertical at Greenwich measured in the plane of the equator. Hence the difference in direction of the verticals at two points may be used to express the distance between them, and the rate of change of direction of the vertical may be used to express speed. In both instances, the angles will be expressed in minutes of arc.

4. It happens that a difference of direction of 1' is roughly a nautical mile at the surface of the Earth and therefore a speed of 1' per hour is roughly a knot. Owing to the shape of the Earth, closer approximations are:

$$\text{(a) } 1' \text{ north or south} = (6077 - 31 \times \cos (2 \times \text{lat.})) \text{ ft}$$
$$= 6046 \text{ ft at the equator or}$$
$$6108 \text{ ft at the poles.}$$
$$\text{(b) } 1' \text{ east or west} = (6098 - 10 \times \cos (2 \times \text{lat.})) \text{ ft}$$
$$= 6088 \text{ ft at the equator or}$$
$$6108 \text{ ft at the poles.}$$

ARITHMETIC

5. A scale marked in equal increments of addition, so that 100, 50, 0, −50 and −100 are at equal intervals, is said to be linear. A scale marked in equal increments of multiplication so that 100, 10, 1, 0·1 and 0·01 are at equal intervals is said to be logarithmic. Log-linear paper is ruled with one axis linear and the other logarithmic, as shown in Fig. 6. Log-log paper has logarithmic scales in both axes.

6. Multiplication and division may be performed on a slide-rule, two scales graduated logarithmically which register against each other. For multiplication and division involving distances, speeds and times, the navigator may use a circular slide-rule as shown in Fig. 7. The figure shows 15 nautical miles on the inner logarithmic scale registered against 60 minutes on the outer logarithmic scale. The slide-rule has thus been set to 15 knots. The distance covered in any number of minutes at this speed can be read on the inner scale of nautical miles against the outer scale of

minutes. Alternatively, the time taken to cover any distance can be read on the outer scale of minutes against the inner scale of nautical miles.

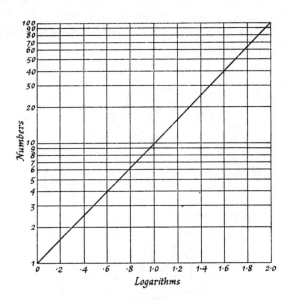

FIG. 6 Connection between numbers and logarithms drawn on log-linear graph paper

Example. From Fig. 7:

In 10 minutes, a distance of 2·5 n. miles will be covered.

To cover 3 n. miles, the time taken would be 12 minutes.

7. It will be noted that the graduation marked 60 on the minute scale has to do duty for 6 minutes or for 600 minutes or, indeed, for 0·6 minutes, and that the position of the decimal point has to be estimated. The position of the decimal point is said to define the 'order' of an answer. A quantity that is ten times bigger than another is said to be an order bigger, and a quantity that is a hundred times smaller is said to be two orders smaller. The term 'order' only implies limited accuracy, so that if a quantity is stated to be of the order of 3 knots, it is implied that the size is nearer proportionally to 3 knots than to 30 knots or 0·3 knots.

3—P.N.

8. Although it is quite plain what is meant by the statement 'of the order of 3 knots', a statement such as 300 knots may be ambiguous. It could mean 3 hundreds of knots, a figure somewhere between $2\frac{1}{2}$ and $3\frac{1}{2}$ hundreds. Alternatively, it could mean exactly 300 knots, a figure between $299\frac{1}{2}$ and $300\frac{1}{2}$. For this reason it may be safer to write 3×10^2 in the first instance or $3 \cdot 00 \times 10^2$ in the second instance.

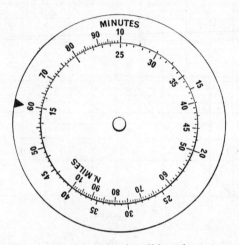

FIG. 7   Circular slide-rule

9. In nature, many quantities change logarithmically with time rather than linearly. Objects tend to cool logarithmically, losing half their excess temperature at regular intervals of time. Fig. 8 shows a quantity that halves itself every minute and is therefore said to have a half-life of 1 minute. The quantity dies away following an exponential curve which may be known as the curve of normal decay. Had the exponential been plotted on log-linear graph paper, it would have appeared as a straight line.

10. It can be shown that, if it were possible to keep the rate of decrease constant, the whole quantity would disappear in about one and a half times the half-life, which will be $1\frac{1}{2}$ minutes in this particular instance. Fig. 8 also shows that this period of $1\frac{1}{2}$ minutes will apply whether the constant rate of decrease is started at 0 minutes or at 2 minutes, or at any other instant.

The period of $1\frac{1}{2}$ minutes is therefore known as the 'time constant' of the particular exponential. In navigation, an exponential is generally defined according to the time constant rather than according to the half-life of the quantity.

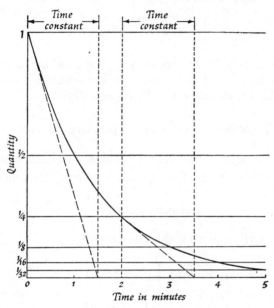

FIG. 8 Exponential curve of normal decay

CALCULUS

11. Calculus is the mathematics of change. On page 3, para 7, the meaning of differentiation and of integration with respect to time was explained. More generally:

(a) *Differentiation* (*symbol D*). The breakdown of a changing quantity into a rate of change. Thus:

$$\text{velocity} = D \text{ (distance)}$$

If the differentiation is with respect to time, it may be written:

$$\text{velocity} = \dot{\text{distance}}$$

Similarly:

Acceleration $= D$ (velocity) or velocity
$$= D^2 \text{ (distance) or } \ddot{\text{distance}}$$

(b) *Integration (symbol 1/D)*. The build-up of a total quantity from rates of change. However, the equation:

$$\frac{1}{D} \text{ (velocity)} = \text{distance}$$

is true only for that part of the velocity that is changing and does not take account of a constant distance from which a craft may start. Thus generally:

$$\frac{1}{D} \text{ (velocity)} = \text{distance} + \text{a constant distance}$$

The navigator often uses the symbol $\int$ to mean integration and may write the above formula, ignoring the constant, as:

$$\int \text{velocity} = \text{distance}$$

Similarly, ignoring the constants:

$$\frac{1}{D} \text{ (acceleration) or } \int \text{acceleration} = \text{speed}$$

$$\frac{1}{D^2} \text{ (acceleration) or } \iint \text{acceleration} = \text{distance}$$

12. Integration is used to find the mean value of a quantity that is fluctuating. If a number of observations are taken at intervals of time, added together and divided by the number of observations, the result will be an average observation. If the observations are continually integrated over the period of time and then divided by the time interval, the result will be the mean value of the observation. The mean value will obviously be more representative than the average.

TRIGONOMETRY

13. The basic ratios are sine (sin) and cosine (cos). Using the right-angled triangle in Fig. 9:

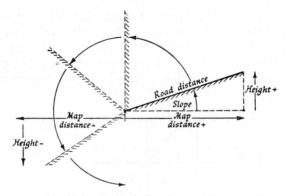

FIG. 9 Trigonometrical ratios and large angles

sin (slope) = height/road distance
i.e.   sin = opposite/hypotenuse
cos (slope) = map distance/road distance
i.e.   cos = adjacent/hypotenuse

14. With a slope of 0°, the height will be 0 and sin 0° will therefore be 0. As the slope increases to 90°, height will increase until,
at 90°, it will equal the road distance so that sin 90° = 1. If the
slope were increased past the vertical, the height would decrease
until at 180° it would be 0. Increasing past 180°, the height
would now become a depth, the sine would become negative and
sin 270° would be −1. This negative height would then decrease
until at sin 360° or sin 0° the value would again be 0. The complete sine curve is shown in the upper half of Fig. 10.
15. The cosine curve will be identical with the sine curve in
shape but displaced 90° ahead of it. At 0°, map distance equals
road distance so that cos 0° = 1. At 90°, map distance is 0 and cos
90° = 0. Past 90°, map distance is being measured negatively so
that cos 180° is −1. At 270°, map distance is again 0 so that
cos 270° = 0. The curve is shown in the lower half of Fig. 10.
16. It will be noticed that at 0° the sine curve is at its maximum
upwards rate and the cosine curve is at its maximum upwards
point. At 90° the sine curve has neither an upwards nor a downwards rate and the cosine curve is at 0. The cosine curve thus
shows the rate of change of the sine curve and is therefore the
differential of the sine curve. The cosine curve is 90° advanced

in phase compared to the sine curve and, therefore, the process of differentiation may be known as 'phase advance'. Since differentiation is inevitably imperfect in practice, the term phase advance will generally be used when the advance is less than 90°, and the term differentiation retained for the theoretical phase advance of 90°.

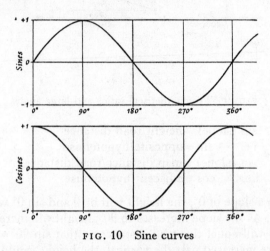

FIG. 10   Sine curves

17. The sine and cosine curves are probably the most significant curves in navigation and are known generically as sine curves. Sine curves represent wave motion, either the slow swing of a pendulum or the very high frequency vibrations of radio or light waves. Any curve can be shown to be built up from a number of sine curves. The process of breaking down a curve into its component sine curves is known as harmonic analysis or Fourier's analysis.

18. In addition to sines and cosines, there are four other basic trigonometrical ratios:

cosecant (cosec) = hypotenuse/opposite = 1/sine
secant (sec)   = hypotenuse/adjacent = 1/cosine
tangent (tan)   = opposite/adjacent   = sine/cosine
cotangent (cot) = adjacent/opposite   = 1/tangent

19. The navigator frequently deals with small angles. If the slope shown in Fig. 9 is very small, map distance and road

distance will be nearly equal and may be regarded as the radii of a circle with height as the arc of the circumference, as shown in Fig. 11. A complete circumference $= 2\pi \times$ radius, so that an arc

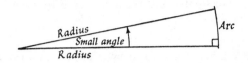

FIG. 11   Trigonometrical ratios and small angles

of about 57°.3 would be equal in length to a radius, and an angle of 57°.3 is consequently known as a radian. The navigator may take an arc of 1° to be roughly 1/60 of a radian, from which the following approximations will emerge ($\simeq$ means approximately equal to):

(a) Sin (small angle°)
   $\simeq$ small angle°/60 (accurate within 5 per cent up to about 43°)
(b) Cos (small angle°)
   $\simeq$ 1 (accurate within 5 per cent up to 16°)
(c) Tan (small angle°)
   $\simeq$ small angle°/60 (accurate within 5 per cent up to about 6°)

The approximations for sines and tangents are sometimes known as 'one in sixty rules'.

20. The position of a point relative to a known fixed point, which may be called the origin, can be measured in one of two ways:

(a) *Polar coordinates.* Direction and distance from the origin. For example, north-west so many miles.
(b) *Cartesian coordinates.* One distance in a fixed direction and another distance at right angles to the fixed direction. For example, so many miles west and so many miles north.

21. The position of a vehicle on a slope compared to the start of that slope can be described either in terms of:

(a) *Polar coordinates.* Slope and road distance (or angle and hypotenuse).

(b) *Cartesian coordinates*. Map distance and height (or adjacent and opposite).

Hence, trigonometry provides a means for converting from polar to cartesian coordinates and from cartesian to polar coordinates.

DYNAMICS

22. It is often necessary to know the acceleration that results when a craft is made to travel in curve. This acceleration, if removed, would allow the craft to travel straight so that it would seem to move outwards. Hence the misnomer 'centrifugal force'. It can be shown that:

$$\text{acceleration} = \text{speed}^2/\text{radius of curvature}$$

23. It is important to note that accelerations set up as a result of changes of direction of a craft will be according to the square of the speed. Put in another way, the radius of a turn in a craft travelling at 100 knots will have to be a hundred times the radius of turn of a craft travelling at 10 knots if the turn is to have no greater effect on the passengers.

24. The force required to accelerate depends not only on the acceleration that is required but also on the mass that has to be accelerated. That is:

$$\text{force} = \text{mass} \times \text{acceleration}$$

25. It is essential to differentiate between mass and weight. A craft may have a certain mass which, on the surface of the Earth, will result in a certain weight. If it travels sufficiently fast over the curved surface of the Earth, its weight will be reduced until eventually it will travel in orbit and be virtually weightless. Nevertheless, the mass will remain unaltered.

CONIC SECTIONS

26. If a cone is cut at right angles by a plane, the section of the cone will be a circle. If the cut is oblique, the conic section will be an ellipse as shown in Fig. 12 (a). An ellipse is a circle whose dimensions in one axis have been increased by a certain ratio as compared to the dimensions in the other axis. A feature of the ellipse is that, from two focal points within it, the sum of

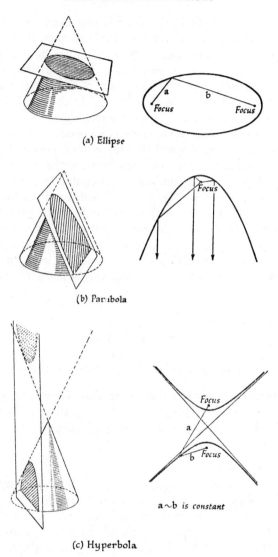

(a) Ellipse

(b) Parabola

(c) Hyperbola

FIG. 12 Conic sections

the distances to any point on the edge of the ellipse will be constant. An object in space generally orbits around a larger object in an ellipse with the larger object at one focus.

27. If the angle of cut of the cone is increased, the ellipse will become longer until eventually the angle of cut will be parallel to the edge of the cone. The section will then be a parabola as shown in Fig. 12 (b). A parabola is the path that would be followed by a projectile on the surface of the Earth if the Earth were flat. Also, from a focal point inside the parabola, rays of light would be reflected in parallel lines.

28. If the angle of cut of the cone is increased past the parallel, the shape of the section will become a hyperbola and the plane will not only cut the cone but will also cut the mirror image of the cone. Therefore a hyperbola in its complete form consists of two curves as shown in Fig. 12 (c). A feature of the hyperbola is that, from two foci, one within each half of the hyperbola, the difference of the distances to any point on the hyperbola will be constant. The hyperbola, if extended sufficiently, will eventually meet a pair of intersecting straight lines. A straight line that eventually represents a curve in this way is known as an asymptote.

2. COMPUTERS

1. Computers are generally divided into two types:

   (a) *Analogue computers* that continuously combine quantities.
   (b) *Digital computers* that operate by counting in discrete units so that the answers are produced at intervals.

ANALOGUE COMPUTERS

2. Various analogue computers used for specific purposes will be described in the course of the book. The slide-rule on page 16, para 6, is a simple mechanical analogue computer with a visual output. Other mechanical computers may have outputs in the form of shaft rotations. Alternatively, an analogue computer may operate on electrical inputs. Generally it will operate on a combination of electrical and mechanical signals and be known as an electro-mechanical computer. Hydraulic and pneumatic computers have also been built but are not prominent in navigation, though they have appeared in missiles.

3. Mechanical movement involves friction and the energy absorbed generates heat and causes wear. Heat introduces distortion, and wear leads to looseness in the joints and possibly the formation of minute particles of swarf. Hence a mechanical computer may not maintain an accuracy greater than around 1 per cent. For many applications, this standard of accuracy will be adequate.

4. The components of an electronic computer do not induce friction but they absorb electrical power and become heated. The characteristics of components also tend to change with time so that, for high performance, the analogue computer needs to be recalibrated at intervals. A newly calibrated computer using high quality components may have an accuracy of the order of 0·1 per cent or 1 in 10^3, and this may be improved to around 1 in 10^4 by maintaining the components at an exact temperature. However, the accuracy of the computing may depend on the accuracy of the input voltages, and it is not easy to measure voltage in a craft to an accuracy of much better than 1 in 10^4.

5. It now appears that there are many problems in the design and operation of a very accurate analogue computer. Therefore, analogue computing is chiefly used where the accuracy requirements are not high and where the computing is relatively simple. Under these conditions, an analogue computer can handle a large number of inputs and produce continuous answers for a relatively small size and cost.

DIGITAL COMPUTERS

6. The digital computer represents numbers by a succession of electronic impulses, known as pulses, with intervals or spaces in between. Each pulse or space element is known as a bit (bi(nary uni)t). Hence, 10 bits can represent any number less than 2^{10}, that is up to 1023. For example:

	Pulse	Pulse	Pulse	Pulse	Pulse	Space	Pulse	Space	Space	Space
=	2^9	2^8	2^7	2^6	2^5	(2^4)	2^3	(2^2)	(2^1)	(2^0)
=	512	256	128	64	32	—	8	—	—	—
=	1000									

Since each bit is an on-off element, it will not deteriorate with time and therefore a digital computer will not need recalibration.

7. The computer is driven by a clock so that the pulses and spaces can be counted in terms of time. The clock may operate in fractions of a second so minute that the time for a calculation may be negligible in terms of a practical navigation system. The duration of each bit may be measured not in milliseconds (ms, thousandths of a second) nor in microseconds (Ms, millionths of a second) but in nanoseconds (kMs, thousand millionths of a second).

8. The bits are collected together into blocks known as words. Thus a word of 10 bits can count up to 1023 and a word of 20 bits up to over a million. According to the length of the word, a digital computer may be made as accurate as desired. A word of 10 bits can be accurate up to 1 part in 10^3 and a word of 20 bits up to 1 part in 10^6.

9. A computer which counts in twos is known as a binary computer. Alternatively, a decimal computer may be used which works in tens, representing the figures from 0 to 9 by blocks of 4 bits thus:

8	4	2	1	
Space	Space	Space	Space	= 0
Space	Space	Space	Pulse	= 1
Space	Space	Pulse	Space	= 2
Space	Space	Pulse	Pulse	= 3 and so on up to
Pulse	Space	Space	Pulse	= 9

There will be six combinations available in each block for other types of information.

10. A digital computer has four main elements linked together by a central controller. These elements are:

(a) *Inputs*
(b) *Arithmetic Unit*
(c) *Store or Memory*
(d) *Outputs*

INPUTS

11. If a cam fitted to a shaft were to operate an on-off switch for each rotation of the shaft, the result would be an elementary form of digital input. In order to be able to record 1° of rotation, the shaft would have to be geared up by 360 to 1. Apart from the friction in gearing, the mechanical switch would wear, and dirt

from the wearing could foul the switch contacts. However, special devices may detect movements without any sliding contacts. For example, a mask could be fitted to the shaft with holes at intervals through which light could pass and impinge on a light sensitive cell. Devices such as these are known as digitizers. The greater the number of bits that have to be transmitted to indicate a given movement, the greater the accuracy but the more complex the digitizer.

12. If the digital computer has a great many inputs, the cost, size and weight of the digitizers may be excessive. Hence the preference for the analogue computer where there are many inputs and low accuracy is acceptable. However, this limitation does not apply when inputs are in the form of punched cards, punched tape, direct key inputs or inputs transferred from magnetic tapes.

ARITHMETIC UNIT

13. The essential feature of the arithmetic unit is the ability to count. Counting may be arranged by a special circuit, such as a 'flip-flop', which registers a pulse when a pulse is injected into it but registers a space when a second pulse is injected into it. It can be made to operate a second circuit so that when two pulses make a space a pulse is carried forward.

14. For simplicity, a binary computer with a word of 10 bits may be imagined. Suppose that 19 and 50 have to be added. If P represents a pulse and — represents a space:

	512	256	128	64	32	16	8	4	2	1
19 =	—	—	—	—	—	P	—	—	P	P
50 =	—	—	—	—	P	P	—	—	P	P

Starting from the right-hand side, a pulse and space will produce a pulse. Moving to the left, two pulses will produce a space and a pulse will be carried to the left. Hence, the addition will become:

	512	256	128	64	32	16	8	4	2	1	
19	—	—	—	—	—	P	—	—	P	P	
+50	—	—	—	—	P	P	—	—	P	—	
	—	—	—	P	—	—	—	P	—	P	= 69

carry carry   carry

15. This example illustrates series addition, in which addition is performed in sequence starting from the right-hand side. An alternative system operates in parallel, adding all the pulses simultaneously, taking care of the carried pulses in a subsequent operation. The parallel system tends to be the faster but requires more equipment.

16. Subtraction may be arranged by a process of reversed addition. Alternatively, all the figures in the number to be subtracted may be reversed by flip-flops and then one added at the right-hand end. Adding this reversed set of figures to the original number will result in subtraction. Thus, to subtract 50 from 69:

		512	256	128	64	32	16	8	4	2	1	
50	=	—	—	—	—	P	P	—	—	P	—	
Reversed	=	P	P	P	P	—	—	P	P	—	P	
one added	=	P	P	P	P	—	—	P	P	P	—	
69	=	—	—	—	P	—	—	—	P	—	P	
add	=	—	—	—	—	—	P	—	—	P	P	=19

17. Multiplication is a process of shifting pulses up to the left. To multiply 19 by 50, 19 is first shifted one space to the left to multiply by 2, then another three spaces to multiply by 16 and then one more space to multiply by 32. Thus:

		512	256	128	64	32	16	8	4	2	1	
19	=	—	—	—	—	—	P	—	—	P	P	
19×2	=	—	—	—	—	P	—	—	P	P	—	
19×16	=	—	P	—	—	P	P	—	—	—	—	
19×32	=	P	—	—	P	P	—	—	—	—	—	
Add	=	P	P	P	—	P	P	—	P	P	—	=950

It is evident that, in order to multiply by a large number, a great many shifts and additions will be required. Hence, the process will not be as fast as addition. It is possible to speed up the process by short cuts. For example, the memory to be described in para 20 may be provided with multiplication tables.

18. Division can be achieved by a process of continual subtraction. Since subtraction is not so fast as addition, division will not be so fast as multiplication. By means of the four basic

processes, it is possible to calculate squares, square roots, cubes, cube roots and so on. Inevitably, the more complex the calculation, the less short will be the time it must take. Fortunately, a computer is able to calculate figures very quickly by a process of hit and miss. It can solve complex problems by making a guess, working out what the error will be as a result of the guess, and recalculating again and again until the answer is produced to the required order of accuracy.

19. An arithmetic unit can perform complex processes using a number of simple circuits. All that is needed to change from one calculation to another is to use the circuits in a different sequence. The arrangement of the sequence is a process known as programming the computer.

STORE

20. By operating in discrete units in the form of pulses, digital computers are able to store arrangements of pulses in a memory unit. The passage of time may cause the pulse to decay in size, but it will continue as a discrete unit. The memory can store not only numbers but also instructions regarding the processes to be applied to those numbers and the programmes to arrange for the calculations. It can also store tables which may be entered by these numbers.

21. In order that the memory shall be used, some form of 'filing' system is necessary. 'Filing' may be of one of two types:

(a) *Parallel*. Words can be numbered and arranged in numbered blocks so that any required word can be quickly extracted. A computer memory of this type may be known as a quick access store, and is useful for holding figures in calculations.

(b) *Series*. Words may be stored as in a book so that it is necessary to run through all the 'pages' to find the right word. A computer memory of this type will have a long access time but will be reasonably compact. The arrangement will therefore be applied where a great deal of information has to be available as in the main store of a computer.

22. *Quick Access Stores.* These commonly use magnetic cores in the form of small ferrite rings arranged in strings according to the number of bits in a word and threaded on to wires that carry pulses. A core will be magnetized by a pulse passing through it. Subsequently, this magnetism will be recognized by whether a second pulse causes magnetization or not. In certain computers, charges imprinted on the face of a cathode ray tube (page 483, para 21) may be used as a quick access store.

23. *Main Stores.* These commonly use magnetic tapes, drums or discs which, like the discs of a juke-box, may provide a measure of quick access. The words to be stored are fed into the magnetic element and run through in a fraction of a second when a particular word has to be recalled. Alternatively, a system of electro-sonic storage units may be used. There are also types of store that act as intermediates between the main store and the quick access store. At the other end of the scale, certain large ground computers may use very large but relatively slow back-up stores.

OUTPUTS

24. The flashing lights of the visual 'read out' of a digital computer are well known. Alternatively, a computer may cause electrically lit numbers to appear or may operate a cathode ray tube to produce signals. However, it may be necessary for the computer to operate powered outputs, such as a shaft with a load attached.

25. The method of using an input device to drive an output will be described in detail on page 145, para 7. Briefly, a digitizer is fitted to the output shaft which is then driven by a motor until the output of the digitizer agrees with the output of the computer. Any difference is passed into a power amplifier which drives the motor until the difference is taken up. Thus the digitizer and the shaft is driven by the motor to follow up the computer output.

DIGITAL COMPUTER CHARACTERISTICS

26. The digital computer has been shown to have the following characteristics:

(a) *Unlimited accuracy.* The greater the accuracy the longer the time required for calculations. This is negligible except perhaps for very fast control systems.

(b) *Great flexibility*. A digital computer used for navigation may not differ basically from one used for business purposes. It can be used as the central 'brain' of the system. It can tackle problems connected with the management of the operation. It can make decisions and it can store information.

(c) *Modular construction*. The computer is built up from a large number of a small variety of circuits. This makes construction and miniaturization simple and economical. The arithmetic unit is steadily decreasing in size and weight as electronic techniques develop.

(d) *Input-output complexity*. In practice the size and weight of the input and output devices for the digital computer are often greater than the computer itself and miniaturization is extremely difficult. Hence, for simple operations with a large number of inputs and outputs, an analogue computer may be cheaper even though a digital computer be already available.

(e) *Self-checking*. The arithmetic unit of a digital computer can very readily be developed to include self-checking devices that can detect errors. These errors can arise, for example, from electrical noise either inside or outside the computer which can cause fleeting pulses to appear in circuits. These transients can cause large errors under certain circumstances unless there is some self-checking facility. Fortunately, the complexity of the arithmetic unit can be increased to allow for self-checking without greatly altering the overall size of the computer.

27. The development of the digital computer is towards special thin film devices in which layers of materials are deposited on bases in order to produce circuits. The semi-conductor elements may be fixed to the thin film devices, or may be integrated into the devices themselves to attain extreme microminiaturization. It is worth noting that this extreme miniaturization tends to produce elements extremely resistant to shock and vibration.

3. ERRORS

ACCIDENTS

1. It can be argued that, where human life may be at stake, accidents cannot be tolerated. However, risks are inseparable from all human activity and travel is no exception. The requirement is that the risks shall be small compared to the advantages to be gained. On any other basis, life itself would be impossible.

2. The navigator will be concerned with the chances of an accident arising during his working life. He will therefore tend to be interested in the connection between accidents and hours of travel. However, the object of travel is to move passengers and cargo from one point to another. It may therefore be more logical to relate accidents to passenger-miles or cargo-miles. Typical indices will be:

passenger index = deaths/(passengers × miles carried)
cargo index   = cargo damage/(cargo × miles carried)

3. These indices do not apply in the many instances where time is of importance. For example, if cargo is perishable, speed will be a factor in the cargo index. Since man has only a limited span of life, he is in that sense a perishable cargo and speed may be valuable.

4. Man can walk a million nautical miles in a lifetime. It can therefore be argued that the passenger index need only be better than one death per million nautical miles. Travel by private car is probably ten times as safe as this, travel by air is probably a hundred times as safe and travel by sea perhaps a thousand times as safe. However, a factor in accidents may be the sentiment aroused by publicity. Hence, special emphasis may have to be placed on avoiding accidents which have a strong element of drama, such as collisions between large craft and accidents involving new types of craft or new techniques.

5. Accidents will be caused by errors in equipment, by mistakes in human operation or by failures of instruments and systems. It will therefore be necessary to study the problems of errors and faults. It will be unwise to leave this entirely to the professional statistician for the reason that occurrences in everyday life cannot be translated simply into numbers. It is therefore

essential that those concerned with navigation shall understand the basis of statistics and errors.

STANDARD DEVIATION

6. In order to consider the allowances that have to be made for errors, it will be useful to define a parameter that will describe them. The single figure used to describe a range of errors is based on the 'golden rule' of errors which states that the effect of a random error is proportional to the square of its size. This rule will have to be taken on trust but it means that, if there are a number of errors, the average error will be found by adding their squares together, dividing by the number of errors and then finding the square root. This quantity is known as the root mean square.

7. For reasons too complex to be tackled in a treatise on navigation, the statistician uses a slight modification of the root mean square and divides by one less than the number of errors, calling this quotient the variance. The square root of the variance is known as the standard deviation of the errors, or sigma (symbol σ). In the instance of a large number of errors, sigma and root mean square are almost identical.

Example. Suppose that ten instruments all measure a known quantity and that the errors of the instruments are as follows:

Errors:	+4	−1	0	+2	+1	−7	0	+3	+1	−3
Errors^2:	16	1	0	4	1	49	0	9	1	9

Sum of errors ^{2} $= 90$
Number of errors $= 10$
Mean square $= 90 \div 10 = 9$ (Variance $= 90 \div 9 = 10$)
Root mean square $= \sqrt{9}$ $= 3$ (Sigma $= 3 \cdot 16$)

ERROR DISTRIBUTIONS

8. Although the standard deviation will give a measure of the size of the error, it will not tell what proportion of the errors can be expected to be bigger than a certain size. The probability of an error being small will be high, since many of the inaccuracies will tend to cancel each other out. The large errors that will result when most of the inaccuracies happen to act in the same direction

will have a low probability. The pattern or distribution of probability may therefore be in the form of a hump centred on the correct value as shown in Fig. 13 which illustrates what is known as the gaussian distribution.

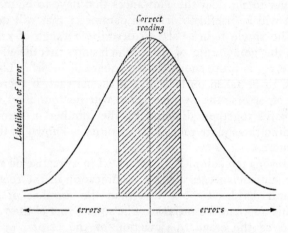

FIG. 13   Gaussian or 'normal' distribution

9. The curve in Fig. 13 is not complete and should be extended to left and to right. The shaded area in the figure will then be 50 per cent of the complete area. An error has a 50 per cent chance of falling within the limits of this shaded area. Therefore these limits can be said to represent the 50 per cent error of the distribution. If the limits were increased, they would cover a greater percentage of the curve and represent a bigger percentage error.

10. The gaussian distribution is known as the 'normal' distribution because it results if a large number of small individual errors are combined irrespective of the distributions of the individual errors. In practice, the gaussian distribution is far from being normal. In certain instances, the ends of the distributions may be cut down by limiting devices. More commonly, large errors will occur far more frequently than the rapidly collapsing skirts of the gaussian distribution would suggest, particularly when errors from widely differing sources are mixed or when expanding errors are generated at different times.

11. When errors ignoring the signs are plotted on log-linear graph paper, the gaussian distribution appears as half a parabola, whereas the pattern produced in practice is more commonly a straight line as shown in Fig. 14. This straight line would naturally produce a double exponential on normal graph paper, with a sharp peak at the centre. This peak may be rounded off in

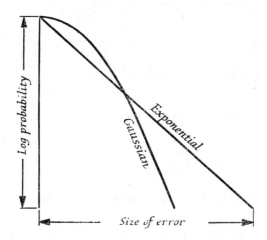

FIG. 14   Gaussian and exponential distributions

practice. Nevertheless, although no one distribution can claim to be normal, it will be sensible for the navigator to base his first approximations on the exponential rather than on the gaussian distribution in the absence of any better statistical information. At least the exponential will be more pessimistic and therefore safer than the gaussian.

12. Fig. 15 gives the connections between percentage errors and standard deviation (sigma) for the gaussian and the exponential distributions, and shows that an error of 5 sigma will occur roughly once in a thousand times with the exponential but only once in a million times with the gaussian. A mental extension of the exponential line shows that for a similar reliability, the exponential distribution would have to have a value of about 10 sigma. Hence, in general, an equipment with an exponential distribution will need to have a sigma of half that of a gaussian

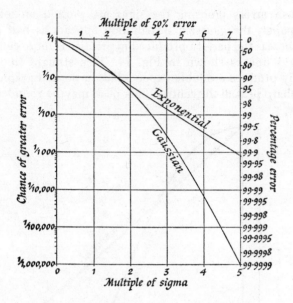

FIG. 15   Gaussian and exponential errors

distribution or, in simpler words, would need to be twice as accurate. Only if the probabilities were to be as low as one in a million million would the exponential need to be three times as accurate as the gaussian. It will have been noted that if the 95 per cent error of an exponential distribution is, say, 1 n.m., this means that the 1 in 20 chance is 1 n.m., and the 1 in 20^2 chance or 99·7 per cent error is 2 n.m. and the 1 in 20^3 chance or the 99·99 per cent error is about 3 n.m. Ease of conversion from one percentage error to another is another advantage that follows from assuming an exponential distribution.

TYPES OF ERROR

13. In general, three types of error are recognized. These are:

   (a) Systematic errors that can be foreseen and corrected.
   (b) Random errors that can neither be foreseen nor corrected.
   (c) Faults and mistakes.

In addition the navigator recognizes the existence of semi-systematic errors half-way between systematic and random errors.

14. The navigator is not concerned with numbers of equipments but with the behaviour of a particular equipment in a particular craft. Hence, he may recognize in the types of error the following characteristics, as suggested in Fig. 16:

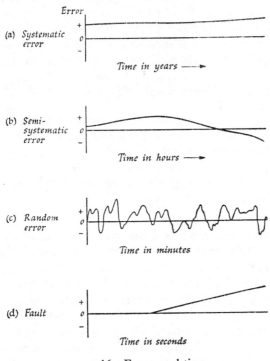

FIG. 16 Errors and time

(a) *Systematic errors* change so slowly with time that they may be measured and corrected.
(b) *Semi-systematic errors* change slowly with time and, over a short period, may be virtually constant. However, these errors change too quickly to be measured and corrected.
(c) *Random errors* change quickly and continuously so that they can neither be foreseen nor corrected.

(d) *Faults* appear as abrupt changes to the pattern of errors either in the form of a rate of error or, in the instance of a mistake, in the form of a large step in the error.

SYSTEMATIC ERRORS

15. There are two common types of systematic error:

(a) *Zero error*, which applies equally to all readings of the instrument, including the zero reading. A tape-measure that has lost the first $\frac{1}{4}$ inch would be a simple example.
(b) *Scale error*, which increases in proportion to the reading and therefore alters the scale of measurement. A tape-measure that has stretched uniformly by one-sixtieth of its length will have a scale of error of 1 in 60 or 1·7 per cent.

16. If an equipment is subject to two or more systematic errors, the total systematic error will be their sum. For example, a length of 30 inches measured on the tape mentioned in the previous paragraph would have a zero error of $+\frac{1}{4}$ inch, and a scale error of $-\frac{1}{2}$ inch, making a total systematic error of $-\frac{1}{4}$ inch.

SEMI-SYSTEMATIC ERRORS

17. It is not possible to define when an error ceases to be systematic and becomes semi-systematic. In the same way, it is impossible to draw a line between semi-systematic errors and random errors since the difference is entirely a matter of time scale as shown in Fig. 16. Certain errors are, however, generally regarded as semi-systematic. Personal error, due, for example, to a tendency to read an instrument too high or too low, tends to change abruptly and unpredictably with time and circumstance.

18. *Tilting Errors.* The existence of tilting errors can be forecast, but generally their appearance cannot be anticipated so that they are virtually semi-systematic. Fig. 17 shows the effect of tilting a shadow-pin mounted on a circular protractor. The error in direction recorded by the shadow will depend on the angle of elevation of the object above the plane of the protractor. The higher the elevation, the greater the error due to tilt. The error also depends on the direction of tilt. If the tilt is towards or away from the object, there will be no error. If it is at right angles to

the direction of the object, the error will be a maximum. As a first approximation:

tilting error° = tilt° × cos (direction of tilt compared to object)
× tan (elevation of object)

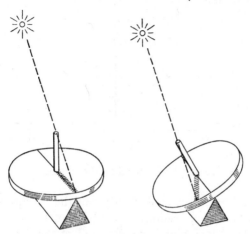

FIG. 17 Tilting error

19 The complete tilting formula is complex. From the approximation it might be imagined that if the object were in the plane of the protractor so that its elevation is nil, there would be no tilting error. If the tilt is large, a second-order error will appear, unless the object is in line with the tilt or exactly at right angles to the tilt. The maximum error will arise with an object at 45° to the line of tilt, the approximate formula being:

tilting error° = − (tilt°)²
× sin (2 × direction of tilt compared to object)/230

RANDOM ERRORS

20. Random errors cannot generally be foreseen. There are, however, two particular instances of random error which commonly arise:

(a) *Rounding-off error*. When an instrument is read to the nearest graduation, this graduation does duty for all readings from half-way up to the next graduation to half-way down to the previous graduation. The error in reading to the nearest graduation will therefore be equally likely to be anywhere between these limits and the distribution of errors is therefore rectangular as shown in Fig. 18. The

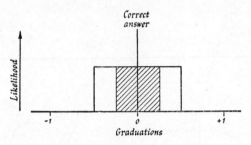

FIG. 18   Rectangular distribution

50 per cent error is obviously half the maximum error or a quarter of a graduation, and it can be shown that the standard deviation is roughly 0·7 of the maximum error or roughly one-third of a graduation.

(b) *Periodic error*. When the reading of an instrument is swinging from side to side, it will be changing quickly as it swings across the correct answer and will be unlikely to be read. However, it will be changing slowly at the extreme ends of the swings and so will be likely to be read. Thus the error will have a U-shaped distribution with the ends fixed according to the extent of the swing.

21. *Combining Random Errors*. Just as the 'golden rule' (page 35, para 6) is used to find the standard deviation of an error, so the 'golden rule' is used to add deviations together:

total standard deviation
$$= \sqrt{}(\text{sum of squares of standard deviations})$$

If errors are expressed as percentage errors, they must be converted to standard deviations before being combined. 95 per cent gaussian and exponential errors must be halved and maximum rounding-off errors reduced by a factor of two-thirds. The combined error may be reconverted to a 95 per cent error by doubling it, provided that any rounding-off error in the combination is not too large.

Example: An instrument with a 95 per cent error of 2° and hence a standard deviation of 1° is read to the nearest degree.

Maximum rounding-off error $= \frac{1}{2}°$
Standard deviation of
  rounding-off error $= \frac{1}{2}° \times \frac{2}{3} = \frac{1}{3}°$
Total standard deviation $= \sqrt{(1^2 + (\frac{1}{3})^2)}°$
  $= \sqrt{1\frac{1}{9}}°$
  $= 1°·05$
Total 95% error $= 2°·1$

22. The example shows that reading an equipment with a 95 per cent error of 2 units to the nearest whole number of units does not increase the error appreciably. This emphasizes that a large error increases only by a very small amount if a small error is combined with it, owing to the need to square the small error before adding and finding the square root.

23. *Limits of Random Error.* If a human operator makes a mistake once in a hundred readings, Fig. 15 shows that when an error is much greater than 3 sigma, it is more likely to be a mistake than a random error. In this instance, 3 sigma might be regarded as the limits of random error. Thus the limits of random error will depend on the fault rate of the equipment or system. In practice, an error or more than 2 or 3 sigma may be treated with suspicion and an error of more than 4 or 5 sigma may be rejected unless supported by other evidence.

FAULTS

24. Faults may be one of three types:

(a) Mistakes or blunders caused by human operators at the time.

(b) Malfunctions of the equipment which may or may not be recognized as such.

(c) Breakdowns in which the equipment behaves in such a way that it is known to have a fault. A breakdown is often less serious than a fault because no answer is generally better than a wrong answer. Equipment on whose operation the safety of the craft may depend may be designed to break down or to disconnect itself in the event of a fault developing.

25. A fault may be of any size and therefore the distribution may be represented by a straight line, as suggested in Fig. 19. The

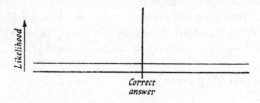

FIG. 19 Fault distribution idealized

fault may be limited by circumstances. For example, a measurement of direction can never be more than 180° in error. Also, a small fault is probably more common than a large fault because the latter will generally take more time to develop. Mistakes, however, may follow no such pattern but may tend to occur at certain points. In the measurement of direction by a compass, a peak commonly occurs at a reciprocal, a blunder known as setting red on blue, red and blue being the opposite poles of a magnet.

26. If a fault arises in one observation out of a hundred, the fault rate may be said to be 1 per cent. If a second fault arises in one observation out of a thousand, or 0·1 per cent, the total fault rate will naturally be 1·1 per cent. If two such faults should occur, the resultant reading will be no more unpredictable than if one fault had occurred.

27. If the breakdown rate of an equipment were such that, over a period of 2000 hours, half the equipments were to become unserviceable, it would be reasonable to expect that half of the remaining equipments would break down in the next 2000 hours if the breakdowns were random. The graph of the number of equipments remaining serviceable would therefore be an exponential. The rate of breakdown may be defined by the average time an equipment remains serviceable, known as the mean time between failures (M.T.B.F.). In a random distribution, the

M.T.B.F. will be roughly one and a half times as long as the time at which 50 per cent of the equipments become unserviceable.

28. If the serviceability of a number of equipments is plotted on log-linear paper as shown in Fig. 20, a truly exponential or random fault rate will appear as a straight line. Plotting on log-linear graph paper therefore suggests when the unserviceability is not random. For example, Fig. 20 shows that the breakdown

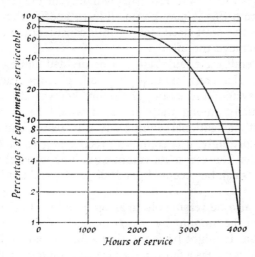

FIG. 20   Serviceability graph

rate of this particular equipment is high initially, which is common since faults in manufacture that have escaped inspection may initially increase the rate. Later on, the rate increases due to wear and tear. Plotting on normal graph paper might not have revealed these changes of fault rate.

SYSTEM FAULT RATES

29. If there are a number of units in a system, the overall breakdown rate can be found from the individual unit rates as follows:

system fault rate per 1000 hours
= sum of unit fault rates per 1000 hours

This can be expressed in terms of M.T.B.F. by:

1/(system M.T.B.F.)
= 1/(unit 'A' M.T.B.F.) + 1/(unit 'B' M.B.T.F.), &c.

30. It will now be necessary to consider how navigation un-serviceability fits into the overall pattern. A craft will have an operational aim. Circumstances outside the control of the navi-gator may lead to a 'fault rate' that will prevent the attainment of the aim. From this it may be possible to specify the reliability expected of the craft itself, taking into consideration the cost of failure to achieve the aim.

31. The overall craft fault rate can be divided among the main elements of the craft, namely, its hull, engines, fuel system, navigation system and so on. If the breakdown rate were to be divided equally among these units, it would be found that a complicated navigational equipment was being equated to a rudder. Accordingly, it is common practice to give each element a number that represents its complexity. The lower the number the less faults can be accepted per 1000 hours, and the longer the M.T.B.F.

32. It may also be reasonable to assign numbers to the elements according to the amount by which unserviceability could affect the operation. It might be found that a fault in an engine would be disastrous whereas a fault in the air conditioning would merely be inconvenient. It may therefore be possible to state factors that bear some relation to the importance of the element, the most important element being given the factor unity and the less important elements higher factors. By multiplying the complex-ity number by the importance factor a relative breakdown rate can be evolved. From this relative breakdown rate, the actual breakdown rate that can be accepted from an element can be indicated by:

fault rate of element/1000 hours
= fault rate of craft/1000 hours

$$\times \frac{\text{relative fault rate of element}}{\text{sum of relative fault rates of all elements}}$$

Example. A craft, consisting of the following elements graded in importance and complexity, is to have an overall fault rate of 1 in 1000 hours.

Element	Importance	Complexity	Relative fault rate
Engine	2	6	12
Body work	4	4	16
Chassis	2	1	2
			30

fault rate acceptable for engine = 12/30 per 1000 hours
$$= 0 \cdot 4 \text{ per } 1000 \text{ hours}$$
$$\therefore \text{ M.T.B.F.} = 2500 \text{ hours approximately.}$$

33. The same process may be used to assess the required M.T.B.F. of an individual equipment within an element of or an individual unit within an equipment. It may, however, be necessary to modify the figures on economic grounds. The expense involved in achieving a certain M.T.B.F. on a very complex and delicate equipment could become exorbitant.

ERROR STANDARDS

34. Scientists and engineers may use sigma to define a navigational error. Unfortunately this may not give a good idea of the accuracy of a system. If the distribution is gaussian, it will represent the accuracy two times out of three, or if it is exponential it will represent the accuracy three times out of four.

35. The 50 per cent error is convenient because a navigator can often estimate it mentally from his experience. Unfortunately it may well give a spurious impression of accuracy and, unless the distribution is specified, cannot be evolved from the standard deviation. However, an error of between 90 and 95 per cent will be approximately twice the standard deviation whether the distribution be gaussian or exponential.

36. It is important that an error should always be stated in terms of percentage or a multiple of sigma. For the purposes of this book, the 95 per cent error will be chosen which is roughly 2 × standard deviation. The odds of 1 in 20 have often been regarded as the quasi-maximum, that is, the order of accuracy always expected and within which a fault is unlikely to

occur. Twice the 95 per cent error will represent odds of one in several hundreds if the distribution is exponential, or several thousands if the distribution is gaussian, and may be regarded as the boundary beyond which faults are likely to arise.

4. REDUCTION OF ERRORS

THE REQUIREMENT

1. A composite picture of errors is shown in Fig. 21. Systematic and semi-systematic errors will displace the hump sideways from the correct reading. Random errors will spread the hump. Faults will add skirts to the hump.

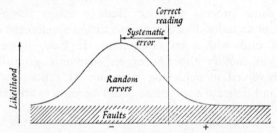

FIG. 21   Composite error curve (fault likelihood greatly exaggerated)

2. The requirement of navigation is that the craft should be conducted within certain limits. It does not matter that the ship is not exactly in the centre of the channel, provided that it does not run on to the rocks either side. The point at which a guided missile warhead explodes is immaterial provided that it is within lethal distance of the target. The requirement for navigation therefore has sharp limits, as suggested in Fig. 22.

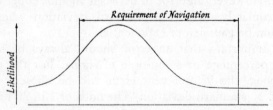

FIG. 22   Composite error curve and navigation requirement

3. On to the sharply limited requirement, the composite error graph has been superimposed. The chance of an error being greater than the requirement will be reduced if the hump is moved sideways by elimination of systematic and semi-systematic errors and if the hump is narrowed by reducing the random error. If the hump is nearly central but very wide, the random error will show the greater return if it can be reduced. If the hump is narrow but displaced sideways by a large amount, it will be the systematic and semi-systematic errors that will need to be tackled first.

4. However carefully the systematic, semi-systematic and random errors may be reduced, the faults will still remain. Furthermore, it is the fault that generally upsets navigation. Hence the efforts to reduce errors must not be such that the fault rate is increased. In the majority of instances, reliability within a band of errors is the requirement, not accuracy accompanied by a high fault rate.

CORRECTION OF SYSTEMATIC ERRORS

5. When a systematic error has been detected, it is best reduced by compensation. Compensation involves feeding into the equipment an effect opposite to that which is causing the error. For example, the errors in a magnetic compass due to the presence of iron in the craft are best eliminated by arranging for compensating magnetism. Compensation generally has a better chance of correcting the systematic error under all conditions.

6. If compensation is not possible, it will be necessary to correct. Automatic correction makes no demands on the human operator and avoids human mistakes, but may increase the danger of malfunction. In many instances, automatic correction is not provided and the navigator uses correction graphs or tables. These arithmetical corrections are of four types which are stated in order of decreasing accuracy but also in order of decreasing chance of mistakes:

   (a) *Correction graph.* If the graph has a large scale it will be
       unwieldy. If small, it will be difficult to read, particularly
       in conditions of vibration, and may easily lead to blunders.

5—P.N.

(b) *Correction tables.* An example is shown in Table I (A). Interpolation will be necessary to achieve the same accuracy as a graph, but it will be easier to read.

(c) *Critical table.* An example is shown in Table I (B). This table reduces the accuracy of the correction but removes the need for interpolation. In a critical table, if there is any doubt, the lower figure in the right-hand column is used. Thus the correction for 117 will be -2, not -2.5.

TABLE I. TYPICAL CORRECTION TABLES

(A) CORRECTION TABLE		(B) CRITICAL TABLE		(C) CONVERSION TABLE	
Instrument reading	Correction to be applied to instrument reading	Instrument reading	Correction to be applied to instrument reading	Instrument reading	Corrected reading
110	-2.75	110		110	$107\frac{1}{2}$
112	-2.6		-2.5	115	$112\frac{1}{2}$
114	-2.5	117		120	118
116	-2.3		-2	125	119
118	-2.1	122		130	130
			-1.5	135	136
120	-1.9	125			
122	-1.7		-1		
124	-1.4	128			
126	-1.1		-0.5		
128	-0.8	131			
			0		
130	-0.4	133			
132	$+0.1$		$+0.5$		
134	$+0.5$	135			

(d) *Conversion tables.* If an equipment may have to be set to a certain figure as well as read, a conversion table as shown in Table I (C) will prevent the correction being applied the wrong way. For example, suppose that there was a need to set the engines of a craft so that the correct reading was 115. The conversion table shows that a reading of about $117\frac{1}{2}$ on the instrument should be used. Had any of the previous tables been used, this $2\frac{1}{2}$ might have been applied the wrong way.

REDUCTION OF SEMI-SYSTEMATIC ERRORS

7. Semi-systematic errors change too quickly to be calibrated but may be reduced by methods similar to those which will be suggested for random errors, except that the corrections will have to be spread over longer periods of time. Of the special instances of semi-systematic errors mentioned on page 40, para 17, personal errors cannot generally be reduced by tabulation since they change unpredictably, but tilting errors can be reduced by stabilizing or maintaining the level of the instrument that is measuring direction.

8. Many semi-systematic errors can be reduced by symmetry. Observations taken on a number of objects symmetrically disposed about the craft tend to reduce semi-systematic errors. Instruments which are constructed symmetrically tend to suffer less from semi-systematic errors. Such instruments also suffer less from errors due to vibration. Vibration errors may be semi-systematic but often appear as temporary faults occurring when the vibration happens to be of a certain critical frequency.

REDUCTION OF RANDOM ERRORS

9. Over a long period of time, random errors are likely to be distributed equally about the correct value, otherwise a systematic or a semi-systematic error would result. If a number of observations are truly random, the reduction of error resulting from averaging will be according to the square root of the number of observations. The average of four readings will be twice as accurate as one reading. In general terms:

average error
= (error in one observation)/$\sqrt{}$(number of observations)

10. If a series of observations be taken on one instrument, each reading will be affected by the previous reading according to the rate at which the readings change. The errors will not be random and the formula in the previous paragraph therefore no longer applies. If a continual input of readings be taken or if a large number of consecutive readings be averaged, the error may be reduced with time, as suggested in Fig. 23. The actual shape of this curve will depend on a number of factors, but it may not

differ greatly from an exponential at least over a short period of time.

11. It will often be necessary to support an observation by another taken on a different equipment with a different accuracy. For example, suppose that one equipment has a 95 per cent error of 1 n.m. and another has a 95 per cent of 2 n.m. The former can be regarded as the average of four errors each of which has a 95 per cent scatter of 2 n.m., and therefore the two errors combined can be regarded as the average of five errors each with a

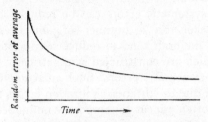

FIG. 23   Reduction of random error
resulting from integrating a number
of readings

95 per cent scatter of 2 n.m., making a total 95 per cent error of $2/\sqrt{5}$ n.m., which is 0·9 n.m. approximately. This emphasizes that the addition of a less accurate observation will do little to increase the accuracy of an observation, another example of the 'golden rule'. However, the second observation, though less accurate, may greatly increase the reliability of the first by providing a check against faults.

12. The rectangular rounding-off error is generally accepted on the basis that to strive for high accuracy will increase the fault rate. The U-shaped error is reduced by averaging the observations spread over this period. Generally, the period will not be known, but it will be sufficient if the observations are averaged over a period long enough to cover the longest possible swing of the readings.

DETECTION OF FAULTS

13. The existence of a fault or a mistake may be detected in one of two ways:

(a) *Cross check.* The cross check comprises an alternative source of information independent of the information to be checked so that a mistake is not repeated. The cross check must be reliable even if not supremely accurate. For example, a navigator will often guess at the result of a calculation beforehand because, being in real quantities rather than dead figures, the 'guestimate' may be the more reliable although much less accurate.

(b) *Consistency.* The navigator may compare present information with past information to check that the sequence is sensible. For example, he may difference a series of observations. Had differencing been applied to the conversion Table I (c), on page 50, 119 would have appeared as a blunder.

14. Dead reckoning as a means of checking position-finding aids is seen to have ideal qualities. As a cross check, it is independent. It also links the present with the past to ensure consistency. In addition, it uses instruments that are simple and reliable. As a result, navigation has been likened to a picture painted by means of position-finding aids on a canvas of dead reckoning.

15. *Mistakes.* The likelihood of human mistakes depends partly on the way in which information is presented. The presentation must be unambiguous, non-irritating and in line with normal habits. For example, because time increases clockwise, instrument readings should increase clockwise. Errors can also arise in transmission. 'Four' and 'nought' can sound similar against a background of noise so that 'zero' will be used. 10 and 1° may be mistaken so that the degree symbol will be avoided. The navigator develops many habits to reduce errors of this nature, and examples will appear in the book.

16. *Malfunction.* Measures taken to deal with malfunction will depend on whether time is of the essence in detecting and correcting. If time is important, it will be necessary to provide an automatic cross check with arrangements for a warning should disagreement arise. If action has to be taken immediately, the automatic comparator may have to take immediate action to inhibit a dangerous situation. For example, it may be necessary to disconnect the faulty equipment on the basis that no information

is better than wrong information. If an essential equipment is to be disconnected, it will be necessary to provide an alternative. Thus fault detection implies redundancy.

REDUNDANCY

17. The following are common applications of redundancy techniques:

(a) *Fault can cause no immediate danger.* The aid may be supported by a second equipment that is extremely reliable even if less accurate. Since an error will only be indicated when the readings of the two equipments differ by an amount that is greater than would be expected according to the least accurate equipment, it follows that the two equipments together can only be *relied on* to give a position as accurate as that which would be given by the less accurate, although generally the accuracy may be much higher.

(b) *Fault must be detected.* Two equipments of a similar accuracy must be continuously compared. In the event of a difference, a third source of information will have to act as an umpire. However, until the two accurate equipments disagree by an amount which is large compared to the accuracy of the umpire, it will be impossible to tell which is wrong.

(c) *Fault must not develop.* Two equipments of a similar accuracy must be compared and both must be disconnected in the event of a major discrepancy. Often one will be a main equipment and the other will be a monitor.

TABLE II. RELIABILITY AND REDUNDANCY
(ASSUMING EQUIPMENT M.T.B.F. $= A$)

Number of equipments	M.T.B.F. OF SYSTEM				Notes
	One fault	Two faults	Three faults	Four faults	
1	A				No redundancy
2	$A/2$	A^2			Fault not located
3	$A/3$	$A^2/3$	A^3		Logical system
4	$A/4$	$A^2/6$	$A^3/4$	A^4	High level of reliability

(d) *Fault must be prevented.* At least three equipments of equal accuracy must be used so that any one which is not working correctly may be discarded. The systems could of course comprise two equipments and a monitor, two equipments and two monitors or four equipments. Table II shows that a system with triple or quadruple redundancy where all equipments have the same level of accuracy is potentially very safe.

18. Redundancy is also of value is assessing the reliability of a complex equipment. For example, suppose that an equipment must not develop a fault more than once in a million journeys. Without redundancy, many millions of journeys would have to be undertaken before this capability could be demonstrated and the equipment would probably be out of date before it could be accepted in service. However, if it were to comprise a number of redundant elements each with a low mean time between faults, the chance that one element would break down in a given time could be found without danger and, from this information, the overall reliability of the equipment could be demonstrated in a short time.

5. TWO-DIMENSIONAL ERRORS

CIRCLE OF ERROR

1. If a measurement indicates that a craft is on a certain line, the errors in the measurement imply that it has a certain chance of being within a certain distance of that line. A line may therefore be regarded as a ridge of probabilities as shown in Fig. 24(a). The 95 per cent error may be portrayed as a band within which the craft can be expected to be on 95 per cent of occasions.

2. A position in navigation may be regarded as being the point where two lines cross. Since each line may be represented by a band of errors, the craft will probably not be at the point where the two lines cut but somewhere in an area around that point. If the errors of each line were rectangular in distribution and the lines were to cross at right angles, the error distribution at the crossing point might be visualized as a rectangular block which

could be represented in plan as a rectangle. If the errors of each line were gaussian in distribution, the error distribution at the crossing point might be visualized as a heap as shown in

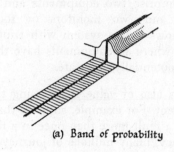

(a) Band of probability

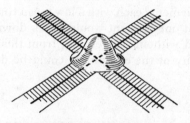

(b) Probability heap

FIG. 24 Two-dimensional errors

Fig. 24 (b). In plan, the heap could be represented by a circle, provided that the lines had equal bands of probability and crossed at right angles.

3. The 50 per cent error of a linear distribution is defined by the limits of a central area equal to half the area of the distribution curve (page 36, Fig. 13). Similarly, the 50 per cent error of a heap is according to the limits given by cutting out a central cylinder equal to half the volume of the heap. The radius of this cylinder is known as the radial error.

4. A linear distribution can be regarded as a number of vertical strips as in a histogram. Similarly, a two-dimensional heap

distribution can be regarded as a number of concentric rings whose volume increases according to the radius as well as the height. Hence the way in which percentage errors are linked to standard deviations will not be the same in a two-dimensional heap as in a linear distribution. This has been well illustrated in

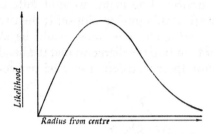

FIG. 25　Radial distribution

Fig. 25, which shows how the probability of an error varies with distance from the centre of a typical two-dimensional heap. It is extremely unlikely that a reading will fall exactly in a small circle centred at the correct point, and far more likely that it will fall in a ring of equal width a short distance around the correct point, since the area of the ring will be many times as great as the area of the small circle.

5. It is now obvious that, if two lines with the same error cut at right angles, the radial error of the resulting heap will be a multiple of the linear error which will vary with the percentage error and with the type of distribution. However, for distributions between the gaussian and the exponential, the following approximate table will apply:

TABLE III. CALCULATION OF RADIAL ERRORS

Percentage error	Linear error to be multiplied by this factor to give radial error
50 per cent	2
Sigma	$\sqrt{2}$
95 per cent	$1\frac{1}{4}$
99 per cent	1

Hence if the two position line bands of error were widened by these factors, the radial error of the circular heap would fit exactly inside the square that the bands contained.

ELLIPSE OF ERROR

6. If the two position line bands were of different widths, the circle would be distorted into an ellipse. If the two position lines were to cut at an angle, the circle would be skewed into an ellipse in order to fit into the diamond that the bands contained.

7. Fig. 26 shows the construction of a 95 per cent ellipse. The

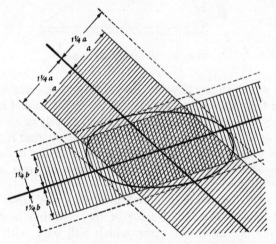

FIG. 26   Construction of 95 per cent probability
ellipse, from 95 per cent probability bands

95 per cent bands of probability are widened by a factor of $1\frac{1}{4}$ (see para 5). The ellipse is then the maximum that will fit into the diamond formed by these widened bands of position. However, this will only apply if the distributions are between the gaussian and the exponential.

RADIAL ERROR

8. To specify an ellipse of probability, it is necessary to state at least three parameters such as length, width and direction of

length. To avoid this complication, it is usual to define a two-dimensional error in terms of the radius of that circle within which the position can be expected to fall on 95 per cent of occasions, and the radius of this circle is known as the radial error. The circle will not be quite as long as the ellipse and will be considerably broader. Furthermore, a position will be more likely to fall within those smaller areas of the ellipse outside the circle than within those larger areas of the circle outside the ellipse. Nevertheless, the approximation is satisfactory except for very elongated ellipses.

9. If two lines cut at right angles, the standard deviation of the combined error will follow the 'golden rule' and be the square root of the sum of the squares of the two linear errors. If the lines do not cut at right angles, the errors are increased. Fig. 27 shows a very accurate position line cutting an inaccurate

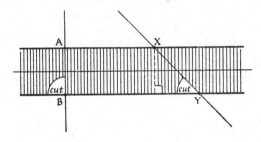

FIG. 27   Error and angle of cut

position line at right angles forming an ellipse which appears as a straight line AB if the cut is at right angles, but a longer ellipse which appears as the straight line XY if the cut is at an angle. The ratio of the two ellipses is obviously according to the cosecant of the angle of cut. Hence, if two lines with linear standard deviations of a and b cut:

Radial standard deviation depends on $\sqrt{(a^2+b^2)}/\sin$ (cut)

10. If the navigator is concerned with the cut of two position lines whose errors are expressed in percentage errors rather than in standard deviation, it will be necessary to convert them to

standard deviations and then to reconvert them back to radial percentages. In the instance of 95 per cent errors, it is found that on a pessimistic basis:

95 per cent radial error
= √(sum of squares of 95 per cent linear errors)/sin (cut)

It is possible to produce figures for other percentages. However, in practice, large errors will seldom be required on an area basis but will be expressed as two linear errors each with a separate significance to navigation. It will, however, be essential to be able to handle 95 per cent errors both linear and radial.

EQUAL AREA CIRCLE
11. It has been suggested that the 95 per cent ellipse would be better represented by a circle of the same area. The 95 per cent ellipse is the smallest area within which a position has a 95 per cent chance of falling. Therefore the circle of the same area, known as the equal area circle, will be smaller than the circle represented by the radial error.
12. The radial error is used by navigators and not the equal area circle, for two reasons:

(a) The radial error is larger and therefore more pessimistic and safer.
(b) With a very long thin ellipse, only a small percentage of errors might fall within the equal area circle. The correct percentage of errors will always fall within the radial error.

REDUCTION OF TWO-DIMENSIONAL ERRORS
13. Two-dimensional errors have been regarded as comprising two linear errors. Each of the two linear errors may be reduced by methods described in the previous section of this chapter. There will therefore be no need to describe the reduction of two-dimensional errors as such. It will, however, be worth noting that the radial errors cannot be retranslated into two linear errors unless the relative size of the errors of the two lines is known and their angle of cut.

6. SUMMARY

MATHEMATICS

The nautical mile, or occasionally 1′ of change in the direction of the vertical, is the unit of distance used in navigation.

The knot, or occasionally 1′ of change in the direction of the vertical per hour, is the unit of speed.

The curve of normal decay is an exponential or logarithmic curve which is defined by the time constant. The time constant is about one and a half times the half-life of a quantity that is decaying.

Integration may be used in navigation to find the mean value of a quantity that is continually changing. A cosine curve is the differential of a sine curve and is a sine curve advanced by 90°. In practice a phase advance of less than 90° is achieved.

Any curve may be built up from a number of sine curves.

For small angles, the 1 in 60 rule applies to sines and tangents and the cosine equals one.

Acceleration in a curve equals $speed^2/(radius of curvature)$. A mass needs a certain force to accelerate it. Weight is the force exerted by a mass which is being accelerated by gravity (32 feet per second per second).

According to the angle at which a plane cuts a cone, an ellipse, a parabola or an hyperbola will result. In an ellipse, the sum of the distances from two foci is constant. In an hyperbola, the difference of the distances from two foci is constant.

By trigonometry, polar coordinates and cartesian coordinates are interchanged.

COMPUTERS

The digital computer compared to the analogue computer has possibilities of accuracy that are not limited, great flexibility, stability and the ability to remember instructions and to follow programmes involving alternatives. It can be made self-checking without great additional complication and is built up from a large number of similar bricks.

The digitizers that convert mechanical movements and electrical quantities into pulses are complex, expensive and bulky if they are to achieve accuracy. For computing involving a number of inputs which have to be combined in relatively simple ways without high accuracy, the analogue computer may be preferred.

ERRORS

The distribution of errors is defined by standard deviation known as sigma or by percentage errors. Throughout this book, the 95 per cent error will be taken as the standard.

Errors are of four main types:

(a) Systematic errors that change slowly with time and may be compensated or corrected.

(b) Semi-systematic errors that change too quickly to be compensated or corrected. Symmetry of observation may help to reduce them.

(c) Random errors that change quickly with time and may be reduced by averaging. The results of averaging over a period of time will depend on the rate at which the random errors change and whether they have a distinct period.

(d) Faults that develop abruptly. They appear as a lack of consistency of readings. Redundancy can reduce the arising of faults that can affect the safety of the craft, two equipments being necessary to establish that a fault exists and a third to establish which of two equipments is at fault.

If an error is such that its likelihood is less than the fault rate, it may be assumed that a fault has occurred. Errors and faults can cause accidents which can be related to passenger miles or to cargo miles.

Reliability may be expressed as an M.T.B.F. which is roughly $1\frac{1}{2}$ times the length of time at which 50 per cent of the equipments will become unserviceable. Serviceability plotted on logarithmic graph paper will reveal random and systematic unserviceability.

Errors, including radial errors, follow the 'golden rule' of squares.

The area within which an error in two dimensions can be

expected to fall will generally be defined by the radial error, although this is larger in area than the probability ellipse. The 95 per cent radial error is approximately equal to the square root of the sum of the squares of the linear errors divided by the sine of the angle of cut.

CHAPTER II
Environment

1. THE WORLD

THE UNIVERSE

1. The universe includes a number of galaxies each composed of millions of stars. The stars, even within a galaxy, are extremely remote from each other. The Sun is a typical star in a galaxy with a near neighbour about 25 million million miles away.

2. Around the Sun, a number of planets travel in elliptical orbits generally close to the plane of the Earth's orbit, which is known as the plane of the ecliptic. The Earth, which is one of the planets close to the Sun, travels in orbit at an average distance from the Sun of 93 million miles. The Earth is closest to the Sun in January and furthest from the Sun in July. The speed along the orbit varies inversely as the distance from the Sun, and therefore the Earth is moving faster in January than in July. This causes the time of the Sun's zenith at Greenwich to vary throughout the period of the orbit.

3. The Earth rotates on its axis at an angle to the ecliptic of about $66\frac{1}{2}°$. The angle of the axis is not absolutely constant but nutates about a central axis which is taken to be the true axis of the Earth for purposes of mapping. The amount of nutation is so small that it can generally be ignored.

4. The Earth rotates on its axis once every 23 hours, 56 minutes and 4 seconds, but as it travels around the Sun in the same direction as that in which it is rotating, the Sun only passes overhead once every 24 hours on the average. The Moon travels round the Earth once a month and rotates once a month so that the same face is always seen.

TIDES

5. The mutual attraction of the Earth and the Moon pulls the water away from the Earth on the side towards the Moon and

the Earth away from the water on the side away from the Moon, thus forming two heaps or tides. As the Earth rotates once a day, and the Moon orbits once a month, these two tides move round the Earth approximately once every 24 hours and 50 minutes, giving an interval of 12 hours and 25 minutes between tides.

6. The mutual attraction of the Earth and the Sun also causes tides, but these are much weaker than the lunar tides. However, at full or new moon, when the Sun and Moon are in line, the solar and lunar tides are cumulative and form spring tides. At half Moon, when the Sun and Moon are at right angles, neap tides result. In between, when the Sun and the Moon are pulling at an angle to each other, the tides are midway between spring and neap tides, and the times of high and low water are slightly modified.

7. Ignoring the effects of winds, the times of high and low water are calculated for certain major ports and appear in tide-tables. Corrections for near-by points are also provided. Alternatively, on a nautical chart, the delays in the hours of the spring tides, which would otherwise be at midday or midnight, are printed in roman figures. By adding to these printed figures 50 minutes for each day since the last full moon or new moon, very reasonable estimates of the times of high water can be made for any other day.

8. On a chart, tidal streams will be marked with half-feathered arrows for rising tides and straight arrows for falling tides. The maximum speed, which is generally 3 hours before or after high water, is also printed alongside the arrow. The speed 2 hours before or after high or low water is generally reckoned to be two-thirds of this maximum, and the speed 1 hour before or after high or low water is generally reckoned to be one-third of this maximum.

TIME

9. The mean time at which the Sun passes overhead at Greenwich is calculated, and this time is taken to be midday Greenwich Mean Time, generally written 1200 G.M.T. G.M.T. is the standard time for navigating, and navigators use a 24-hour clock.

10. Man generally prefers that his midday should be around

6—P.N.

12 o'clock. In theory, this could be managed by advancing time at the rate of 1 hour for each 15° of longitude east of Greenwich and retarding time at the rate of 1 hour for each 15° of longitude west of Greenwich. In practice, man is organized into countries or states which do not fit exactly into these 15° of longitude intervals. Hence countries and states tend to work in their own local Standard Times. These usually approximate to the 15° of longitude per hour relationship but, for ease of conversion, are generally an exact hour or an exact half-hour ahead or behind G.M.T. Typical examples connected with major cities are given in Fig. 28.

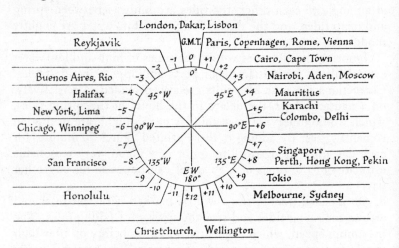

FIG. 28 Local Standard Times and G.M.T.

11. *Clocks and Watches*. Timepieces are sometimes divided into those which are driven mechanically and those which are driven by electricity. However, the important consideration is not the power that drives the hands but the precision with which this power is released. The mechanism that releases the driving power is generally known as an escapement.

12. The accuracy of an escapement will be affected by the driving power if the escapement is mechanical. Hence the need for regular winding of navigation watches and chronometers. However, the most important problem is temperature. The

accuracy of any type of escapement is limited by the extent to which it can be kept at a constant temperature or compensated for temperature changes. The wristwatch has a particular advantage as the temperature tends to be maintained constant.

13. There are two main types of escapement:

(a) *Pendulum.* This is not suitable for a moving craft because the swing will be modified by sideways acceleration. Nevertheless, on terra firma and in a suitable temperature-controlled environment, pendulum escapements have achieved accuracies measured in a few seconds a year. Even relatively simple temperature-compensated pendulums can achieve accuracies of the order of a few seconds a week.

(b) *Balance-wheel.* The balance-wheel, which rotates and contra-rotates against a hair spring, can be compensated for temperature changes but is generally less stable than a pendulum. However, accuracies of better than a second a day can be achieved provided the ambient temperature is reasonably constant. These accuracies can be achieved in a moving craft since the only accelerations that affect the balance-wheel are angular and are seldom of any duration or extent. Balance wheels demand great care in regulation. Marine practice is to establish, by comparison with radio time signals, the rate of losing or gaining of the chronometer. A correction is then applied arithmetically without altering the chronometer. However, if the balance wheel is electrically driven, it may be possible to reset without losing accuracy.

14. *Crystal Control.* Provided a piezo-electric crystal, generally a quartz crystal, is kept at a constant temperature and pressure, it will oscillate at a very exact frequency. Unlike the balance-wheel or pendulum, it can measure minute fractions of a second. If carefully controlled, it has a performance comparable to a very high-class pendulum. Its only weakness is that it tends to be bulky compared with the balance-wheel.

15. *Atomic Control.* By this means, it is possible to achieve an accuracy of the order of a second of time in several hundreds of years. The equipment is relatively heavy and costly and the

standard of time is not generally necessary for navigating. Nevertheless, the ability to measure time to 1 part in 10^{10} is a reminder that man can measure time more precisely than he can measure any other quantity.

ROTATION OF THE EARTH

16. At the equator, the surface is tilting at 360° a day or 15° an hour, but it is not rotating. At the poles, the surface is rotating at 15° an hour, but it is not tilting. Fig. 29 illustrates what will happen at the intervening latitudes. In 1 hour A will move to A′ and $\angle$ AOA′ will be 15°. Hence:

$$\angle ACA' = 15° \times AO/AC = 15° \times \cos \angle OAC$$
$$\therefore \text{ rate of tilt} = 15° \times \cos \text{ (latitude) per hour}$$

17. In Fig. 29, AP is the horizontal line at A which meets the Earth's axis at P. Hence:

$$\angle APA' = 15° \times AO/AP = 15° \times \sin \angle OPA$$
$$\therefore \text{ rate of rotation} = 15° \times \sin \text{ (latitude) per hour}$$

18. At the equator, the surface is moving eastwards at 15×60 minutes of angle per hour or about 900 knots. To north and south, this speed is reduced as the radius of the latitude becomes less than the radius of the Earth. Hence, from Fig. 29,

$$\text{speed at A due to Earth's rotation} = 900 \text{ knots } \times OA/CA$$
$$= 900 \times \cos \text{ (latitude) knots}$$

19. If a craft is at rest on the surface of the Earth, the rotation will reduce the force of gravity. At the equator, the rotation will cause an acceleration acting directly against gravity but, at other latitudes, the acceleration will act at an angle. It can be shown that:

$$\text{gravity} = 32 \cdot 155 \ [1 - 2\tfrac{1}{3} \times \cos(2 \times \text{latitude})/1000] \text{ ft/s}^2$$

which works out to 32·09 at the equator and 32·26 at the poles. As a result, the Earth is wider at the equator than between the poles by rather less than 1 part in 300 (1 in 298¼), the ratio being known as the figure of the Earth. Although gravity changes with latitude, it is generally taken to be 32 ft/s² (page 15, para. 2 (c)).

Gravity also changes as the surface of the Earth is left. At 40,000 feet, it is ¼ per cent less than at sea-level. Eventually, gravity decreases as the square of the distance from the centre of the Earth.

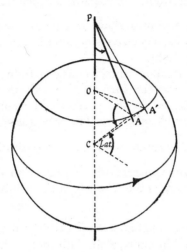

FIG. 29   The rotating Earth

EFFECTS OF MOVEMENT OF CRAFT

20. If a craft moves over the Earth at high speed, the weight will change owing to the curvature of the surface. A large, fast ocean liner steaming eastwards on the equator may lose a ton or may gain a ton steaming westwards. A supersonic aircraft may lose 1 per cent of its weight.

21. *Coriolis.* If a ball starts to roll from the centre of a turn-table which is rotating anti-clockwise, the path that the ball will mark on the surface as it travels outwards will be a curve to the right. The greater the rate of rotation, the greater the curvature of the path of the ball. The faster the ball is moving, the less the path will curve.

22. In the northern hemisphere, the surface of the Earth is rotating anti-clockwise, and therefore a craft travelling in a straight line will veer to the right as seen from the Earth. In the southern hemisphere, a craft will veer to the left. The curvature will depend on the rate of rotation, which has been shown

to be $15° \times \sin$ (latitude) (page 68, para 17), and on the speed. It can be shown that the radius of this curvature will be approximately:

$$[2 \times \text{(speed in knots)}/\sin \text{(latitude)}] \text{ nautical miles}$$

Hence the curvature of a slow craft or of slow-moving air or water due to coriolis may be considerable, but that of an extremely fast craft will be slight.

23. As a result of this curvature, a craft constrained to travel along a straight line across the surface of the Earth will have to be accelerated to the left in the northern hemisphere and to the right in the southern hemisphere. The acceleration will be roughly:

$$0.000008 \times \text{(speed in knots)} \times \sin \text{(latitude) ft/s}^2$$

This will cause an apparent tilt of gravity to the right in the northern hemisphere and to the left in the southern hemisphere of:

$$0.00044 \times \text{(speed in knots)} \times \sin \text{(latitude)} \quad \text{degrees, or}$$
$$0.026 \quad \times \text{(speed in knots)} \times \sin \text{(latitude)} \quad \text{minutes of angle}$$

STRUCTURE OF EARTH AND ATMOSPHERE

24. Three-quarters of the surface of the Earth is covered by water, most of which has a salt content of 3 or 4 per cent. The surface has mountains up to nearly 5 miles high and ocean deeps more than 6 miles deep. The average depth of the sea is over 10,000 feet, whereas the average height of the land is less than 2500 feet.

25. Air is composed of a mixture of gases, about three-quarters being nitrogen and a little over one-fifth being oxygen. As the surface of the Earth is left, the air becomes gradually less dense. Half the atmosphere is concentrated below 20,000 feet, and almost all the rest below 10 miles.

26. Water vapour is concentrated in the lower levels of the atmosphere, known as the troposphere. The upper limit of the troposphere, known as the tropopause, may be as low as 3 or 4 miles over the poles and as high as 8 or 10 miles over the equator. Above the tropopause, the atmosphere is known as the stratosphere.

27. At heights of about 30 or 40 miles by day, rising to about 200 miles at night, layers of electrically charged particles are found in the rarified air. These layers stretch upwards several

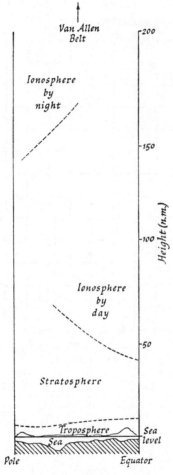

FIG. 30 The Earth's atmosphere

hundred miles, the whole forming the ionosphere. Further out, at distances of between 5000 and 15,000 miles, are layers of radiating particles known as the Van Allen belt. Fig. 30 illustrates

the distances of the atmospheric layers compared to the irregularities on the Earth's surface.

28. *Standard Atmosphere*. The way in which the density and
temperature of the air changes with height above sea-level will

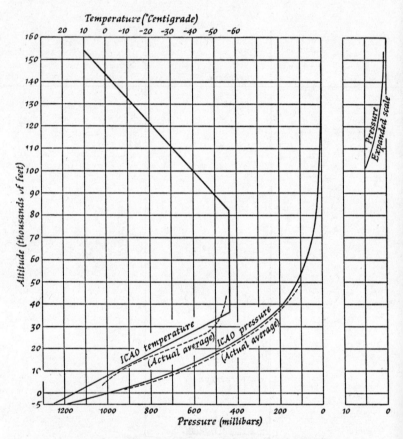

FIG. 31   The ICAO standard atmosphere (ISA)

vary from place to place and from time to time. The graph in
Fig. 31 shows a standard atmosphere reasonably close to the
overall average which has been agreed by the International Civil
Aviation Organization (ICAO). In this ISA atmosphere, air
pressure is measured in millibars, and air temperature in degrees

celsius (°C), generally known as centigrade. It is assumed that sea-level pressure is 1013 millibars at a temperature of 15°C. (A millibar (mb) is the pressure per square centimetre which would accelerate 1000 grams at 1 cm/s².)

THE ALTIMETER

29. The altimeter consists of a barometric capsule from which the air is exhausted. The capsule is mounted within an air-tight case into which pressure is led from outside the craft by a vent,

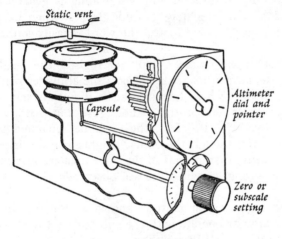

FIG. 32 Barometric altimeter

known as a static vent, so placed that no additional pressure resulting from the motion of the craft is fed into the altimeter case. The tube leading from the static vent to the case is known as the static tube. The capsule is connected to a pointer that registers against a dial which is marked not in millibars but in feet according to the standard atmosphere (para 28). The instrument may be fitted with three hands, the outer measuring 1000 'feet' in one revolution, the hand inside measuring 10,000 'feet' in 1 revolution, and the innermost hand reading 100,000 'feet' in 1 revolution. A simplified diagram with only one hand is shown in Fig. 32. Today, counters replace inner hands.

30. The altimeter is provided with a mechanical zero setting known as a sub-scale which is calibrated in millibars. If this

sub-scale be set to actual sea-level pressure, the altimeter will read 0 feet at sea-level. If set to the pressure of an airfield runway, it will read 0 feet on the runway. The altimeter will become progressively less accurate as the height above or below the datum increases, unless the change of pressure and temperature with height happens to vary exactly as the standard atmosphere. A closer approximation to height can be arrived at by making an allowance for the air temperature, but the estimate tends to be so inaccurate that it is not made by navigators. Since an altimeter cannot readily measure height, its reading is generally known as altitude. Unfortunately altitude has another navigational meaning (page 419, para 3) and the word is easily confused with attitude.

31. Although the altimeter will not register the height of an aircraft, the airman invariably selects the altimeter reading as a standard against which to fly because, if two aircraft are flying with sub-scales set to the same figure but with altimeters differing by, say, 1000 feet, they will be separated by about 1000 feet even though the actual heights may be in error. In order to ensure that aircraft in the same area are using the same sub-scale setting, certain rules are observed:

(a) Above a certain altitude known as the transition level, all aircraft operate with the sub-scale set to the standard pressure of 1013 millibars.

(b) Below the transition level, the area may be divided into zones, and a point on the Earth roughly in the centre of each zone chosen as the standard. The authorities that control air traffic in each zone may advise each aircraft by radio of the sub-scale setting for 0 feet at that point. This setting is known as the QNH.

(c) For an approach to landing, the airfield will advise the aircraft by radio of the setting that will give 0 feet at the airfield itself. This is known as the QFE.

32. Unfortunately, readings of barometric altimeters have inaccuracies due to errors in calibration of the altimeter, position errors due to the siting of the static vent, and hysteresis or lag inevitable in a barometric capsule. Hence the altimeter may have

a 95 per cent error of 100 feet at low level which may double for each 20,000 feet of altitude.

2. WEATHER

1. The navigation of a craft on or above the surface of the Earth is affected by the weather, mainly in one of three ways:

    (a) Vertical air currents and the resulting winds may affect progress directly by wind pressure or indirectly, for example, by causing waves at sea.

    (b) Poor visibility at the surface of the Earth can hamper navigation, particularly terminal navigation.

    (c) Ice can form on the craft or on the land or the sea.

2. In order to limit a review of meteorology to these particular items, it may be possible to restrict the broad study of the weather largely to a study of:

    (a) *Cold air masses*, in which the air is colder than the ground below and from which vertical air currents and winds are commonly derived.

    (b) *Warm air masses*, in which the air is warmer than the ground below and from which poor visibility may result.

3. These sharp distinctions are somewhat artificial and the meteorologist will need to qualify them considerably. Nevertheless, they may serve to illustrate the basic causes of winds, of poor visibility and of icing.

COLD AIR MASS

4. The rays of the Sun pass through the atmosphere without losing a great deal of heat but they warm the surface of the Earth. As a result, the ground becomes warmer than the air above it. Thus the air above may be regarded as a cold air mass.

5. *Upward Air Currents*. The warm Earth heats the lowest layers of air. Warm air, being lighter than cold air, rises. As it rises, the air expands and therefore cools, thus following the general pattern of the atmosphere which becomes colder and more

rarified with height. If the rising air is moist, the cooling will cause some of the moisture to condense. The process of condensation will release additional heat, and the air will be additionally warmed and will continue to rise. The result will be the formation of clouds with a heaped appearance, known as cumulus (Cu) clouds.

6. Within a cumulus cloud, a few water droplets that are bigger than the others will collect smaller droplets, eventually growing into raindrops. Upward currents of air will prevent small raindrops from falling but they will collect other water droplets until they become too large to be supported. If the temperature is so low that the droplets freeze directly, they will form snow flakes, but if large water droplets are carried upwards into freezing levels they may form into hailstones which may fall, collect more water, be lifted up by stronger upward currents and freeze again into large hailstones.

7. If the upward currents in the cumulus cloud are of the order of 15 knots, raindrops with a diameter of about $\frac{1}{4}$ inch may be prevented from falling but may be torn apart by the air flowing past. As a result, the negative electric charge on the outside may be carried up to the top of the cloud while the positive charge remains below. A great difference in electrical potential may develop between the top and the bottom of the cloud or, if the droplets fall to the ground, between the cloud and the ground. If this potential exceeds a certain amount, it will discharge in a flash of lightning. A craft can, to a large extent, discharge itself through lightning conductors but, if in the line of a discharge, it will provide a good path for the flow of electricity and, as a result of this flow, it may become magnetized.

8. Thunderstorms are associated with strong vertical air currents which cause bumpy conditions for aircraft and may make it necessary to reduce speed for comfort or for safety. In the cloud, visibility will be low but, below the cloud, visibility will generally be good although heavy rain may obscure the windshield.

WINDS

9. As the warm or moist air rises, the air above it at height moves out sideways. As a result of this outward flow, the total weight of

air above the warm area is reduced so that the air pressure at the surface is lowered, forming a Low (symbol L).

10. The air that drifts out sideways at height above the Low is not only cold but also much of the moisture that it originally held will have been condensed. Dry air is heavier than moist air and therefore cold dry air will tend to be heavy and will sink. The subsidence of cold dry air will evidently cause a high pressure area or a High (symbol H) at the surface of the Earth. Air at the surface tends to flow from a high pressure to a low pressure. As the cold dry air flows back towards the Low it may pick up moisture, so that when it reaches the low pressure area it may be moist once more and ready to repeat the process of circulation.

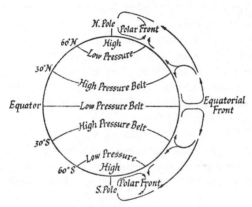

FIG. 33   World circulation of air

11. This idealized circulation is illustrated by the cross-section of the world in Fig. 33. The Sun beats down on the equator, the air rises and upper winds flow north and south from the equatorial low-pressure belt. Some of the air eventually drifts outwards to the poles where it descends and forms two high-pressure areas. This air starts to drift back towards the equator, becoming warm and collecting moisture, so that a low-pressure belt develops at about 50° to 60° of latitude.

12. Some of the air that drifts north and south at height from the equator sinks down around latitudes 30° north and south, forming two high-pressure belts. From these high-pressure belts,

air flows back towards the equator, picking up moisture as it goes. Air also flows from these high-pressure belts away from the equator towards the poles, absorbing moisture and so becoming lighter. Eventually this air meets the cold air coming down from the polar Highs at about 60° north and south.

13. *Fronts.* When two air masses meet, they tend to form a discontinuity known as a front. The air masses that flow towards the equator from latitude 30° north and from latitude 30° south meet at what is known as the equatorial or intertropical front, a line of storms with towering cumulus clouds and heavy rain. Similarly, the cold air from the polar Highs meets the warm air from latitudes 30° north and south to form two belts of polar fronts at latitudes 50°–60°.

14. *Cold Front.* The polar front advances and recedes, divides and splits into a number of scattered fronts. Along each front, the cold air from the poles sweeps under the warm air coming from latitude 30°. The cold air undercuts the warm air at an angle of about 1° and lifts it up, forming what is known as a cold front. The rising warm moist air condenses, is rewarmed and accelerates upwards, cumulus clouds appear and a line of storms is built up along the cold front.

15. *Effects of Coriolis.* The flow of winds will be deviated by coriolis to the right in the northern and to the left in the southern hemisphere. As a result, the circulation of winds over the surface of the Earth tends to follow the pattern shown in Fig. 34. For

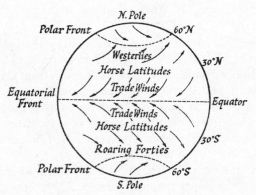

FIG. 34   General pattern of surface winds

the same reason, the winds at height, being due to the general drift from equator to the poles, are warped westwards.

16. The surface winds that blow from the east towards the equator are known as the trade winds. To the north and south of the trade winds, the winds are westerly. The belts of calm air between the trade winds and the westerlies are known as the horse latitudes, particularly the northern belt, the name resulting from the habit of sailors of consuming livestock when becalmed. The westerlies at latitude 40° south blow unimpeded for long stretches over open sea and are known as the roaring forties.

17. *Seasons.* The basic pattern of winds is modified in practice by two main factors:

(a) The inclination of the Earth's axis to the ecliptic causes the seasons. The water on the Earth acts as a savings bank, storing up summer heat against the winter and winter cold against the summer. Hence the seasons are delayed so that midsummer and midwinter occur in the months of July and January.

(b) The variation of temperature over the land is at least three times that over the sea. The quarter of the Earth's surface which is above the oceans is concentrated into large land masses which become very hot in summer and very cold in winter. The hottest place in the world is south central Asia in midsummer, and the coldest place in the world is north central Asia in midwinter. The winds that flow into Asia in summer and out from Asia in winter are known as monsoons.

18. As a result of these modifications, the circulation of winds over the surface of the Earth tends to follow the general pattern shown in Fig. 35 and Fig. 36. The frontal belts are shown as pecked lines.

EFFECTS OF WINDS

19. Winds affect navigation directly by impeding or assisting the progress of the craft. Also, in the instance of surface winds over the land, dust storms may build up or haze, defined as visibility of less than 2200 yards due to particles of solid matter

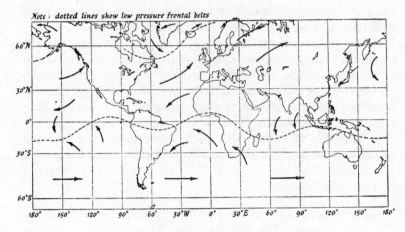

FIG. 35   January surface winds

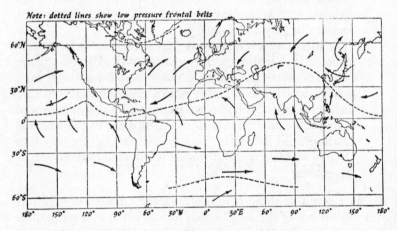

FIG. 36   July surface winds

in the air, may form. Winds also affect the movement of the surface of the sea.

20. The effects of winds increase very rapidly at high speeds because the pressure (in pounds per square foot) generated is given approximately by (windspeed in knots)^2/300. Table IV is a summary of various rules used for estimating wind strengths.

TABLE IV. EFFECTS OF WINDS

Windspeed knots	EFFECTS
0	Smoke rises straight upwards. Sea is glassy.
5	Breeze felt in face. Leaves rustle. Small wavelets at sea.
10	Small branches and twigs sway. White horses may start to appear at sea.
20	Small trees sway. Many white horses at sea.
30	Effort needed to walk into wind. Trees sway. Foam blows in streaks over surface of sea.
40	Walking hindered. Twigs break. Edges of waves at sea begin to break.
50	Trees may be uprooted and damage caused to buildings. Sea mostly white and waves have long overhanging crests.
60	Widespread damage over land. Sea covered with foam and spray so that visibility is affected.

21. Windspeed is sometimes measured according to the Beaufort scale which was based on the amount of sail that a man-of-war could carry. The connection between the Beaufort scale and speed in knots is as follows:

TABLE V. BEAUFORT WIND SCALE

Beaufort scale number	0	1	2	3	4	6	7	8	9	10	11	12
Wind speed knots	0–1 (calm)	1–3 (light air)	4–6	7–10 11–16 17–21 22–27 (breeze)			28–33 34–40 41–47 48–55 (gale)				55–65 (storm)	over 65 (hurricane)

OCEAN CURRENTS

22. The direction *towards* which a current flows is known as the set, and the speed of the flow as the drift. Even without winds, the waters of the ocean would drift. The Sun causes evaporation which makes the sea more salty so that the water tends to sink. Cold water also sinks unless it is close to freezing point, when it rises. Currents are caused by the flow of water off the land, particularly from the melting of the ice-caps that cover large areas of high ground in arctic and antarctic regions.

23. The prevailing winds, shown in Fig. 35 and Fig. 36, tend to set up a clockwise circulation in the northern oceans and an anti-clockwise circulation in the southern oceans as shown in

Fig. 37. The speed at which these currents flow is seldom more than 3 knots and generally about 1 knot. In addition, the local surface wind will drift the water at the surface. The movement will be deflected by coriolis to the right in the northern hemisphere and to the left in the southern hemisphere so that the movement of water may differ from that of the wind by as much as 45°.

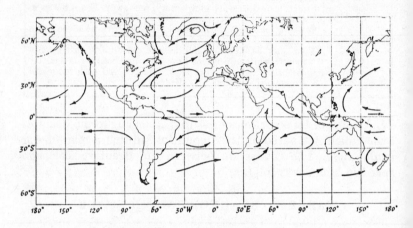

FIG. 37   Ocean currents

WAVES

24. The height of a wave is measured from the crest to the trough. The height will depend on the fetch, which is the distance over which the wind has been blowing, and on the time for which it has been blowing. The waves in a sea may vary considerably in height and the calculation of wave heights is an extremely complex process. However, it has been estimated that in open water the height of a wave in feet will seldom be greater than 10 feet less than the speed of the wind in knots except at low wind speeds. Hence 50-foot waves are rare.

25. If the wavelength—the distance between successive wave crests—is less than twelve times the height, the waves break. If the wind dies down, the waves will persist, and in this instance will be known as swell. Owing to the energy in waves, swell may travel over the sea for thousands of miles.

26. Waves will tend to break if the depth of water is much less than six times their height, and the intervals between crests are close to their minimum value. However, the effects of waves are hardly felt at a distance below the surface of twelve times the height of the waves. Hence a submarine at 600 feet or 100 fathoms will hardly be affected by waves.

WARM AIR MASS AND VISIBILITY

27. Since the air in a warm air mass will be warmer than the ground below, the lower layers will be cooled by contact. Under such conditions, air will not rise. In the limit, the air may be cooler low down than it is higher up, a condition known as an inversion.

28. If the lower layers of the air are moist, the cooling will cause condensation. If the air is absolutely still, the cooling may be limited to the air in contact with the ground and dew will form. The temperature at which condensation occurs is accordingly known as the dew point. If the wind is strong, the cooling effect of the ground may be spread by eddies to such a level that the air generally is cooled but not sufficiently to cause condensation. However, if the wind is light, the cooling may be concentrated in a layer just above the surface of the Earth and condensation will occur. This is known as:

(a) Fog, if visibility is less than 1100 yards.
(b) Mist, if visibility is less than 2200 yards.

29. There are many conditions that cause the ground to be colder than the air just above it. Common examples of these conditions are:

(a) *Radiation fog.* On a clear night, ground temperature may be lowered by radiation. Although this type of fog must form over land, it may drift out across estuaries and narrow channels. As the sun rises next day, the temperature of the top of the fog layer will rise, moisture will be reabsorbed and the fog dispersed. If the air is polluted by smoke, the reabsorption of water droplets will be hindered and the resulting 'smog' may persist for long periods.

(b) *Advection fog.* Warm moist air may be blown over cold

land or sea. Air from the warm sea may blow across frozen ground or across a cold current such as that which flows along the Labrador or the Californian coast. This leads to dense sea fog. For the same reason, fog will form in the presence of icebergs.

30. *Warm Front.* It has already been explained that the cold air from the poles may meet and undercut the warm air from latitudes 30° north and south. Alternatively, the warm air may meet receding cold air and overrun it. The slope of the discontinuity is generally not much more than a $\frac{1}{4}$° and, though the warm air may be damp, it will not rise up sufficiently quickly to cause cumulus cloud. Instead, layers of flat sheets of cloud known as stratus (St) will appear. As the warm air runs up the cold air, these clouds will appear at increasing heights. If over 8000 feet, they are known as alto-stratus (As) and if over 18,000 feet as cirro-stratus (Cs).

31. Since the formation of stratus clouds occurs in the absence of strong upward currents of air, the moisture will fall as soon as it forms into small raindrops. Hence stratus clouds may cause drizzle or light rain but cannot lead to heavy rain, hail or thunderstorms.

32. Stratus clouds also occur when, owing to eddies, the air at low heights becomes so thoroughly mixed that the moisture is evenly distributed. The cloud will form at the level where the temperature is sufficiently low. Broken stratus cloud, known as fracto-stratus, may occur when rain falling from a height is reabsorbed in the air at lower levels. Clouds of a stratus type may also occur when moist air is blown up a slope. Such clouds are known as orographic clouds.

STABILITY

33. When air rises, it cools, and therefore in the troposphere the temperature generally decreases with height. The rate at which it decreases is known as the lapse rate.

34. If the lapse rate is low, the air above is very little colder than the air below. Should air start to rise, it will cool so that it will be colder than the surrounding air and will fall back again to its own level. In such conditions, the air is said to be stable.

However, if the lapse rate is high, the air above is much colder than the air below. Should air start to rise, it will cool but not to the extent of the surrounding air and so its upward motion will be accelerated. In these conditions the air is said to be unstable.

35. The true nature of the cold air mass and the warm air mass may now be better appreciated. In a warm air mass, the lower layers will be cooled by contact with the ground and the lapse rate will be low. The consequence will be stability and lack of upward air currents. In a cold air mass, the lower layers will be warmed by contact with the ground and the lapse rate will be high. The consequence will be instability and development of upward air currents.

ICE

36. If snow is sufficiently deep, the lower layers will be compressed into ice. In arctic and antarctic regions, whole areas are covered in sheets of ice known as ice-caps, a notable example being Greenland. On the surface of these ice-caps, ridges of snow and ice, known sometimes as sastrugi, may be formed by the wind.

37. From about 80° north to the North Pole, the Arctic Ocean is not navigable, as it is covered with pack-ice, generally around 5 feet thick but broken by winds and ocean currents into floes. As the floes are driven together, pressure ridges are formed and leads of open water appear where the floes have been blown apart. Some of the floes are so large that they are known as ice islands, and may be sufficient in size for aircraft to land and take-off.

38. The ice drifts out from the Arctic Ocean, mainly down the east coast of Greenland as a result of the ocean current (Fig. 37, page 82). In addition, icebergs break off the glaciers where the ice-caps flow down to the sea and float southwards into the North Atlantic, appearing in particular off the Newfoundland coast. These bergs vary greatly in size but can be several hundred feet high with lengths of the order of 1000 yards. As the icebergs enter temperate regions, they break up into sodden lumps of ice known as growlers.

39. In the Antarctic, the situation differs from the Arctic. Ice-shelves form along the coasts of Antarctica stretching as far as

70° south in winter but receding in summer. This ice is continually being broken up by the strong circumpolar currents and the extremely high seas resulting from the westerly winds. Very large icebergs break off the antarctic ice-shelves and may drift as far as 50° south before disintegrating into growlers. Fortunately, the strong winds tend to discourage the formation of fog.

40. *Icing on Craft.* When a craft is moving through air holding water particles which has a temperature of between $+2°$ and $-15°C$, water droplets struck by the leading edges may form clear ice. Below $-15°$ and down to $-40°$, the water droplets will increasingly tend to form into snow, though where the air is very clean and free from solid particles, water droplets can exist at even lower temperatures.

41. The effect of this icing is obviously of great significance to aircraft. Clear ice may form at the rate of $\frac{1}{4}$ inch in a minute on the wings of an aircraft flying in cloud, adding to the weight and upsetting the aerofoil shape of the wings. Ice can likewise form on propeller blades and pieces may fly off into the fuselage, leaving the blades so unbalanced that they may vibrate to destruction. Ice may also form on engine air-intakes, and inside carburettors, causing loss of power. It may build up on the inlets to air-pressure instruments, causing major errors.

42. Aircraft may be fitted with strips of material in the leading edges of the wings which may either vibrate and break off the ice or may be heated so that the ice is melted. Rings may be fitted on to propeller hubs that can sling anti-freeze on to the blades. Inlets to air-pressure instruments may be heated. Fortunately, as aircraft speeds and heights of operation tend to increase, the time spent climbing through critical freezing-levels is reduced. Apart from airborne icing, snow falling on the wings of parked aircraft may need to be removed to avoid spoiling the aerodynamic shape and affecting take-off.

3. FORECASTING

THE METEOROLOGICAL CHART

1. At meteorological stations, air-pressure readings are taken and corrected to a common datum, generally sea-level. The readings

are then plotted on charts and smooth curves drawn at intervals. Fig. 38 shows a typical chart with the isobars, lines of equal pressure, plotted. The chart represents a situation in latitude 50° north. A mirror image from top to bottom could represent a situation in latitude 50° south.

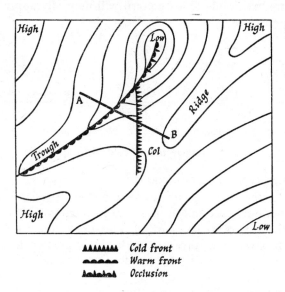

▲▲▲▲▲▲	Cold front	
━━━━━	Warm front	
▲▬▲▬▲	Occlusion	

FIG. 38   Meteorological chart

2. On the chart can be seen a High, a Low, a ridge of high pressure, a trough of low pressure and a col, an area between two Highs and two Lows. In temperate latitudes, a High is often known as an anticyclone and a Low as a depression. A cold front and a warm front are also shown together with an occlusion, which is where the cold air behind the warm air has caught up with the cold air ahead of the warm air. As a result, the warm air is lifted and the low-pressure area tends to fill up and disappear. It will be noticed that the discontinuity of direction of the isobars marks the discontinuities in air masses and therefore the positions of the fronts.

3. Fig. 39 shows a cross-section of the two fronts along the line AB in Fig. 38. Since at both 50° north and 50° south the prevailing winds are westerly, these fronts will move across from west to

east. Hence, to an observer on the ground, the weather will tend to change from that shown on the right-hand side of Fig. 39 to that shown on the left-hand side. The warm front will appear first as cirro-stratus, gradually lowering to stratus, possibly with drizzle at the warm front. The cold front will be a line of storms with cumulus clouds. This pattern will naturally apply to both hemispheres.

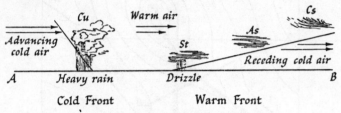

FIG. 39   Cross-section of cold and warm fronts

CALCULATION OF WIND VELOCITY

4. Where the isobars are close together, pressure changes rapidly with distance and the pressure gradient is said to be steep. Where the isobars are far apart, the pressure gradient is said to be slack. The steeper the pressure gradient, the greater the acceleration of the air. If an average air density is assumed, it follows that:

pressure gradient acceleration = closeness of isobars

5. *Geostrophic Wind.* Except on the equator, coriolis will deflect the wind to the right in the northern hemisphere and to the left in the southern hemisphere. This deflection will build up until it balances the acceleration caused by the pressure gradient, and this will happen, in theory, when the air is flowing parallel to the isobars. Any tendency for the wind to blow inwards towards the low pressure will cause it to accelerate and the coriolis deflection to increase until once more the air is flowing parallel to the isobars. Any tendency for the wind to blow outwards away from the low pressure will cause it to slow down and the coriolis deflection to decrease until once more the air is flowing along the isobars. Thus:

pressure gradient acceleration = windspeed × sin (latitude)
(see page 70, para 23)

From the previous paragraph:

pressure gradient acceleration = closeness of isobars

and hence

closeness of isobars = windspeed × sin (latitude)

so that

windspeed = closeness of isobars/sin (latitude)

6. The geostrophic wind scale is a transparent rule that can be placed across the 2000-foot isobars to measure their closeness. Separate scales are used for the various latitudes to allow for sin (latitude), and therefore each scale can be calibrated to read directly in geostrophic windspeeds for that particular latitude.

7. Because winds tend to blow along the isobars, air circulates anti-clockwise round a depression in the northern hemisphere and clockwise round a depression in the southern hemisphere. Above the area between the cold and the warm front, which is known as the warm sector, there will be a tendency for the air to flow outwards, as if from a High, so that the circulation will be reversed. As a result, the westerly winds will tend to arc around the warm sector travelling rather towards the pole on the western side of the depression at height and rather away from the pole on the eastern side. These features are illustrated in Fig. 40.

8. At height over a front, strong temperature gradients may produce narrow ribbands of very strong winds known as jet streams. Speeds reaching hundreds of knots may be concentrated in strips of up to 1000 or 2000 miles in length with widths of only 100 miles or so and depths of 10,000–20,000 feet. Jet streams are rarely powerful below 20,000 feet, although similar effects on a less violent scale have been noted occasionally down to 2000 feet. In addition, close to the tropopause, clear air turbulence can appear due to the top layers of air cooling and falling.

9. *Cyclostrophic Effect.* Curvature of the isobars introduces a centrifugal effect known as the cyclostrophic effect. Like all accelerations caused by movement in a circle, the effect is proportional to speed^2 and to radius of curvature (see page 24, para 22). The cyclostrophic effect, when combined with the geostrophic wind, gives an approximation to the wind at 2000 feet which is known as the gradient wind. In the instance of winds

circulating around a High, the cyclostrophic effect assists the outward motion of the air. In the instance of winds circulating about a Low, the cyclostrophic effect acts against the inwards suction.

(a)   2000 feet

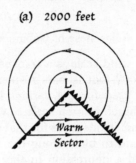

(b)   At height

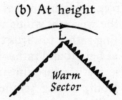

FIG. 40   Winds around a depression
in the northern hemisphere

10. In latitudes a few degrees away from the equator, the air is often very warm and damp so that very strong low-pressure areas develop. The geostrophic effect may be just sufficient to start a rotation and the cyclostrophic effect arising from the fast-flowing converging air may result in the building up of a tropical revolving storm or cyclone, known as a hurricane in the West Indies and as a typhoon in the South China seas. These revolving storms are generally small, with diameters measured in a few hundred miles. The centre or eye of the storm, where the winds are light, may be only a few tens of miles across, but the winds outside may reach speeds of up to 100 knots at the surface and even more at 2000 feet. At any considerable distance from the

equator, the air is seldom sufficiently warm and moist for cyclones to develop, although small twisters and waterspouts can appear.

11. *Surface Winds.* Below 2000 feet, winds are slowed down by friction between the air and the surface of the Earth. Over the sea, the surface wind tends to be about two-thirds of the speed of the 2000-foot wind. The reduced speed lessens the coriolis deflection, so that the winds blow in towards the low pressure at an angle of 10° or 20°. Over the land, the effects are more irregular. Eddies can carry surface friction up into the 2000-foot layer and, if the ground is rough, the surface wind may be less than half the 2000-foot wind and may blow in towards the low pressure by up to 50° or 60°. The change of wind with height, which is known as wind shear, can be as much as 1 knot for each 10 feet of height close to the ground.

12. In addition, gusts will occur, particularly over the land. These gusts may lead to temporary increases and decreases in the strength of the winds which may be doubled or halved momentarily. The direction may also change so that, in strong winds, strong cross-wind gusts will appear. Over the sea, gusts may build up into short-period squalls.

13. *Local Winds.* During the day, the land warms up more quickly than the sea and, particularly during the afternoon, breezes will blow from the sea. At night, the land cools more quickly so that breezes will blow from the land. Land breezes are generally impeded by friction and weaker than sea breezes. Also, when mountains become hot by day, air currents flow up their sides and these are known as anabatic winds. However, katabatic winds, downward currents of cold air from high ground, are much more powerful, particularly in high latitudes.

PROBLEMS OF FORECASTING

14. The accuracy of the meteorological forecast depends on whether there is ample meteorological information available not only in the area but also in the adjacent area from which the weather comes. The information at height is frequently incomplete but, fortunately, the weather at height is generally less unpredictable.

15. The forecaster may also be aided by prognostic charts based upon how weather situations have developed in the past. The

way that the weather develops is generally more predictable in tropical regions than in temperate regions where the unexpected can occur, such as the development of a depression along a long, straight, cold front or the sudden coincidence of all the factors that lead to the formation of radiation fog.

16. Although the forecaster may be able to predict what the weather will be, it may be even more difficult to judge where it will be. Therefore, in interpreting a forecast in the light of the weather actually experienced, the navigator may relate his position to the weather chart and, so to speak, mentally shift the weather chart until it agrees with his geographical position. This will be particularly necessary when flying at height in the vicinity of a jet stream.

17. It is doubtful whether the navigator of any craft except possibly a very high-flying aircraft or a deep-cruising submarine can avoid taking account of the weather forecast. Even in these two special instances, weather will affect the terminal phase of the journey. Although the craft itself may be able to dock or to land, fog, ice and strong winds may disrupt surface transport to an extent that there is no support available to the departing or arriving craft.

FORECASTING ACCURACIES

18. *Wind Forecasts*. Errors in wind forecasts may be expressed in terms of vector errors. Thus, if a forecast wind were 4 knots east and the actual wind were 3 knots north, the vector error would be the third side of the vector triangle, an error of 5 knots.

19. The 95 per cent vector error of a wind forecast based on information provided to the meteorologist 18 hours previously will depend on the strength of the winds in the area and on the extent to which they tend to change. However, the following may serve as a guide to the likely order of 95 per cent errors (given in knots):

    (a) *Except in the tropics*
        (i) Close to the surface, 20
       (ii) 10,000 feet, 25–30
      (iii) 30,000 feet, 40–45
      (iv) 50,000 feet, 25–30

(b) *In the tropics*
(i) Close to the surface, 10
(ii) 10,000 feet, 10–15
(iii) 30,000 feet, 15–20
(iv) 50,000 feet, 10–15

20. For periods further ahead than 18 hours, the accuracy of a forecast will deteriorate rapidly so that, except in very settled conditions, a three- or four-day forecast may not be very much better than the seasonal average. This suggests that, in temperate regions, three or four days is the limit of useful forecasting. However, in the tropics, the divergence from the seasonal average is generally relatively small, and long-term planning can be based on monthly averages.

21. The forecast accuracies in para 19 are values for 'spot' winds. Over an area, the errors in winds tend to average out until they approach more closely to the general world circulation expressed by monthly averages. It has been suggested that the errors in forecasting become random over a distance of the order of 500 or 1000 miles. On this basis, one would expect the error over a route to be only half the 'spot' error if the route were between 1500 and 3000 miles long.

22. *Wave Forecasts*. The accuracy of an 18-hour wave-height forecast may be 95 per cent within 10 feet with skilful forecasters. As with wind forecasts, errors increase when the forecast is for a time further ahead. However, the errors increase less quickly since a large part of the energy in waves will have been developed by past winds. Forecast wave charts are generally prepared for less than a week ahead, a normal limit being around five days in temperate waters.

23. *Ocean Current Forecasts*. Ocean currents are sufficiently steady to be plotted on charts as if they were permanent. The errors will generally be small since the currents themselves are generally less than 1 knot. However, the general direction of the wind blowing for the past 24 hours tends to drift the surface with a speed of the order of 2 per cent of the average windspeed. Since surface winds may be forecast with an accuracy that even outside the tropics will be 95 per cent less than 20 knots, it follows that the 95 per cent error in the forecast of ocean drifts

due to winds will be around $\frac{1}{2}$ knot. However, if the ocean wind-drift and the ocean currents are both to be represented by the charted values, the 95 per cent overall error may not fall short of 1 knot.

4. SUMMARY

THE WORLD

Tides rise and fall at intervals of about 12 hours 25 minutes.

Time-keeping accuracies are of the following orders:

(a) Mechanical watch or chronometer, a second per day.

(b) Crystal controlled clock, a second in months.

(c) Atomic clock, a second in centuries.

The Earth, as a result of rotation:

(a) tilts at 15° cos (latitude) per hour;

(b) rotates at 15° sin (latitude) per hour;

(c) causes coriolis acceleration in a moving craft which distorts the direction of gravity by 0·00044 × speed in knots × sin (latitude) degrees.

WINDS

Close to the surface of the Earth, winds depend on:

(a) Geostrophic effect, which causes wind at 2000 feet to flow parallel to the isobars. The winds blow anti-clockwise round a depression in the northern hemisphere and clockwise round a depression in the southern hemisphere at a speed depending on:

closeness of isobars/sin (latitude)

(b) Cyclostrophic effect, which when added to the geostrophic effect gives the gradient wind at 2000 feet.

(c) Surface friction, which causes the surface wind to be slower than the gradient wind and to flow in towards the low pressure.

At height, winds are generally westerly. Narrow ribbands of wind known as jet streams appear between 20,000 and 40,000 feet, particularly in the vicinity of cold fronts.

Waves depend on windspeed, fetch and time for which the wind has been blowing.

VISIBILITY

A cold air mass implies unstable air and results in good visibility, cumulus clouds and, sometimes, heavy rain and thunderstorms.

A warm air mass implies stable air and can result in mist or fog, stratus cloud and, sometimes, drizzle or light rain.

There are four types of front:

(a) *Equatorial front*, a line of cumulus clouds rising up to 5 or 10 miles with torrential rain.
(b) *Cold front* to the west of a depression, a line of storms with cumulus cloud.
(c) *Warm front* to the east of a depression, a gradual lowering of stratus cloud with drizzle or light rain at the front.
(d) *Occlusion* where the cold front catches up the warm front and causes a front at height. Rain may not reach the ground.

ICE

Icebergs flow south from the Arctic Ocean down the coast of Labrador and north from the Antarctic continent. Icebergs break into growlers and disappear in temperate waters.

Aircraft that fly for periods in cloud at temperatures between $+2°C$ and $-40°C$ can suffer from ice accretion.

WIND FORECAST ACCURACIES

The 95 per cent errors of typical wind forecasts for 18 hours ahead can be expected to be of the following orders of accuracy:

(a) *Sea surface.* Spot wind, 20 knots. 2000 n.m. average, 10 knots.
(b) *Land surface.* Spot wind variable.
(c) *At height.* Spot wind, 30 knots. 2000 n.m. average, 15 knots. Greater errors between 30,000 and 40,000 feet, and less errors above and below these levels.

The following points should be noted:

(a) Errors in tropics are generally half the world average and long-term forecasting is more accurate.

(b) Tropical storms and jet streams may introduce major errors.

(c) The weather may be accurately forecast but errors in its geographical position may introduce large spot wind errors.

SEA-SURFACE DRIFT FORECAST ACCURACIES

The 95 per cent errors for two or three days ahead may be of the order of 1 knot at any point and may average less than $\frac{1}{2}$ knot over 2000 n.m.

WAVE FORECAST ACCURACIES

The 95 per cent errors for two or three days ahead may be of the order of 10 feet in any one area.

CHAPTER III

The Craft

1. Navigation has been defined as the business of conducting a craft as it moves about its ways. Satellites in fixed orbits, missiles that are aimed and not steered, and vehicles that travel on rails, are unable to move about their ways and cannot be navigated. Vehicles travelling along roads are also largely constrained. There may be a strong element of navigation in certain sporting events such as motor rallies and route-finding competitions. Nevertheless, road navigation will not be considered in this book. Nor will the navigation of balloons be considered since these are not a means of transport.

2. In general, craft that are navigated may be classified according to the medium on which or in which they operate. This gives four classes:

(a) *Land vehicles*. These may travel on wheels, tracks or skids. Navigation applies to operations over untracked country such as deserts or arctic wastes.

(b) *Marine vessels*. These include:
   (i) Power-driven surface craft which may be large ships or small boats. They may also be skimming craft that either plane on their hulls or are supported by hydrofoils.
   (ii) Sailing craft.
   (iii) Submarines.
   (iv) Under-water missiles.

(c) *Aircraft*. Discounting balloons and airships, the main categories will be:
   (i) Aeroplanes: supported by aerodynamic lift, generally from wings, and power driven.

    (ii) Gliders: supported by wings but not powered.

    (iii) VTOL (vertical take-off and landing) craft: includes rotating-wing craft such as helicopters.

    (iv) Missiles that operate in the air. These are either offensive missiles launched from the ground (SSM, surface-to-surface missiles) or from the air (ASM, air-to-surface missiles) or defensive missiles launched from the ground (SAM, surface-to-air missiles) or from the air (AAM, air-to-air missiles).

(d) *Space craft*. Initial lift-off is by launchers similar to those used for launching long-range ballistic missiles. The main classes will be:

    (i) Navigational satellites which follow fixed orbits.

    (ii) Controlled satellites of which the orbits can be varied.

    (iii) Space craft that operate in areas where the Earth's gravitational field does not predominate.

3. Inevitably, the divisions between types of craft are not exactly definable. A submarine may operate on the surface as a normal ship. A VTOL aircraft may be fitted with wings to cruise normally. Nor can the classes be clearly separated. A particular instance is the air-cushion vehicle (ACV) or ground-effect machine (GEM) sometimes known as a Hovercraft. These craft may operate over land or water supported on a cushion of air. However, since operations over land will be impeded by obstructions, they may generally be regarded as power-driven marine craft. Indeed, the side-wall ACV, which has a keel each side immersed in the water, behaves like a skimming craft.

1. THE HULL

ASPECT

1. For structural reasons, for concentration of propulsive power and, in most instances, for reduction of resistance, a craft is designed to be driven in a certain direction. In most instances, this direction is along the length of the main element or hull of the craft, which is defined by:

(a) *Head*. The forward end of the length of the hull. In a marine craft, the water is cut by the stem of the craft and the two sides that comprise this cutting edge are known as the bows. Hence an object on the bow is at an angle to the head of the craft.

(b) *Stern or tail.* The after end of a craft is known as the stern in the instance of marine craft, and as the tail in the instance of aircraft. An object on the quarter is at an angle to the stern of a craft.

2. The remaining aspects of a craft are generally related to its attitude when at rest on the ground with the length parallel to the surface. The directions at right angles, which are known as beams, are named:

(a) *Port.* The left-hand side of the craft looking ahead. The colour associated with port is red and the connection can be remembered by the jingle 'a little *red port left* in the bottle'.

(b) *Starboard.* The right-hand side of the craft looking forward. The colour associated with starboard is green. The term originates from the mounting of the steering oar on the right-hand side or board of the ship convenient to the helmsman's right hand.

3. When a craft is moving, directions to either side of the direction of movement may be named:

(a) *Left* (L);
(b) *Right* (R).

When moving ahead, left and right correspond to port and starboard; but, when moving astern, left and right correspond to starboard and port. In the instance of aircraft that never move backwards, left and right have become synonymous with port and starboard.

4. Change of alignment of a craft is related to aspect and, like aspect, applies to the craft irrespective of its alignment with the outside world. Thus:

(a) *Yaw.* Rotation about the vertical axis of the craft. When the head of the craft moves to the left, this is known as yawing left.

(b) *Pitch.* Rotation about the athwartships axis. When the head of the craft moves up, this is known as pitching up.

(c) *Roll*. Rotation about the length or the longitudinal axis of the craft. When the rotation is clockwise as seen from inside the craft looking ahead, this is known as rolling to the right. It is the direction in which the seaman sees the top of the mast move when he is facing forward.

Fig. 41 summarizes the various aspects of a craft.

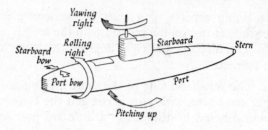

FIG. 41   The aspects of a craft

SUPPORT OF CRAFT

5. The support of a craft may depend on its speed. When a surface is driven at an angle through water or air, a force is set up at right angles to the surface. This force may be the result not only of pressure on one side of the surface but also of suction on the other side of the surface. If the surface is driven through the medium at an angle, which is known as the angle of attack or incidence, one component of the force at right angles acts in opposition to gravity and produces lift as shown in Fig. 42. The

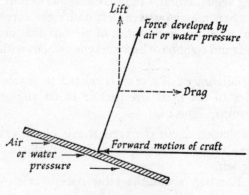

FIG. 42   Lift and drag

other component of the force at right angles to the surface opposes the forward motion of the craft. This opposing force is known as drag.

6. If the angle of attack is too fine, the force at right angles to the surface will be small and the lift will be reduced. If the angle of attack is too coarse, the drag will be increased disproportionately, the forward motion will be reduced and the lift will consequently be reduced. It is therefore important that a lifting surface be driven through the water or the air at the designed angle of attack or incidence.

7. In aircraft, most of the lift is generated by suction due to the flow of air over the upper surface. If the angle of attack is too great, eddies form, the suction is destroyed and the wing will cease to provide lift relatively suddenly. This condition is known as a stall. It is possible to measure the angle of attack to provide warning of the stall. In practice, it is difficult to find a position where the flow is representative, and the devices used for measurement tend to be troubled by dust and water and may become iced up.

8. The lift on the top surface of the wing will depend on the speed of the airflow and on the density of the air. Similarly, the pressure on the nose of an aircraft will depend on the speed of the airflow and the density of the air. Hence, a measure of pressure due to the forward motion of an aircraft will be a measure of the lift generated on the top surface of the wing. This forward pressure can be led into an open-ended tube projected forward into the air-stream, and known generally as a pitot head, and fed through a pitot tube to a barometric capsule as shown in Fig. 43. The capsule is mounted in a case which is kept at atmospheric pressure by means of a static tube (page 73, para 29).

9. The capsule works a pointer that registers against a dial calibrated in units of speed as if the aircraft were flying in air at standard ISA sea-level pressure and temperature (page 72, para 28). The instrument is therefore known as an air-speed indicator (ASI) although it is used as a lift indicator. It is obvious that an air-speed indicator will be an essential instrument for aircraft handling because it can give warning of a stall.

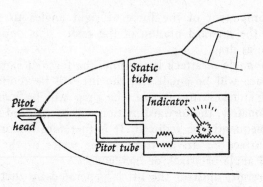

FIG. 43   Principle of air-speed indicator

10. The air-speed indicator is subject to the inaccuracies that affect the altimeter, namely:

(a) *Position error* due to the air not striking the open end of the pitot tube squarely when the aircraft is pitched up or down. In practice, changes of pitch are normally due to flying slowly or fast, and therefore position error is corrected according to the air-speed indicator reading.

(b) *Calibration or instrument error* inevitable in any instrument.

(c) *Lag* due to the barometric capsule. This is generally unimportant.

11. The lift that a wing will have to generate will depend on the weight that it has to support. Hence the stalling 'speed', the reading of the air-speed indicator at which a stall occurs, will be lower at landing when some of the fuel has been burnt off. The stalling speed can be reduced by the use of auxiliary aerofoils known as flaps, or by reducing the weight of the aircraft directly by directing engine thrust downwards or by using special lift engines. These devices are employed by STOL (short take-off and landing) aircraft.

RESISTANCE

12. With the exception of those that travel into space, craft have to overcome resistance due to the medium that supports them. There are two particular instances of this resistance:

(a) *Wash*. As a ship is driven through the water, the displacement due to the motion of the hull forms waves which appear astern in the form of wash. With increasing speed, power is increasingly diverted to the formation of wash. The energy in a wave is proportional to the cube of the height so that a wash of 10 feet will absorb a great deal of power. As a result, the speed of a craft through the water is limited to a few tens of knots. If the craft has to travel at over 50 knots, the hull will have to be lifted out of the water by planing which involves lifting the nose so that the water presses against the bottom of the hull and generates lift as shown in Fig. 42. Alternatively hydrofoils may be fitted. These are sloping surfaces mounted on stilts below the hull which raise the hull out of the water when sufficient speed is gained. However, to attain speeds of the order of 100 knots, a craft has to be lifted off the surface of the water on an air cushion. Air-cushion vehicles leave little wash once their speed has exceeded a critical amount known as the hump speed, which is generally about 20 knots.

(b) *Air resistance*. Surface craft that travel at more than a few tens of knots will benefit from streamlining. The benefit will be great for aircraft that travel at speeds measured in hundreds of knots. Fig. 44 shows that air resistance increases very rapidly as the speed of sound is approached, owing to the increasing inability of the air molecules to move out of the way sufficiently quickly. At supersonic speeds, the molecules have to be driven aside by the craft and this causes shock waves and supersonic bangs. The shock waves can cause damage or even destruction to the aircraft and, accordingly, high-speed aircraft are fitted with mach-meters which measure speed as a fraction or as a multiple of the speed of sound, mach 1 being the speed of sound in the air of the particular temperature at the time. The hotter the air, the faster a craft can travel for a given mach number. In practice, a mach-meter may not measure temperature but may be built with a complex of capsules and cams operated by pitot and by static pressure.

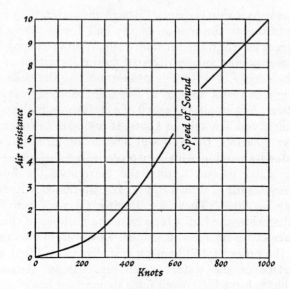

FIG. 44   Air resistance and speed

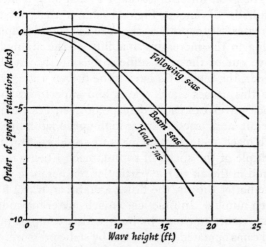

FIG. 45   Typical effect of seas on speed of ship

13. Planing and hydrofoil craft consume power not only to overcome air resistance but also to offset the drag that must accompany lift. Similarly, the lift demanded by an air-cushion vehicle demands power. In the air, winged aircraft demand power to offset drag, and STOL or VTOL machines require power to produce the necessary direct lift.

14. *Roughness.* If the supporting medium be rough, resistance to the motion of the craft will be increased and speed will have to be reduced to avoid structural damage and discomfort to crew and passengers. Thus bumpy surfaces slow down land vehicles and bumps in the air, caused by vertical air currents, slow down aircraft. In particular, rough seas slow down ships, the effects being particularly noticeable in the instance of head seas as suggested by Fig. 45. This figure refers to large vessels, and small vessels are naturally affected by smaller waves. High-speed marine craft, such as planing craft, may not be able to operate properly in waves of over a certain height, and difficulties may also be caused to hydrofoil craft. Air-cushion vehicles may, however, be able to raise themselves above the level of most waves by the fitment of flexible curtains or skirts that will give to the motion of the water. Nevertheless, only a submarine well below the surface can travel fast through very rough seas.

STABILITY

15. Craft that operate in space have neither stability nor instability apart from a slight tendency for the distribution of mass to align itself along a line of gravitational force. Stability or instability is, however, a characteristic of craft that are supported on land, sea or air. A tendency to keep level in pitch and roll whether a craft is moving or not is generally of one of two types:

(a) *Absolute stability.*
(b) *Metacentric stability.*

In addition, in a moving craft, there may be an element of stability that depends on the flow of the medium past the craft.

16. *Absolute Stability.* For absolute stability, two conditions have to be satisfied:

(a) The centre of gravity must be below the centre of support.

(b) Any disturbance in the level of the craft must move the centre of gravity out of line with the direction of support.

17. Absolute stability is the only stability available to a stationary submarine, which keeps upright for the same reason that a diver with heavy weights in his boots keeps upright. Balloons, airships and old-fashioned sailing boats with very deep hulls and heavy keels possess this type of stability. Vehicles supported on land cannot possess absolute stability because their centres of gravity must be above the ground on which the wheels of the vehicle are supported. Nor can aircraft possess this type of stability because the direction of the lift must pass through the centre of gravity if the craft is not to be continually pitching or rolling over.

18. In the instance of absolute stability, as soon as a craft is disturbed, the reaction is initially small, but gradually increases until the craft is heeled on to her beam ends. It continues even if the craft turns turtle and will restore a craft to the level position unless the action of turning turtle has destroyed the absolute stability, for example by allowing water to enter the hull.

19. *Metacentric Stability.* In general, the centre of support of a craft shifts when the alignment is disturbed. To take an extreme example, if a force tends to roll a catamaran, the hull on one side will become immersed more deeply and the hull on the other side will be lifted out of the water. The centre of support has therefore shifted from the central point between the two hulls to one of the hulls.

20. Fig. 46 illustrates that as the craft rolls the centre of flotation shifts sideways. The point where the vertical through the centre of support meets the direction of support when the craft is level is known as the metacentre. The height of this point above the centre of gravity is known as the metacentric height.

21. Fig. 46 shows that the metacentre is above the centre of gravity and that any disturbance in the level of the craft will move the centre of gravity out of line. Therefore, the craft will be stable (para 16). A large metacentric height means a stiff ship that will keep level with the surface of the water but will roll violently in response to waves from the beam. A small

metacentric height means a tender ship which will be more comfortable but with an increased risk of capsizing.

22. By using the metacentric principle, a ship can be made far more stable than a craft with absolute stability, since the metacentric height can be much greater than the distance of the centre of support of a deep-hulled craft above the centre of gravity. However, if the roll exceeds a certain limit, the centre of support will cease to move sideways, the metacentric height will be reduced and eventually the ship will turn turtle. In the absence of absolute stability, there will be no restoring force.

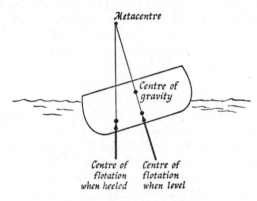

FIG. 46   Metacentric stability

23. *Aircraft Stability.* In the instance of aircraft, the centre of lift passes through the centre of gravity and therefore there can be no metacentric stability. However, when an aircraft is moving, weathercock stability comes into play. The extreme example is the stability of a parachute which keeps upright for the same reason that a dart with a heavy pin forward keeps upright. In an aircraft, there is generally a design feature, often a simple upward tilt of the wings known as dihedral, so that, as the aircraft moves through the air, it keeps upright in much the same way that an inverted cone would keep upright.

24. In the instance of VTOL craft and helicopters that are hovering, there is neither forward speed nor downward speed to produce weathercock stability. If a craft should start to tilt, it will continue to tilt and will start to move sideways until the pressure

of air on the side exercises a weathercocking effect. This will restore the tilt but at a greater rate so that the process will be repeated in the other direction at a greater rate. In this way, unless checked, the swinging from side to side will build up until the VTOL craft goes out of control. The effect will be particularly noticeable with a helicopter that has its rotating wings well above the fuselage and the centre of gravity. The effect may, however, be masked close to the ground.

25. *Dynamic Stability*. In addition to the type of stability that restores a craft to a level position, the shape of the craft may reduce the rate of roll or pitch. For example, bilge keels are commonly fitted to the hulls of ships to reduce rolling. Similarly, long wings in aircraft can reduce rates of roll. Length of hull or of fuselage similarly affect rate of pitch or of yaw. These effects may be called dynamic stability.

SPECIAL PROBLEMS

26. *Noise*. High-speed craft invariably cause a great deal of noise. The jet engines of aircraft taking off are objectionable to those that live close by, and special quick climbs are instituted to achieve noise abatement. Another serious problem is the supersonic bang. At 15,000 feet a large aircraft travelling at mach 2 (about 1200 knots) may cause widespread damage, and even at 30,000 feet panes of glass may be broken. Not until the aircraft has reached 45,000 feet is the bang likely to be acceptable and even then perhaps not in urban areas.

27. *Temperature*. Very-high-speed craft tend to become hot, so that special metals have to be used for speeds much in excess of mach 2. The problem becomes progressively worse as speeds increase, and is crucial for space craft re-entering the atmosphere, reaching a climax in the nose cone of a ballistic missile which may travel at around mach 25 or 15,000 knots and become incandescent.

28. A particular problem in helicopters is the vortex-ring condition which corresponds to the stall in the fixed-wing aircraft (para 17), and arises when making a vertical descent. The condition is marked by some loss of control, increased rate of descent and vibration, corresponding closely to the symptoms of a stall. As a result, the heavily laden helicopter may

prefer to approach its landing point at an angle that is not unduly steep.

2. PROPULSION

SAILING AND GLIDING

1. Certain craft are driven by air currents, the classic example being the sailing craft. The boat may be blown along by the wind from aft or it may make progress at an angle into the wind as shown in Fig. 47. To sail into wind, the sails are set at a narrow

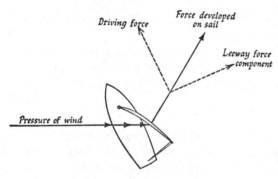

FIG. 47   Sailing 'into' wind

angle to the fore and aft line of the craft and the craft is steered so that the sail is kept at a fine angle of attack. The resulting force at right angles to the sail has a large component tending to drive the hull sideways, but the shape of the hull and, in particular, the keel, will reduce this unwanted sideways movement, which is known as leeway. There will also be a smaller component tending to drive the craft ahead and, provided that the angle of attack is not too greatly reduced, this forward component will be sufficient to offset the wind pressure on the hull. Thus the craft will make way in a direction 'into wind' or 'close hauled'.

2. The glider relies on upward currents of air either from air rising off warm ground, known as thermals, or from air blown upwards over ridges known as 'standing' waves. A well-designed glider may travel at an angle of less than 2° to the horizontal at a forward speed of around 45 knots so that the rate of sink may be

between 1 and 2 knots. Since upward currents of 10 knots are common, the pilot is able to gain height in one upward current and then glide to the next, thus proceeding on his way across country.

3. Today, craft that rely on meteorological power are used only for sport or pleasure. Craft concerned with the business of carrying passengers or cargo are power-driven. In low-speed craft, the power will be exerted against the supporting medium. In this instance, there will be three facets of propulsion:

(a) *Fuel*. The energy latent in fuel is first converted into heat.

(b) *Engine*. The heat from the fuel is converted into a mechanical rotation.

(c) *Transmission*. The rotation of the engine is translated into a force that acts against the medium supporting the craft or through which the craft is moving.

FUEL

4. *Atomic Fuel*. The greatest possible energy will be derived by converting the matter of which the fuel is composed into energy. The conversion requires an atomic reactor and the dangerous radiation has to be shielded. As a result, atomic propulsion is more suited to large surface craft such as ships, and to submarines. However, space craft and very-high-speed aircraft, which would otherwise have to carry disproportionate loads of fuel, may be forced to use atomic propulsion.

5. *Chemical Fuel*. Generally, craft will be driven by chemical energy released by burning fuel in oxygen. Space craft, or craft that travel at great heights, will need to carry oxidizing agents whose weight will generally exceed the weight of the accompanying fuel. These oxidizing agents may be either liquid or solid according to whether the fuel is liquid or solid. Liquid fuels and oxidizing agents are easily metered, but solid fuels and oxidizing agents are more conveniently stored.

6. Oil in the form of petrol or kerosene is the universal fuel for vehicles and aircraft and has almost supplanted all other forms of fuel at sea. Normally, passengers and freight will be carried around the centre of gravity of a craft so that the fuel will need

to be offset. The change in balance that can result when a small amount of fuel is being consumed will not disturb land vehicles or short-range marine craft and aircraft. However, in long-range craft and ACV's, it may be necessary to distribute the fuel about the craft and to pump from one tank to another to maintain balance.

7. *Fuel Gauge.* A float can measure the fuel in a tank. In order to transmit the information to a convenient point, the float may be mounted on a hinged arm which works a potentiometer so that a voltage is produced according to the position of the float. This voltage may be made to work an instrument similar to a voltmeter but with the dial calibrated in gallons.

8. Fixed plates may be used in place of a moving float. The electrical capacity between two plates will be greater when there is liquid between. By measuring the capacity, the depth of the fuel at that point can be recorded electrically. Systems such as these are particularly suited to tanks of a complex shape. The capacity of several pairs of plates may be averaged electrically so that the amount of fuel can be measured even though the craft may not be level. It is also possible to introduce corrections so that the fuel may be registered in pounds.

9. *Flowmeter.* The amount of fuel in a craft can also be measured by ensuring that the journey begins with a known amount of fuel in the tanks and, subsequently, by measuring how much fuel has flowed out from the tanks. A flowmeter generally consists of vanes that rotate in the fuel pipe so as to drive a form of speedometer. The instrument can be made not only to display the flow in gallons per hour or gallons per minute but also to clock up the integrated total flow. This simple type of flowmeter can cover a wide range of flow rates with an accuracy better than 1 per cent.

10. The energy in fuel does not depend on the volume, which will alter with temperature, but on the mass. For surface craft, the difference between measuring by volume and measuring by mass may not be significant. However, in craft that operate in extremes of temperature and consume fuel at great rates, such as high-flying aircraft, fuel flow needs to be measured in pounds per minute rather than in gallons per minute.

11. The simplest mass flowmeter consists of a restriction with

means for measuring the difference of pressure on each side. Such a flowmeter can have an accuracy as high as 1 per cent but generally only over a limited range of flow rates. Other flow-meters spin or deflect the fuel and measure the consequent angular energy. However, flowmeters that depend on inertia operate less efficiently in high-speed craft where there may be considerable and long sustained accelerations. Alternative systems have been developed based on marking the fuel with radio-active particles which can be counted as they flow down the fuel pipe.

12. *Gauges and Flowmeters.* Evidently the fuel gauge and the flowmeter form a good combination. The flowmeter is accurate during the early stages of the journey when the percentage of fuel consumed is low. The gauge is accurate in the critical final stages of a journey because the measurement is made on a small quantity of fuel. The flowmeter can provide immediate informa-tion regarding the performance of the engines. The fuel gauge can give warning of fuel leaks and can show fuel levels if fuel has to be jettisoned to lighten the craft or reduce fire risk.

ENGINES

13. The power that an engine will produce depends on the pressure generated by the heat and on the rate at which this pressure is released. The rate at which this pressure is released will generally be according to the rate of engine rotation. Hence the fundamental engine instruments are:

(a) *Pressure gauge.* This may measure pressure directly or, more commonly, indirectly according to the pressure of the air entering the engine through the inlet pipe. In a jet engine it may be better to measure the pressure ratio between inlet and jet pressures.

(b) *Tachometer.* Rate of revolution can be measured by driving a form of mechanical speedometer from the engine shaft. Alternatively, a very precise electrical generator, known as a tacho-generator, may be driven by the shaft and the rotations recorded on an instrument similar to a voltmeter but calibrated in revolutions per minute (r.p.m.).

TRANSMISSION SYSTEMS

14. A craft will be driven at low speeds by wheels or tracks on land and by propellers in water or air. The marine propeller or screw may tend to deflect the craft because the upper blade will grip the water less firmly than the lower blade, particularly if the hull is lightly loaded. Hence with a single screw and the usual clockwise rotation as seen from the stern, the stern will be deflected to starboard when driving power is applied to move the craft forwards. This is known as paddle wheel effect. The aircraft propeller or airscrew, which when viewed from ahead generally rotates clockwise, will cause the nose to dip if the air-craft turns to port or to rise if the aircraft turns to starboard. The reason will be explained in the section on gyroscopes on page 153, para 4.

15. At high speeds, the transmission of power to the medium that supports the craft tends to be unsatisfactory:

   (a) Wheels bounce at speeds of over 100 knots.
   (b) Marine screws lose power at speeds of over 50 knots. Suction on one side of the blades forms bubbles that escape into the compression on the other side of the blades and causes a loss of grip known as cavitation.
   (c) Air propellers that travel at the speed of sound, which is around 600 knots, form shock waves. As a result, the speed of a propeller-driven aircraft is limited to about 400 knots.

16. *Gearing.* An engine works best when it is rotating within a certain range of speeds and, in the instance of a high-performance petrol- or kerosene-driven engine, this range may be small. Accordingly, land vehicles are fitted with gears to enable the engine to run at a suitable speed while the vehicle is moving slowly, as when climbing a hill. For the same reasons, aircraft, which need to climb, and marine craft, that may need to alter speed, may be fitted with variable pitch propellers so that the angle of attack of the blades can be altered, and the propulsive force consequently increased or decreased or even reversed.

REACTION MOTORS

17. Where the speed required is too great for the transmission system to act against the medium that supports the craft, the

reaction motor is used which blows out burning gas from a jet nozzle aft. This propels the craft forwards just as a gun recoils when a shot is fired out of the muzzle. The recoil will not be lessened when the gun is travelling at high speed and neither will the thrust of a reaction motor fall off. Indeed, in air, the faster the craft is moving, the faster the hot gas can flow out of the nozzle without hindrance and the greater the reaction thrust or recoil.

18. Back pressure will prevent the reaction jet motor from operating underwater, although submarines may be driven by jets of water pumped out aft. Owing to reduced back pressure, a jet aircraft is three times as economical in fuel at 40,000 feet as it is at sea-level. At heights measured in tens of miles, however, the jet engine will need an oxidizing agent. If solid fuel is used, the resultant rocket motor will consist of a simple container that will form part of the jet pipe and will need to be able to stand heavy pressure. The solid-fuel rocket motor is therefore heavy but is so cheap and reliable that it is universally used for short-range missiles, and for launching all types of craft into the air.

FUEL ECONOMY

19. In a cargo ship travelling at not much over 10 knots, the weight of fuel consumed in a couple of weeks may only be a fraction of the cargo carried. In an aircraft travelling at nearly 10 miles a minute for hours, the fuel may weigh more than the pay-load. In a space craft, blasted off the Earth at a speed of several miles a second, the fuel may weigh a hundred times as much as the capsule. This emphasizes that the faster the craft, the greater the proportion of fuel to load and therefore the greater the possibilities of increasing this load by a large proportion as a result of a small improvement in fuel consumption.

20. All craft operate most economically at their designed speed. Increasing the speed of a marine craft beyond this speed is wasteful because it greatly increases the wash and may lead to cavitation. In aircraft, the designed speed varies with the all-up weight. In the instance of piston-engined aircraft, which work best at certain heights, the speed is reduced in proportion to the square root of the all-up weight as the fuel is burnt; in the instance of jet aircraft, which work better the higher and faster

they fly, the aircraft maintains its speed and can climb in steps or 'cruise-climb' as fuel is burnt; thus aircraft operate with different 'flight profiles', as shown in Fig. 48. Supersonic aircraft profiles will be similar to subsonic jets, but modified according to air temperatures to a far greater extent so that height may be decreased as well as increased sharply during the cruise.

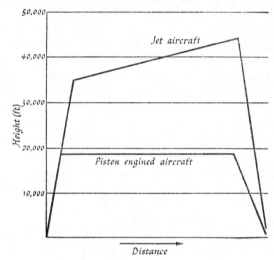

FIG. 48 Typical flight profiles for fuel economy

GROUND EFFECT

21. In certain instances, the efficiency of a propulsion system can be reduced by proximity to the ground. In shallow water when moving slowly, a ship's propeller may set up confused eddies and cause an excessive paddle-wheel effect. A jet VTOL aircraft will have the speed of the downward gasses reduced close to the ground so that the lift will decrease as the ground is approached. However, certain craft may operate with increased efficiency close to the ground, in particular, helicopters and fixed-wing aircraft. The wings of the latter may obtain additional lift and this may affect landing.

GENERATORS

22. Navigational equipment demands the generation of hydraulic, electric or, in certain instances, pneumatic power. Many craft

are fitted with auxiliary motors that drive hydraulic pumps or electric generators which feed into accumulators that store up hydraulic or electric power so that it will be available in large amounts when required. Craft with multiple engines may have generators driven from individual engines and these generators are usually electric because electric current is easily carried from one point to another. These electric generators may carry current to drive electric motors that operate pumps, the pumps feeding hydraulic power into hydraulic accumulators.

23. Generators may produce either direct current (d.c.) or alternating current (a.c.). Alternating current has the advantage that it can be converted by means of a transformer into the higher voltages required for operation of certain equipment, notably cathode ray tubes. Direct current has the advantage that it can be stored in an accumulator and is therefore used for emergency or stand-by systems. If stand-by systems need to produce alternating current, this can be arranged by an equipment known as an inverter which transforms direct into alternating current. An equipment that transforms alternating into direct current is known as a rectifier.

24. Space craft may use special solar cells that develop power from the Sun's rays, for example by boiling mercury and driving a generator. It is generally necessary to orient the space craft so that the Sun is in the correct direction although the angle is not critical. Special accumulators, possibly of the nickel–cadmium type, may be required so that the power will be available when the craft is in the shadow of the Earth or a planet.

3. STEERING

STABILITY

1. Driving power is exerted along the length of a craft, and therefore to accelerate the craft in a different direction it is necessary to alter the alignment. Changes of alignment involve overcoming the inertia of the craft, but this is generally small. More important is the inherent stability of a craft that tends to resist a change of alignment. This stability is necessary to prevent the craft from running wild if control should break down.

2. Craft that travel over land or through water or air have a tendency to keep on a steady alignment provided that the centre of gravity of the craft is ahead of the centre of resistance. This is known as weathercock stability, the extreme example being a dart with a heavy pin forward and feathers aft. If thrown point forwards, the dart is stable and stays pointing forward, but if thrown backwards with the centre of resistance ahead of the centre of gravity, it is unstable and turns round. Hence craft that are stable when travelling in one direction become unstable when travelling in reverse.

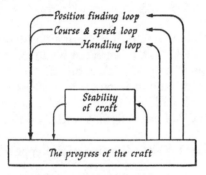

FIG. 49   The stability loop

3. Weathercock stability is possessed by a land vehicle. If the drive is from the back wheels, the front wheels provide the main resistance and, being ahead of the centre of gravity, the vehicle will be unstable. However, if the drive is from the front wheels, the vehicle becomes stable. In braking, if the rear wheels grip the more strongly, the centre of resistance moves back behind the centre of gravity and the vehicle is stable until the rear wheels lock. In a back wheel skid, the resistance of the rear wheels tends to disappear, the centre of resistance once more becomes the front wheels, and the vehicle will be unstable. By contrast, a front-wheel skid will not of itself cause instability.

4. *Stability Loop*. Weathercock stability may be regarded as an additional loop as shown in Fig. 49. It will also be found that the steering of winged aircraft is affected by the stability in roll which may be increased by the shape of the craft, particularly

by long wings. Hence the shape as well as weathercock stability may affect the ease with which a craft can manœuvre.

5. The stability of a craft not only affects the speed of manœuvre but also the amount of effort required to manœuvre. A stable craft may be steady but may need considerable force if alignment is to be altered and will be sluggish. An unstable craft may be difficult to control but will be lively. Hence the amount of steering stability will depend largely on the functions of the craft. In particular, if the craft needs to go into reverse at speed, it cannot be given much stability when travelling ahead.

CONTROL SURFACES

6. A motor vehicle is steered by altering the alignment by turning the front wheels. A ship is steered by altering the alignment in yaw by means of a rudder. A submarine or an aircraft may have the alignment altered in pitch as well as in yaw and will therefore be fitted with elevators as well as a rudder. In addition, an aeroplane will have ailerons working differentially to give control in roll.

7. When alignment is altered, three effects appear:

(a) The medium that supports the craft causes the craft to travel in a circular path.

(b) The change of direction of propulsion conforms to the circular path.

(c) The resultant forces slow up the craft. In a large ship, a prolonged turn may reduce speed by as much as a half. In an aircraft, the engines are normally opened up in a turn or else height may be lost.

In order to illustrate these effects and the problems of arrangement of control surfaces, it will be convenient to use the steering of a ship as the example.

8. *Trailing Steering.* When the rudder is FIG. 50   Trailing   moved to port, as shown in Fig. 50, the water steering   pressure sets up a force at right angles that

rotates the hull about a point some distance from the bows. As a result, the stern is moved a considerable distance to starboard. The rotation of the ship causes the flow of water due to the forward movement of the hull to press on the starboard side and this pressure accelerates the craft to port. The initial swing of the stern in the wrong direction, which is a feature of trailing steering, is accepted by ships because a rudder fitted forward would be too vulnerable.

9. In the instance of planing or hydrofoil craft, the initial turn of the rudder does little but skid the craft sideways and only gradually is the alignment changed. This means that the centre of rotation is well ahead of the bows. Indeed, the less the grip on the water provided by the hull, the further ahead will the centre of rotation become. This is a particular feature of air-cushion vehicles which have no sidewalls.

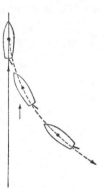

10. *Leading Steering*. Fig. 51 shows a ship travelling in reverse. With the rudder leading, the initial movement of the craft is in the same direction as the turn. For this reason, land vehicles use leading steering and so also

FIG. 51 Leading steering

do high-speed defensive missiles which may be steered by a small cruciform of elevators and rudders mounted at the nose.

11. *Wing Steering*. A missile has so little air resistance that a turn initiated by a rudder mounted either fore or aft must cause a large amount of skidding, though this may be reduced by fitting wings. Certain missiles use ram jet engines that rely for their thrust on the ramming of air directly into the engine intakes. Such craft must keep their hulls aligned to the airflow. They therefore use central-wing steering as shown in Fig. 52. The wing is tilted so that a direct sideways force is applied. The tail fins are fixed and weather-cock the body in line with the airflow.

FIG. 52 Wing steering

12. Wing-steering mechanisms are heavy and

consume considerable power. Therefore only two wings may be fitted. The wings may operate differentially to roll the body into a position from which the wings, acting together, can steer the missile in the required direction. Such an arrangement is known as twist and steer. Even if the missile is only making small changes of direction, it may still be necessary to roll violently. Also the missile may hesitate whether to roll left and steer up or roll right and steer down.

13. *Bank Steering*. An aircraft has little sideways air resistance and therefore is steered by banking to one side so that the lift of the wings introduces a sideways component as shown in Fig. 53.

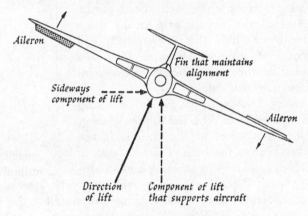

FIG. 53   Turning by banking

The fin and the rudder keep the fuselage aligned with the airflow and prevent any skidding or 'sideslipping'. Sideslip can be detected by a simple pendulum mounted in the craft. In practice, an agate ball is allowed to roll in a glass tube that is curved in the form of an arc. This instrument is known as a ball-bank indicator.

14. The rate of turn will be determined by the angle of bank. A rate one turn means a turn through 180° in 1 minute. A rate two turn means a turn through 360° in 1 minute and a rate half turn is a turn through 90° in 1 minute. At moderate bank angles:

$$\text{bank angle}° = \text{speed (knots)} \times (\text{rate of turn})/7$$

Example. A 350-knot aircraft is turning at rate half:

$$\text{bank angle} = 350 \times \tfrac{1}{2}/7 = 25° \text{ approximately}$$

15. It is worth noting that between 20° and 30° is the maximum angle of bank that passengers generally wish to accept. The example in the previous paragraph shows that this limits a 300–400 knot aircraft to a rate half turn. The formula also shows that a mach 3 aircraft will be limited to a turn of rate one-tenth or about 20° per minute. In a military aircraft, however, the rate of turn is limited only by the acceleration that the airframe and the human pilot are able to withstand. This acceleration in terms of g will be g.sec (bank), so that a 60° bank will impose $2g$ on the craft and its crew.

16. *Steering Surface Stability.* There is no difference in steering stability whether the control surfaces are leading, trailing or central. Stability of steering depends on how far the centre of resistance of the craft is behind the centre of gravity. A parallel criterion applies to the steering surface. Stability depends on how far the centre of pressure due to steering is behind the centre of support. If too far behind, it will take power to move the surface and the surface will be unstable in reverse. In practice, a limited stability is generally provided when the craft is moving forwards so that the craft will not run wild if the steering should break down. Alternatively some self-centring mechanism may be provided.

17. *Steering and Speed.* In a very-high-speed craft under certain conditions, the operation of a steering control may warp the craft initially and, by so doing, cause the craft to turn in the wrong direction, a condition known as reversal of control. At low speeds, it is impossible to arrange for the surfaces to exercise sufficient power, although, in aircraft, matters can be assisted by blowing air over the surfaces. In a ship, if the speed drops too low, the ship loses steerage way, and becomes uncontrollable. Control will then have to depend on deflected thrust.

THRUST DEFLECTION

18. *Marine Craft.* When a ship has lost steerage way, control may be regained by accelerating the engine and deflecting the flow of water from the propellers by using the rudder. If a ship has two

or more propellers, turning may also be assisted by differential thrust. In general, ships have contra-rotating propellers to reduce paddle-wheel effect (page 113, para 14) so that, when one propeller is reversed, both may paddle-wheel in the same direction and this can assist the turn. Another result of reversing one screw is that it will upset the flow over the rudder and reduce the outward heel which would otherwise tend to assist the turn.

19. Certain vessels are fitted so that they may be steered directly by thrust. The best-known example is the outboard motor which is turned in order to steer. Special types of propeller such as the Voith-Schneider will drive the water in any direction and enable the craft to be steered directly but are rather vulnerable to grounding. This type of propeller is particularly useful in tugs. Large ships may use one Voith-Schneider propeller in the bows and a normal propeller astern. Alternatively they may be fitted with impellers fore and aft so that water may be ejected to move the bows or the stern sideways. By such means the ship may be controlled in alignment if she is stationary, but impellers are ineffective when under way.

20. Air-cushion vehicles pose particular problems. At low speeds, control may be exercised by auxiliary outboard motors mounted fore and aft. However, once over the hump speed, a turn will be affected by a tilt which will cause additional air to escape from below the raised side and will drive the craft in the opposite direction. For this reason, a keel will be ineffective since it would tilt the craft outwards in a turn. The air-cushion vehicle is therefore steered at speed by a rudder in the slip-stream of the air propellers that drive the craft forwards. An exception is the sidewall vehicle in which the sidewalls act as keels and also prevent the air from escaping sideways so that the craft can be steered by a rudder in the water.

21. *Aircraft*. The air-cushion vehicle is an example of a craft which, when supported on air, steers by deflecting air thrust. Similarly, when a VTOL aircraft is hovering it will be controlled as well as supported by thrust. The engines or the jet pipes may be tilted or fixed lift engines may be fitted and the whole craft tilted by air jets mounted in wing-tips or tail. These air jets are known as puffers and may be fed by air from the lift-engine compressors.

22. In the instance of a helicopter, the pitch of the blades can be varied at different parts of the cycle of rotation by means of a cyclic-pitch control. This will increase the lift in one direction and tilt the helicopter accordingly. The over-all lift produced by the rotating wing will then cause the helicopter to travel in the direction of the tilt. During these manœuvres, yaw is generally controlled by a separate propeller mounted athwartships in the tail.

23. *Space Craft and Missiles.* Space-craft launchers and ballistic missiles are steered by thrust in order to provide control during the very slow speed at lift-off and subsequently when the Earth's atmosphere is left behind. At least two steering motors are necessary each of which may be tilted in one axis only so as to control the vehicle by twist and steer (page 119, para 12). However, it is generally inconvenient to roll the vehicle and therefore either each of the two motors is mounted so that it can be tilted in two axes, or three or more motors are fitted each of which can tilt in one axis. In practice, since only a small amount of power is needed to control the vehicle, whereas a very large amount is needed to accelerate it, a main motor will often be fitted which does not tilt, and auxiliary motors will provide the control.

24. The very small field of battle weapons used to attack armoured vehicles travel so slowly that they may have to be controlled by thrust deflection. Generally, deflector vanes are mounted in the rocket-motor effluxes.

INERTIA

25. The force needed to accelerate a craft will depend on its mass (page 24, para 24). The turning force or torque needed to rotate a craft or to stop a craft rotating will similarly depend on the mass and on the leverage that this mass exerts about the centre of gravity. A ship with the load concentrated right forward and right aft will take more force to turn and more force to stop turning than will a ship with the load concentrated at its centre. The torque or angular force will depend on (mean distance from centre of gravity) × (mass), this quantity being known as the moment of inertia.

26. In a surface craft, the effects of inertia may be largely masked by the friction of the medium that supports the craft.

However, in a space craft, it is possible to provide control of alignment by inertial means. Rotating a small mass at high speed in one direction can cause a heavy space craft to turn slowly in the opposite direction.

27. A space craft weighing a ton with the mass distributed on an average 5 feet from the centre will have a moment of inertia of 5 ft.tons or about 10,000 ft.lb. A wheel within the craft weighing 1 lb with its weight distributed about 1 inch from the axis of rotation will have a moment of inertia of 0.1 ft.lb approximately. To alter the alignment of the craft through 1°, the wheel would have to be turned through 100,000° or nearly 300 revolutions. To correct a rotation of the craft of say 1° per second, the wheel would have to spin at nearly 300 revs/sec. Hence the rotating wheel is generally used as a fine control in space craft, the main control being exercised by differential thrust.

4. HANDLING PROBLEMS

BERTHING

1. There are three different types of problem each of which is surrounded by circumstances which are particular to the locality as well as to the craft:

  (a) Berthing alongside a wharf or quay.
  (b) Mooring to a buoy.
  (c) Anchoring. This may be compared to mooring to a buoy in a position selected by the craft.

2. In all these problems, the object is to arrive at the chosen position aligned in the required direction and with the way taken off the craft. In the instance of mooring to a buoy or anchoring, the alignment must be such that the craft will subsequently tend to drift backwards, otherwise the craft may over-run the buoy or the anchor and catch the chain on the stem or pull the anchor out of the ground. It is, however, important that as the craft drifts backwards the strain on the cable shall be maintained, otherwise the drift may have to be checked suddenly, the process being known as bringing up with a round turn, which puts an unreasonable strain on the cable.

3. The anchor may be pulled out of the ground by a sudden

strain or a strain in the wrong direction. Unless there is sufficient length of chain to give the effect of a spring, pitching of the
craft may jerk the cable. Anchors may be laid in various patterns
and attached to the vessel aft as well as fore. They may also be
used to pull a craft off a bank on which she has grounded, the
process being known as kedging.

4. A ship coming slowly to her berth is supported by water
which may be moving relative to the bottom or the dockside.
She is affected by wind which will move in a direction completely
independent of the water and the dockside and may blow in
gusts or eddies. The way in which she will answer to her helm
will depend on her speed, on her draught and the way in which
she is loaded, and on whether her screws are accelerating or
decelerating her and the extent of the paddle-wheel effect. In
addition, the screws may interact with the bottom if the water is
shallow, and the bows may be forced away from a bank owing to
the build up of pressure signified by the bow wave. This effect
is sometimes preceded by a swinging towards the bank, a
characteristic known as 'smelling the ground'.

5. It follows that the berthing of a vessel will involve a very large
number of factors which may interact in a most subtle fashion.
It will be important to appreciate this in relation to the control of
the vessel during these critical phases of terminal navigation.

6. *Getting Under Way*. The problems of setting out from a
berth are naturally simpler than the problems of berthing. The
major requirement is so to align the vessel that she can move off
safely. This can demand the towing of a ship to another point. In
particular, it may involve the movement of a sailing craft by other
means so that the bows may be headed into wind.

LANDING AND TAKE-OFF

7. Landing an aircraft involves a steady descent to a point 50 or
100 feet over the threshold of the runway at a speed as close to
the stalling speed as is safe and into wind so as to reduce speed
compared to the ground as much as possible. The final descent
is completed by a rotation in pitch known as a flare-out which
reduces the rate of descent to a smooth touch-down. Simultaneously, power is cut so that the aeroplane virtually stalls on to
the ground.

8. If there is a wind blowing across the runway, the aircraft will have to head slightly towards it to follow down the centre line. Just before touch-down, the aircraft must be aligned with the runway by yawing with the rudder, a process known as decrabbing or kicking off drift (KOD), otherwise the aircraft wheels would land at an angle to the runway and the sideway forces could collapse the undercarriage. If the decrab is too early, the yawing will develop a sideways acceleration and may run the aircraft off the runway sideways. If the decrab is too late, the aircraft may not have time to yaw.

9. Decrabbing can be avoided by approaching with a bank so that the aircraft is skidding sideways to offset the wind, but this will require the aircraft to be levelled on landing and is not commonly adopted as a landing procedure. Decrabbing may not be needed for landing on a grass airfield and will not be required for landing on a carrier since the carrier can be aligned into the wind. Aircraft have also been built with castoring wheels, but these introduce a number of problems including the steering of the aircraft subsequently along the ground.

10. The process of landing an aircraft is a complex manœuvre demanding rapid and precise control. There is little margin for error and the results of mishandling may be catastrophic. Nevertheless, compared to berthing a ship, the process is basically a matter of repeating a manœuvre with minor modifications. Only two mediums are concerned so that the factors are relatively limited. However, if these two mediums are in conflict, and there are strong gusts or cross-winds, landing can be extremely difficult.

11. *Take-off*. The problem is to acquire sufficient speed for lift-off. The speed will depend on the head wind, the all-up weight, and the air density. The attainment of that speed will depend on the engine performance, possibly on the temperature, and certainly on the length of the runway available. At some stage during the take-off run, the aircraft may be travelling so fast and be so far down the runway that it will be impossible to stop without an accident. The problem will be to ensure that the aircraft can in fact take-off before that critical point is reached.

12. It will be possible before take-off to calculate according to the known factors whether the aircraft can safely get airborne.

However, if the margin for error is not large, the development of reduced power by an engine may make it necessary to break off. The decision can be extremely difficult to take and ground-run predictors have been designed which measure speed and distance down the runway so as to assist the pilot. A major difficulty is to measure speed, particularly in conditions of slush.

13. There are several stages in the take-off. As soon as the aircraft gathers way, she may be put into a level attitude to reduce air resistance to the minimum. When speed has built up sufficiently, she can be rotated in pitch, lifted off the runway and then allowed to gather further forward speed before being made to climb away. The rate of rotation may be critical in a jet aircraft.

5. SUMMARY

CRAFT

The following is a summary of types of craft and their major characteristics from the navigation point of view. The speeds mentioned are very approximate maximum speeds.

LAND VEHICLES

Propulsion: Internal combustion and gears.
Speed: 30 miles per hour across country, 100 miles per hour on roads are normal maxima.
Steering: Leading.
Stability: Metacentric. Unstable in yaw with rear-wheel drive or in rear-wheel skid.

MARINE CRAFT

(a) *Submarines*
Propulsion: Oil fuel (or atomic reactor).
Speed: Generally a few tens of knots.
Steering: Elevators and rudder, generally trailing.
Stability: Absolute.

(b) *Ships* (including powered boats)
Propulsion: Oil fuel (or atomic reactor for large ships).

Speed: Wash excessive over 50 knots. Speed reduced by heavy seas, particularly head seas.

Steering: Trailing. May be aided by impellers or special propellers.

Stability: Metacentric. Bilge keels for dynamic stability.

(c) *Skimming Craft* (includes sidewall ACV)

Propulsion: Internal combustion engines and marine propellers.

Speed: Cavitation probably limits speed to about 100 knots. Minimum speed about 20 knots.

Steering: Rudder, trailing.

Stability: Metacentric.

Note: Operation limited by seas.

(d) *Air-Cushion Vehicles*

Propulsion: Internal combustion engines and air propellers.

Speed: Over 100 knots possible.

Steering: Aerofoil rudder.

Stability: Metacentric.

Note: Operations limited by seas according to size of craft.

(e) *Sailing Craft*

Propulsion: Wind.

Speed: Up to about 20 knots according to size.

Steering: Rudder (unbalanced).

Stability: Metacentric.

Note: Progress impossible within about 45–60° either side of wind direction.

AIRCRAFT

(a) *Aeroplanes, Propeller driven*

Speed: Up to about 400 knots; then air propellers form shock waves.

Steering: By ailerons and elevators.

Stability: Weathercock.

Note: For economical cruise a steady height is maintained.

(b) *Jet Aeroplanes* (includes wing-borne missiles)
Speed: Up to 2000 knots or above. Then shock waves occur in air inlets and higher-speed aircraft may require rocket motors.
Steering: By ailerons and elevators or by elevons.
Stability: Weathercock.
Note: Cruise climb for economy.

(c) *Gliders*
Propulsion: Upward air currents and gravity.
Speed: Up to about 60 knots but may be much higher.
Steering and Stability as with aeroplanes.

(d) *Vertical Take-off and Landing* (includes helicopters)
Propulsion: Lift engines, tilting or rotating wings.
Steering: By thrust.
Stability: Unstable.
Note: A VTOL aircraft may be a normal aircraft with a VTOL capability, and the above characteristics apply only when operating in the VTOL regime.

(e) *Missiles* (except ballistic missiles)
Propulsion: Generally solid rockets.
Speed: A few hundred to a few thousand knots.
Steering: Generally by elevators and rudders placed fore and aft with wings to reduce skid. Ram-jet missiles use twist and steer. Slow missiles may be steered by thrust deflection.
Stability: Weathercock.

SPACE CRAFT

(a) *Launchers* (and ballistic missiles)
Propulsion: Solid (or liquid) rockets.
Speed: Up to 20,000 knots or more.
Steering: By thrust.
Stability: Neutral except close to the ground.

(b) *Space Craft*
Propulsion: Solid, liquid or atomic rockets.
Speed: According to orbit.
Steering: By auxiliary thrust and rotating masses.

Stability: Neutral. Tendency for mass to align itself along line of gravitation force.

HANDLING INSTRUMENTS

(a) Engine power is measured by pressure gauges and revolution meters.
(b) Liquid fuel is measured by gauges and flowmeters.
(c) Angle of attack in aeroplanes is generally inferred by air-speed indicator.
(d) Speed in high-speed aircraft is limited with the help of a mach-meter.
(e) Sideslip is detected by a ball-bank indicator.

BERTHING AND LANDING

Berthing involves the interaction of a large number of factors. Landing requires precise control of a few factors.

BIBLIOGRAPHY: BACKGROUND

MATHEMATICS AND ERRORS

Anderson, E. W., and J. B. Parker, Observational errors. *J. Inst. Navig.*, **9**, 105.

Berkeley, E. C., and L. Wainwright, *Computers, their operation and applications*, Blackwell, Oxford, U.K.

Bowley, A. L., *Elementary manual of statistics*, Macdonald & Evans, London.

Brownlee, K. A., *Industrial experimentation*, H.M.S.O.

Gaskell, R. E., *Engineering mathematics*, Staples Press, London.

Hogben, L., *Mathematics for the million*, Unwin & Allen, London.

Institute of Navigation meeting, Blunders and gross human errors in navigation, *J. Inst. Navig.*, **12**, 28.

Ivall, R. E. (Editor), *Electronic computers*, Blackwell, Oxford, U.K.

Parker, J. B., see Anderson, E. W.

Renwick, W., *Digital storage systems*, Reinhold Publishing, New York.

Wainwright, L., see Berkeley, E. C., and L. Wainwright.

Wesley, R., *Mathematics for all*, Odhams Press, London.

ENVIRONMENT AND ALTIMETRY

Bannon, J. K., Strong winds in the upper atmosphere above 15,000 ft., *J. Inst. Navig.*, **9**, 282.

Cronin, J. G., Some practical applications in flying the western and central Pacific jet streams, *Navigation (U.S.A.)*, **6**, 217.

Crossley, A. F., Hail in relation to the risk of encounters in flight, *Met. Mag., Lond.*, Vol. 90.

Darbyshire, J., Prediction of wave characteristics over the North Atlantic, *J. Inst. Navig.*, **14**, 339.

Durst, C. S., The probable errors in forecast winds, *J. Inst. Navig.*, **11**, 180.

Durst, C. S., The statistical variation of wind with distance, *Quart. J. R. Met. Soc.*, 1960.

Durst, C. S., and G. W. Hurst, *Gusts over short periods of time*, Meteorological Research Committee, H.M.S.O.

Halpine, C. G., and H. H. Taylor, *A mariner's meteorology*, Van Nostrand, New York.

Honick, K. R., and A. Stratton, Presentation of height information, *J. Inst. Navig.*, **14**, 308

Hurst, G. W., see Durst, C. S., and G. W. Hurst.

King-Hele, D. G., The shape of the earth, *J. Inst. Navig.*, **17**, 1.

Meteorological Office, *Charts of flow lines and isotachs over the world and standard vector deviations*, H.M.S.O.

Meteorological Office, *The handbook of aviation meteorology*, H.M.S.O.

Meteorological Office, *The marine observer's handbook*, H.M.S.O.

Meteorological Office, *Meteorology for mariners*, H.M.S.O.

Reiter, E. R., *Jet stream meteorology*, University of Chicago Press, Chicago.

Stratton, A., see Honick, K. R., and A. Stratton.

Taylor, H. H., see Halpine, C. G., and H. H. Taylor.

Wallington, C. E., *Meteorology for glider pilots*, John Murray, London.

THE CRAFT

Ardley, R. A. E., *Harbour pilotage and the handling and mooring of ships*, Faber and Faber, London.

Cotter, C. H., *The master and his ship*, Maritime Press, London.

King, E. R., and J. V. Noel, *Ship handling*, Van Nostrand, New York.

Noel, J. V., see King, E. R., and J. V. Noel.

Troup, Sir J. A. G., *On the bridge*, Hutchinson, London.

United States Hydrographic Office, *Handling a vessel in ice*, H.O.

Wynne-Edwards, Capt. J. C., Handling ships in narrow waters, *J. Inst. Navig.*, **9**, 198.

PART TWO

INSTRUMENTATION

CHAPTER IV CONTROL. The chapter deals very briefly with the principles of servo control and explains their application to power controls and the possibilities afforded by servo-driven instruments for improved displays. The second half of the chapter is mainly concerned with stabilization and, in particular, with the principles of simple gyroscopes used for short-term integration and smoothing. The problems of long-term references in general and of gravity monitors in particular are discussed and particular reference is made to the increase in monitoring time constants made possible by the reduction of apparent gyro drifts. The chapter concludes with notes on stabilizers and on the applications of redundancy for increase of safety.

CHAPTER V. HEADING. The three types of reference, true, grid and magnetic, and the relevant heading references, gyro compass, directional gyro and magnetic compass, are discussed separately. The pattern of gyro errors that appeared in stabilization systems due to the Earth's rotation and to transport errors is seen to repeat itself in these systems. It has not been possible to deal fully with magnetic deviation corrections but notes on remote reading compasses and gyro-magnetic compasses have been included. The chapter finishes with a brief description of autohelmsman and autopilot elements.

CHAPTER VI. SPEED. This relatively short chapter deals briefly with measurement of speed through water and air and over land, and touches on the principles of doppler, the radio aspects of doppler being reserved for Chapter XV. The second half of the chapter is taken up with a description of the Schüler tuned inertial platform with its marine, aircraft and missile variations and the consequent development of sophisticated gyroscopes. The combination of inertia with measured water speed and with airborne doppler is discussed and also the improvements in heading reference accuracy made possible by the Schüler tuned platform.

CONTENTS

CHAPTER IV

Control

1. SERVO CONTROL

1. The speed with which a human learns to control his craft tends to disguise the complexity of the problems that he masters. To understand the way in which a craft is controlled in yaw, roll and pitch, it may be helpful to consider the hypothetical instance of a device designed to steer a ship automatically down the centre of a canal.

POSITION TERM
2. Suppose that the equipment were able to measure the position of the ship compared to the centre line of the canal and were to turn the rudder according to the distance off the centre line. If the ship should drift to the left, the rudder would turn to the right and steer the ship back towards the centre line, the amount of turning of the rudder being proportional to the distance of the ship from the centre of the canal. Information of position used in this way to control a craft may be referred to as a 'position term' in a control system.
3. Fig. 54(a) shows that, with a position term only, the ship will weave from side to side across the centre line. If the ship veers off to the left, as in this illustration, the rudder turns to the right and by the time that the ship has returned to the centre line the rudder will have returned to amidships. The ship will therefore continue across the centre line until the rudder starts a turn to the left. Thus the ship will weave from side to side across the centre line. The frequency of this weaving is known as the natural frequency of the system.

DAMPING
4. The swinging of the ship from side to side across the canal may be compared to the swinging of a pendulum. The swing of a

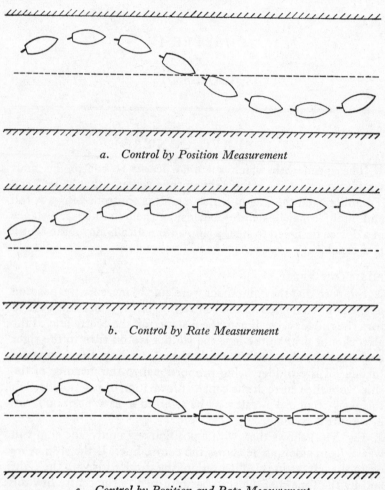

a. Control by Position Measurement

b. Control by Rate Measurement

c. Control by Position and Rate Measurement

FIG. 54　Characteristics of control terms

pendulum may be reduced by immersing the bob in oil so that the viscosity cuts down the successive movements. This is known as frictional damping. In the instance of a ship in a canal, frictional damping might delay the response of the rudder and allow the original error to build up further and likewise to delay the correction of the consequently increased overshoot. The weaving from side to side might build up and the ship go out of control.

5. *Rate Term.* Fig. 54(b) shows what would happen if the equipment were made to turn the rudder according to the rate at which the ship was departing from the centre line. As the ship starts to drift to the left, the rudder will turn to the right, the amount of turning gradually decreasing as the rate of drift off the centre line decreases. Eventually the ship will straighten up, with the rudder amidships, travelling along the canal but to one side of the centre line. Information of rate used to control a craft in this way may be referred to as a 'rate term' in a control system.

6. If the position term and the rate term are combined, the result will be as shown in Fig. 54(c). When the ship drifts to the left, both the distance and the rate will combine to turn the rudder to the right. When the drift to the left ceases, the rate term will cease to take effect but, because the ship is to one side of the centre line, the position term will hold the rudder to the right.

7. As a result of the turning of the rudder due to the position term, the ship will start to move back towards the centre line. In so doing, a rate will build up in the opposite direction so that the rate term will begin to oppose the position term. As the ship moves in towards the centre line, the position term will decrease but the rate term will increase until the rudder will be driven amidships. The position term will continue to decrease and therefore the rate term will overcome it, and the rudder will turn to the left as if anticipating arrival at the centre line. As the rate and distance terms both become smaller, the craft will settle down on the centre line.

8. If the rate term were unduly powerful, the settling of the craft on the centre line could be delayed as shown in Fig. 55(a). Such a system is said to be aperiodic. If the damping were weak, the craft would overshoot but the oscillations would die away as suggested in Fig. 55(b). In practice a slight oscillation may produce a faster overall correction than the theoretically ideal balance between position and rate which is shown in Fig. 55(c). A system with this balance is said to be critically damped or dead-beat. It is impossible to measure when a control system settles absolutely and therefore the settling time is taken to be when the

original error has been corrected by a certain percentage, generally 98 per cent.

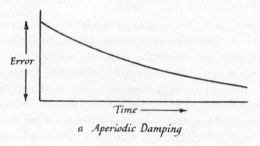

a Aperiodic Damping

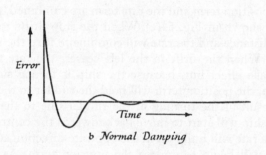

b Normal Damping

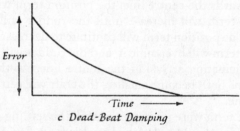

c Dead-Beat Damping

FIG. 55 Types of damping

ADDITIONAL TERMS

9. *Integral Term.* If position and rate terms only are used to control a craft, a 'hang-off' error may develop. Suppose that the canal were to turn to the left. Initially, the ship would travel straight ahead until the position and the rate term pulled the rudder to the left. The rate of departure from the centre line would soon be balanced but the position term would be absorbed in keeping the ship following the bend to the left. Therefore the ship would follow the bend round the outside.

10. Hang-off error can be reduced by adding an integral term. If the ship begins to travel consistently to one side of the centre line, the integral term will build up and produce an additional turning of the rudder, which will go far to restore the ship to the centre line.

11. *Rate of Rate Term.* It was explained on page 21, para 16, that differentiation results in phase advance. The expression phase advance is appropriate because a rate of departure will always precede a measurable positional departure. For the same reason, a rate of rate term will have a phase advance beyond that of a rate term and may be useful in a control system in which very quick action is necessary.

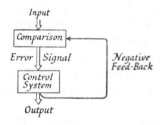

FIG. 56   Basic servo-loop
elements

SERVO LOOP

12. The servo loop has already been mentioned on page 4. A simple example is the domestic heating system. The thermostat is set to the required temperature and this setting may be regarded as the input to the system. The temperature of the building may be regarded as the output of the system. The thermostat compares the output with the input. If the output is lower, the thermostat switches on the heat. When the output becomes higher, the thermostat switches off the heat. This simple on-off control system is known as a bang-bang servo.

13. The feeding back of the output in opposition to the input as a means of comparison is an essential feature of a servo loop and is

known as negative feed-back. A servo system therefore comprises the elements shown in Fig. 56. The difference between the input and the output produces an error signal which is used to drive the control system. In order to make the output follow the input precisely, negative feed-back may include a rate term in addition to a position term and, in certain instances, an integral and a rate of rate term.

14. The ratio of the feed-back to the input signal is known as the gain of the servo. If the gain is high, the response of the servo will be powerful. If the gain is low, the response of the servo will be weak. A high gain is therefore an advantage. The natural frequency is also important as it will determine the ability of the servo to react quickly to disturbances.

15. *Stability*. If the servo system is responding to a sine wave input, it will tend to lag behind by a slight amount according to the natural frequency. Thus the output will be slightly out of phase with the input. If the input frequency equals the natural frequency, the output will be exactly 180° out of phase with the input. The feed-back will therefore be positive instead of nega-tive. If the gain of the system is greater than unity, the positive feed-back will be greater than the input signal and the oscillations will build up until the whole system is vibrating at the natural frequency.

16. Fortunately, at frequencies close to the natural frequency of servo, the gain tends to decrease so that a gain of three or four at normal operating frequencies may introduce a gain of only a half at the natural frequency. However, if the gain of the servo is increased past a certain limit, the gain at the natural frequency will become unity. There will inevitably be a little noise at the natural frequency to start the loop oscillating, whereupon it will oscillate wildly irrespective of the input signal.

SERVO ENGINEERING

17. Servo engineering is a problem for the servo engineer. The only reason for a brief mention of some of the problems is to emphasize that there are many pitfalls in the design of servo loops. An improvement in one direction may lead to a degrada-tion of performance in another, so that the solution to any problem must be a matter of compromise.

2. ACTUATORS AND DISPLAYS

1. A navigation equipment may be illustrated by means of a block diagram that shows the elements that it contains. In Fig. 57, symbols which are often used for some of the more common elements are shown.

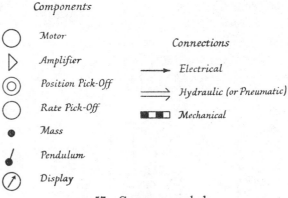

FIG. 57　Common symbols

2. Even more important than the symbols for components are the symbols for the flow of information and action. Fig. 57 shows typical symbols for electrical, for hydraulic or pneumatic and for mechanical connections. Each symbol may represent a number of wires or pipes, and will be marked with arrows to show the direction of flow, except in the instance of the mechanical linkages which will inevitably be both ways. These linkages form what are known as transmission systems within the navigation equipment.

TRANSMISSION SYSTEMS

3. An electrical potential divider, known commonly as a pot or potentiometer, produces a voltage proportional to the rotation of a shaft and, when used in this way, it may be known as a position pick-off. The symbol is shown in Fig. 57. The signal from the transmitting pick-off may be reproduced by a simple electro-magnetic moving-coil device which will act as a receiver. Such an instrument is basically an electric motor and can use the same symbol.

4. Unless the slider of a potentiometer presses hard on the wire, it may jump off if the craft vibrates. If the slider presses hard, minute particles of swarf may be rubbed off and may lodge between the turns of wire and cause short circuits. It is possible to use a pick-off with no sliding contacts such as a capacity pick-off shown in Fig. 58. The capacity between the rotating plate and the

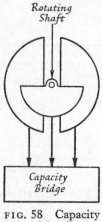

FIG. 58 Capacity
pick-off

two fixed plates is varied by rotating the shaft and the differences in capacity can be detected by an electrical device known as a capacity-bridge. In practice systems that avoid sliding contacts use alternating current.

5. *Synchro*. The alternating current synchro is a common form of position pick-off. As shown in Fig. 59, alternating current is passed through the moving coil of the transmitting synchro. This current sets up ripples in the three fixed coils of the transmitting synchro, and these ripples are passed to the three fixed coils of the receiving synchro. The alternating field from the transmitting synchro is thus reproduced in the receiving synchro. If the same current that was passed through the moving coil of the transmitting synchro is also passed through the moving coil of the receiving synchro, the latter will align itself with respect to the fixed coils in the same direction as the former. The a.c. synchro transmitters and receivers are identical so that both can be designated by the same pick-off symbol.

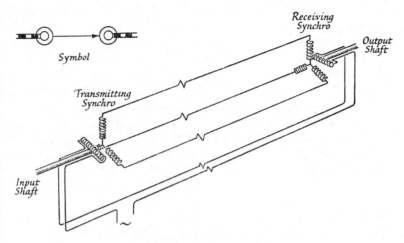

FIG. 59   Synchro transmission

6. *Tacho.* A rate pick-off measures a rate of movement, generally the rate of rotation of a shaft. The tacho-generator is a common form. A tacho is usually similar in design to a motor and may use the same symbol. The direction of flow of information and action will serve to distinguish between a motor and a tacho.

7. *Power Output.* The current produced by a pick-off and the torque exerted by the receiver is not always sufficient. In this event, a power transmission may be used. Fig. 60 shows a power

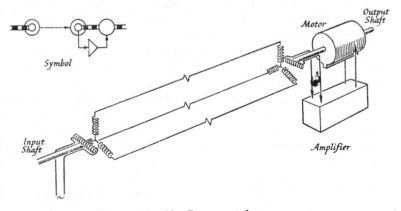

FIG. 60   Power synchro

synchro. If the receiver synchro is not aligned with the transmitter synchro, the difference is amplified and made to drive a motor which turns the receiver synchro until the misalignment is eliminated. The motor simultaneously drives an output shaft.

8. In place of two position pick-offs, two rate pick-offs could be used. By fitting tachos instead of synchros to the system of Fig. 60, the receiving shaft can be made to rotate at the same rate as the transmitting shaft. Phase advance or, if necessary, an integral term, could be included in the amplifier. Alternatively, a tacho could be fitted in addition to the synchro to provide rate damping of the feed-back.

ACTUATORS

9. In small craft, human muscles may power the steering. In large craft, or in missiles, it will be necessary to use either:

(a) Hydraulic power.
(b) Electric power.
(c) Pneumatic power.

Pneumatic power may control small missiles but, because gas is compressible, lags are apt to appear. The equipment is similar to that used in hydraulic systems.

10. *Hydraulic Actuators.* The hydraulic motor generally consists of a piston or ram driven by hydraulic pressure. The fluid is admitted by a control valve which may resemble the valve used in a steam engine and is generally known as a spool valve. Fig. 61 shows a typical hydraulic ram and spool valve in section.

11. The hydraulic motor is quick-acting as it has relatively little inertia of its own. Only a small effort is needed to move the control valve, which accordingly acts as an hydraulic amplifier and can be shown as such on a schematic flow diagram. The rams move only when pressure is directed by the control valve and therefore the system is irreversible and cannot be driven by external force in the wrong direction. Hydraulic pressure is readily stored in a reservoir, known as an accumulator, by means of a pump working when steering is not required. There can thus be ample power available to operate the actuator when necessary.

12. *Electric Motors.* Electricity can flow from one point to another more readily than hydraulic fluid, and there are no valves with

small openings that are difficult to manufacture and may get
clogged up. Unfortunately, electrical actuators have two disadvantages. It is not easy to store large amounts of electricity in
an accumulator and to release this power suddenly, and the
electric motor has to spin fast if it is to develop the necessary
power in a small volume. The necessity to spin fast can be
accommodated by interposing gearing but this will introduce
inertia.

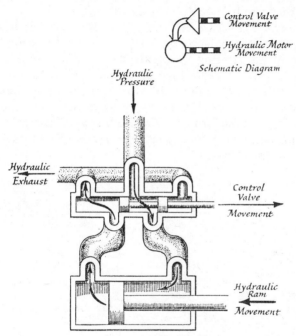

FIG. 61   Hydraulic actuator

13. *Rate Feed-back.* To spin an electric motor quickly up to the
speed necessary to move a mechanism at the required rate, a
heavy current is required. However, once the motor has reached
the correct speed, only a relatively small amount of current is
needed to maintain the spinning. A rate pick-off, such as a
tacho-generator, is therefore attached to the output shaft of the
motor. As the motor speed starts to build up, the tacho-generator
begins to feed back an opposing signal to the amplifier that is

driving the motor. By this means, the incoming signal is reduced as the motor speeds up to the required rate.

14. *Complex Actuators.* Where the power required is very great, the control valve of the actuator may itself be worked by a smaller pilot valve, thus giving two stages of hydraulic amplification. Alternatively, the control valve may be driven by a powerful electric motor. The pilot valve may, however, be so light that it is possible to drive it with a simple type of motor which has so little inertia that rate feed-back is not necessary.

15. *Actuator Feed-back.* All steering systems include feed-back from the actuator to the controller. In a car, the driver can feel the position of the steering-wheels by the force he needs to exert, though he may go gravely astray in the event of a front-wheel skid. In an aircraft, a pilot is able to feel the force on the control surfaces or, if powered controls are used, he is provided with artificial 'feel' in the form of spring loading to his control column. In the instance of a small boat, the helmsman can sense the position of the tiller.

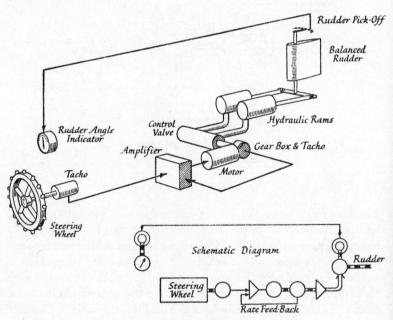

FIG. 62 Powered steering (rate-rate system)

POWERED STEERING

16. Fig. 62 illustrates a marine powered steering system. The rate pick-off on the steering-wheel drives an electric motor through an amplifier. The motor drives a control valve which operates rams that turn the rudder. On the rudder shaft is a position pick-off that feeds a signal to the rudder-angle indicator. The actuator loop is then completed through the helmsman's eyes, brain and hands.

17. The system illustrated in Fig. 62 is known as a rate-rate system because the rudder is turned at a rate according to the rate at which the steering-wheel is turned. An alternative would be a position system in which the rudder would be made to follow the position of the wheel. A block diagram of a position system is shown in Fig. 63. It will be noticed that in order to

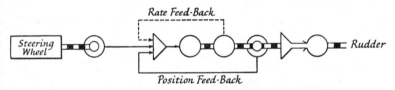

FIG. 63   Powered steering (position system)

improve control, a rate feed-back is included, but this rate feed-back will be weak compared to the major position feed-back.

18. The rate-rate system and the position system may appear to produce the same result, but in practice there are certain differences. For example, if the position system were to be disconnected and the wheel was subsequently moved and, at some time later, the position system was engaged, the rudder would be driven quickly back to the new position assumed by the wheel. In a rate-rate system, the rudder would be engaged smoothly and would not move until the wheel was moved. On the other hand, the position of the rudder would have to be determined separately by a rudder-angle indicator.

REMOTE INDICATING INSTRUMENTS

19. The rudder-angle indicator shown on page 148, Fig. 62, is an example of a remote indicating instrument. Remote indicating

instruments, if the moving parts are sufficiently light, may be worked by synchros or other position transmissions. If the moving parts are heavy or make irregular demands on torque, the instruments may be servo driven.

20. The altimeter and the air-speed indicator have been described in the form of direct-reading instruments. However, both these instruments may be servo driven from barometric capsules. For instance, the altimeter needs a pointer on a wide scale, generally one revolution to 1000 feet, and yet has to read up to many tens of thousands of feet. The use of a number of hands, as in a clock, tends to cause confusion so that counters will be preferred, but these have too much friction at change-over points to be driven directly from a capsule.

21. The availability of servo-driven instruments makes it possible to design displays for maximum efficiency. However, direct-reading instruments are less complicated and may therefore be more reliable. They will generally be used as stand-by instruments.

PRINCIPLES OF DISPLAYS

22. Information is presented to the navigator through three senses:

  (a) *Touch*. Only a limited amount of tactile information can be passed. The sense of feel is, however, an important factor in handling a craft.

  (b) *Hearing*. Aural information can only be passed at a slow rate, and the human voice is used for communication within the craft and between the craft and the outside world. Sound is therefore generally reserved for warnings and seldom used for general navigation.

  (c) *Sight*. A great deal of information can be passed extremely quickly by a visual display. The eye absorbs two types of information:

    (i) *Direct vision* from the most sensitive part of the eye, the fovea. No known navigational aid has the discrimination of the human eye.

    (ii) *Parafoveal vision* from the sides of the eye. This is not able to distinguish shapes and sizes readily but is very sensitive to movements. It can therefore be used to provide information to control the movements of the helmsman or pilot.

23. Visual displays are ideal for control since the eye is adept at judging not only distances but also rates. Visual information may be provided by :

(a) Symbolic display.
(b) Pictorial display.

24. *Symbolic Display*. In many instances a symbolic display has to be accepted. For example, time cannot be displayed pictorially. A symbolic display will generally bear no relation to the actual situation but relies on convention. Thus, the clockwise rotation of a pointer is invariably taken to mean an increase in the quantity. A pointer is a good symbolic display because the human being is quick to notice small changes of alignment. The progress of a quantity represented by a pointer can therefore be followed by occasional glances without necessarily reading the dial against which the pointer registers. Nevertheless, symbolic displays are not ideal for control since they involve an element of interpretation.

25. *Pictorial Display*. Pictorial presentation may be one of two types:

(a) *Outside-in or true*. This will show the situation of the craft as it would appear from the world outside. An error to the right is shown as a movement to the right. The human controller finds it natural to try to oppose an unwanted movement. Hence, the outside-in presentation calls for the natural 'oppose to correct' response.

(b) *Inside-out or relative*. This shows the world as it would appear from inside the craft. The world outside moves in the opposite way to the craft so that a movement of the world outside to the right has to be offset by a movement which assists rather than opposes. The inside-out presentation therefore involves an unnatural 'follow to correct' response which makes control harder. Certain inside-out presentations may attempt to project a representation of the world outside on to the wind shield in order that the human controller can marry the display with reality. This is known as a contact analogue.

26. The human eye receives inside-out information but the brain instinctively corrects the impression that the outside world is moving. However, the craft tends to become the individual's 'world' and the world outside appears as a detached impression moving the wrong way. Hence the helmsman on the bridge of a ship and the pilot of an aircraft has to learn to control his craft by 'follow to correct' movements when looking out. In order to avoid reversing control, control instruments likewise use inside-out presentations. Fig. 64 shows a typical example used by a helmsman to steer a ship. Turning to the left causes the compass scale and the objects on the horizon to seem to move to the right.

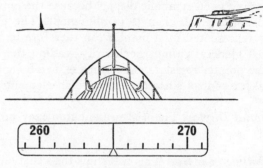

FIG. 64   Inside-out presentation

LIGHTING

27. If an instrument has only to be read under full lighting conditions, it can be painted white with the figures printed in black. However, navigation instruments often have to be read at night under conditions when the eye also needs to look outside the craft. To reduce the effect on the fovea to a minimum, the instrument is generally painted black and only the figures and pointers are picked out in white.

28. For night work, the dials and switches should be lighted internally so that the minimum amount of light is emitted where it is not wanted. This is generally known as integral lighting.

In certain instances, red lighting is used in order that the vision of the eye be affected as little as possible. In other equipments, the paint is made fluorescent. Fluorescent markings can be arranged to depend on ultra-violet lighting. The latter is invisible but the strength can be adjusted so that the luminescence may be as required by the user.

3. SENSORS

1. The human helmsman is adept at introducing the necessary terms to achieve dead-beat control of his craft. Provided that the visibility is sufficiently good, information can generally be obtained from the eyes. A headland jutting out into the sea can be aligned with a part of the craft so that control in yaw can be obtained; the line of the horizon can provide pitch and roll information.

2. In the absence of good visibility, the helmsman may be unable to rely on his semilunar canals since the accelerations of his craft will introduce misleading sensations. Nor is it possible to use positional aids for handling, for reasons already mentioned on page 4, para 10. Therefore, a self-contained system will be necessary for all weather operations. Such a system commonly includes a gyroscope.

GYRO WHEEL THEORY

3. A rotating wheel tends to maintain alignment by virtue of its angular momentum. Angular momentum depends on the mass of the wheel, on the radius of gyration which is the mean distance that the mass is distributed away from the axis of rotation, and on the rate of rotation. This may be expressed as the product of the angular inertia and the rate of rotation. In order to develop the maximum angular momentum, a gyro wheel is spun at a high rate.

4. *Precession.* Fig. 65 shows a gyro wheel spinning in a direction indicated by a thick arrow. If a force is applied to the wheel to tilt it sideways as shown by the two thin arrows, this force will produce an upwards acceleration on each part of the wheel as it

travels from A to B, a downwards acceleration as each part travels from B through C to D, and an upwards acceleration from D to A. Thus the wheel will tilt towards the alignment shown by the dotted line. This tilt at right angles to the tilting force or torque is known as precession.

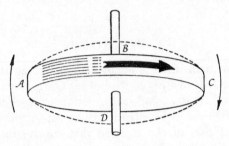

FIG. 65   Gyro precession

5. The faster the wheel is rotating, the greater the angular momentum and the slower the wheel will precess when a given torque is applied. Hence, when a gyroscope is started up, it will precess readily. It is important to note that the *rate* of precession is also according to the torque.

6. *Toppling.* If the precession of the gyro wheel is prevented, a constraining torque will have been applied. This will cause a precession at right angles to the original precession which will be in the same direction as the original torque. Hence, if precession is prevented, the gyro wheel will offer no resistance to a torque. The effect is known as toppling. By holding a gyroscope so that it cannot precess, it can be tilted into any desired alignment.

SIMPLE GYROSCOPE DESIGN

7. Simple aircraft gyro wheels have been spun by air jets. In small field-of-battle missiles with short flight times, the wheels may be blown up to speed by explosive cartridges and allowed to coast for the duration of the flight. However, normally, the wheel of a gyroscope is driven by an electric motor.

8. The wheel is generally supported by ball bearings. Any friction acts around the axis of the gyro wheel and therefore will not cause precession but will develop heat and increase wear.

9. Since the gyroscope can only measure change of alignment by precessing and will topple if this precession is inhibited, the gyro wheel has to be mounted so that it can precess. In a simple gyroscope, the wheel is mounted in gimbals. If mounted in one gimbal as shown in Fig. 66(a), it can precess in only one axis and can

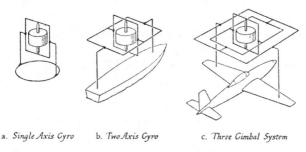

a. *Single Axis Gyro*   b. *Two Axis Gyro*   c. *Three Gimbal System*

FIG. 66   Gimbal systems

measure change of alignment only in the axis at right angles. Such an instrument is known as a single axis gyroscope or a single degree of freedom gyroscope.

10. If the gyro wheel is mounted in two gimbals at right angles, as shown in Fig. 66(b), it can precess in two directions at right angles. It is then known as a two axis or a two degrees of freedom gyroscope. Since precession fore and aft and athwartships means precession in any intermediate direction, a two-axis gyroscope may be known as a free gyroscope.

11. In practice, a third gimbal may be required. In Fig. 66(b), if the nose of the craft were tilted up through a right angle, the inner and the outer gimbals would become aligned. If the nose of the craft were now to move to the left or to the right, the gyro wheel would be violently precessed. This situation is known as gimbal lock. In practice, a tilt of 60° can cause very large precessions. However, the problem can be resolved by providing a third gimbal as shown in Fig. 66(c). This third gimbal may be made to turn so that the two inner gimbals are kept at right angles. Redundant gimbal systems will be required in a craft that has to be fully manœuvrable in all axes.

12. The gimbal bearings need to be as free as possible from friction otherwise the tilting of the craft will set up torques leading

to unwanted precessions. The gyro wheel and gimbals need to
be balanced otherwise the force of gravity or an acceleration of
the craft will set up torques. The wheel has also to be held
securely by the gimbals because, if it shifts, balance will be
upset.

RATE GYROSCOPE

13. The rate gyroscope is a single axis gyro which consists of a
wheel mounted in one gimbal, the rotation of which is constrained by a spring, as shown in Fig. 67. The amount of rotation

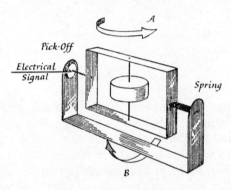

FIG. 67   Rate gyroscope

of the gimbal is measured by a pick-off. If the rate gyroscope is
rotated about the axis of the gyro wheel, as indicated by the
arrow marked A in Fig. 67, there will be no precession. If the
gyroscope is rotated about the axis shown by the arrow marked B,
the wheel will be tilted by the spring and will start to precess at
right angles. This precession is inhibited because there is only
one gimbal and therefore the wheel will topple and will offer no
resistance. However, if the gyroscope is tilted about the third
axis, that is about its length, the wheel will precess at right angles
against the constraining spring and the amount of precession will
be registered on the pick-off. Thus the faster the rate of lengthwise rotation, the greater the movement against the resistance of
the spring and the greater the rate of turning registered by the
pick-off.

14. The rate gyroscope is a simple instrument and, having only one gimbal, can be made robust and is easily balanced. However, when measuring change of alignment, the wheel will tilt and will become affected by rotations shown by the arrow A in Fig. 67. This disadvantage is known as cross-coupling, cross-talk or cross-feed. It can be reduced by increasing the strength of the spring and the sensitivity of the pick-off to lessen the amount of rotation of the gimbal.

POSITION GYROSCOPE

15. The position gyroscope is a two-axis or free gyroscope as illustrated in Fig. 68. The gyro wheel is not intended to precess.

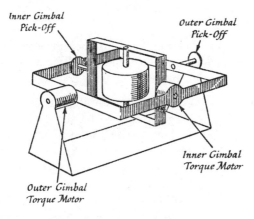

FIG. 68   Position gyroscope

The misalignment of the inner wheel with the outer case is measured by the angle that the outer gimbal makes with the outer case and the angle that the inner gimbal makes with the outer gimbal. Generally, pick-offs are mounted on the inner and outer gimbals so that the position of the gyro wheel within the outer case may be recorded electrically.

16. To align the position gyroscope in the correct direction, torque motors which exert a rotational force are mounted on the gimbal axes. The torque motor on the inner gimbal axis will set up a force tending to precess the wheel in the direction of the

outer gimbal. Hence, the inner gimbal torque motor is used to align the outer gimbal. Similarly the outer gimbal torque motor is used to align the inner gimbal.

17. When the wheel is not spinning, an angular acceleration could cause it to roll wildly within the gimbals. Accordingly, position gyroscopes are fitted with caging mechanisms that grip the inner gimbal and hold the wheel steady when it is not running. The wheel can then be run up and set in the correct direction.

18. It is evident that, compared with a rate gyroscope, the position gyroscope is more complex and, therefore, less robust. However, it measures alignment in two axes. It therefore has to be balanced simultaneously in two axes, a problem which may demand special care in manufacture.

GYRO DRIFT

19. A gyroscope, whether used to measure position or rate, tends to drift from its original alignment. The drift will generally be due to four basic causes:

(a) *Mechanical imperfections*. Gimbal friction can cause precession. Also torques may be set up by the electrical conductors that carry power to the motor of the wheel.

(b) *Unbalance*. If the wheel within its gimbals is not balanced, any acceleration will set up a tilting force. Even a slow craft will be affected by gravity, and this can cause large torques if there is any unbalance. The unbalance can arise if the gimbals are not extremely close fitting. If gimbals are close fitting, gimbal friction errors will arise.

(c) *Dynamic unbalance*. If the gyroscope is subjected to an angular vibration, a very high drift rate can appear temporarily if the vibration happens to be of a certain frequency. The cure will be to balance the wheel and gimbals dynamically.

(d) *Anisoelasticity*. Accelerations can affect the shape of the gyro wheel, its mountings, or its gimbals. The effect is normally small but it depends on the square of the acceleration. It can therefore cause errors in craft that are subjected to high accelerations for long periods, such as guided missiles.

20. The simple gyroscope will generally have a drift rate of tens of degrees per hour. A well-made instrument may have the error reduced until it can be measured in a few degrees per hour. However, the law of diminishing returns tends to make it uneconomic to produce a simple gyroscope that will have a drift rate as low as 1° per hour. For very accurate gyroscopes, special design features have to be included, and these are described on page 186, para 9 and page 227, para 11.

21. Drift rate, particularly in a high quality gyroscope, tends to be constant but to change each time the instrument is switched on like a fault rather than a random error (page 39, para 14). There is therefore no reason to assume that the drift rate of a gyroscope will necessarily tend to average out over a period of time. If a gyroscope has a drift rate of 2° per hour, it may have to be assumed that over 10 hours the error will build up to 20°.

SPECIAL GYROSCOPES

22. A gyroscope means, literally, an instrument that looks at turning. Although the rotating wheel is the most common type, there are others such as:

(a) Dumb-bell gyroscopes which have wheels with the mass concentrated at two opposite points on the circumference. These have not been greatly developed, owing to the complexity of the associated electronics.

(b) Vibrating reeds, known generally as vibros.

23. *Vibros*. In certain flies, vibrating reeds known as halteres are used for control in flight. Such devices operate in a manner analogous to a dumb-bell gyroscope with only one mass, but they operate only in one plane. Unfortunately the single reed sets up vibration. Supporting the mass at each end reduces vibration but the performance tends to change with temperature. The most promising development is the tuning-fork. It is robust, has no sliding parts to cause wear, and responds accurately to continual and considerable rates of rotation. It is vulnerable to minor irregularities in material so that miniaturization may be more difficult than with the rotating wheel. Also, the response is

affected by temperature. Nevertheless, where long life and low power consumption are more important than lightness, the vibro may have particular applications.

MONITORS

24. The drift of a gyroscope can be reduced by a correcting system. For example, the drift of a vertical gyroscope may be corrected by gravity. A correction system of this type is known commonly as a monitor. However, the word 'monitor' implies an equipment that watches and warns. The correcting system may therefore be described as a 'reference' or a 'long-term reference' if the term 'monitor' could cause confusion.

25. In order to correct the alignment of a gyroscope in one axis, a torque has to be applied to the other axis to cause precession. The greater the misalignment, the greater the torque that will have to be applied and, as the gyroscope returns to the correct alignment, so the torque will decrease. Hence the gyroscope will be corrected in an exponential pattern. If half the misalignment is removed each minute, the time constant of the reference system can be said to be $1\frac{1}{2}$ minutes (page 18, para 10).

26. The use of a gyroscope implies that the long-term reference system is noisy. For example, a pendulum that measures the direction of gravity will be disturbed by sideways accelerations. Since the rate of precession will be according to the torque and the torque according to the disagreement with the reference, the final gyroscope alignment will be the integral of the long-term reference indications. The longer the time constant, the longer the period of time over which the indications of the reference will be integrated.

27. It is evident that the time constant of the reference must be a matter of compromise. If it is short, the gyro will react to the irregularities. If it is long, the reference system may be insufficiently powerful to offset the effect of gyro drift. If the gyro drift were $\frac{1}{2}°$ per minute and the time constant of the reference were 2 minutes, simple multiplication shows that the gyroscope would settle at a constant hang-off error of $1°$. Hence the time constant can only be as long as the gyro drift will allow.

28. *Apparent Drift*. A system that uses a long-term reference to control a gyro is known as a slave system. It is possible to reduce

gyro drift by using a better gyroscope, but apparent drift will often arise. Typical causes of apparent drift are:

(a) *Rotation of Earth.* This will rotate the gyro in azimuth at the rate of 15° cos (lat.) per hour and tilt it eastwards in the vertical plane at the rate of 15° sin (lat.) per hour. These drifts can be as much as $\frac{1}{4}$° per minute.

(b) *Transport error.* As the craft moves over the surface of the Earth the direction of the vertical changes by about 1' of arc for each nautical mile.

Sophisticated systems correct for apparent drift so that the long-term reference only has to offset the random gyro drift.

29. *Variable Time Constant.* It may be useful to be able to vary the time constant of a reference. For example, when starting up, it may be necessary to align the gyro quickly by using a short time constant. Alternatively, if the reference is known to give a false signal under certain conditions, it may be better to disconnect the reference temporarily.

30. It will probably be difficult to change the time constant of a reference by direct means. However, if the reference be mounted remotely and signals from it used to correct the gyroscope, these signals may be strengthened to produce a short time constant for starting up, and disconnected in special circumstances, such as violent manœuvres. In high-speed craft, remote references and special switching arrangements to alter the time constant are invariably fitted.

ACCELEROMETER

31. An accelerometer consists of a mass mounted on a spring so that it can move along one direction as suggested in Fig. 69. The amount of displacement of the mass against the spring will be proportional to the force exerted by the mass (Hooke's law). This force is proportional to the acceleration. Hence a linear pick-off of the type shown in Fig. 69, which produces a signal proportional to the displacement of the mass, will produce a signal proportional to the acceleration.

32. A change of alignment of a craft will cause it to accelerate in a direction at right angles to the original direction. The amount of acceleration will depend on a number of factors that may include

engine thrust, forward speed, shape of body of craft and nature of medium through which the craft is travelling. Accelerometers may therefore be fitted to missiles in which the sideways acceleration has to be controlled.

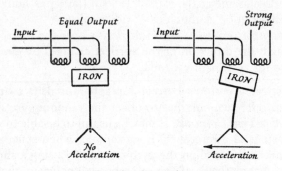

FIG. 69   Simple accelerometer

33. An accelerometer will react to the acceleration of gravity as well as to the acceleration of the craft. If gravity should pull the mass to one side, it will appear that the craft is accelerating in the opposite direction and causing the mass to lag behind. Thus, if the accelerometer is measuring fore and aft or athwartships accelerations, a tilt will cause a false acceleration to appear in the opposite direction, the amount of the acceleration being:

g.sin (tilt) which for small angles is nearly
$\frac{1}{2}$ (tilt °) feet per second.

If the accelerometer is measuring vertical accelerations, the effect will only be:

g.cos (tilt) which for small angles is nearly 0 feet per second.

34. An accelerometer of the simple type already described has another disadvantage. In the left-hand illustration of Fig. 69, gravity will not affect the mass mounted on an upright spring. However, when the mass moves, gravity will start to affect it, and this is suggested by the right-hand illustration of Fig. 69. The effect is another example of cross-talk already mentioned on page 157, para 14.

35. *Differential Accelerometers.* If one accelerometer is sited in the nose of the craft and a second accelerometer in the stern, each measuring accelerations at right angles to the line of the craft, the difference between the signals from the two pick-offs will be a measure of the angular acceleration of the craft. This signal will therefore have phase advance compared to the rate gyroscope. Unfortunately, between the nose and the stern of a craft there will inevitably be a good deal of flexion and vibration. It is therefore necessary to bring the accelerometers close together and they will then be less sensitive to angular acceleration. For this reason, differential or angular accelerometers are not commonly used.

AERODYNAMIC SENSORS

36. *Burgee.* In a craft at sea, a small flag or burgee or even a piece of cloth can be streamed to show the direction of the wind. Indeed, wind is the prime control sensor of the sailing boat supported by the long-term reference afforded by a magnetic compass.

37. *Pressure detector.* In light aircraft, the flow of air has been detected by pressure-difference measurements and used for control of the craft. Very sensitive height-measuring capsules have also been fitted in the wings of gliders. An upward air current due to a thermal through which only one wing of a glider passes will tend to bank the glider away from the thermal. If detected barometrically, it may be made to turn the glider into the upward-moving current of air.

4. CONTROL EQUIPMENT

RATE OF TURN INDICATOR

1. The rate of turn indicator is a typical control instrument used for control in turns. It consists of a rate gyroscope, the inner gimbal being constrained by a spring but linked to a pointer which works across a dial as shown in Fig. 70. The greater the rate of yawing or turning the greater the movement of the pointer from the central position. In an aircraft, the rate of turn indicator is often combined with a ball-bank indicator (page 120, para 13). The combined instrument is known as a turn and slip indicator.

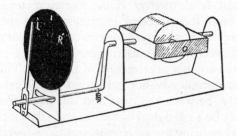

FIG. 70   Rate of turn indicator

VERTICAL REFERENCE

2. In a craft that travels on or above the Earth, stabilization generally means keeping upright. This may be arranged by gyroscopes monitored by gravity. Such an equipment is known as a vertical reference.

3. The simplest system will be a mass at the lower end of the axis of a gyro wheel. If the wheel drifts out of the vertical, the mass will tend to pull it upright and the wheel will respond by precessing at right angles. This precession will itself be opposed by the righting effect of the mass so that the gyro wheel will partly precess and partly topple back towards the vertical. It will thus return to the upright in a decreasing exponential spiral.

4. *Artificial Horizon.* A simple vertical reference may be used in an artificial horizon as shown in Fig. 71. This instrument helps a pilot to keep his aircraft level when the real horizon is not

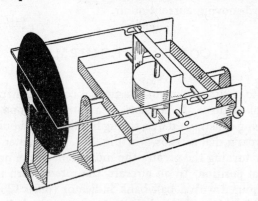

FIG. 71   Artificial horizon

visible. It has an 'inside-out' or relative presentation, which consists of a model of an aircraft fixed behind a bar which is maintained parallel to the real horizon. The bar also moves up and down with the real horizon when the aircraft is pitched down or up. The bar is shown controlled through links by a vertical gyroscope, and a simple mass is fitted below the gyro wheel axle to give erection.

5. An example of an aircraft with 25° bank turning through 180° in 2 minutes has already been quoted (page 120, para 14). With a 1-minute time constant, the error at the end of a turn through 60° would be $12\frac{1}{2}°$, and this would take over 2 minutes to be restored to around 1°. Hence, in a high-speed craft, a variable time constant is necessary, and this can only be achieved by mounting the mass remotely.

6. *Pendulum.* A pendulum may be used to monitor a vertical gyroscope. The bob may be immersed in oil to prevent it swinging about wildly. Any deviation of the bob from its central position can be measured by a pick-off similar to that shown on page 162, Fig. 69, and the signal passed to the appropriate torque motor on the vertical gyro gimbals. Two pendulums at right angles will maintain the vertical.

7. *Disconnect Switch.* The pendulum that records the athwartships acceleration can be disconnected during a turn by means of a disconnect switch. This can take the form of a mercury level mounted on the inner gimbal of the vertical gyroscope, which will tend to unbalance the gimbal as it operates. It may be better to use a turn discriminant in the form of a switch operated by the rate of turn indicator or by a separate rate gyro. Alternatively, a rate pick-off may be fitted to the heading reference of the craft.

STABILIZATION

8. To make the artificial horizon easier to see out of the corner of the eye, the bar may be replaced by a plate or roller blind with a light coloured 'sky' and a dark 'ground'. Such a display generally has to be driven by power synchros, and these are linked to synchros on the gimbals of a vertical reference gyro.

9. A vertical reference may similarly be used to stabilize any instrument. If the instrument is very light, for example, a prism or a mirror, it may be mounted directly on the inner gimbal of the

vertical gyroscope. However, if the instrument is heavy, it may be mounted on separate gimbals driven by power synchros so as to maintain exact alignment with the gimbals of the vertical reference unit. For precision, it is essential that there be a rigid mechanical connection between the mounting of the vertical gyroscope gimbals and the mounting of the stabilized instrument gimbals.

10. *Stable Platform.* The performance of a vertical gyroscope may be improved if it can be given a steady ride. This maintains the gimbals in their normal alignment so that there is less likelihood of unbalance. The gyroscope can be fitted to a platform mounted on gimbals driven by power servos from pick-offs on the gyro gimbals. Such a device is known as a stable platform, and is illustrated in Fig. 72. A platform may alternatively be stabilized

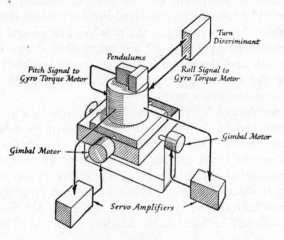

FIG. 72   Stable platform

by two rate gyroscopes. Signals necessary to stabilize instruments can be taken from pick-offs mounted on the power-driven gimbals of the platform.

11. *Apparent Drift.* The accuracy of a simple platform depends on gyro drift. The lower the drift, the slower the time constant of the gravity monitor and the steadier the platform. A stable platform will be affected by apparent drift due to the Earth's rotation and, in high-speed craft, to transport error (see page 160,

para 28). If corrections for apparent gyro drifts are provided, the accuracy of the vertical will be improved.

12. *Coriolis.* The accuracy of the indications from gravity will be affected by coriolis which may tilt the vertical by more than $\frac{1}{4}°$ at speeds approaching the speed of sound. For a high-performance platform in a high-speed craft, it may be worth while to feed in this additional correction.

MARINE AUTOSTABILIZERS

13. A reduction in the rolling of a ship will add to the comfort of passengers, reduce damage to cargo and strain on the ship and make steering easier, particularly in a following sea. Small bilge keels may only reduce roll by a small proportion and large bilge keels greatly increase the resistance to forward movement. However, relatively small moving fins with an area in square feet roughly 1 per cent of the tonnage of a ship can, if driven to the correct angles, reduce roll by a factor of about five.

14. The metacentric height will exert the necessary long-term leverage to correct a roll and therefore the fins have to act mainly as rate dampers and, in early equipments, were controlled by rate gyroscopes alone. In modern marine autostabilizers, the rate of roll may be supported by a roll acceleration 'term'. However, in a following sea, when the surface of the water may be at an angle for a longer period, the ship will tend to remain heeled unless a position 'term' is fed in to offset the metacentric heeling. Hence the two types of control 'law':

(a) *Following sea.* Roll rate and heel.
(b) *Head or beam sea.* Roll rate and roll acceleration.

15. For the following sea, roll rate and heel can be fed in by a rate gyro and a position gyro working together. However, for a head or beam sea, the requirement is to replace heel by a roll acceleration term. Since a roll generally follows a sinusoidal pattern, it is evident from page 21, para 16, that roll acceleration will be 180° out of phase with 'roll position' and can be provided by reversing the input from the position gyroscope. Hence the simple marine stabilizer will be fitted with a 'sea switch' to reverse

the position gyro signal and may follow the pattern shown in Fig. 73.

16. In practice, the roll of a ship will not follow an exactly sinusoidal pattern and therefore roll acceleration may have to be derived independently from attitude either by differential accelerometers or by differentiating the rate input, and the ship may then be controlled by all three terms. The control may also need to be modified according to the speed at which the ship is moving.

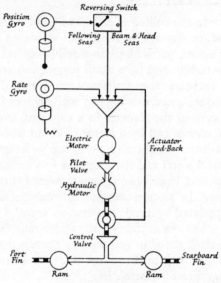

FIG. 73   Marine stabilizer

17. The effect of a fin increases up to a certain angle of attack and then dies away very quickly although the drag greatly increases. Therefore the fins must not turn by more than a certain amount. Unfortunately, the water may flow past each fin at a different angle due to the conditions of the sea. Each fin may need to have its own actuator which can take account of the flow of water on that side of the hull.

18. The flow of water could in theory be measured by a simple vane. Such devices are easily damaged and can readily become fouled. The angle of flow can, however, be measured by the force

exerted on the fin by the water. This force can be signalled by a strain gauge which is basically a length of wire doubled to and fro which becomes stretched under strain, the stretching altering the electrical resistance. A diaphragm in the surface of the fin with a strain gauge attached can measure force and this signal, when modified by the speed of the ship, will give the fin angle. This fin angle compared with the actual angle of the fin will give the flow of water compared to the horizontal which can be fed into the main actuator amplifier. A sketch of such a system is given in Fig. 74.

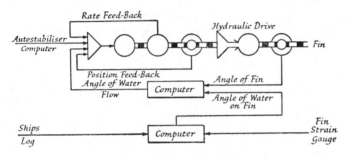

FIG. 74   Marine stabilizer actuator

19. *Safety Devices.* In the event of a break down, it is important that the fins should level themselves, in other words that the actuator should be self-centring. In addition, safety devices in the form of slipping clutches may have to be fitted to ensure that damage is not caused to the fins themselves as a result of sudden strains.

AIRCRAFT AUTOSTABILIZERS

20. The instability of a VTOL aircraft while hovering has already been mentioned. Other types of aircraft become unstable at high speed, particularly in pitch. Many develop rhythmic motions as they fly. A tendency to oscillate in pitch is known as a phugoid oscillation. A combined yaw and roll is known as a Dutch roll.

21. An autostabilizer is only intended to help the pilot to fly the aircraft and not to fly it for him. It will therefore be connected in

parallel with the pilot's flying controls as shown in Fig. 75. It will be connected irreversibly, for example through a screw-jack; otherwise, if the servo drive should break down, the pilot's stick might have nothing to push against. It may be controlled, like a marine stabilizer, by a rate gyroscope with a position term or by differentiating the position term. The position term will be according to the channel:

(a) *Roll channel.* Long-term control of ailerons by a vertical reference.

(b) *Pitch channel.* Long-term control of elevators by a vertical reference.

(c) *Yaw channel.* In winged aircraft, the rudder has the function of eliminating sideslip (see page 120, para 13) and therefore a simple pendulum can give long-term control.

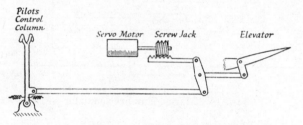

FIG. 75   Aircraft autostabilizer channel (pitch)

SAFETY DEVICES

22. Although a marine stabilizer is a great convenience, it may not cause danger if it should go wrong. On the other hand, if an aircraft autostabilizer should go wild or run away, not only can it damage the aircraft but also the pilot might not have sufficient time to disengage it and take correcting action. It may be possible to reduce the severity of a runaway by reducing the power of the servo drives or by fitting some form of mechanical fuse, known generally as a limiter, so that the power exerted by the servo will be limited. In either event, the limitation of power or 'authority' of the autostabilizer will decrease the ability to maintain the aircraft level in turbulence. Systems with limited authority may be known as 'fail soft' systems because they cannot run away violently.

23. *Redundancy.* When close to the ground, the authority of an aircraft system must be adequate and yet any runaway may be disastrous. Monitors can be developed that disconnect the system in the event of a serious malfunction. In the limit, such a monitor may take the form of a second system working in parallel and known as a duplex system. Very close to the ground, it may be impossible for the pilot to take over, and therefore a complete second system with its own monitors may have to be provided and the combination will form a duplicated system. Alternatively, a third autostabilizer working in parallel may be added to a duplex system to form a triplex system.

SPACE CRAFT STABILIZATION

24. A space craft or a controlled satellite may need to be stabilized, and so also may an uncontrolled satellite used, for example, for photographing the ground below. Stabilization is effected on a short-term basis by motors that drive wheels so that the space craft rotates in the opposite direction (page 123, para 26). The motors may be operated by signals from gyroscopes, which are first passed through electronic filters. If the signals are above a certain level, so that the wheels cannot provide enough angular momentum, the filters will pass signals to auxiliary jets set at angles so as to rotate the space craft. The system has to be simple to ensure reliability and bang-bang servos may be used. In certain circumstances it may be adequate to stabilize in two axes only and allow the craft to spin in the third axis.

5. SUMMARY

ELEMENTS

The elements of a control system are shown in Fig. 76. The controller, whether human or automatic, operates an actuator that moves the steering mechanism, and the resulting position is signalled to the controller by negative feed-back. The consequent alteration in the alignment of the craft is detected by sensors and also fed back to the controller. The alteration in the alignment of the craft may be hindered by its natural stability.

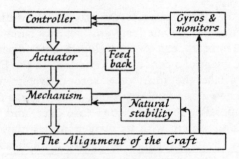

FIG. 76   Basic control loops

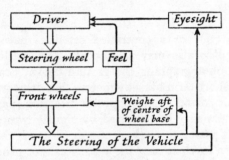

FIG. 77   Road vehicle control loops

These elements appear in all craft. In Fig. 77 their appearance in a motor vehicle is shown.

GENERAL PRINCIPLES

For dead-beat control, rate damping is needed in addition to positional information and, if there is hang-off, an integration term may have to be included. Frictional damping can lead to instability.

Natural frequency and damping are generally the two most important measures of the performance of a servo system.

If the gain of a servo system is increased past a certain limit, the system will become unstable.

SENSORS

The basic control sensors are listed in Table VI.

TABLE VI. BASIC CONTROL SENSORS

SENSOR	MEASUREMENT	ALTERNATIVE
Postion (free) gyro	Angle or alignment in two axes	Two rate gyro signals integrated
Rate gyro (or vibro)	Change of angle or change of alignment in one axis	Position gyro signal differentiated
Differential accelerometers	Rate of change of alignment or angular acceleration. Two accelerometers for one axis	Rate gyro signal differentiated
Accelerometer or pendulum	Linear acceleration, direction of gravity or sideslip	

When a force is applied to change the alignment of a gyro wheel, the wheel precesses at right angles or, if constrained, topples. For full manœuvrability, three gimbals are needed in a free gyroscope.

LONG-TERM REFERENCES

(a) Short time constant offsets apparent and real drift.
(b) Long time constant integrates reference signals.
(c) Very short time constant needed for quick starting up.
(d) Reference may need to be disconnected during manœuvres.

ACTUATORS

Three types of drive are used:

(a) *Hydraulic.* Simple, reliable and irreversible. Hydraulic accumulators can store considerable power for short periods.
(b) *Electric.* Introduce inertia and generally need gearing and rate feed-back. Are easily fitted into craft owing to the absence of piping. Electric accumulators cannot deliver a great deal of power quickly.
(c) *Pneumatic.* Used only in small missiles.

A rate-rate system will connect smoothly to the craft but used alone will not ensure that the position of the steering mechanism agrees with the position of the steering wheel or control column.

STABILIZATION

A system using a vertical gyroscope slaved by gravity has a limit of accuracy of about $\frac{1}{4}°$ in a slow craft. In a high-speed craft the errors will be much greater, particularly after turns or other manœuvres.

Performance is improved by the use of remotely mounted long-term references so that the time constant can be varied. By mounting the gyroscope on a platform which it stabilizes, performance is further improved. In a high-speed craft, a correction for coriolis will be needed.

INSTRUMENTATION

Displays. Symbolic presentation may be insufficiently instinctive for control of craft. Inside-out presentations demand a 'follow to correct' action, but there is no reversal of control when attention is transferred from the instruments to the real world.

The turn and bank indicator and the artificial horizon are used to control an aircraft. A rate of turn indicator is used in marine craft.

Instruments, particularly the altimeter, may be driven remotely from sensors.

AUTOMATIC STABILIZERS

Marine autostabilizers need different 'terms' according to whether the seas are coming from astern or not.

Aircraft autostabilizers operate in parallel with the human pilot. Control may be exercised in three channels, roll, pitch and yaw. If used close to the ground, a runaway must instantly disconnect the autostabilizer. If the pilot cannot take over, redundancy must be provided.

CHAPTER V

Heading

ELEMENTS

1. *Definitions.* The heading of the craft is the alignment of the fore
and aft axis in the plane parallel to the surface of the Earth. This
plane is known as the azimuth plane.

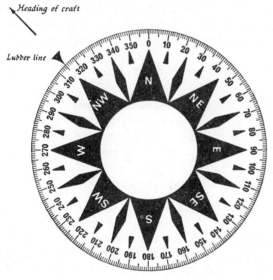

FIG. 78   Compass card

2. *Compass Card.* The alignment of a craft in the azimuth plane is
recorded on a compass card. A compass card of a type that is
sometimes used at sea is shown in Fig. 78. It has a clockwise scale
of degrees and is also divided into thirty-two 'points', each point
being $11\frac{1}{4}°$ from the next. N., E., S. and W. are known as the
cardinal points and NE., SE., SW. and NW. as the intercardinal
or quadrantal points. The heading of the craft is registered

against the card by means of a heading marker, known sometimes as a lubber line. Although points are still referred to at sea, directions are usually stated as a three-figure number with the sign for degrees omitted. Thus north will appear as 000 and east as 090, south as 180 and west as 270. North may also be referred to as 360 when counting past 359.

3. The simplest type of compass consists of a moving magnetized needle mounted above a fixed compass card. This is an outside-in presentation which shows the alignment of the craft as looked at from outside and therefore it may be used by the navigator who is working on a map or chart. The helmsman or pilot, looking out from his craft, will prefer an inside-out or relative presentation, a rotating compass card with a fixed heading marker, as in Fig. 78.

4. Since the helmsman or pilot may have to look ahead, it may be convenient to use a moving compass card in the form of a cylinder as shown in Fig. 79. Ideally, the observer ought to be

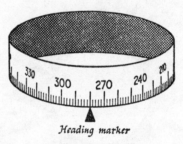

Heading marker

FIG. 79   Cylindrical compass card

inside the cylinder to achieve the real effect of an inside-out presentation. The cylindrical card may therefore be less natural than the normal compass card, though the latter may need to be tilted up by optical means, as suggested in Fig. 64 on page 152, to enable the helmsman to read it looking ahead.

1. THE GYRO COMPASS

TRUE DIRECTIONS

1. The gyro compass measures directions according to the direction of the north geographic pole, known as the true north

pole. A line on the surface of the Earth running towards the true
north pole is known as a meridian because the Sun reaches the
zenith at midday at the same instant all along it. In contradistinction to a line of longitude, which is a reference of position
and has no direction, a meridian is not a reference of position
and is only a reference of direction in the azimuth plane.

2. Directions measured according to the meridian are known as
true directions and are suffixed T. Thus in Fig. 78, if the compass
card were aligned to the meridian, the heading would be 315T.

PRINCIPLES

3. As the Earth rotates, the surface, except at the poles, tilts.
The tilt at any point was shown on page 68, para 16, to be
$15 \times \cos$ (latitude) an hour. If a gyro wheel is mounted so that it
can rotate in azimuth but has its axis kept parallel to the surface
of the Earth, the tilting of the Earth will precess the wheel until
it is at right angles to the direction of tilt. In this alignment, it will
be pointing along the meridian. Any change of alignment will re-
introduce the tilting effect of the Earth's rotation and precess the
wheel until it points along the meridian once more.

4. A moving craft will not keep level, and gravity must be used to
maintain the axis of the gyro wheel parallel to the surface of the
Earth. The wheel will be mounted in gimbals as a free gyroscope
(page 157, para 15) and a mass will be fitted below the wheel to
pull it parallel to the Earth's surface. A simple mass could set up a
continual swinging and, therefore, damping is introduced. The
mass may be a liquid in a tube with a constriction as shown in
Fig. 80(a).

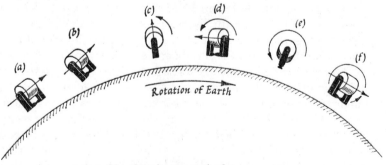

FIG. 80   Gravity control of gyro compass

5. In Fig. 80(b), the tilting effect of the Earth is shown acting on the gyro wheel. The mass will tend to pull the wheel back to the level alignment, causing precession, as shown in Fig. 80(c), but without correcting the tilt. The continuing pull of the mass will cause the wheel to precess past the meridian whereupon the tilting of the Earth will start to correct the tilt of the gyro wheel. As a result, the wheel will finish its swing as shown in Fig. 80(d), pointing to the opposite side of the meridian. The tilting of the Earth will now pull the gyro wheel in the other direction and the precession resulting from the mass will drive the wheel back to the meridian. The far end of the wheel, as shown in Fig. 80(e), will now be tilted downwards and the mass will continue to cause it to precess until it reaches the alignment shown in Fig. 80(f), which is the same as that in which it originally started. The axis of the wheel will have described an ellipse about the meridian.

6. *Schüler Pendulum.* The rate at which the gyro wheel swings from side to side will depend on the righting effect of the mass. In practice the righting effect is adjusted so that the period of swing is 84 minutes. A pendulum with this period is known as a Schüler pendulum. It acts like a pendulum whose length is 3400 n. miles so that, if supported on the surface of the Earth, the bob would be at the centre of the Earth. With a bob at the centre of the Earth, acceleration over the surface would not disturb it. Similarly, with a period of 84 minutes, a gyro compass will not be disturbed if the craft is accelerated over the surface of the Earth.

7. *Damping.* The continual rolling of the gyro wheel either side of the meridian is to be expected if there is no rate term in the gravity correction. Rate can be introduced by causing the mass partly to decrease the tilt by arranging that it shall also act to rotate the gyro wheel in azimuth. This torque in azimuth will cause the wheel to precess at right angles so that the tilt is reduced.

8. The mass can be made to exert a force tending to turn the gyro wheel in azimuth in a number of ways. It can be made to act at an angle to the tilt gimbal so that it has an azimuth as well as a tilting effect. It can be made to open or shut orifices so that air pressure or oil pressure is applied to the gyro wheel to exert a force in azimuth. By such devices, the swing can be damped so that, at the end of each 84-minute cycle, the angular displacement will be

only a third of the value at the start of the swing. This rate of correction can be expressed as a time constant of an hour and a half.

GYRO COMPASS ERRORS

9. *Apparent Drift.* Apparent drift due to the rotation of the Earth is known generally as latitude error. It amounts to:

$$15 . \sin \text{ (latitude)}° \text{ an hour (page 68, para 17)}$$

Since the gyro compass follows the meridian with a time constant of about $1\frac{1}{2}$ hours, it is necessary to correct for this rotation to avoid hang-off. This can be arranged by mounting a mass on the gimbal to precess the wheel in azimuth. It may be possible to arrange to adjust this mass according to latitude. If not, a latitude correction table may be used. Alternatively, if torque motors are fitted to the gimbal, the precession may be arranged electrically.

10. *Course and Speed Error.* Page 68, para 18, showed that due to the Earth's rotation the surface moves at a speed of $900 \times \cos$ (latitude) knots in an easterly direction. If the craft is moving either due east or due west, this movement will appear to increase or decrease the speed of the Earth's surface. However, if the craft is moving north or south, it will be as if the speed of the surface had a northerly or southerly component and therefore as if the Earth were rotating in a direction slightly north or south of due east. This will cause the gyro compass to point in a direction either to the west or to the east of true north.

11. From Fig. 81, it can be seen that:

$$\text{error}° = \tan^{-1} \frac{\text{speed (knots)} \times \cos \text{(course)}}{900 \cos \text{(latitude)} + \text{speed (knots)} \times \sin \text{(course)}}$$

If the speed of the craft is low compared to the speed of the surface of the Earth, from the one in sixty rule (page 72, para 19):

$$\text{error}° = \frac{\text{speed (knots)} \times \cos \text{(course)}}{15 \times \cos \text{(latitude)}}$$

It is possible to feed in a mechanical correction for this error from a setting of latitude and speed, the gyro compass providing information as to the course. Alternatively, a correction card may be used or, if there are torque motors on the gimbals of the gyro wheel, the correction may be fed in electrically.

12. *Change of Course and Speed.* From the previous paragraph, if a ship is travelling at 15 knots due north at latitude 60°, the course and speed error will be 2° west. If the ship were to turn due south, the course and speed error would change to 2° east and the gyro wheel would begin by pointing 4° too much to the west. The time constant of about $1\frac{1}{2}$ hours would mean that this error would not be corrected for a matter of hours. Turning introduces accelerations that correct this error to some extent. Nevertheless, a residual ballistic error or deflection, which in this particular instant will be roughly 1°, will appear initially.

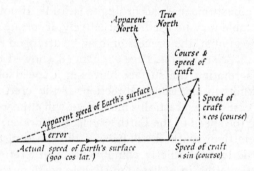

FIG. 81   Course and speed error

13. *Rolling Error.* A ship will have a rolling motion which will act on the unsymmetrical gravity control that damps the swing of the gyro compass and, as a result, an error may arise. If the ship is headed either north, south, east or west, the roll will act either along or directly across the gyro wheel axis and there will be no rolling error. However, if the heading is in an intervening direction, rolling error will appear and, accordingly, is known as quadrantal or intercardinal rolling error. It can generally be reduced to negligible proportions by design.

GYRO COMPASS DESIGN

14. Apparent drift due to latitude together with course and speed error can be corrected mechanically, electrically, or by means of

tables. In Fig. 82, these corrections are shown applied electrically. The gravity monitor of the gyro compass, though mounted on the gimbal of the gyro wheel, is a pendulum with a pick-off feeding to torque motors on the gimbals of the gyroscope. This allows the the use of a start-up switch. Since the normal monitoring time constant is roughly $1\frac{1}{2}$ hours, starting up will take a long time unless some system of rapid alignment is provided.

15. It has already been mentioned that, owing to the long time constant, it is important to reduce the real as well as the apparent drift of the gyro wheel. Since any forces in azimuth acting on the wheel will build up errors that will reach a maximum 21 minutes

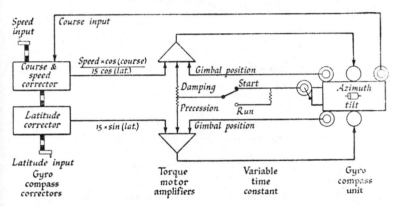

FIG. 82　Electrical gyro compass

later, it will be necessary to reduce these and other parasitic forces by mounting the gyro wheel quite freely. This can be arranged by hanging the wheel within a frame by fine wires, or by supporting it on oil jets, or by mounting it in a can and floating it in a liquid, generally fluorlube. Any misalignment between the gyro wheel and the frame can be detected by pick-offs and signals can be passed to an amplifier so that motors will drive the frame back into alignment with the gyro wheel. Such a frame is known as a follow-up frame.

16. The power-driven follow-up frame of the gyro compass can act as the master unit. The compass card may be linked to it mechanically and the complete frame and gyro can be mounted in gimbals within a pedestal known as a binnacle. The follow-up

frame may also be made to drive a transmission system so that the compass card reading may be repeated in various parts of the craft.

17. *Transmission Systems.* A typical transmission system used for driving repeaters from a gyro compass is shown in Fig. 83. The transmitter is a rotating switch with three pairs of contacts, each pair connected to one of the three coils of the motor in the repeater. With the switch in the position shown, the vertical coil in the repeater motor will be energized and the magnet that drives

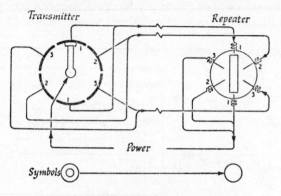

FIG. 83   Step-by-step transmission

the repeater will accordingly be aligned vertically. If the switch were to move 30° clockwise, contacts one and two would be energized in the transmitter and current would flow through coils one and two in the repeater so that the magnet would turn through 30° clockwise. As the transmitter continues to turn, the repeater will follow in 30° steps. Hence the name step-by-step transmission.

18. To make the repeater follow the compass card with sufficient accuracy, it may be geared by sixty to one. It will then operate in half-degree steps instead of 30° steps. However, there is always a chance that the repeater motor may miss a step, jump backwards and be in error by 180° or, taking into account the gearing, by 3°. Hence it is necessary to check or synchronize a step-by-step transmission system at regular intervals, or use a monitoring system involving, for example, a synchro transmission.

19. The power that can be developed by the repeater of a step-by-step transmission is limited only by the power that passes through

the transmitter switch and the ability of the repeater motor to handle this power. Therefore one transmitter may drive a number of repeaters each having to develop a considerable amount of power. In marine systems, it is common for repeaters to be installed in various parts of a vessel. For example, a sight known as a bearing plate may be driven by a repeater so that the direction of an object outside the craft can be measured.

ACCURACY

20. In a ship travelling at only a few tens of knots, a carefully corrected gyro compass can probably maintain alignment with the meridian with a 95 per cent accuracy of about 1° up to 60° latitude. At higher latitudes, the accuracy deteriorates owing to the reduced rate of tilt of the surface of the Earth.

21. Many of the gyro compass errors will be semi-systematic and the accuracy over a journey will tend to improve. If the errors become virtually random over a period of a day or so, the error averaged over 2000 miles, even allowing for some residual systematic error, might be 95 per cent within half a degree on a 20-knot vessel.

22. In a high-speed craft, the errors will be greatly magnified. Accelerations tend to depend on the square of the speed. Even if course and speed errors can be corrected, changes of course and speed will cause large ballistic errors. It will therefore be very difficult to design a gyro compass for an aircraft although a complex system able to discriminate between sideways accelerations and gravity, such as will be described in Part 3 of the next chapter, could be made north-seeking. A system of this type could seek north even if the aircraft were to fly westerly at a speed equal to the speed of the Earth's surface (450 knots at 60° latitude).

2. THE DIRECTIONAL GYROSCOPE

GRID DIRECTIONS

1. Outside the range of latitudes 75° north to 75° south, the gyro compass cannot be used because the tilting of the Earth is insufficient to align the gyro wheel to the meridian. Furthermore, in polar regions, the meridians converge too rapidly to be convenient

as steady references of direction for a moving craft. Accordingly, an arbitrary reference line is chosen and all directions are referred to this line. For convenience, navigators generally draw a series of lines on their charts parallel to the arbitrary reference line. From this practice, the name grid steering has come to be applied to this arbitrary direction reference.

2. In Arctic regions the Greenwich meridian is used, often reversed and taken to run from the North Pole southwards towards Greenwich. Steering by this reference line is known as Greenwich grid steering, and directions are suffixed G to distinguish them from true directions. For a craft on longitude 0°, 000T will be 180G. For a craft on longitude 90 east, 000T will be 090G and for a craft on 90 west, 000T will be 270G. Hence it follows that:

$$\text{Greenwich grid direction} = \text{True direction} + 180 \begin{cases} -\text{long. east} \\ +\text{long. west} \end{cases}$$

3. Grid steering may be used by high-speed craft in normal latitudes. In such instances, the reference line may be the planned path of the craft so that the grid will be marked transversely across the surface of the Earth. Direction may be maintained by a directional gyroscope (DG), a simple gyroscope on which is fixed a compass card. A directional gyroscope may also be used for short-term steering using any type of reference.

DIRECTIONAL GYRO ERRORS

4. *Earth's Rotation.* An apparent drift due to the rotation of the Earth will be corrected either by fitting a weight to unbalance the inner gimbal or by applying a precession electrically. The former system is only used in simple gyroscopes which will not suffer large accelerations and in craft that operate at a reasonably constant latitude. Electrical correction, which can be varied according to sin (latitude) is used in long-range craft.

5. *Convergency.* Drift will also arise if the craft is moving east or west over the surface of the Earth in high latitudes and it is necessary to keep the directional gyroscope aligned with true north rather than with a grid reference line. The meridians run together towards the pole and, as the pole is approached, the

rate at which they converge increases. The extent of this meridian convergency is given by:

Convergency°/hour = 0·013 × speed (knots) × tan (latitude) × sin (track)

6. Near the pole, convergency is such that a directional gyroscope can no longer be used pointing along the meridians. Hence grid directions become essential. The effect is found in the gyro compass used in relatively slow craft at latitudes less than 70°. However, the drift will not be more than 0°2 an hour, assuming a 20-knot ship, and may therefore be ignored.

7. *Tilting Errors.* A directional gyroscope can suffer from tilting errors. The tilting errors can be caused by gyro drift or, unless the axle of the wheel happens to be aligned north and south, may result from the rotation of the Earth tilting the wheel axis. From page 41, para 19, this tilting error will be in degrees:

$$-(\text{tilt}°)^2 \times \sin (2 \times \text{direction of tilt compared to gyro axis})/230$$

8. An error will also arise if the craft is tilted. Fig. 84(a) to (d)

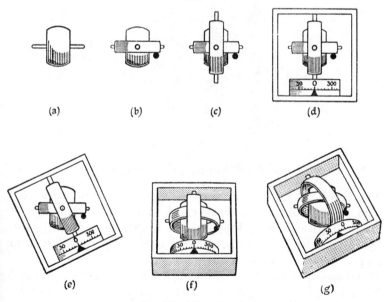

FIG. 84   The directional gyro

shows the build up of elements of a simple directional gyroscope. Fig. 84(e) and (f) shows the effects of sideways and of fore and aft tilts of the craft which will be fixed to the outer case of the gyroscope. Although there is no error if the tilt is in these directions, Fig. 84(g) shows the error that results when the tilt is in an intermediate direction. The misalignment is known as gimballing error and, as might be expected, is another manifestation of the tilting error mentioned in the previous paragraph.

Example. A directional gyroscope is aligned due north. The craft is tilted 30° in a north-easterly direction.

Gimballing error $= -30^2 \times \sin (45 \cdot 2/230 = -4°$ approximately

GYRO HEADING REFERENCE

9. To reduce gyro drift and to eliminate gimballing errors, the gyroscope may be stabilized on a platform as shown in Fig. 85.

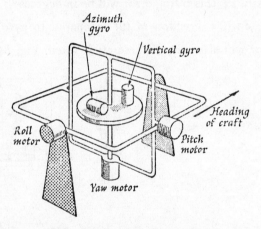

FIG. 85   Stabilized heading reference

The stable platform has already been described (page 166, para 10), and also the use of a third gimbal in a gyroscope to avoid gimbal lock (page 155, para 11). For the same reason, if full manœuvrability is a requirement, the stable platform will have to be provided with a fourth gimbal.

10. Gyroscopes for accurate heading references may be calibrated for drift before the journey starts and temperature may be controlled accurately thereafter. An alternative system using two

gyros has been tried, control being switched from one to the other, the gyro not being used for control having the wheel rotation reversed during the interval. Unfortunately, the greatest changes in gyro drift occur during run-up. The method of rotating the case of the gyroscope at a few revolutions per minute does, however, improve performance by reducing unbalance in one axis.

11. The gyroscope will be affected by sideways accelerations that will displace the wheel. For high performance, the wheel should be mounted so that it cannot shift. If gimbals are used to support the wheel, friction may be reduced by dithering the bearings or rotating them to and fro. Gyroscopes with this feature may maintain alignment to within the order of a degree per hour. If lower drift rates are needed, special devices may be used to support the wheel (see page 228, para 11).

12. In place of the vertical gyroscope and the azimuth gyroscope, it is possible to use two free gyroscopes each measuring azimuth but arranged at right angles so that one gyroscope is also stabilizing the platform in one plane and the other gyroscope is also stabilizing the platform in the other plane. Such a system improves the accuracy of the heading reference, which will be the average of the two gyroscopes. It is generally known as a twin-gyro platform.

ALIGNMENT

13. Unlike the gyro compass, which uses the tilting of the Earth to monitor alignment, the directional gyroscope is unmonitored. It is therefore an open-loop equipment and the accuracy must depend on the accuracy with which the gyro heading reference is aligned initially. Initial alignment can be achieved by lining up the gyro with some other heading reference in the craft or by aligning the gyro with some object outside the craft, generally using optical equipment.

14. The gyro may be aligned either with the Sun or a star or with a distant object on the surface of the Earth. Alternatively, two objects in line with each other may be used. If such means are not available, it may be practicable:

(a) To use the heading reference when stationary to find its own heading by gyro compassing. This may take a considerable fraction of an hour and can only be used at latitudes of less than 75°.

(b) To carry the heading to the craft from a reference on the ground by means of a transfer gyroscope. The transfer gyroscope may be aligned against a fixed marker, carried to the craft, and aligned with the gyro heading reference in the craft. The gyro heading reference may then be precessed until the reading agrees with that of the transfer gyroscope.

ACCURACY

15. The accuracy of a gyro heading reference may be summarized as follows:

(a) Unstabilized gyroscope: 95 per cent error of less than 10° per hour may be achieved.

(b) Stabilized gyroscope: with simple stabilization, a 95 per cent error of the order of 1° per hour may be achieved but not in high-speed craft.

16. The errors caused by initial alignment of the directional gyroscope may be small. However, the drift of a simple gyroscope will be as likely to accumulate as to average out with time since the error tends to have the characteristics of a fault. The mean value in degrees over a period may therefore be:

$$\tfrac{1}{2} \, (\text{drift rate } (°/\text{hour})) \times (\text{hours of period})$$

Example. 20-knot ship on 2000 n. mile voyage. Directional gyroscope with 1°/hour drift.

$$\text{Mean error} = \tfrac{1}{2} \times 1 \times 100 = 50°$$

(This example suggests why directional gyroscopes are not used on ships.)

Example. 200-knot aircraft on 2000 n. mile flight. DG 1°/hour drift.

$$\text{Mean error} = \tfrac{1}{2} \times 1° \times 10 = 5°$$

Example. 1000-knot aircraft on 2000 n. mile flight. DG 1°/hour drift.

$$\text{Means error} = \tfrac{1}{2} \times 1° \times 2 = 1°$$

3. MAGNETIC COMPASS

EARTH'S MAGNETISM

1. The Earth acts as a magnet, the lines of force following a pattern shown in cross-section in the sketch, Fig. 86. At a magnetic pole, the Earth's field dips vertically downwards. At the magnetic equator, the Earth's field is parallel to the surface and the dip or inclination is zero. To north or south of the magnetic equator, the dip gradually increases.

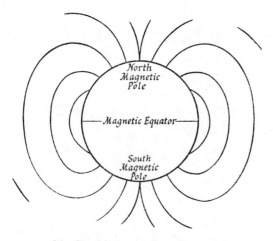

FIG. 86   Earth's magnetism, lines of force

2. If the Earth were completely symmetrical, the north and south magnetic poles might coincide with the axis of the Earth. In fact the magnetic poles are separated from the true poles by about 1000 miles, the north magnetic pole being in the area 70–75°N. and roughly 95° W., and the south magnetic pole being in the area 70–75° S. and about 155° E. If isoclinals, lines of equal dip, are plotted over the surface of the Earth, they will form an irregular pattern as shown in Fig. 87.

3. The greater the dip, the less the horizontal component of the Earth's magnetic field. The connection is not simple. Fig. 88 indicates the strength of the Earth's horizontal magnetic field in gauss units. The gauss unit represents the magnetic flux density whereas the strength of the magnetic field depends on the material

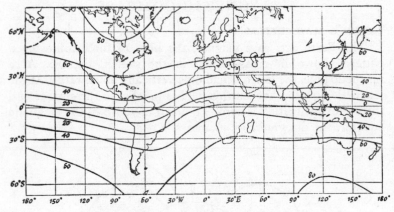

FIG. 87   World isoclinals (lines of equal dip)

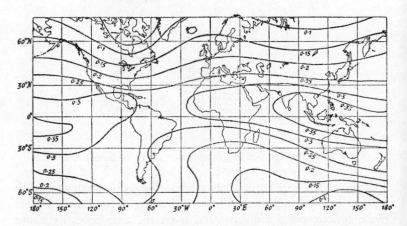

FIG. 88   Strength of horizontal magnetism (in gauss units)

through which the magnetic flux is passing. However, in the atmosphere, the gauss unit is also a measure of field strength. The field strength decreases with height initially at about 1 per cent per 50,000 feet.

4. The magnetic meridian at any point on the Earth is the direction of the horizontal component of the Earth's magnetic field running towards the north magnetic pole. The displacement of the magnetic poles and variations in the structure of the

Earth will cause the magnetic meridian to differ from the true meridian. The difference of angle is known as the variation and is named east or west according to whether the magnetic meridian points to the east or to the west of the true meridian. Fig. 89

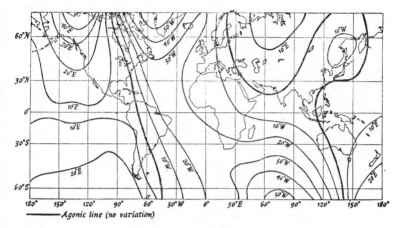

FIG. 89　World isogonals (lines of equal variation)

shows the variation plotted on a world map by means of isogonals, which are lines along which the variation is constant. Along one isogonal, known as the agonic line, the variation will be 0 and the magnetic and true meridians will coincide. Variation may be known as magnetic 'declination', but unfortunately the term declination also has another meaning (page 435, para 19(a)).

MAGNETIC DIRECTIONS

5. Directions measured according to a magnetic meridian are known as magnetic directions and are written in three figures with the suffix M. To convert magnetic directions into true directions, it is necessary to add clockwise or easterly variation or to subtract anticlockwise or westerly variation. The navigator uses a jingle to remind him whether true or magnetic ought to be the greater:

Variation east, magnetic least.
Variation west, magnetic best.

Example. Heading is 030M and variation is 10° east.

$$030M + 10 E. = 040T \quad \text{(check: magnetic least)}$$

6. On page 183, para 1, grid direction was described. In polar regions, the true meridians converge rapidly and so also do the isogonals as shown on the left-hand side of Fig. 90. However, if

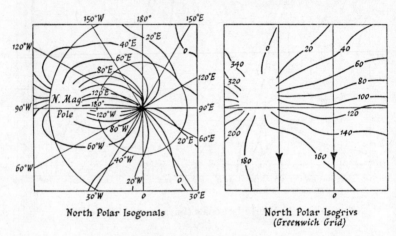

North Polar Isogonals

North Polar Isogrivs
(*Greenwich Grid*)

FIG. 90   Polar variation

grid navigation is being used, the isogrivs, that isogonals converted into grid directions, are relatively simple, as can be seen from the right-hand side of Fig. 90. As neither east nor west exists in grid directions, the grid variations, known as grivations, are counted from 000 clockwise to 360 and always subtracted from the magnetic direction in order to give grid direction. Hence:

No east, no west, magnetic best.

Example. Heading is 070M and grivation is 100.

$$070M - 100 \text{ grivation} = -030G \quad \text{(check: magnetic best)}$$
$$= 330G$$

VARIATION ERRORS
7. Variation has been recorded only at certain points on the surface of the Earth and isogonals drawn by interpolation. The accuracy of charted variation is therefore not high. In addition,

anomalies may occur owing to minerals in the Earth's crust. These anomalies extend only a short distance upwards so that they are not noticeable in ships in deep water, but can cause errors in charted variation overland or in shallow water. Variation also changes slightly with height, tending generally to reduce as the distance from the Earth increases.

8. The magnetic poles travel round the geographic poles in a westerly direction about once in 500 years. As a result, isogonals on a map or chart will only refer to a certain year and, for other years, a date correction will have to be applied. This correction is printed on the chart together with the year for which the isogonals were drawn.

9. In addition, there are changes in magnetic variation brought about mainly by the Sun and the Moon:

(a) *Diurnal changes.* Variation changes twice daily due to lunar and solar tides in the Earth's atmosphere.

(b) *Magnetic storms.* These appear generally in 27-day periods, the period of rotation of the Sun, and have an 11-year cycle, the cycle of increased sunspot activity. These magnetic storms generally produce magnetic fields that are horizontal around the poles and vertical around the equator. Hence they cause very large changes of variation in polar regions, where the Earth's horizontal magnetism is also weak, but have very little effect in the tropics.

THE SIMPLE MAGNETIC COMPASS

10. The simple magnetic compass consists of a card supported by a jewelled cone on a hardened steel point. To the card a number of short magnets are fitted. If one long magnet were fitted, the dip of the Earth's magnetic field would tilt the card at a large angle. There will always be a slight tilt except on the equator and, as a result, the centre of gravity of the card and the magnets will not be directly below the centre of support. Any acceleration at right angles to the magnetic meridian will therefore rotate the card.

11. In order to damp the swinging, the card and magnets are generally supported in a liquid and wires fitted to increase the friction. The liquid is generally some form of alcohol.

12. The simple compass is supremely reliable and, provided the craft is steady, can work in flux densities of less than 0·1 gauss.

14—P.N.

To avoid errors due to the card being misaligned with the lubber line when the craft tilts, the compass may be mounted on gimbals in a binnacle. For use at night, it may be provided with integral lighting.

DEVIATION

13. Magnetic material within a craft, or magnetic fields set up by electrical currents, may deflect the magnetic compass. Deviation is the difference in angle between the compass alignment and the magnetic meridian and is named east or west according to whether the compass aligns itself to the east or to the west of the magnetic meridian. As the craft turns, the magnetic material will alter its relationship to the magnetic meridian and the deviation will change. Hence, deviation caused by magnetic material varies according to the heading of the craft. Deviation caused by electrical currents will appear as a fault when current is switched on, but this should not occur with adequate shielding of wiring.

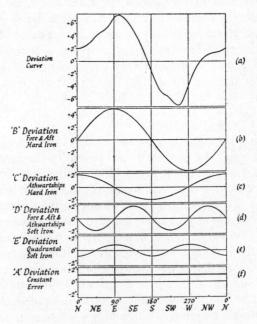

FIG. 91   Analysis of compass deviation

14. The process of measuring deviation is known as 'swinging'. The craft is turned on to a number of headings and the compass readings compared with the magnetic headings. Magnetic heading can be found:

(a) Directly by sighting along the fore and aft line of the craft by means of a magnetic compass placed at a distance from the craft so as not to be affected by disturbing magnetism.
(b) Indirectly, by measuring the true heading, using a bearing plate sighted on a distant object. Having found the true heading, an allowance can be made for the local variation.

15. A typical deviation curve produced by a swing is shown in Fig. 91(a). In order to correct for deviation, it is necessary to identify the types of magnetic disturbances. It has already been shown (page 22, para 17) that all curves can be built up from a series of sine waves. The deviation curve is built up mainly from:

(a) Constant error.
(b) Two sine waves.
(c) Two double sine waves.

The process of correction of these errors is known as compass adjustment.

COMPASS ADJUSTMENT

16. The constant or A error can arise when the lubber line is not correctly aligned with the fore and aft axis of the craft. This error can be found by adding the deviations on N., S., E., and W. and dividing by 4, or including the deviations on the intercardinal points and dividing by 8. By this means, the sine wave and double sine wave errors will cancel out. The A error can then be compensated by rotating the compass mechanically.

17. *Horizontal Hard Iron Deviation.* The hammering that occurs when a craft is being built tends to align magnetic particles in the materials with the Earth's magnetic field. After the craft is built, this magnetism may be reduced by electrical hammering known as demagnetizing. Nevertheless, some magnetism may persist and is known as '*hard*' magnetism. A material with magnetic permanence is sometimes known as '*hard iron*'.

18. The compass will be affected by hard iron in the horizontal plane which may be regarded as equivalent to two bar magnets placed close to the compass, one aligned fore and aft and the other athwartships, the former generally being the larger. In the instance of the fore and aft 'hard iron' there will be no effect on the compass when the craft is headed magnetic north or south as the 'hard iron' will be in line with the compass, but a maximum effect when the craft is at right angles to the magnetic meridan. The deviation is therefore of the pattern shown in Fig. 91(b). In the instance of the athwartships 'hard iron' the effect will obviously be a maximum on north and south and nil at right angles to the magnetic meridian as shown in Fig. 91(c).

19. In order to compensate for 'hard-iron' deviation, bar magnets may be inserted close to the compass of a strength that will exactly offset the 'hard iron' in the craft. Fore and aft compensating magnets are known as B 'correctors' and athwartships compensating magnets as C 'correctors'. In place of bar magnets, pairs of bar magnets arranged in an X and pivoted at the centre may be used. Opening or closing the X will affect the amount of magnetism produced by the pair.

20. To discover the compensation to be provided by the B and C correctors, deviation has to be measured on the four cardinal points of the compass. By subtracting the deviation on west from the deviation on east and halving the result, the extent of the peak of the B correction can be measured, the process of subtraction eliminating the double sine wave errors and the constant A deviation, the C deviation being nil on these headings. The B correctors can then be adjusted with the craft heading either east or west so that the correct amount of deviation is removed. The process can be repeated for the C correctors except that the compensation will depend on half the difference between deviations on north and south.

21. *Horizontal Soft-Iron Deviation.* In certain craft, some of the magnetic particles align themselves readily to the Earth's magnetic field and equally readily change their alignment when the craft changes its heading. This can be regarded as a '*soft-iron*' bar placed either fore and aft or athwartships and a '*soft-iron*' bar placed halfway between fore and aft and athwartships.

22. In the instance of a soft-iron bar placed either fore and aft or

athwartships, there will be no error when the craft is aligned with the magnetic meridian because the soft iron will be aligned in the same direction as the compass magnet. Nor will there be an error when the craft is at right angles to the magnetic meridian because the bar will not pick up the Earth's magnetism. The deviation known as *D* deviation will therefore follow the pattern shown in Fig. 91(d). In the instance of a soft-iron bar placed diagonally across the craft, the effect will be to alter the phase of the deviation by 45°. The pattern of the resulting *E* deviation will be as shown in Fig. 91(e).

23. *D* and *E* compensation is achieved in ships by soft-iron spheres aligned in the right direction and at the correct distance from the compass. The amount of compensation can be found as follows:

D compensation = ¼(sum of deviations on NE. and SW.
                    − sum of deviations on SE. and NW.)

E compensation = ¼(sum of deviation on N. and S.
                    − sum of deviations on E. and W.)

It will be noted that, in these calculations, *A*, *B* and *C* deviations are eliminated by the subtractions.

24. If the horizontal soft iron is so disposed about the craft that it is unsymmetrical about the compass, a deviation will arise that will have a constant effect on all headings. For example, if the soft iron were to attract the north-seeking end of the compass clockwise when heading in one direction, the same soft iron placed to one side could attract the south-seeking end clockwise if the heading were reversed. As a result, the normal double sine wave of the soft iron will also produce an apparent *A* that will be corrected by mechanical rotation.

25. *Vertical Iron.* When a craft rolls, the vertical hard iron will develop a sideways effect on the compass. The consequent heeling error can be compensated by vertical hard-iron magnets. This error will also arise when deviations are measured in a craft which, at rest, is pitched at an angle differing from that in motion. Since the change in pitch will affect the fore and aft magnetism, the deviation must be measured on east or west with the craft in its operating attitude and the compensating magnet adjusted for

any difference in reading when the craft is at rest. In a ship, the vertical hard iron can be measured by a magnetometer, sometimes known as a varioscope, and the appropriate corrector magnets inserted.

26. Vertical soft-iron deviation caused by the vertical component of the Earth's magnetic field will not change with the heading but will act as if it were hard iron. Unlike horizontal hard iron, its strength will change as the vertical component of the Earth's magnetic field changes. It is compensated in ships by a vertical soft-iron bar known as a Flinders bar. This adjustment is a matter for a specialist and in practice is often based largely on experience with a particular type of craft. The adjustment has to be made before the B and C compensations and the bar has to be placed on the side of the compass opposite to the main soft-iron mass of the craft.

27. *Correction Cards.* After compensation, residual deviation will be revealed by a final check swing of the compass and may be corrected by a correction card. A correction card may only apply to a particular magnetic latitude. It may therefore be necessary to swing the compass again and to prepare a fresh correction card if the craft should change magnetic latitude.

28. In aircraft, the correction card may have to allow for B and C deviations. In any event, it invariably has to allow for D and E corrections. In an aircraft, there is seldom much soft iron. Furthermore, since the horizontal component of the Earth's magnetic field determines the directive force on the compass and equally determines the force exerted by the horizontal soft iron, a numerical D and E correction may not be affected by changes of magnetic latitude.

TRANSMITTING COMPASS

29. If a magnetic detecting element is placed on the bridge of a ship or in the cockpit of an aircraft, it may be unduly affected by magnetic structures or electrical currents. The magnetic detector of the compass may have to be moved to a part of the craft where the deviation is likely to be a minimum and the indications led to a compass card on the bridge or in the cockpit.

30. The remote or transmitting compass element may consist of a magnet whose position is followed up by a frame driven by a

motor, the system being comparable to that used for the gyro compass (page 181, para 15). The misalignment between the magnet and the frame may be detected by a capacity pick-off and a capacity bridge. The difference signal may be fed into an amplifier which drives a motor so that the frame is rotated until it is aligned once more. The motor that drives the follow-up frame can also drive a transmission system of the type described on page 182, para 17.

31. *Fluxvalve*. The fluxvalve is an example of a magnetic detector. It can be compared to a synchro in which the moving coil is replaced by the magnetic field of the Earth. Each fixed coil has a soft-iron core and alternating current passed through is of such a strength that the soft iron is saturated with magnetism by each

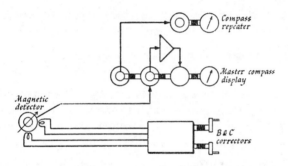

FIG. 92   Transmitting compass

swing of the current. The addition of a component of the Earth's horizontal magnetism will distort the response of the core and will introduce a ripple of twice the original frequency. This distorted signal is passed to the receiver synchro where it will reproduce the magnetic field of the Earth. The moving coil in the receiver can then be rotated until it is aligned with the Earth's magnetic field. Fig. 92 shows such a system.

32. The fluxvalve may be fitted in a remote part of the craft where it is impossible to operate corrector magnets. Electrical *B* and *C* correctors may therefore be fitted as shown in Fig. 92. Alternatively, two magnetic detectors may be fitted, one of which is twice as far from the centre of disturbing magnetism as the other. The difference between the signals from the two detectors

may be applied to the nearer detector to give a measure of the deviation. The method has been applied to armoured vehicles in which the magnetism may change considerably, for example following the firing of a gun.

TILTING ERROR

33. The magnetic element in a compass will be pendulously mounted so that any tilt of the craft will not introduce an error according to magnetic heading and magnetic latitude. However, accelerations will tilt the magnetic element. In particular, during a turn, an error will arise which can be expressed by:

$$\text{turning error}^\circ = (\text{speed (kt)} \times \text{rate of turn} \times \cos (\text{heading}) \\ \times \tan (\text{magnetic dip})/7$$

Example. A 200-knot aircraft heading north at latitude 30°N., where the dip is about 45°, starts a rate one turn to the east:

$$\text{Turning error} = -200 \times 1 \times \cos 0 \times \tan 45°/7 \\ = -200 \times 1 \times 1 \times \tfrac{1}{2}/7 = -14° \text{ or } 14° \text{ westwards}$$

34. The example of para 33 shows that an aircraft starting a turn to the east will register a 14° turn to the west. This is known as northerly turning error. The formula shows that northerly turning error will have four manifestations:

(a) Under-reading in turns on northerly headings north of magnetic equator.

(b) Over-reading in turns on southerly headings north of the magnetic equator.

(c) Over-reading in turns on northerly headings south of the magnetic equator.

(d) Under-reading in turns on southerly headings south of the magnetic equator.

35. The elimination of tilting error by stabilizing the magnetic detector has not been very successful. Apart from the difficulty of direct stabilization of an element mounted in a remote part of a possibly flexible craft, the stabilization has to be extremely good if northerly turning error is not to appear in high magnetic latitudes. The more usual solution is to smooth the signals of the magnetic detector by a directional gyroscope.

GYRO-MAGNETIC COMPASS

36. Fig. 93 shows a simple gyro-magnetic compass system. The remotely mounted detector unit is fitted with B and C correctors. The signals are disconnected in a turn by a turn discriminant worked from the main shaft of the compass system so that, when the rate of turn exceeds a certain limit, the detector is disconnected from the gyro.

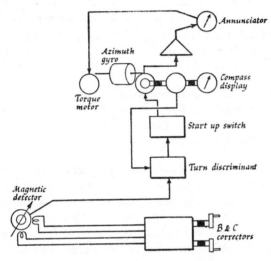

FIG. 93   Gyro-magnetic compass (compare with Fig. 92)

37. The signals from the detector pass to a synchro on the main shaft of the compass to which the gyroscope is attached. If the synchro is not aligned with the fluxvalve, the difference generates a signal in the synchro which is amplified and passed to the torque motor so that the gyro wheel is precessed accordingly. Thus the gyroscope integrates the indications of the magnetic element.

38. A display known as an annunciator is shown between the amplifier and the torque motor. If the gyro is seriously misaligned with the magnetic detector, a strong current will flow to the torque motors and this will cause the annunciator to move, thus providing a warning. The misalignment can be corrected

quickly by using a start-up switch, as shown in the illustration, to shorten the detector time constant.

39. In a moving craft, if the time constant is short, the directional gyroscope will respond too readily to false readings in magnetic detectors due for example to temporary tilts. Also a form of northerly heading error may appear when steering polewards. On the other hand, if the time constant is long, hang-off error will result due to the real and apparent drift of the gyroscope.

40. The real drift of the directional gyroscope can be reduced by improvements in design, by arranging that the gyro itself is not precessed but that the shaft is turned instead, and by stabilizing the gyroscope. However, the main problem will be apparent drift which will generally be from three causes:

(a) *Rotation of the Earth* (page 184, para 4).
(b) *Convergency of meridians* (page 184, para 5).
(c) *Variation.* In a high-speed craft it may be difficult to feed in this correction manually.

41. *Automatic Variation Correction.* If a craft were to fly only along one parallel of latitude, a cam could be cut according to the variation along the parallel and could be made to operate a roller so that the variation could be fed in according to the longitude. A number of cams placed together could provide variation for a range of latitudes and, if the roller could be moved across the cams according to the latitude, variation could be fed into the system on a world-wide basis. The ways in which such a three-dimensional cam could be driven according to longitude and the roller moved according to latitude will be described on page 301, para 5(d).

42. *Coriolis Correction.* An error can arise owing to the tilt of the magnetic detector in high-speed craft due to coriolis (page 69, para 21). The error in degrees would be:

$$0{\cdot}00044 \times \text{speed (knots)} \times \text{sin (latitude)} \times \text{tan (magnetic dip)}$$
$$\times \text{cos (magnetic heading)}$$

43. A vertical magnetic detector with a proportion of magnetic effect applied as an additional C correction will automatically deal with the last two terms of this complex expression, and the

first two terms, speed and latitude, can be fed in manually or automatically.

ACCURACY

44. *Variation*. The errors at any point are probably of the following order.

TABLE VII. VARIATION ERRORS AND LATITUDE

	95 PER CENT ERRORS	
Latitude	Charted variation	Magnetic anomalies
°	°	°
70	3	1
60	2	$\frac{1}{2}$
50	$1\frac{1}{2}$	$\frac{1}{4}$
40	$1\frac{1}{2}$	$\frac{1}{4}$
30	$1\frac{1}{2}$	small
20	$1\frac{1}{2}$	small
10	$1\frac{1}{2}$	small
Equator	$1\frac{1}{2}$	small

45. Charted variation has a semi-systematic error which reduces over a distance rather than over a time. It may be that, at latitudes less than 60°, the error averaged over a distance of 2000 miles may be not much more than half the error at any point. The anomalies, on the other hand, probably reduce over a period of time rather than over a distance, and when averaged over a period of 6 hours are probably only half their value at any particular instant. Hence the effect of anomalies may be expected to average out during a voyage lasting several days.

46. Because errors in charted variation change relatively slowly with distance, it follows that, if a magnetic compass can be corrected at any instant during a journey, the correction will apply over a considerable distance though it may vary with anomalies over a period of time. It is this characteristic that gives the magnetic compass a well-earned reputation for stability.

47. *Deviation*. Unlike variation, deviation tends to be systematic provided the craft is travelling along a reasonably steady path. A compensated compass may have an error in deviation that is less than $\frac{1}{2}°$ on 95 per cent of occasions. A poorly compensated

compass, or a compass close to a magnetic cargo, may have much greater deviation errors and a 95 per cent value of the order of two degrees is not uncommon.

48. *Compass System Errors*. The mechanical errors of a simple magnetic compass in a slow craft may be as much as $\frac{1}{2}°$ on 95 per cent of occasions but these errors average out very quickly. In a fast craft, the compass quickly becomes too unsteady and the simple gyro-magnetic compass has to be used. Such a compass may have errors of the same order as the simple magnetic compass but, in addition, there will be systematic and other errors introduced by the increasing speed of the craft. For example, failure to correct for coriolis may add a 95 per cent error of $\frac{1}{2}°$ at latitude 50° in a craft travelling at 500 knots and a similar error at 70° in a craft travelling only half as fast.

49. *Total Magnetic Heading Errors*. It may be useful to calculate a few typical magnetic compass and gyro-magnetic compass errors for craft covering distances of the order of 2000 miles. Although these results are only able to give the order of error, they may provide a useful comparison with other systems.

Example (a). 20-knot ship, latitude less than 60°, using a normal magnetic compass.

Source of error	95 per cent error °
Charted variation	$\frac{1}{4}$
Anomalies	very small
Deviation	$\frac{1}{2}$
Equipment errors	very small
∴ Total mean error =	1°approximately

This will be found to be about twice the error introduced by a gyro compass under similar conditions (page 183, para 21).

Example (b). 200-knot aircraft, latitude less than 60°, using a simple gyro-magnetic compass.

Source of error	95 per cent error °
Charted variation	$\frac{3}{4}$
Anomalies	small
Deviation	$\frac{3}{4}$
Equipment errors	$\frac{3}{4}$
∴ Total mean error =	$1\frac{1}{3}°$ approximately

This will be found to be about a quarter of the error of a 1° per hour gyro heading reference (page 183, para 16).

Example (c). 500-knot aircraft, latitude about 70° using a sophisticated gyro-magnetic equipment.

Source of error	95 per cent error $^\circ$
Charted variation	$1\frac{1}{2}$
Anomalies	$\frac{1}{4}$
Deviation	$\frac{1}{2}$
Equipment errors	$\frac{1}{4}$
∴ Total mean error =	over $1\frac{1}{2}°$

This will be found to be rather greater than the error resulting from a $\frac{2}{3}°$ per hour gyro heading reference.

4. AUTOMATICS

AUTOHELMSMAN

1. As with the majority of servo systems (page 137, para 2) three terms are needed to maintain the ship on a chosen heading:

  (a) Heading error.
  (b) Rate of change of heading.
  (c) Integral of heading error.

2. *Heading Error.* The difference between a signal representing required heading and a signal representing the heading derived by a gyro compass or other heading reference may be fed into an amplifier and a heading error signal provided.

3. *Rate of Change of Heading.* This could be produced by differentiating the heading error signal. However, this signal can be noisy and it may be better to use a rate gyroscope. This rate signal is essential to damp the heading error term, and to provide phase advance that will anticipate the swinging of the ship.

4. *Integral of Heading Error.* When the wind blows against the ship from one side, the hull will generally have a tendency either to weathercock or to fall off. To counteract this, a steady application of rudder will be necessary. This steady application will consume some of the steady input from the heading error term so that a hang-off error will result. This hang-off can be offset by feeding in the integral of heading error.

5. Fig. 94 shows an autohelmsman of this type. The heading error is derived from a comparison of the required heading (which is fed in manually) and the compass heading. The error

signal passes to the main servo amplifier and also to an integrator whence the integral of heading error also goes to the servo amplifier. The damping signal from the rate gyroscope is also fed in, together with rate feed-back from the servo drive.

6. Two additional refinements are also shown in the Fig. 94. The heading error signal goes also to an off-course warning lamp which

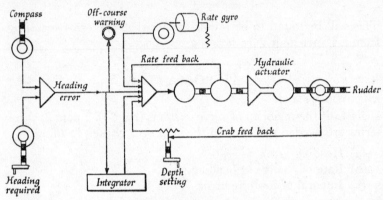

FIG. 94   Autohelmsman

will light up when the error exceeds a certain figure. This is a warning of temporary divergencies from heading and of the development of a fault or runaway. The amount of error that causes the light to appear has to be carefully adjusted. If it is too small, the light will continually be crying 'wolf'. If it is too large, the ship may go seriously off course before the man on the bridge is warned.

7. It has been explained that in order to deal with a beam wind the rudder may have to be kept at an angle. This will force the stern to one side and the ship will go sideways or crab slightly through the water. The amount of crab will depend on the depth of the hull and therefore the rudder position signal is modified according to the depth in order to produce a signal to offset crabbing.

8. The control system may operate the rudder with undue force particularly in the event of a runaway. To prevent this, safety devices such as friction clutches may be fitted. These safety devices inevitably reduce the authority of the system (page 170, para 22).

9. An autohelmsman acts in the same way as a 'lazy helmsman', which means a good helmsman. The rudder will respond at once to a tendency to swing off course and will give a small correction. Nevertheless, in a quartering sea, when the ship may have a tendency to turn to one side or broach-to, only a complex autohelmsman with ample authority will be able to perform as well as the experienced man.

AUTOPILOT

10. The basic autopilot includes an aileron channel to steer the aircraft by controlling it in roll, and a rudder channel to prevent sideslip by controlling the aircraft in yaw. An elevator channel controls the aircraft in pitch and ensures the correct attitude in elevation.

11. Fig. 95 shows the flow diagram of a simple autopilot. The ailerons, elevators and rudder are each shown controlled by

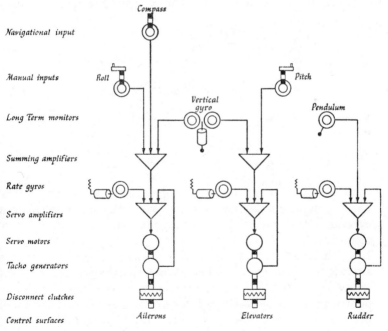

FIG. 95   Simple autopilot

identical servos damped by rate gyros and with rate feed-back from the servo drives, disconnect clutches being fitted so that the pilot can revert to manual control. The positions of the control surfaces are determined by a vertical reference in the instance of the aileron and elevator channels and by a sideslip pendulum in the instance of the rudder channel and these signals could be differentiated to give rate signals to replace the rate gyros. For steering the aircraft in the azimuth plane, a manual input of roll is illustrated also a compass input known as a heading lock or heading hold. For steering the aircraft in elevation, a manual input of pitch is shown. Alternatively, manometric instruments (page 218, para 20) could provide inputs for control of height or air-speed, such controls being known as height- or air-speed locks or holds. For other inputs see page 374, para 13.

12. Unlike the aircraft autostabilizer, which operates in parallel with the pilot, the autopilot drives the whole of the control system including the pilot's control column. It therefore operates in series as shown in Fig. 96. Hence, by watching his control

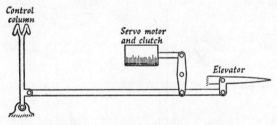

FIG. 96   Autopilot control run (pitch)

column, the pilot can see the autopilot controlling his aircraft. Arrangements may be made so that, if the pilot exerts an effort to overcome the autopilot, the autopilot is automatically disconnected.

13. The autopilot may be used for high-level cruise in a fast aircraft flying in marginal conditions of stability. Accordingly, safety devices (page 170, para 22) will need to be fitted. The autopilot may also be used close to the ground, in which event it will need ample authority for control in turbulence and redundancy to provide immunity from runaway.

SAILING CRAFT AUTOMATIC CONTROL

14. It is possible to set the sails of a well-balanced craft so that she will sail herself. However, when the wind increases, the craft may tend to turn head into wind. This tendency can be offset by linking the rudder mechanically to a small sail aft so that the increased wind gives an offsetting turn to the rudder.

5. SUMMARY

REFERENCES OF DIRECTION

Directions may be:

(a) True (T), with reference to meridians.
(b) Magnetic (M), with reference to magnetic meridians.
(c) Grid (G), with reference to great circles.

The angle through which the magnetic meridian is misaligned with the true north meridian is known as the variation and is measured east or west from the true meridian. The angle through which the magnetic meridian is misaligned with the grid great circle is known as grivation and is measured clockwise from the grid direction.

Directions are generally recorded by a lubber line against a moving card so as to provide an inside-out presentation for helmsman or pilot.

HEADING ERRORS

The following errors affect all heading systems:

(a) *Apparent drift* due to rotation of the Earth.
(b) *Course and speed or transport error*. A compass in a high-speed craft will be affected by meridian convergency.
(c) *Tilting errors*. These introduce gimballing errors in gyroscopes and deviations in magnetic detectors in high latitudes. Coriolis acceleration will cause tilts at high speeds and in high latitudes.

GYRO COMPASS

The gyro compass loses accuracy above 75° latitude. Owing to ballistic errors, the gyro compass tends to be inaccurate in high-speed craft.

15—P.N.

The 84-minute period of the gravity monitor reduces acceleration errors. The gyro wheel may be specially mounted to reduce forces that tend to set up torques in azimuth.

DIRECTIONAL GYROSCOPE

A directional gyroscope needs to be aligned initially and tends to drift with an error that generally increases with time.

Gimballing and other tilting errors may be reduced by stabilizing the gyroscope on a platform.

MAGNETIC COMPASS

Up to about 70° latitude, the magnetic detector is satisfactory, but the directive force thereafter weakens rapidly and the effects of tilt and of magnetic storms increase.

Deviations are due to hard and soft iron and are reduced by compensating magnets. In steel craft, the detector may be mounted in one of the extremes of the hull and made to operate a remote indicator. Deviations may also be caused by unshielded electrical wiring.

GYRO-MAGNETIC COMPASS

Acceleration errors and particularly northerly turning errors increase with the speed of the craft. The magnetic detector may therefore be made to slave a directional gyroscope.

The time constant cannot be short or acceleration errors will appear. If it is long, hang-off errors will appear unless true and apparent gyro drifts can be reduced.

HEADING REFERENCE ACCURACIES

Slow Craft. In craft whose speeds are measured in a few tens of knots, compasses will be used whose performance can be summarized as follows:

TABLE VIII. COMPASS ERRORS

Characteristic	Magnetic compass	Gyro compass
95 per cent errors	2°	1°
95 per cent errors averaged over 2000 n. miles	1°	$\frac{1}{2}$°
Coverage limits	1000 n. miles from magnetic poles	1000 n. miles from geographic poles

High-speed Craft. In craft whose speeds are measured in hundreds of knots, gyro-magnetic compasses are necessary. As speeds increase so the time taken to cover a distance decreases and the directional gyroscope becomes relatively more accurate.

AUTOMATICS

An autohelmsman may use an integral term to reduce hang-off due to weathercocking or falling off.

An autopilot operates in parallel with the pilot and will control an aircraft in roll, pitch and yaw.

CHAPTER VI

Speed

REFERENCES
Speed is always relative. It is generally measured relative to one of three frames of reference:

(a) *The medium that supports the craft.* For convenience, this may be referred to as measured speed. It is recorded in knots.

(b) *The surface of the Earth.* This will generally be measured by doppler equipment. It is normally recorded in knots.

(c) *The direction of the vertical.* Inertial platforms measure speed as a change of the direction of the vertical on the surface of the Earth. This speed may be measured in minutes of arc per hour and will differ from knots as shown on page 16, para 4.

1. MEASURED SPEED

1. Speed relative to the medium that supports the craft is generally measured in one of three ways:

(a) By speed of the engine that drives the craft.
(b) By speed of the medium past the craft.
(c) By the force set up as a result of movement through the medium.

ENGINE SPEED
2. In a land craft, the speed will be according to the rate of revolutions of the engine and the gear ratio. In an aircraft, the power settings can be expected to produce a certain speed according to the all-up weight and the altitude at which the aircraft is flying, and this is sometimes used as a check on speed

found by other means. In a marine craft, speed can be calculated from engine revolutions and may be measured on a tachometer with an accuracy of about 1 knot in a slow craft.

3. In order to find the speed of a ship from the engine revolutions. allowance has to be made for the following:

(a) *Draught.* The depth of the hull underwater will affect the forward speed that results from the rotation of the screw.

(b) *Condition of hull.* A hull which is fouled will travel more slowly for the same rate of revolutions of the engine.

(c) *Amount of roll.* The rolling tends to increase the resistance to forward motion roughly in proportion to the amount of roll.

4. The speed of a ship can be calculated by means of tables that take these factors into account. Alternatively, the corrections could be made automatically. Fig. 97 shows a theoretical system

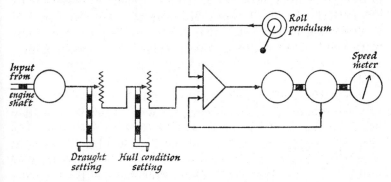

FIG. 97   Theoretical engine revolution speed meter

for correcting engine revolutions according to draught, condition of hull, and rolling, and may be useful as a summary of the corrections.

SPEEDOMETER

5. The speed of a craft is commonly recorded by the motion of the supporting medium past the craft. The driving wheels of a motor vehicle measure speed in this way and so do the trailing wheels fitted to sledges. In essence, the devices measure the distance

travelled and as such are correctly known as odometers (or hodometers). Speed is derived by a process of differentiation and therefore is apt to be noisy.

6. A speedometer can record speed from the wheels of a vehicle in many ways. For example:

(a) A tacho generator fitted to the shaft may produce a voltage proportional to the speed of rotation of the wheel.

(b) A magnetic element on the shaft may pull round a pointer against a spring, the faster the rate of rotation the greater the angle of pull. Speedometers of this type suffer from eddy currents and tend to be unsteady.

(c) The rate of rotation may cause a weight to fly outwards against a spring. The amount of outward movement will be a gauge of the speed.

The error in the record of speed depends partly on the amount of wheel skid and is therefore affected by weight, by speed and by the surface on which the vehicle travels. The 95 per cent accuracy is generally better than 5 per cent of the speed at any instant and rapidly improves when averaged over a period of time.

LOG

7. In a marine craft, speed may be measured by a small propeller that will rotate as it passes through the water, the rate of rotation being measured in the same way as in a speedometer. The propeller may be a towed log, which is streamed behind the craft on a wire traditionally attached to the taffrail or it may be fixed to the hull in a submerged position. Provided that the propeller is not fouled, speed may be registered over a period of time with a 95 per cent accuracy of the order of 1 per cent of the speed through the water.

8. A similar system has been used in aircraft. However, the propeller is not placed in the slip-stream but the air is led through a pitot tube (page 101, para 8) to a diaphragm on the opposite side of which is a fan driven by a motor which corresponds to the propeller in the log. When the movement of the aircraft sets up pressure in the pitot tube and causes the diaphragm to cave in, a contact is closed and current is passed to the motor. The fan speeds up until the air pressure is equalized whereat the

diaphragm returns to its normal position and the current is cut off. By this type of bang-bang servo, the fan can be made to rotate at a rate proportional to the speed of the aircraft. The device is known as an air-mileage unit and the accuracy over a limited range of speeds on a 95 per cent basis is generally around 3 per cent of the speed through the air.

9. The accuracies quoted for the marine log and the air-mileage unit are essentially averages over a period of time. The instantaneous errors may be far greater. This is only to be expected since the system is basically distance measurement and speed has to be evolved by a form of differentiation introduced by a rate-measuring device.

10. A special form of electro-magnetic (E.M.) marine log consists of a pulsating magnet mounted on a probe pointing downwards with two contacts each side of the probe. The movement of the water through the magnetic field is detected by the contacts, and the ripple of voltage thus induced can be converted to measure the speed of the craft. The saltiness of the water appears to have little effect on the accuracy of the indications which are comparable to that of the marine log.

PITOT PRESSURE

11. On page 101, para 8, the way in which the air-speed indicator worked was explained. A similar system for measuring speed through the water can be used in marine craft, the pressure resulting from the forward motion being led from the pitot head through the pitot tube to a capsule.

12. The speed recorded by the instrument may be known as the indicated speed or IAS (indicated air speed) in aircraft. It will first be corrected for instrument errors and position errors (page 102, para 10). The corrected speed may be known as the calibrated speed, or in aircraft the term rectified speed may be used.

13. The calibrated or rectified speed will not represent the true speed of the craft unless the density of the medium is the same as the density for which the instrument was calibrated. The density of water depends on temperature and salinity but the variation is generally not great. However, air density decreases very considerably with height.

14. It can be shown that the speed registered on the air-speed indicator depends on the density of the air relative to the density of air at 1013 millibars and 15°C, and this ratio is known as the relative air density. The formula for converting calibrated air speed (CAS) or rectified air speed (RAS) to true air speed (TAS) is approximately:

True air speed
= (calibrated or rectified air speed)/$\sqrt{}$(relative air density)

Example. At 40,000 feet, where the air density is roughly a quarter the air density at sea-level, an air-speed meter reads 200 knots with negligible instrument and position errors.

$$\text{True air speed} = (200/\sqrt{\tfrac{1}{4}}) \text{ knots} = 400 \text{ knots}$$

15. In order to convert calibrated or rectified air speed to true air speed, pressure is recorded in terms of height with the altimeter set to 1013 millibars, and the air temperature is read. The two quantities are applied to a simple form of slide-rule from which true air speed can be read against calibrated or rectified air speed. A simple approximation accurate to within about 5 per cent up to 10,000 feet is obtained by adding one-sixtieth of the speed for each 1000 feet of height.

16. As the speed of the craft approaches the speed of sound, the ability of the molecules to move aside decreases and the compressibility of the air consequently changes. Rectified air speed and calibrated air speed corrected according to this change of compressibility is known as equivalent air speed (EAS). In practice shock waves begin to form ahead of the pitot tube so that pitot pressure can no longer be registered by the air-speed indicator. However, if pitot pressure could be measured, it would be found that:

$$\text{TAS}[1 + \text{TAS}^2/(2 \times \text{speed of sound})^2]$$
$$\simeq (\text{CAS or RAS})/\sqrt{}(\text{relative air density})$$

17. *True Air-Speed Indicator.* By assuming that the atmospheric pressure follows the ISA pattern, a capsule that registers static air pressure can modify, by means of a cam, a capsule movement that registers pitot pressure and thus can produce a movement of a pointer that is approximately proportional to true

air speed. It is, however, impossible to make an adequate correct-tion for compressibility, and the instrument can only be expected to be accurate over a relatively small range of speeds even if the atmospheric pressure and the air temperature happen to be linked together in the same way as the corresponding values in the ISA pattern. Alternatively a mach-meter (page 103, para 12(b)) may be corrected for temperature so that it can give true air speed in place of speed compared to the speed of sound.

VERTICAL SPEED INDICATOR

18. A barometric instrument may be used to indicate the rate of climb or descent. The capsule is supplied with atmospheric pressure through a static tube in the same way as the altimeter. However, the case is provided with a leak, as shown in Fig. 98,

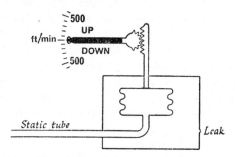

FIG. 98   Vertical speed indicator

so that the deflection registered by the pointer depends on the rate at which the pressure is changing. Thus the pointer registers rate of climb or descent against a dial.

19. A vertical speed indicator (VSI) tends to have the usual faults associated with barometric instruments. In particular, it will suffer from lag. This lag can be reduced by means that will be described on page 239, para 43. Apart from the lag, the simple rate of climb and descent indicator in an aircraft can register changes of height at low levels to within about 50 feet per minute for the first 1000 feet per minute on the scale. A glider may use a specially sensitive vertical speed instrument known as a vario-meter, which shows small changes of pressure and thereby indicates the presence of thermals.

AIR-DATA COMPUTER

20. Five different aircraft manometric instruments have been described:

Page	para.	Instrument	Basic pressure inputs
73	29	Altimeter	Static
101	8	Air-speed indicator	Static and pitot
103	12(b)	Mach-meter	Static and pitot
216	17	True air-speed indicator	Static and pitot
217	18	Vertical speed indicator	Static

21. An air-data computer accepts inputs of static and pitot pressure and produces outputs of height, indicated air speed, mach number, true air speed and vertical air speed. The capsules that sense static and pitot pressures will generally be fitted with pick-offs and the signals will be electrically mixed to provide the necessary outputs. The capsules may be mechanically balanced so that accelerations cannot affect the indications.

22. The mixing of the pressure signals may be achieved in a relatively crude fashion by power synchros driving specially shaped cams that adjust the outputs in the same way that cams act as altimeter settings (page 73, para 30). Hence the term air-data computer may give a picture rather more grandiose than is warranted by the basic simplicity of the equipment itself.

AUTOMATIC SPEED CONTROL

23. The measurement of speed in its various forms and in particular the presentation of speed as an electrical signal enables a required speed to be set and the difference to be amplified and produced as an error signal. This error signal may be made to operate actuators that move the throttles of the engines accordingly. Thus the power settings can be adjusted automatically so that the craft is travelling at the required speed.

24. In the instance of an aircraft, the required speed may be set into the manometric system, which may be an air-data computer, and the error signal produced passed to an amplifier that drives a motor as shown in Fig. 99. On the motor shaft will be a rate and a position pick-off to provide the necessary feed-back for steady control. The motor shaft will be coupled to the throttle lever to drive it according to the required speed that has been set in. Such a system is known as autothrottle.

25. In practice, a rate gyroscope that records changes of pitch of the aircraft is generally included as an additional input. The rate gyroscope provides a measure of phase advance so that the system is able to anticipate the changes of speed that will result from changes of pitch and can introduce the necessary throttle adjustments before the changes of speed can build up.

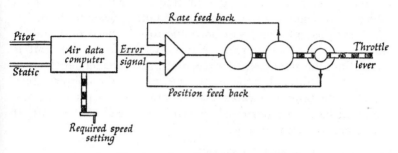

FIG. 99   Autothrottle (greatly simplified)

AIR-CUSHION VEHICLES

26. The air-cushion vehicle presents a particular problem. At low speeds on the water it can be regarded as a normal marine craft whose motion is affected directly by the motion of the water. However, when the speed exceeds the hump speed (page 103, para 12(a)), the craft becomes affected only by the motion of the wind. Any extrusion downwards to measure water speed would be too vulnerable, and a pitot tube in the air above the craft would be ineffective at low speeds and during turns. The preferred solution may be a simple doppler as described on page 224, para 14. These problems do not, of course, apply to sidewall air-cushion vehicles.

ACCURACY

27. The accuracy of measured speed for both marine and aircraft has been shown to be 95 per cent between 1 and 3 per cent. It is likely that half this error is random and will disappear relatively quickly so that, over a distance, the average may be of the order of 1 per cent on a 95 per cent probability basis.

2. DOPPLER

PRINCIPLES

1. When a motor vehicle approaches, the sound of each cylinder firing is emitted a little closer to the listener than the sound of the previous firing so that the sounds arrive bunched more closely together and the note appears to be higher. As the vehicle recedes, each sound of firing is emitted a little further away than the previous sound so that the engine note appears to drop.

2. The apparent change in note due to the speed of a craft is known as the doppler shift. Naturally, the faster the craft is travelling, the greater the doppler shift. Also, the higher the note being transmitted by the craft, the greater the doppler shift, whereas the faster the waves that carry the note are travelling, the less will be the proportional effect of the speed of the craft. It therefore follows that:

Doppler shift in cycles a second
  = (speed of craft) × (transmitted frequency)/(speed of waves)

3. If the craft is regarded as stationary and the listener is given a relative speed towards the craft, the frequency shift due to doppler will obviously depend on how many of the waves the listener covers in a second. If the listener is closing with the craft at the rate of 10 wavelengths a second, the note will obviously increase by 10 cycles a second. Hence a simpler version of the fundamental formula will be:

Doppler shift in cycles a second = (speed of craft)/wavelength

MEASUREMENT OF SPEED

4. Doppler systems alone cannot measure the speed of a craft instantaneously. Fig. 100(a) shows a craft whose doppler speed has been measured by a ground station. This speed can only be represented by a circle around the craft since the direction of the speed is not measured by doppler. The true speed of the craft cannot be smaller than the doppler speed. With this proviso, however, it can be of any size and in any direction. In Fig. 100(a), a typical speed vector is shown and, by drawing a tangent to the doppler speed circle, it can be shown that this speed selected at

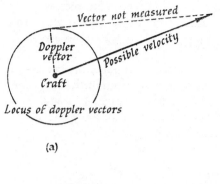

(a)

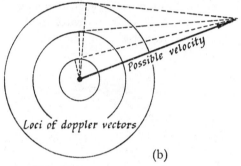

(b)

FIG. 100   Instantaneous speed measurement

random is consistent with the doppler speed that has been
measured.

5. Fig. 100(b) shows a number of doppler speeds. The speeds can
still only be represented by a series of concentric circles and the
true velocity of the craft can still be in any direction and of any
speed provided that it is not less than the greatest doppler speed.

6. In order to measure the speed of a craft instantaneously, it is
necessary to add further information. For example, if two ground
stations simultaneously measure bearing and doppler speed, then
there will be two doppler speed vector lines instead of two circles,
and where two lines at right angles to the ends of these doppler
speed vectors cut will be the end of the true speed vector. Hence,
by measurement of two bearings as well as two doppler speeds, it
is possible to measure instantaneously not only the speed of the
craft but also the direction of that speed.

7. Simultaneous measurements of direction and doppler speed from ground stations have been used to measure the trajectories of missiles during trials. However, radio waves cannot penetrate far under water, and sound waves are not easily beamed over any distances. Hence, marine craft generally cannot use sound waves to measure speed over the bottom of the sea, though submarines running deep can achieve some accuracy. However, aircraft using radio beams can and do measure speeds very successfully both over land and sea.

AIRBORNE DOPPLER

8. Fig. 101 shows two doppler beams each at an angle of 70° to the horizontal line of the aerial, which measure the speed of an aircraft over the ground. The aerial is pitched up or down until the

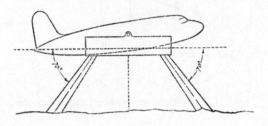

FIG. 101   Doppler in elevation

doppler shift from the beam ahead equals the doppler shift from the beam astern. The line of the aerial will then show the path of the aircraft in elevation and, if the average of the two doppler shifts is multiplied by secant 70°, the speed along this path may be measured. In practice, the aerials may be tilted electronically rather than mechanically.

9. Measurement of the slope of the path of an aircraft is less useful than might be expected. In civil aviation in particular, height is measured in terms of barometric pressures and not in true height. Nor will the measurement of the slope of the flight path give an indication of the angle of attack or incidence since this will also depend on the speed of the air relative to the sloping path.

10. By using four beams as shown in Fig. 102, doppler can measure the path of an aircraft in the azimuth plane. For example, the aerial may be rotated in azimuth until the doppler shifts each side are equalized. By this means doppler drift, the direction of the path measured by doppler compared to the heading, can be found. The mean of all the shifts can be multiplied by the secant of the angle that each beam makes with the line of the aerial, so as to measure speed over the ground. Alternatively, the four aerials may be fixed and the drift and ground speed computed from the four shifts. In theory, such a system would need only three beams but the computing would be more complicated.

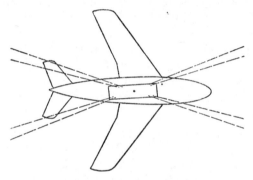

FIG. 102   Doppler in plan

11. Measurement of velocity in the azimuth plane is of extreme value in air navigation since it is the wind that causes problems. Over the land, the accuracy will be very high, probably 95 per cent within $\frac{1}{4}$ knot. Corrections will have to be made if the aircraft is high, to allow for the Earth's curvature. At any instant, errors may appear due to the contours of the ground. For example, in Fig. 101 the forward beam will be seen to be striking a mountain face. As a result, the lower edge of the beam will be reflected more strongly and the angle temporarily will be more than 70°.

12. Over the water, the sporadic errors due to the contours of the ground will be replaced by continuous errors due to waves so that the beams may not effectively be at 70°. This sea-state error can be reduced by feeding in a correction. Movements of

surface spray will occur which have been estimated as roughly one-fifth of the surface wind. Unless the navigator has some means of measuring surface wind, the forecast error of the order of 20 knots (95 per cent) will lead to an error of 4 knots. To this must be added a small error due to ocean currents and perhaps 5 per cent of the wind that has been blowing for the past 24 hours. The total errors will be of the order of 5 knots (95 per cent) but, over a long 2000-mile run, this might be reduced by averaging to about 2 or 3 knots. At any one point, on the other hand, the error might well be as much as 10 knots, particularly over tidal streams.

13. Sea errors will largely disappear if the wind is light. However, if the wind is less than 2 knots, the sea will become glassy and the radio waves will not be reflected back to the aircraft. The doppler equipment will then cease to measure speeds. This characteristic is known as unlocking. Fortunately, except in certain special localities, the sea is seldom flat over wide areas.

AIR-CUSHION VEHICLES

14. It was explained on page 219, para 26, that air-cushion vehicles, except sidewall ACV's, find difficulties in speed measurement by log or by pitot head. Doppler has been used with one transmitter aimed at a point generally behind the craft and two receiver aerials separated by a wide angle so that they look inwards at about 45°. Comparison of the two doppler shifts enables drift to be calculated and the mean shift gives the speed compared to the water with an accuracy of the order of 2 per cent (95 per cent probability).

3. INERTIAL PLATFORM

FORCE FEED-BACK ACCELEROMETERS

1. Inertial navigation systems measure and integrate accelerations in order to find speed. Since accelerations are absolute, the speed found as a result of accelerations is related absolutely to the speed of the craft when the measurements of acceleration began.

2. On page 161, para 31, it was shown that acceleration may be measured by the movement of a mass against a spring. A

mechanical spring is neither sufficiently sensitive nor sufficiently consistent to achieve high accuracy and therefore an electro-magnetic spring is commonly used as shown in Fig. 103.

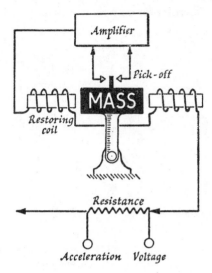

FIG. 103   Force feed-back accelerometer

3. The mass is freely mounted so that if the instrument accelerates from left to right, inertia will cause the mass to lag behind to the left. This will be detected by the pick-off and a signal will be passed to the amplifier so that current will be driven through the restoring coils of an electro-magnet to drive the mass back to the original position. The current flowing through the restoring coils will be proportional to the restoring force required, and therefore proportional to the acceleration. By passing this current through a resistance, a voltage proportional to the acceleration will be produced. An instrument of this type is known as a force feed-back accelerometer.

INTEGRATORS
4. A tacho-generator, if driven according to *rate* by a power synchro, could be directly coupled to a *position* pick-off, such as a potentiometer, and the combination would form an integrator as

16—P.N.

shown in Fig. 104. An electro-mechanical integrator of this type can be made very accurate and reliable. Unfortunately, accelerations change extremely quickly in certain types of craft, and mechanical inertia may prevent the integrator following the output of the accelerometer sufficiently closely.

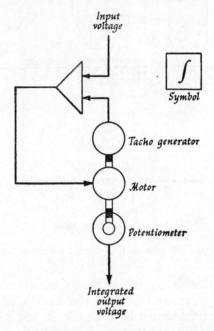

FIG. 104   Electro-mechanical integrator

5. An electronic integrator cannot suffer from mechanical inertia. A resistance is connected to the voltage output of the accelerometer. According to the acceleration voltage, current will flow through the resistance. This current then charges up a capacitor so that the total charge across the capacitor will be directly proportional to the total flow of current. If a simple capacitor were used, it would have to be extremely large. However, an amplifier can be arranged which effectively multiplies the size of the capacitor. An integrator of this type is sometimes known as a Miller integrator.

6. Although the Miller integrator can respond to very fast changes of acceleration, the capacitor has a limited size and therefore the integrated total is limited. This may not matter when integrating acceleration since the speed of a craft will be limited. The capacitor has to be specially designed and maintained at an exact temperature. Temperature control is also needed for the high-precision electro-mechanical integrator, but generally the requirements are not rigid.

INTEGRATING ACCELEROMETERS

7. If an acceleration can be measured as a rate, a position pick-off will provide an integrated total. For example, a piston may be fitted into a cylinder filled with a viscous liquid. Acceleration will force the piston along the cylinder at a rate proportional to the acceleration and the total movement of the piston will give a measure of speed.

8. A type of integrating accelerometer commonly used in ballistic missiles is the integrating gyro accelerometer which consists of a single-axis gyroscope which is unbalanced by means of a mass. Acceleration will tilt the mass and the tilting will be measured by a pick-off which will rotate the accelerometer so that the gyro precession resulting from the rotation exactly offsets the tilt. Thus acceleration is balanced by a rate of rotation and a position pick-off on the same shaft will give an output of speed. The instrument is very accurate but somewhat bulky.

9. Other types of accelerometers use masses supported by wires or mounted on crystals that vibrate electrically. The strain resulting from an acceleration will change the rate of vibrations. The total vibrations may be counted and these will be a measure of the integrated speed.

PRECISION GYROSCOPES

10. The accuracy with which the accelerometer and integrator will measure accelerations will depend on the accuracy with which the alignment of the accelerometer can be maintained. A gyroscope drift rate of the order of 1° per hour (95 per cent) may be satisfactory as a short-period heading reference, but for an inertial speed measurement over a matter of a few hours, an accuracy of between 0°1 and 0°01 per hour (95 per cent) is needed.

11. *Floated Gyroscopes*. It was explained on page 158, para 19(b), that one of the major difficulties was to support the gyro wheel absolutely firmly so that accelerations will not unbalance it and yet absolutely freely so that tilting of the outer case will not torque the gyro wheel. The dilemma can be resolved by supporting the wheel in liquid. The centre of support can be maintained far more constant by flotation than by gimbals. Accordingly, the gyro wheel may be mounted in a can and floated in a liquid, generally fluorlube, within an outer can. The inner and outer can may be kept apart by mechanical links but these will not have to take weight or exert any force.

12. Fig. 105 shows a single-axis floated gyroscope of a type commonly used on inertial platforms. It is a rate integrating

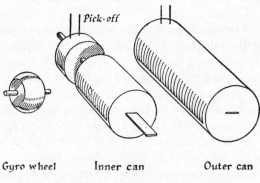

Pick-off

Gyro wheel   Inner can   Outer can

FIG. 105   Floated single-axis gyroscope

gyro. The wheel is mounted in an inner can and the precession is detected by a pick-off. The platform is driven by motors until the precession has been cancelled out by an exactly opposite precession. A rate gyroscope of this type can be miniaturized and is so sensitive that it can record the rate of rotation when fixed to the hour hand of a clock.

13. Floated gyroscopes may be rate gyroscopes or position gyro-scopes. The wheel may be supported by liquid, by wires or by air jets. However, the wheel may shift on its bearings and become slightly unbalanced. To reduce this shift, the wheel may be supported on a self-generating film of air known as an air

bearing. Although the film of air will absorb power, there will be no wear except when starting and stopping. Slight torques arising from the leads that bring power to the motor will now become significant. These torques can be avoided by arranging that a motor shall drive the wheel externally by means of eddy currents, and a sketch of a gyroscope of this type is shown in Fig. 106. It will be noted that this is a two-axis gyroscope with an extremely simple support for the spinning element that acts also as a gimbal system.

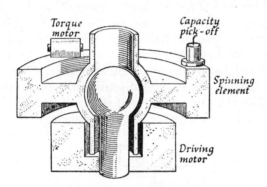

FIG. 106 · Free gyroscope with air bearing rotor

14. *Sophisticated Gyroscopes*. For an inertial-speed measurement over a matter of days or weeks rather than hours, a drift rate of $0°.001$ to $0°.0001$ per hour is needed. Even if leads to the wheel are dispensed with, the driving motor will cause precession if the gyro wheel is temporarily misaligned with the outer case. This can be avoided if, once started up, the wheel will spin without demanding power.

15. If the wheel is supercooled to a temperature close to absolute zero ($-273°$C) electrical resistance disappears. The wheel, generally in the form of a hollow sphere, will then spin indefinitely in a vacuum supported by electrical eddy currents or electrostatic forces. Displacements can be detected by light-sensitive cells that look at markings on the surface of the sphere. This is the principle of the cryogenic gyroscope. Other developments include the particle gyroscope that uses the spinning of atomic nuclei and the ring laser described on page 413, para 31.

GRAVITY MONITORING

16. An accelerometer and integrator can measure speed with an error of the order of 1 per cent, or, with precise manufacture and temperature control, $0\cdot1$ per cent or 1 in 10^3. An accuracy of 1 in 10^4 is, however, difficult to achieve, the main limitation being the performance of the accelerometer. Since an acceleration of 10 knots per second will be common, being a bank angle of a little over $25°$, even 1 in 10^4 will represent in 1 hour nearly 4 knots and in 2 hours over 7 knots. Therefore, on the surface of the Earth, gravity will be used as a long-term reference.

17. To explain how gravity is used, an example will be taken of an accelerometer mounted on a platform stabilized by a gyroscope with an accurate heading reference so that the accelerometer senses accelerations. If the north end of the accelerometer were raised, the mass would be pulled southwards by gravity. This would produce the same effect as if the craft were accelerating northwards and the mass were lagging behind.

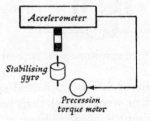

FIG. 107   Initial levelling
of platform

18. *Levelling.* In order that gravity shall not introduce a false acceleration, it will be necessary to maintain the platform level. When the craft is about to start the journey, the acceleration caused by gravity can be fed back into the gyroscope to precess it until the false acceleration disappears. A flow diagram is shown in Fig. 107. As soon as the craft starts on its journey, the direct link from accelerometer to gyroscope must be broken, otherwise the platform would be tilted as soon as the craft accelerates on its journey.

19. *Schüler tuning.* Because the surface of the Earth is curved, it will be necessary to tilt the platform by 1 minute of arc an hour

for every minute of arc an hour of speed registered by the accelerometer and integrator. The arrangement which achieves this is shown as a simplified flow diagram in Fig. 108.

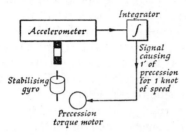

FIG. 108 Schüler-tuned system

20. If the speed recorded is in error, the precession will not allow correctly for the curvature of the Earth and therefore the platform will develop a tilt as shown in Fig. 109(a). This tilt will

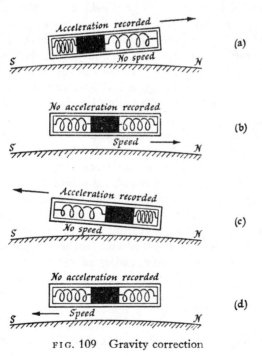

FIG. 109 Gravity correction

cause a false acceleration to be recorded in a northwards direction as explained in para 17. The false acceleration will develop a correcting speed until the platform is eventually levelled as shown in Fig. 109(b). The correcting speed will persist and a tilt will develop in the opposite direction. Gravity will take effect so that the overswing will be slowed down, halted (see Fig. 109(c)), and eventually the accelerometer will return to the level position (Fig. 109(d)). Thus the platform will continue to oscillate from side to side about the correct vertical. The speed registered will also oscillate from side to side about the correct value.

21. From the platform it will be as if the Earth were swinging to and fro below like a gigantic pendulum the length of which will be the radius of the Earth. It is therefore not surprising that the oscillations of the platform have the period of 84 minutes, which has already been mentioned on page 178, para 6, as a Schüler pendulum period. Hence a system in which the platform tilts through 1 minute of arc an hour for 1 minute of arc an hour of speed recorded by the integrator is said to be Schüler tuned.

22. Although gravity can monitor the accelerometer and integrator outputs, it cannot monitor gyro drift. Even in a stationary craft, a gyro drift of 1′ an hour will have to be counterbalanced by a false speed of 1′ an hour in the opposite direction. However, initially, the change in level of the platform will build up a compensation in the form of an 84-minute oscillation which will be superimposed on the steady drift rate. A similar 84-minute oscillation will be introduced if, for any reason, the platform becomes disturbed from its level.

23. The three effects, accelerometer and integrator errors, gyro drift and platform disturbances, all introduce 84-minute oscillations but only one, the gyro drift, introduces a steady speed error. The accelerometer and integrator errors will change as the heading of the craft alters, and from time to time minor disturbances will upset the rhythm and add further 84-minute oscillations. Hence the formal pattern indicated in Fig. 110 may tend to build up into larger oscillations.

PLATFORM DESIGN

24. The gyroscopes and accelerometers determine the accuracy of the speed measurement. Their size and temperature control

requirements determine the size of the platform, which in turn determines the size of the gimbal motors, the over-all power requirements and the cooling requirements.

25. There are three main types of platform:

(a) *Precessed*, used in aircraft.
(b) *Unprecessed*, used in marine craft such as submarines.
(c) *True*, used in ballistic missiles.

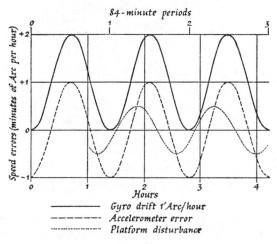

FIG. 110   Errors in inertial platform

26. *Precessed platform.* Accelerometers measuring accelerations east–west and north–south are mounted on a small Schüler-tuned platform stabilized either by two rate gyroscopes, with a third for heading reference, or by two free gyroscopes (page 228, para 12). Three gimbals will be fitted with an additional gimbal for complete manœuvrability (page 155, para 9), and these will be driven directly by motors without intermediate gearing so that angular vibrations from the craft are not carried through to the platform.

27. Fig. 111 shows the basic system. In addition to precessing the gyroscopes, speed signals pass to a coriolis computer whence the E.–W. speeds are fed to precess the N.–S. gyroscope, and the

N.–S. speeds to precess the E.–W. gyroscope according to latitude. Latitude must also be fed into the E.–W. gyroscope to precess it in order to compensate for the rotational tilt of the Earth's surface.

28. A precessed platform is used in an aircraft because it is small and light and may weigh only a few tens of pounds if miniature

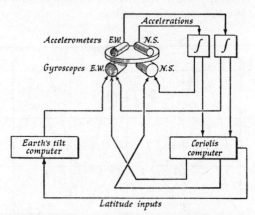

FIG. 111   Precessed platform (gimbals omitted)

gyroscopes and accelerometers are fitted. The journey will seldom last more than a few hours and therefore the drift rate of the gyroscopes need not be better than a minute of arc an hour.

29. *Unprecessed platform.* A marine platform, and particularly a submarine platform, has to operate for days rather than hours so that large, exotic and heavy gyroscopes will be required. To avoid the loss of accuracy inevitable in precessing the gyroscopes, the platform will be maintained in a constant alignment and the accelerometers mounted on a second platform connected to the main platform by gimbals. This accelerometer platform will be tilted for Schüler tuning, for coriolis correction, and for Earth's tilt compensation. A sketch of such a platform, in a theoretical form in order to show the principle, is shown in Fig. 112.

30. *True Inertial Platform.* The ballistic missile platform has to measure accelerations in the vertical axis as well as in the horizontal plane, and the platform with the three accelerometers is maintained steady in space so that it approximates to a true inertia

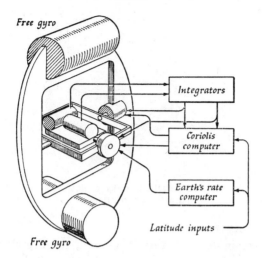

FIG. 112 Unprecessed platform (main gimbals omitted)

system. In fact, the outputs of the accelerometers have to be modified by a computer to take account of the changing direction of gravity as the missile is launched, so that the same element of gravity control applies.

31. The ballistic system only operates for the few minutes before fuel is burnt and thrust is cut off, after which the missile proceeds on its ballistic path unnavigated. For such short periods, gyro drifts will be unimportant, as is shown by Fig. 110. On the other hand, the accelerometers will have no time to take advantage of the 84-minute correction and therefore they have to be extremely accurate. In practice, integrating rate accelerometers may be used. An example of a true inertial system is shown in Fig. 113. The inside-out or knuckle-joint gimbals provide ease of access to components and give the platform the maximum of natural angular inertia. The limitations in manœuvrability are no disadvantage in a ballistic missile or a launcher.

32. *Strapped System.* A feature of engineering is the replacement of mechanical parts by electronics. The platform may be replaced by strapping down all the components to the craft and using electronics to convert the outputs of gyroscopes and accelerometers so that speeds are registered along the correct directions.

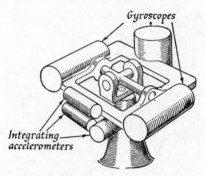

FIG. 113   Ballistic missile platform
(inside-out gimbals)

INERTIAL SLAVING

33. If the 84-minute oscillation is ignored, the overall accuracy of an inertial platform depends on the drift rate of the stabilizing gyroscopes. It may happen that, over a period of time, these drift rates build up until the errors in the inertial measurement of velocity are greater than those of some other form of speed measurement.

34. At sea, measured speed can be recorded to an accuracy of the order of a tenth of a knot. To this measured speed may have to be added a correction for ocean currents, tidal streams and so on. However, over a period of time, measured speed at sea may be more accurate than inertial speed. In the air, measured speed has to be corrected by a large quantity, wind speed, and cannot be expected to be more accurate than inertial speed over the period of a flight. However, airborne doppler is extremely accurate over land, and even over sea the errors are seldom more than a few knots.

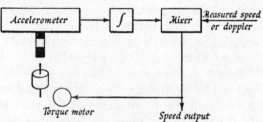

FIG. 114   Slaved inertial platform

35. Marine measured speed or airborne doppler may be used to monitor the inertial platform by means of a circuit similar to that shown in Fig. 114. The monitoring speed and the inertial speed are fed into a mixer which is virtually a summing amplifier. The combined output will be a mixture of the inertial speed and the monitoring speed. Since this mixed signal is used to precess the gyroscope, the platform will be aligned so that the accelerometer output when converted into a speed does not differ from the monitoring speed. The final output will therefore be the monitoring speed smoothed by inertial speed.

INERTIAL DAMPING

36. In high-performance inertial systems, the long-term accuracy may be good but the unwanted oscillations may build up and cause large speed errors. It is, however, possible to use a signal to damp these oscillations. For example, if the output of the accelerometer were mixed with a measure of acceleration obtained by differentiating measured speed or doppler speed, and this acceleration were fed through the integrators to the gyroscopes, any errors in acceleration due to the 84-minute oscillation would be reduced by the absence of a corresponding acceleration appearing in the measured speed or the doppler speed.

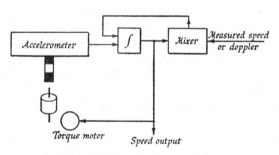

FIG. 115   Damped inertial platform

37. Differentiation introduces noise and, therefore, it will be sufficient to compare inertial speed with marine measured speed or airborne doppler and to feed back the difference to the integrator as shown in Fig. 115. The situation is somewhat different

from that of the slaved system. The main velocity control is by the accelerometer and gravity, and the monitoring velocity will damp the oscillations of the inertial system and will only slave the platform very gradually.

ACCURACY

38. It is evident that, apart from the 84-minute oscillations, the accuracy of an inertial navigation system depends mainly on the gyro drift rate. A drift rate of $0°.1$ to $0°.01$ an hour will mean a speed error of between $6'$ and $0'·6$ an hour. For airborne systems the target accuracy is probably $1'$ an hour. The oscillations can be reduced by doppler damping.

39. For marine applications and, in particular for submarine applications, the target is much higher and security may prevent the final performance being known. It will, however, be safe to assume that at least one order and possibly two orders better than airborne performance will be sought. Once again, oscillations will appear and will need to be damped by measured speed or other means.

ADDITIONAL FACILITIES

40. *Inertial Heading Reference.* The inertial platform measures speed by maintaining a very accurate vertical, the accuracy being between one and two orders better than can be achieved by a non-inertial vertical reference. It follows that, if a high-performance heading reference gyroscope be mounted on an inertial platform, heading may be obtained with an accuracy limited mainly by the drift rate of the gyroscope, $0°.1$ or $0°.01$ an hour (95 per cent).

41. To these errors must be added the error of initial alignment. While an error of $\frac{1}{4}°$ (95 per cent) may not add much to a drift rate of $1°$ an hour, it will be overwhelming in an inertial heading reference. The improvement of initial alignment depends on operational practices, skill of servicing teams and other imponderables. Fortunately, accuracy of gyro compassing also improves with gyro performance, and if the craft can be kept absolutely steady for a fraction of an hour, the heading accuracy may not be many times worse than the random drift rate of the gyroscope measured in degrees an hour.

42. In very accurate inertial navigators, such as may be fitted to naval craft, a form of automatic gyro compassing will occur (page 304, para 18). In less accurate airborne systems, doppler damping may be arranged to assist airborne gyro-compassing but doppler speed errors over the sea will introduce a form of course and speed error (page 179, para 10).

43. *Vertical Speed.* Unlike north–south and east–west accelerations, vertical acceleration is not corrected by gravity. A vertical accelerometer cannot therefore measure vertical speed accurately over a long period. However, over a short period, a vertical accelerometer and integrator will provide a measure of vertical speed that will be of great value in supporting any height-finding device which tends to suffer from lag or is apt to be noisy. In particular, a barometric rate of climb indicator can be designed with an inertial element so that the responses to changes of altitude are faster and more sensitive. Such an instrument is known as an IVSI (instantaneous vertical speed indicat)r).

44. *Vertical Reference.* An inertial platform can provide a vertical reference unaffected by accelerations. The referenc : will be accurate even if the platform has a relatively poor performance provided it be Schüler tuned. It will be even more accurate if monitored by doppler or measured speed. Such a plat;orm will be valuable in very-high-speed craft since either the accelerations will be high or else will be sustained for long periods during climb and descent and in a turn. It will also be valuable in a military aircraft in which continuous high-speed manœuvres would render the normal gravity monitored vertical reference unusable.

4. SUMMARY

MEASURED SPEED

The speed of a craft relative to the medium that supports it may be recorded by:

(a) *Engine revolutions.* In a marine craft, allowance must be made for draught, state of the ship's bottom and rolling.

(b) *Log.* This includes not only the rotating element streamed in the water or attached to the hull but also the electromagnetic log. The air mileage unit is a similar device.

(c) *Pitot pressure.* Allowances must be made for:
  (i) Position and instrument errors in order to convert indicated speed into calibrated or rectified speed.
  (ii) Density of medium, the variation only being serious in the air.
  (iii) Compressibility of medium, which arises in the air at speeds of more than a few hundred knots.

In aircraft, height, air speed and vertical speed may be recorded by an air-data computer, which may also control an autothrottle.

DOPPLER

Doppler can measure the speed of a craft extremely accurately if directional information is also available.

Airborne doppler can record the path of an aircraft in plan and in elevation. Over the sea, corrections have to made for:

(a) State of the sea.
(b) Ocean currents and surface drifts.
(c) Surface winds.

INERTIAL PLATFORM

The key components of an inertial platform are:

(a) *Gyroscopes.* These may be rate or position gyroscopes, the latter being capable of extremely sophisticated development.
(b) *Accelerometers.* Force feed-back or integrating gyro accelerometers will be required.

Accelerometer signals are integrated by electro-mechanical or electronic integrators. The resulting speeds tilt the accelerometers at the rate of 1' an hour for each 1' an hour of speed, and also correct for coriolis.

The effect of gravity is to monitor accelerometer and integrator errors and restore platform tilts with an 84-minute oscillation. Gyro drifts of 1' an hour introduce speed errors of 1' an hour with an 84-minute oscillation superimposed. These oscillations may be damped by measured speed in marine craft or by doppler in aircraft.

There are four types of inertial platform:

(a) Precessed system used in aircraft. Gyros and accelerometers follow the vertical.
(b) Unprecessed system used in marine craft. Gyros are stabilized in space, but accelerometers follow the vertical.
(c) True system used in ballistic missiles. Gyros and accelerometers are stabilized in space.
(d) Strapped system. Gyros and accelerometers fixed to the craft.

An inertial platform can act as short-term speed reference to support doppler. It can also stabilize a sophisticated azimuth gyro that will reduce gyro heading reference errors by more than an order; increased alignment accuracy will be required in consequence.

ACCURACY OF SPEED MEASUREMENT

Fig. 116 shows the level of performance that may be expected from various types of speed measurement. Measured speed is shown as a dotted line because it needs the addition of flow velocity to convert it into a measure of speed over the ground.

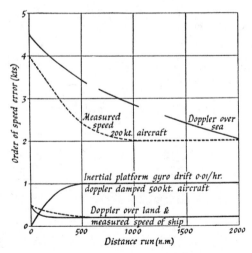

FIG. 116   Speed accuracies

In Fig. 116, doppler speed is shown broken to indicate the possibility of unlocking.

Inertial speed depends on component performance so that no generalization is possible. Also, an undamped system may have low average errors but extremely large momentary errors after a period of time. However, the example indicates the order of performance that may be achieved by a high-grade airborne inertial system with doppler damping. Marine systems will, of course, achieve far higher accuracies.

SPEED REFERENCE

Measured speed and doppler speed will be recorded in knots. Inertial speed will be in minutes of arc an hour, but this will approximate to knots and is shown as knots in Fig. 116.

BIBLIOGRAPHY: INSTRUMENTATION

The basic instrumentation is so much a part of the individual craft that it will be dealt with in any general book on navigating. Accordingly, the books on page 613 may be of use. However, there are certain specialised books and papers which are listed below. It will be noted that the bibliography on doppler will be found separately on page 585, but that there is mention of doppler in many of the papers listed under inertial navigation and at least one of these is specifically concerned with the linking of doppler with inertial navigation.

SERVO MECHANISMS

Braun, L., see Mishkin, E., and L. Braun.

Brown, G. S., and D. P. Campbell, *Principles of servo mechanisms*, Blackwell, Oxford, U.K.

Burdett, G. A. T. (Editor), *Automatic control handbook*, Newnes, London.

Campbell, D. P., see Brown, G. S., and D. P. Campbell.

Conway, H. G. (Editor), *Aircraft hydraulics*, Reinhold Publishing, New York.

Miles, R. B., see Tyers, A., and R. B. Miles.

Mishkin, E., and L. Braun, *Adaptive control systems*, McGraw-Hill, New York.

Porter, A., *Introduction to servo mechanisms*, Wiley, New York.

Savant, C. J., *Basic feedback control systems design*, McGraw-Hill, New York.

Thaler, G. J., *Elements of servo mechanism theory*, McGraw-Hill, New York.

Topopiev, A. (Editor), *Fundamental problems of automatic control*, Blackwell, Oxford, U.K.

Tyers, A., and R. B. Miles, *Principles of servo mechanisms*, Pitman, London.

Van Valkenburgh, Nooger, and Neville Incorporated, *Basic servos and servo mechanisms*, Technical Press, New York and London.

INSTRUMENTS

Barnett, D., see W. A. W. Fox, and D. Barnett.

Burger, W., and A. G. Corbet, *Marine gyro compasses and automatic pilots*, Pergamon Press, London.

Corbet, A. G., see Burger, W., and A. G. Corbet.

Fearnside, K., Instrumental and automatic control for approach and landing, *J. Inst. Navig.*, **12**, 66.

Fearnside, K., Some engineering problems in the design of a multiplex autopilot, *Proc. I.E.E. and R.Ae.S.*, 1962, London.

Fox, W. A. W., and D. Barnett, The vertical reference in aircraft, *J. Inst. Navig.*, **6**, 161.

Majendie, A. M. A., The display and use of navigational intelligence (Presidential Address), *J. Inst. Navig.*, **11, 1.**

Richardson, K. I. T., *The gyroscope applied*, Hutchinson, London.

Savet, P. H. (Editor), *Gyroscopes*, McGraw-Hill, New York.

Williams, C. A., *Aircraft instrument control systems*, Blackwell, Oxford, U.K.

Woodson, W. E., *Human engineering guide for equipment designers*, University of California Press, Los Angeles.

COMPASSES

Admiralty Compass Observatory, *Notes on the correction of magnetic compasses on ships*, H.M.S.O.

Admiralty Compass Observatory, *The theory of the deviation of the magnetic compass*, H.M.S.O.

Brown, C. H., *Deviation and the deviascope*, Brown, Son & Ferguson, Glasgow.

Chapman, S., *The earth's magnetism*, Methuen, London.

Denne, W., *Magnetic compass deviation and correction*, Brown, Son & Ferguson, Glasgow.

Evans, F. J., and A. Smith, *Admiralty manual for the deviation of the compass*, H.M.S.O.

Glenny, A. P., see Green, J. F., and A. P. Glenny.

Grant, G. A., and J. Klinkert, *The ship's compass*, Routledge and Kegan Paul, London.

Green, J. F., and A. P. Glenny, Heading definition in commercial aircraft, *J. Inst. Navig.*, **13**, 196.

Hitchens, H. L., and W. E. May, *From lodestone to gyro compass*, Hutchinson, London.

Klinkert, J., see Grant, G. A., and J. Klinkert.

May, W. E., see Hitchens, H. L., and W. E. May.

Merrifield, F. G., *Ship magnetism and the magnetic compass*, Pergamon Press, London.

O'Hara, W. J., *Mariners gyro navigation manual*, Cornell Maritime Press, Cambridge, U.S.A.

Smith, A., see Evans, F. J., and A. Smith.

INERTIAL NAVIGATION

Adams, D. E., Introduction to inertial navigation, *J. Inst. Navig.*, **9**, 249.

Anderson, E. W., Inertial navigation systems, *J. Inst. Navig.*, **11**, 231.

Collinson, R. P. G., see Stratton, A.

Draper, C., W. Wrigley, and J. Hovorka, *Inertial guidance*, Pergamon Press, London and New York.

Duncan, D. B., Combined doppler radar and inertial navigation systems, *Navigation (U.S.A)*, **6**, 30.

Hovorka, J., see Draper, C.

Parvin, R. H., *Inertial navigation*, Van Nostrand, U.S.A.

Pitman, G. R., Junr., *Inertial guidance*, University of California, Los Angeles.

Stratton, A., R. Whalley, R. P. Collinson, F. J. Sullings, and J. E. D. Williams, The application of inertial navigation systems to civil air transport, *J. Inst. Navig.*, **16**, 265.

Sullings, F. J., see Stratton, A.

Whalley, R., see Stratton, A.

Williams, J. E. D., see Stratton, A.

Wrigley W., see Draper, C.

PART THREE
TECHNIQUES

CHAPTER VII. COURSE. The introduction to the book explained the significance of course. The first half of this chapter deals with choosing a heading to make good a course either to a fixed point, using the triangle of velocities to allow for the flow of water or air, or to another craft, using the triangle of relative velocities to achieve interception. The constant-line course is explained as a special instance of the general problem of interception. In the second half of the chapter, avoidance of collision by changes of course or of speed is described and also the way that rules of the road assist the navigator to estimate the likely actions of the other craft.

CHAPTER VIII. DEAD RECKONING. The chapter opens with the basic finding of D.R. positions by plotting and with the aid of simple analogue computers, and then shows the order of errors to be expected when using these simple techniques. Next, automatic D.R. using doppler or inertial navigation systems is described, together with the characteristics of the errors of positions found by these two types of system. Finally the place of timing in navigation is dealt with briefly, together with its application to fuel management. This chapter shows the difference between basic dead-reckoning systems and dead-reckoning systems which are supported at intervals by position-finding aids.

CHAPTER IX. THE ROUTE. The first section deals with the various projections used for navigational charts with special emphasis on orthomorphy and the correct representation of angles. The connection between the type of projection and the method of steering is also shown. The second section describes the classical calculations of rhumb-line and great-circle distances in minutes of arc and courses. This leads on to the third section which deals with the basic problem of route selection starting with the major problems, avoidance of collision with other craft and with the ground. Planning and preparation before the journey are explained briefly, including the calculation of special points during the journey at which decisions have to be taken. Special tactical routing for search and for air-traffic control purposes concludes the chapter.

CONTENTS

CHAPTER VII

Course

1. VELOCITY

DEFINITIONS

1. Velocity has two elements, direction of motion and speed of motion. Velocity is always measured according to some frame of reference which may be the surface of the Earth, a moving object in space, or the craft itself.

2. The velocity of a craft compared to the surface of the Earth is known as the ground velocity. The speed is known as the ground speed (G.S.) and the direction as the course (Co.). Like heading, course is described by a three-figure number and suffixed T, M or G according to whether it is measured in true, magnetic or grid directions.

3. On level ground, a land vehicle can measure course made good and ground speed directly. The compass measures direction in the azimuth plane but, if the ground is sloping, the speed over the surface may have to be reduced according to the cosine of the slope in order that it may be converted into ground speed.

TRIANGLE OF VELOCITIES

4. A craft can measure its heading and its speed through the water or the air. A ship may make leeway due to the wind or may crab due to the need to apply continual rudder to offset the tendency to weathercock or to fall off. An aircraft may slideslip or crab if bank or rudder has to be applied to offset loss of power from an engine on one side. In such circumstances, the velocity of the craft through the water or the air will be at an angle to the heading.

5. Fig. 117 suggests that the speed of the craft through the water or the air will also be greater than the speed recorded by the the craft, though this will not apply in the instance of the log that

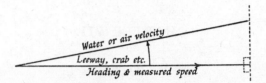

FIG. 117 Effect of leeway, crab or sideslip

is streamed behind the ship. In practice, leeway, crab or sideslip is seldom more than a few degrees except in heavy weather at sea and in a sailing craft. The effect on speed will therefore generally be ignored and the navigator will simply correct for the heading error. Since the correction will only be applied in special circumstances, it is common practice for the navigator to regard heading and measured speed as defining the path of his craft through water or air and leeway or sideslip are treated as if they were corrections to heading.

6. The velocity of the craft through the water or air, when combined with the set (direction) and drift (speed) of the ocean current or tidal stream, or with the wind velocity, will give the ground velocity. The navigator portrays this by the triangle of velocities as shown in Fig. 118. In this figure, the water or air

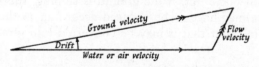

FIG. 118 Triangle of velocities

velocity has been marked with a single-barbed arrow, the ground velocity with a double-barbed arrow and the current, which may be known as the flow velocity, with a triple-barbed arrow.

7. In Fig. 118 the angle between the water or air velocity and the ground velocity has been named 'drift' (dr.). This is the term used in air navigation, but, at sea, 'drift' may mean the speed of the water due to ocean currents or tidal streams. To avoid confusion the term drift angle will be used, unless it is obvious from the context that an angle is being referred to. Drift angle is

measured left or right from the water or air path and suffixed L or R accordingly.

8. Ground velocity may be found by constructing a triangle of velocities on a chart using a nautical mile to represent a knot. The water or air velocity will therefore be represented by the equivalent of an hour's travel through the medium. The flow of the current or the wind for an hour will be added and the total will represent an hour of ground velocity. It is important to remember that the triangle of velocities is a picture of the velocity vectors at a moment of time.

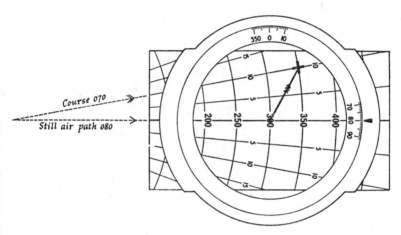

FIG. 119   Graphical computer

9. In aircraft, a graphical computer may be used such as the Dalton computer shown in Fig. 119. It consists of a perspex window on which the wind velocity may be drawn. Behind this window is a template marked with radiating lines that represent courses and arcs of circles that represent speeds. The template can be rotated until it is aligned according to the air velocity, and it can be slid in or out until it registers the true air speed against the centre of the perspex window. In the illustration, an air path of 080 and a true air speed of 300 knots has been set. The wind vector gives a course made good of 070 and a ground speed of 350 knots.

RELATIVE VELOCITY

10. In navigation, the term 'relative' attached to a measurement is taken to mean that the measurement is made as if the craft were stationary and as if direction were measured with respect to its heading. Hence, relative velocity means velocity with respect to the craft.

11. The relative velocity of the water or the air as it flows past the craft is obviously opposite to the water or air velocity of the craft. Fig. 120 shows the flow of water past a marine craft as

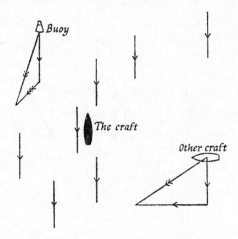

FIG. 120   Relative velocity

she travels due northwards, the flow being represented by a number of arrows all of the same length running southwards. In addition, if the water is moving north-east, a buoy moored to the ground will appear to be forging its way south-westwards through the water. The addition of these two velocities gives the relative velocity of the buoy.

12. The relative velocity of another craft can be found in the same way as the relative velocity of the fixed buoy. Fig. 120 shows another craft travelling westwards through the water. This west-wards velocity is added to the relative velocity of the water to give a south-westerly relative velocity of the other craft. It should be emphasized that the direction of the relative velocity bears no

relationship to the direction of the other craft as seen from the navigator's craft. Relative velocity simply defines the velocity of the other craft as if the navigator's craft were a stationary point in a block of moving water or air.

13. *Relative Wind.* If there is no wind, the smoke trail from a funnel will flow back along the track of the craft. However, if the wind is from the beam, the smoke trail will flow at an angle to the track. Fig. 121 shows the relative wind that causes the smoke

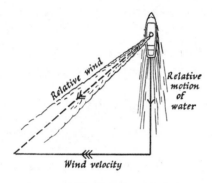

FIG. 121   Relative wind

trail to flow at an angle to the craft. The motion of the water past the ship is drawn, and to this is added the sideways motion of the wind. As a result of the motion of the craft, the relative or apparent wind always blows from a direction closer to the heading than does the true wind. As a consequence, the angle of attack of the sail of a sailing craft is reduced as the craft gathers way.

SETTING COURSE

14. To proceed to a point on the surface of the Earth or to another craft, the navigator may head his craft directly towards the objective if the water or air that supports him is not flowing over the surface of the Earth, or if the other craft is stationary in the water or the air. Thus a ship can head directly towards a buoy if there is no current, and an aircraft can head directly towards a gap in the clouds. In both instances the heading may have to be corrected according to leeway or sideslip.

15. If the water or the air is flowing over the surface of the Earth, by the time that the craft should have arrived at its objective the water or air will have carried it to another position. Similarly if the other craft is moving, by the time that the navigator's craft arrives, the objective will have moved somewhere else. The error may be particularly large in the instance of a course set towards another craft, because the speed of the other craft may be as great as, or greater than, the speed of the navigator's craft. Hence it may be better to consider first the setting of a course towards another moving craft, a problem known as interception.

INTERCEPTION

16. The craft to be intercepted is known generally as the target. In order to intercept, it is necessary to know the direction of the straight line between the target and the craft. This line is known as the line of sight and is correctly a direction fixed in space. In surface navigation, however, the line of sight is generally defined, like a course, in terms of true, magnetic or grid directions.

17. As a first approximation, the craft may head directly towards the target, that is along the line of sight. If the target is moving, the line of sight must be expected to change direction. The heading of the craft must be changed and the rate of this change of heading will be some ratio of the rate at which the direction of the line of sight is changing. This can be expressed by the equation:

FIG. 122   Curve of pursuit

$$\text{heading} = k \times \text{line of sight}$$

where k = the rate at which heading is changing compared to the line of sight.

18. This elementary conception is the basis of interception theory and is known as proportional navigation. If the rate at which the heading changes is less than the rate at which the line of sight changes, the target will drift away and the craft will fail to intercept. If k equals 1, the heading will alter at the same rate as the line of sight. The craft will therefore continue to head towards the target along the changing line of sight. The resulting interception will follow a curved path known as the curve of pursuit, and such a path is shown in Fig. 122.

19. If k is infinitely large, the tendency for the line of sight to drift will be countered before the drift can develop. The line of sight will therefore remain constant and the craft will steer directly towards the target as shown in Fig. 123. Unfortunately, the system will be unstable. It takes time to detect a rate of change of line of sight and still more time to initiate the necessary high rate of turn to offset it. By the time that the effect of this high rate of turn can be detected, the target will have started to drift in the opposite direction, but even faster, and a still higher rate of turn will then be needed, but in the opposite direction. Hence the craft will follow a series of ever-increasing turns unless the value of k is limited. The limitation in the value of k will depend not only on the sensitivity of the line of sight measurement but also on the distance to the target. The closer the target, the lower the value of k that can be tolerated.

FIG. 123   Ideal interception

20. It follows that a craft cannot achieve the ideal interception merely by measuring the direction of the line of sight. However, in the instance of a missile that has to home itself on to a target, line of sight information may be all that is available. Proportional

navigation will have to be used with a moderate value of k. It can be applied to guide the missile in the vertical as well as in the horizontal plane.

CONSTANT LINE OF SIGHT

21. To maintain a target at a constant line of sight, it is necessary to ensure that the velocity of the target relative to the craft is along the line of sight, otherwise the line of sight will drift off to one side. The coincidence of the relative velocity and the line of sight is arranged by constructing the triangle of relative velocities as shown in Fig. 124. The line of sight is drawn so that the

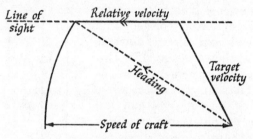

FIG. 124   Triangle of relative velocities

direction of the required relative velocity is established. To a point on the line of sight, the velocity vector of the target is drawn and, centred on the other end of the target velocity vector, an arc is drawn whose length equals the speed of the craft through the water or the air. Where the arc cuts the line of sight will be the third point of the triangle of relative velocities.

22. If the target is continually changing direction and speed, the relative velocity will be continually changing and so will the shape of the triangle of relative velocities. However, it may be possible to choose a mean heading at long range. As the target is approached, it may be necessary to revert to proportional navigation even though the latter can only provide an approximation to the constant line of sight.

23. The triangle of relative velocities can be used to find the course to intercept a moored buoy in a tidal stream, the buoy being regarded as if it were a craft forging its way through the

water as a result of the pull of the mooring chain. However, in practice, such a triangle is drawn relative to the Earth. It will then be known simply as a triangle of velocities.

CONSTANT COURSE

24. The construction of a triangle of velocities is shown in Fig.125. The course is drawn and the water or air velocity vector is added.

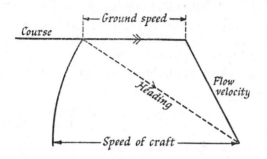

FIG. 125   Triangle of velocities

Centred on the end of this flow vector, an arc is drawn whose radius equals the speed of the craft. Where this arc cuts the course will be the third point of the triangle of velocities. Instead of drawing the triangle, the air navigator commonly uses a computer such as has been illustrated in Fig. 119.

25. If the drift angle can be measured, there will be no need to draw the triangle of velocities. It will be sufficient to add drift angle to course if drift is right and subtract drift angle from course if drift is left. This method is only used in the air since the drift angle is not readily measured at sea. It is particularly useful when the wind is continually changing, but it does not enable the speed of the craft to the destination to be calculated.

26. *Drift measurement.* Drift can be measured in aircraft in three ways:

(a) *Drift sight.* A downward-looking optical device may be provided with grid wires so that it may be aligned with objects on the ground passing below the aircraft. Unfortunately, if the aircraft should roll, the objects will move sideways unless the drift sight is stabilized.

(b) *Doppler-drift*. The use of doppler to measure drift has already been described (page 223, para 10).

(c) *Pressure pattern or Bellamy drift*. If the aircraft is flown at a constant altitude over the sea using the pressure altimeter, and the radio altimeter is used to find by how much the aircraft height has actually increased over a period of time, the principle of the geostrophic wind scale may be used (page 88, para 5) to measure the cross-track wind and hence the drift. In practice, if altitude on the pressure altimeter changes, the change in height may be applied also to the radio altimeter reading, provided it is only a few hundred feet. It can be shown that, in the northern hemisphere:

$$\text{Drift (n.m. left)} = 21.47 \times \text{(increase of height in feet)} / (\text{TAS (knots)} \times \sin (\text{lat.}))$$

For a decrease in radio altimeter height, the drift will be to the right. The directions of drift will be reversed in the southern hemisphere.

TRACK

27. The line along which a craft has travelled is known as its track (Tr.). Although it is important to distinguish between a line, which may be curved, and a direction, navigators often interchange the meaning of the words 'track' and 'course'. Nevertheless, for the purposes of this book, the following definition will be used:

(a) *Past line* will be described as track.

(b) *Future direction* will be described as course.

28. There are evidently two half-way houses between track and course:

(a) *Future line*. This may be described by intended or required track (Tr. Req.). The use of the term course line may obscure the fact that a course is a direction and not a line.

(b) *Past direction*. This may be described by course made good. The use of the terms track angle or track made good (TMG) may obscure the fact that a track is a line rather than a direction.

29. The velocity of a craft may be measured according to the track. Fig. 126 shows two points on the track of a craft. The direction of the straight line from A to B and the distance from A to B divided by the time can be used to find the mean velocity between A and B. There are two main methods:

(a) *True plot.* If a track is drawn with reference to the surface of the Earth, the straight line between two points along it can be used to measure the mean course made good and to find the mean ground speed according to the time interval.

(b) *Relative plot.* If the track is that of a target and is drawn relative to the craft, it is known as a relative track. The direction and length of a straight line between two points on the relative track will give the relative velocity of the target.

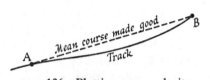

FIG. 126   Plotting mean velocity

30. It is not to be expected that two positions will both be accurate. The velocity AB in Fig. 126 will have an error estimated by adding the errors at A and B according to the golden rule of squares. The rough formula is:

Velocity error (knots) $\simeq 80 \times$ (error in positions (n.m.))
/(interval between positions (mins))

31. Navigation is concerned with finding the way or avoiding collision and not with history. The measurement of a mean velocity over a past period is of no value unless the conditions under which it was measured in the past continue into the future. For example, a measure of velocity of a land craft up a hill will not appertain to the descent at the far side of the hill. A measure of relative velocity of a marine craft will no longer apply if speed is reduced. A measure of ground velocity of an aircraft will be inaccurate if the aircraft flies into a region where the winds are different.

2. COLLISION AVOIDANCE

1. The problem of setting course to arrive at an object generally has a unique solution. On the other hand, the problem of setting course to avoid collision with another craft can have no such unique solution and depends on the subsequent actions of the other craft. Thus, although finding course may be regarded as a matter of simple geometry, the avoidance of collision introduces the complication of co-operation.

2. On land, man is accustomed very early to avoiding collision with static objects. From early childhood, his brain has made allowances for the apparent movement of the world about him as he turns his head and, later on, as he moves about his ways. This allowance is so instinctive that he is able to recognize when an object is moving over the stationary ground, and he learns to recognize when it is on a collision course from its stationary appearance against a background of moving objects.

3. When man sails in a ship in the open seas or flies in an aircraft in the skies, the cabin of his craft becomes his world and it is not easy for him to recognize when another object is on a collision course. If he can see the object and judge its aspect, he may be able to estimate its direction of travel and judge its approximate speed. Even so it may be difficult to decide what action to take.

4. On page 261, paras 30 and 31, the difficulties of accurate measurement of up-to-date velocity were stressed. Unless the navigator measures the relative position of the target over short intervals, he will not know when the target has changed its relative velocity as a result of a change of its heading or its speed. If he measures relative velocity over short intervals, the errors will be magnified.

MISS DISTANCE

5. Collision is avoided when a craft sets a course so that the relative velocity of the target causes it to miss the craft. The miss distance is sometimes known as the closest approach distance and the point at which the target is closest as the closest point of approach (C.P.A.). The time at which the target is closest is known as the time of closest point of approach (T.C.P.A.).

6. On a collision course, the line of sight will remain constant and the closing speed will be equal to the relative velocity of the target. If course is set so that the target will miss the craft, the line of sight will change and so also will the closing speed. The way in which the line of sight drifts and the closing speed changes as the target passes by the craft is identical with the way in which the direction and the rate of closing changes as a craft passes by a stationary object.

7. As the target approaches the closest point of approach, the line of sight deviates further from the direction of the relative velocity until, at the point of closest approach, it is at right angles to the direction of relative velocity. Fig. 127 also shows

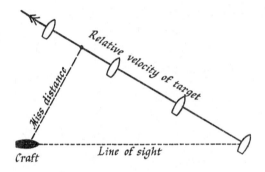

FIG. 127   Target not on collision course

that, at the point of closest approach, the craft must not be assumed to be abeam of the target but only at right angles to the relative velocity. The figure also shows that the target distance decreases until the closest point of approach is reached and thereafter increases.

8. The three graphs in Fig. 128 show the ways in which the direction of the line of sight, the distance between the target and the craft, and the closing speed will change with time and with distance as the target passes by. The units of time have been chosen not as minutes but as multiples of the time that the target, travelling at its relative speed, would take to cover the miss distance. The same units can therefore be regarded as units of distance measured in multiples of the miss distance.

9. The three graphs of Fig. 128 show the following relationships:

(a) The way in which the direction of the line of sight shifts as compared to the direction of relative velocity.

(b) The way in which the distance of the target from the craft changes. The curve is an hyperbola.

(c) The way that closing speed changes. The closing speed is illustrated not in knots but in decimals of the relative speed.

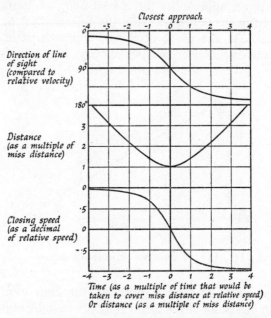

FIG. 128 Changes of line of sight, distance and closing speed

10. It is impossible to use change of direction of line of sight to measure miss distance. The change of line of sight of a target with a relative velocity of 30 knots and a miss distance of 3 miles will be indentical with the change of line of sight of a target with a relative velocity of 10 knots and a miss distance of 1 mile. Nor is it easy to make use of distance or closing speed. Three separate observations spread over a considerable period of time will be necessary in order to define which part of the relevant curve is

being examined and, in any event, when the target is much more than twice the miss distance away, the curves approximate closely to straight lines.

11. Miss distance can be measured in practice by at least two measurements of the position of the target relative to the craft. By joining these two positions by a straight line and producing it, the miss distance may readily be estimated. By measuring the distance and the time interval between the two positions, relative speed may be calculated, and by measuring the distance from the second position to the closest point of approach and dividing by the relative speed, the time of the closest point of approach may be calculated. The process evidently demands some form of plotting unless a computer is available.

12. The next problem will be to decide the action that ought to be taken. It is essential that whatever the action taken by one craft, it shall not be negatived by an action of the other craft. Otherwise both craft may collide as a result of, rather than from a lack of, avoiding action, a process known as the 'dance of death'.

RULES OF THE ROAD

13. Rules of the road have been introduced in various forms on the highways of the countries of the world. An International Convention on the Safety of Life at Sea provides International Regulations for Preventing Collisions at Sea, known as the Collision Regulations. Aircraft are similarly bound by International Rules of the Air. Rules enable each craft to know what the other craft is likely to do. Hence rules generally aim at giving one craft or the other the responsibility for taking avoiding action and enjoin the other to maintain a steady course and speed (Rule 21, Collision Regulations).

14. A major exception is the action to be taken when two craft meet head on. The rule is that both craft shall turn to the right (Rule 18, Collision Regulations), except on the highways of certain countries where the rule of keep to the left still obtains.

15. It is only natural that a craft overtaking another shall keep out of the way (Rule 24, Collision Regulations). The definition of overtaking is that the craft shall be approaching the other from more than $22\frac{1}{2}°$ (two points of the compass) abaft the beam at sea or more than $20°$ abaft the beam in the air. When a crossing

situation arises, the decision as to which craft should give way is more arbitrary. On the roads in certain countries, the vehicle that has the other vehicle on the driver's side keeps out of the way. At sea, the ship that has the other on his starboard side keeps out of the way (Rule 19, Collision Regulations).

16. It may be impossible to decide when a target is meeting and when crossing, and it is not easy to decide when it is crossing and when overtaking. As a result, all rules accept that the craft that should normally maintain course and speed may have to take avoiding action *in extremis* (Rules 21 and 27, Collision Regulations). Unfortunately, this makes it even more difficult for a navigator to be certain what the target is likely to do in the event of a collision becoming imminent.

17. At close quarters, some form of signalling between craft is generally possible. Marine craft use sound signals to indicate what action is being taken. At sea, one short blast signals that the craft is turning to starboard, two short blasts that it is turning to port and three short blasts that it is going astern (Rule 28, Collision Regulations). Also, in poor visibility, a vessel may sound a fog-warning signal such as a horn, siren or whistle.

18. Rules of the road are continually undergoing scrutiny and occasionally are revised. However, there is no real solution to the dilemma of regulations. Unless simple, they cannot be applied under conditions of stress. If simple, they cannot be precise and must be subject to interpretation.

19. Except for a head-on meeting the rules direct which craft should take action but not what the action should be. However, certain principles may be mentioned. For example, it is inadvisable to cross the bows of another craft (Rule 22, Collision Regulations), and keeping clear may include not only altering course but also reducing speed, stopping or even reversing (Rule 23, Collision Regulations).

20. In addition, special rules apply to sailing craft. A powered craft has to keep out of the way of a sailing craft (Rule 20, Collision Regulations), unless he runs into danger by so doing. A sailing craft with the wind aft has to give way to a sailing craft with the wind ahead and the sail at its minimum angle of attack (close hauled). If two close-hauled craft meet, the rule that the craft that has the other on its starboard shall give way naturally

applies, this rule being expressed in the words: 'port tack (wind from port side) gives way to starboard tack'.

AVOIDING ACTION

21. If a navigator has discovered that there is a danger of collision and that his craft is responsible for taking action, the next step will be to decide what action should be taken. It has already been shown in paras 17–19 of the previous section of this chapter that collision will occur if heading $= k \times$ (line of sight), where k is not less than 1. If k is negative so that the craft turns in a direction opposite to that in which the line of sight is drifting, the miss distance will be increased.

22. The formula applies to a craft that is intercepting a target ahead. If the target is astern, the opposite rule will apply. For example, if a craft is overtaking to starboard, the direction of the line of sight will be decreasing from 180 towards 090 and drifting anticlockwise. A turn in the opposite direction, that is clockwise or to starboard, will inevitably increase the risk of collision.

23. Generally, to avoid collision, k must be negative and must vary according to the cosine of the direction of the line of sight compared to the heading of the craft. This allows for the fact that where the target is astern, heading should be altered in the same direction as the change of the line of sight instead of in the opposite direction, and when the target is abeam, no change of heading will be effective. The advantage of a turn away is, of course, that it reduces the closing speed and gives more time for subsequent action.

24. Since alteration of heading will not alter the line of sight while the target is abeam, it may be better to alter speed. A reduction of speed will cause a target on either beam to appear to accelerate forwards and an increase of speed, if such is possible, will cause a target on either beam to appear to decelerate so that the line of sight will travel aft. However, just as alteration of heading will be ineffective initially when the line of sight is on the beam, so an alteration of speed will be ineffective initially if the line of sight is ahead or astern though it can reduce the severity of the collision.

25. If the line of sight is drifting, the theoretical rules for accelerating the drift are now evident:

(a) For a clockwise drift:

    (i) Target ahead, alter course to port.
    (ii) Target on starboard beam, accelerate if possible.
    (iii) Target astern, alter course to starboard.
    (iv) Target on port beam, slow down.

(b) For an anticlockwise drift:

    (i) Target ahead, alter course to starboard.
    (ii) Target on starboard beam, slow down.
    (iii) Target astern, alter course to port.
    (iv) Target on port beam, accelerate if possible.

26. If the target is on a collision course, the rules of the road suggest the following actions:

    (i) Target ahead, alter course to starboard.
    (ii) Target on starboard beam, slow down. Acceleration is often impracticable.
    (iii) Target astern, maintain course and speed.
    (iv) Target on port beam, maintain course and speed.

A comparison with para 25 now suggests that on a collision course the action taken will generally be such as to cause the line of sight to rotate anticlockwise. This rotation will also appear anticlockwise when viewed from the target.

27. If two craft are on a collision course and one alters heading or speed, it is not possible to arrive at the miss distance simply by multiplying this change in velocity by the time interval before collision would have occurred. The effective velocity as far as the miss distance is concerned is less than the change of velocity. Thus:

(a) For a change of heading, effective change of velocity$\simeq$ (heading change°/60) × speed (knots) × cos (angle between line of sight and heading).

(b) For a change of speed, effective change of velocity$\simeq$ speed change (knots) × sin (angle between line of sight and heading).

28. The formulae act as a reminder of the uselessness of small alterations of heading or speed. For example, an alteration of heading of 10°, even for a target dead ahead, can only cause an effective change of velocity of 3 knots in the instance of a ship travelling at 18 knots. To measure the relative velocity of a target within 3 knots by observations taken every 4 minutes means an accuracy of measurement of position and of plotting about 300 yards (see page 261, para 30). Hence the change of heading of 10° could in fact change a near miss into a collision and, in any event, its effect could hardly be distinguished on the plot.

CLOSE-QUARTER SITUATION

29. At close quarters, four elements operate to the disadvantage of the navigator:

(a) *Time.* Less time will be available to assess the situation and decisions may have to be made under pressure. If the craft is travelling slowly, there will generally be more time but low speed may reduce manœuvrability.

(b) *Manœuvre lag.* A craft, particularly a large ship, may take an appreciable time to initiate a manœuvre. Indeed, a large ship may not be able to take any action to avoid a collision that is only 2 or 3 minutes away in time.

(c) *Size of craft.* As the distance between the craft decreases, so the demand for manœuvre increases since the size of the craft becomes a factor in the change of velocity necessary to avoid collision.

(d) *Trailing steering.* If a craft is fitted with trailing steering, any turn away from danger will be preceded by a swinging of the stern towards danger.

30. To show the problem in big ships, suppose that collision will occur in 4 minutes. Allowing for time to start the turn, the effect will be as if heading had been altered immediately by about 10°. Para 28 showed that this alteration will be ineffective if based on observations every 4 minutes.

31. It is now apparent that if two large marine craft find themselves on a collision course while separated by only a few minutes of time before collision occurs, then collision can only be

avoided by a mixture of luck and judgment, unless one or other of the craft has exceptional powers of manœuvre. Hence it is not surprising that experienced seamen insist that a close-quarter situation must not be allowed to develop. With early and bold action, the other craft will have time to assess the results of that action and to take additional action if necessary.

MULTIPLE TARGETS

32. The avoidance of a single target may demand careful and continuous plotting in order to ensure that the miss distance is maintained at a safe value. However, when there are a number of targets, the problem becomes extremely complicated. A decision to alter heading or speed to avoid one craft has to take into consideration the possibilities of increasing the dangers of collision with other craft. Perhaps the one safe action is to reduce speed if this is practicable.

33. There are two main plotting systems used in collision avoidance:

(a) Relative plot in which all the targets are plotted relative to the craft.

(b) True plot in which the water is presumed to be stationary.

In addition, E. S. Calvert has proposed a hybrid plot in which the relative plot is based on a 'ghost' craft maintaining the original course and speed of the craft.

34. *Relative Plot.* Fig. 129(a) shows a craft surrounded by four targets of which two are diverging, one is beginning to fall astern, and one, which is ahead and to starboard, is on a collision course. It is assumed that, in order to avoid this target, the navigator decides to alter heading by 45° to the right so as to pass under the stern of the threatening target. The effects of this alteration of heading on the various targets, assuming that all targets maintain their original courses and speeds, are shown in Fig. 129(b). It is doubtful whether the navigator could have visualized with certainty that his action would have placed two other targets on collision courses, and to discover this by plotting would involve finding the velocities of each target relative to the water and then the velocities of each target relative to the craft on its new heading.

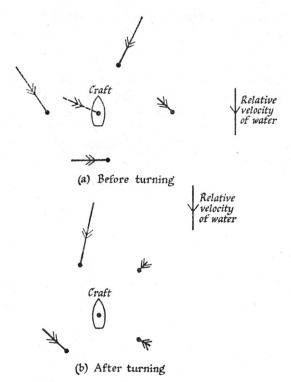

(a) Before turning

(b) After turning

FIG. 129   Effects of alteration of heading, shown
on a plot of relative velocity

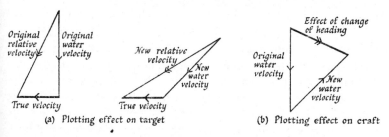

(a) Plotting effect on target

(b) Plotting effect on craft

FIG. 130   Plotting the effects of an alteration of heading

Fig. 130(a) shows the plotting of one target. If four targets are
involved, it may be necessary to construct no less than eight
triangles of relative velocity.

35. Fortunately, it is possible to plot the change of velocity of each target. The original water velocity is plotted and the velocity through the water resulting from the change of heading is applied as shown in Fig. 130(b). The third side of this triangle will be the change of velocity resulting from the change of heading. If this change of velocity be applied to each of the four target relative velocities, but in the opposite direction, the relative velocities of Fig. 129(b) can be plotted with only five triangles.

36. *True plot.* Plotting in true velocities involves no triangles and is shown in Fig. 131. The dotted line shows the new velocity of

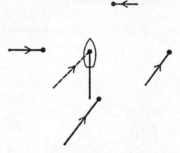

FIG. 131　　True velocity plot

the craft. It is not difficult to visualize from this plot that the two targets that were diverging are now converging. It is, however, less easy to ascertain by how much a target will miss the craft whereas the relative plot shows the miss distance directly and simply.

37. *Calvert Plot.* In the Calvert plot, the vector effect of a change of heading is found as in Fig. 130(b), but this effect can be applied directly to the relative plot as shown by the dotted arrow in Fig. 129(a). The plot shows the danger into which the alteration of heading is leading the craft, and does not alter the velocity vectors of the various targets. Nevertheless, unless the craft can return fairly soon to the original course and speed, subsequent actions may become relatively complicated.

SPECIFIC AVOIDANCE PROBLEMS

38. *Land Craft.* Vehicles that operate across country in remote areas have no real collision problems. However, on roads the

danger of collision is paramount. Yet road traffic is never more than two way, except at junctions, and in many instances it is only one way. The driver of a vehicle is in the element to which he is accustomed, with ample reference marks all around him and with leading steering invariably fitted to his vehicle. Nevertheless collisions continually occur.

39. *Marine Craft.* At sea there may be an absence of reference marks and the target will often be travelling in a direction not easily determined. Errors arise in the estimate of the miss distance and in the estimate of responsibility for giving way, so that a close-quarter situation may develop in which the avoidance of collisions becomes a matter of good fortune as well as good judgment. The problem is not easy when there is only one target, and collisions have occurred in clear weather in the open sea between two large, well-manned ships. The problem is immensely complicated when there are many targets.

40. It follows that when traffic reaches a certain density, it is necessary to limit the possible situations that each craft will have to tackle. This can be arranged by the use of 'one-way streets' in which the only possible situation is overtaking. This, however, is a strategic rather than a tactical solution and will be dealt with in Chapter VIII under the heading of Routing (page 339, para 5).

41. It is possible to devise a computer (see page 32, para 26) that can calculate answers to successive questions according to observations taken of an individual target. If the direction and distance of a target can be measured at intervals, the computer can calculate answers to the following questions:

(a) Is the miss distance too low? If the answer is no, the computer may turn its attention to another target. If the answer is yes, the computer may display an alarm signal or continue to the next question.

(b) Are the two craft meeting? If the answer is yes, the computer can feed a demand into the autohelmsman to turn right. If the answer is no, the computer may proceed to the next question.

(c) Is the target overtaking? If the answer is yes, the computer may turn its attention to another target. If the answer is no, the computer may proceed to the next question.

19—P.N.

(d) Is the craft overtaking? If the answer is yes, the computer has to programme an action according to the situation, turning to the right if in doubt or slowing down. If the answer is no, the computer may proceed to the next question.

(e) Is the other craft to port? If the answer is yes, the computer may turn its attention to another target. If the answer is no, the computer has to programme an action according to the situation, turning to the right or slowing down.

42. A computer is able to ask all these questions, answer them accurately and initiate the consequent actions so quickly that it will appear to be handling a number of targets simultaneously. Nevertheless, it will still not be competent to avoid collision unless it can be programmed to take the correct action whenever the target fails to follow the expected procedures. It will surely be necessary to provide a human monitor.

43. *Aircraft*. An aircraft is generally an order smaller than a marine craft in all dimensions so that the area of an air target is generally about two orders less than the area of a marine target. The speed of an aircraft, on the other hand, may be between one and two orders greater than the speed of a marine craft. The aircraft has to avoid collisions from craft not only flying at its own level but also from craft climbing or diving, and it is not easy for an aircraft to be certain of the height at which another aircraft is flying.

44. Higher speeds, smaller targets and possibilities of collision in three dimensions make the avoidance of air collision by last-minute manœuvres extremely difficult. On the other hand, the fact that an aircraft is a small target operating in three dimensions reduces the chances of a collision to a relatively low value. However, when a collision does occur, it is invariably disastrous. Hence collision avoidance is of sufficient significance for the formation of a complete organization, air-traffic control, which would hardly exist but for the dangers of collision not only en-route but more particularly in the congested terminal areas.

45. *Air-Traffic Control*. As a result of the extreme difficulty in tactical avoidance in the air, air-traffic control (ATC) operates on the principle of avoiding collision by ensuring that sufficient

separation is maintained between aircraft. This strategic solution will be considered further in the chapter that deals with routing (page 339, para 6 and page 351, para 7).

3. SUMMARY

DEFINITIONS

Track means *past line* along which the craft has travelled.
Track intended or required may denote *future line.*
Course means *future direction* in which the craft will travel.
Course made good may denote *past direction.*

VELOCITIES

The triangle of velocities combines velocities relative to the surface of the Earth which are sometimes known as ground velocities. The triangle is used to measure:

(a) Course made good from past measured speed and flow velocity.
(b) Course from intended water and air speed and predicted flow velocity.

In both instances, the measured speed through water or air may have to be corrected to allow for leeway or sideslip.

The triangle of relative velocities combines velocities relative to the craft as if the craft were stationary and as if its heading provided the reference of direction.

INTERCEPTION

Proportional navigation is based on the connection:

$$\text{heading} = k \times \text{line of sight}$$

where:

k is less than 1, interception cannot occur;
$k = 1$, interception will be along curve of pursuit;
$k = $ infinity, interception will be along the shortest path and the line of sight will remain constant in direction. In practice, if k is large, the system tends to become unstable.

COLLISION AVOIDANCE

Miss distance can be found by a relative plot. Changes of line of sight direction, of distance to target, or of closing speed, are generally inaccurate for forecasting miss distance at long range.

Rules of the road are aimed primarily at ensuring that a craft will know what a target is likely to do. At close quarters, signals may be used to advise the target of the craft's intentions.

Avoiding action is aimed at increasing the miss distance. An early and substantial change of heading is readily recognized by the target, and this assists in avoiding misunderstandings.

At close quarters, avoidance of collision is extremely difficult owing to reduced time, slowness of manœuvres and the increased effect of the physical size of the craft. Hence the object must be to prevent a close-quarter situation from developing.

MULTIPLE TARGETS

Multiple targets increase the difficulties of collision avoidance so greatly that, where traffic reaches a certain density, it is necessary either to reduce speed so as to increase the time available to avoid collision or to resort to strategic rather than tactical collision avoidance.

Collision avoidance is assisted by the choice of routes so that the craft will be travelling generally in the same direction as adjacent traffic.

MARINE AND AIR SOLUTIONS

Marine craft move relatively slowly and are generally large targets. As a rule, collision avoidance can be based mainly on tactical action by the individual vessel.

The speed of aircraft is probably more than an order greater than the speed of a marine craft, and as targets their areas are probably two orders smaller. Hence collision avoidance is based on strategic planning by air-traffic control organizations which arrange safe separation between aircraft.

CHAPTER VIII

Dead Reckoning

Dead Reckoning (D.R.) is the business of finding positions according to the progress of the craft from a known starting point. There are three main types of dead reckoning:

(a) *D.R.* of the classical type in which a compass and a measurement of speed are used, allowance being made for the flow of the water or the air or for the slope of the ground in the instance of land craft. A navigator may use a simple computer to assist him.

(b) *Airborne doppler* with a gyro-magnetic or directional gyro heading reference and generally with a computer to calculate positions.

(c) *Inertial navigation* using a platform and a computer.

1. D.R. POSITIONS

PLAIN SAILING

1. The simple basic process of dead reckoning is known as plain (or plane) sailing. The navigator estimates position by drawing a line from the last known position in the direction of his course made good and stepping off a distance according to the distance run. The distance run is obtained by multiplying the time interval by the ground speed.

2. On a chart, the known position may have a circle drawn around it with the time written alongside in four figures, two for the hours and two for the minutes, using a 24-hour clock. The course made good may be marked with a double-barbed arrow and the consequent dead-reckoning with a square and the time alongside. Fig. 132 shows these symbols plotted on a chart.

3. Dead reckoning is essential when it takes time for the navigator to establish his position from observations. For example, in Fig. 132 the navigator might take 3 or 4 minutes to plot his position. He would therefore work out a D.R. position for a time 6 minutes after the found position, 6 minutes being convenient because the distance run in n. miles will be the ground speed in tens of knots. The navigator can then measure the amount of alteration of course necessary on arrival at the D.R. position in order to reach his destination. The process is known as 'advancing' a position.

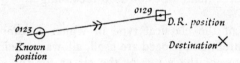

FIG. 132   Advancing a position

4. The maintenance of a dead-reckoning plot of position is of prime importance for two reasons:

(a) If positions can be found at intervals, the comparison of the found position with the dead-reckoning position for the same time will provide an invaluable check of the accuracy of the navigation.

(b) If positions cannot be found, dead reckoning will enable the track of the craft to be estimated so that danger may be avoided until positive information of position is available.

5. When a craft is fitted with navigation aids that give continuous information of position, the dead-reckoning plot may appear unnecessary. In particular, if continuous fixing of position is available, it will not be necessary to advance a position. Nevertheless, the prudent navigator will generally maintain some form of plot, even if only a mental estimate, as a check on his navigation.

TRIANGLE OF VELOCITIES POSITIONS

6. In the instance of a marine craft or an aircraft, the course made good and the ground speed may be found by means of the triangle of velocities and position may then be plotted in the usual way.

However, if the craft changes heading during the period of dead reckoning, it may be easier to plot the path of the craft in still water or air and to add the current or wind effect afterwards.

7. Fig. 133 shows a typical 'water' or 'air' plot. The position of the craft is estimated as if there were no current or no wind and

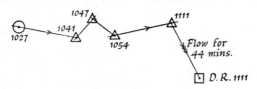

FIG. 133   Water or air plot

the subsequent positions are, at least in air navigation, generally marked with a triangle. When a D.R. position is needed, the water or air position is found by adding the current or wind effect for the whole of the dead-reckoning period.

8. On occasions, the flow vector may change during the period of dead reckoning. This is particularly common during climb or descent in air operations. It will be possible to plot a series of vectors of the various flows, each vector being of a length proportional to the time spent in that flow. The total flow may then be calculated from the total vector as shown in Fig. 134. Note that the total flow speed is *less* than the mean of the individual flow speeds because they tend partly to counteract each other.

9. In Fig. 133 alterations of heading were drawn as if there were a sudden change in direction and this is normal navigational

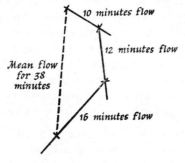

FIG. 134   Vectoring flow velocities

practice. A craft will actually turn along a complex path which will approximate to an arc of a circle once the turn has been established. It will be easier to plot a turn as an abrupt change of course, but it may be necessary to allow for the time saved by cutting the corner. It will also be necessary to start the turn before the dead-reckoning time. A typical table will be:

TABLE IX. ALLOWANCES FOR TURNING

Change of course	15°/min (rate $\frac{1}{12}$) turn	
	Time saved by turn (minutes)	Time to start turn (minutes early)
30°	small	1
60	$\frac{1}{2}$	2
90	$1\frac{1}{2}$	4
120	5	$6\frac{1}{2}$

10. For faster rates of turn, the figures have to be decreased thus:

for a rate 1 turn (180° per minute), divide figures by 12.
for a rate $\frac{1}{2}$ turn (90° per minute), divide figures by 6.

Also, for a large ship add between 1 and 3 minutes to allow for the time taken to initiate a turn. For an aircraft, only a few seconds need be added to initiate a turn.

MEASUREMENT OF FLOW VELOCITY

11. In order to estimate the position of a ship or an aircraft by dead reckoning, a knowledge of the flow velocity of the water or of the air is needed. This knowledge is also needed in order that a course may be set to a destination. In section 3 of Chapter II, the forecasting of flow velocities was described. The navigator may be able to modify these forecasts so that they agree more closely with the actual flow velocities experienced by the craft. Flow velocities can be found by the navigator by two main methods:

(a) Extrapolation from past 'fixes' or found positions.
(b) Measurement of elements of triangle of velocities on the spot and subsequent extrapolation into the future.

12. 'Flow velocity' can be found from fixes over an interval of time using one of three techniques:

   (a) *Course and ground speed.* The course made good between two fixes may be measured and the ground speed calculated according to the distance between the fixes and the time interval. 'Flow velocity' can be found by drawing the triangle of velocities as illustrated in Fig. 135(a). In the air, a graphical computer may be used of the type illustrated in Fig. 119 on page 253.

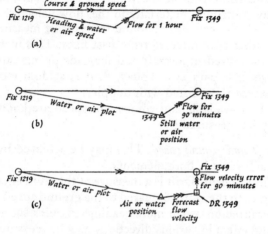

F I G. 135   Flow velocity from fixes

   (b) *Water or air plot.* Position is reckoned from the first fix as if there were no 'flow velocity' as shown in Fig. 135(b). The difference between the still water or air position and the second fix will be the 'flow velocity' vector for the period between the fixes. This method will be convenient if there have been a number of alterations of heading or speed between the two fixes, or if there is an automatic plot of the water or air position available.

   (c) *D.R. position and fix.* The D.R. position according to the forecast currents or winds may be plotted for the period of the second fix. The 'flow velocity' error can then be found a shown in Fig. 135(c). This compares the forecast position to the fix and acts as a check on the validity of the fix itself. The method is cumbersome if there are alterations of heading or speed between the two fixes which have to be converted into tracks and ground speeds before being plotted.

13. In the previous paragraph, the words 'flow velocity' have been placed in inverted commas. This will serve as a reminder that when 'flow velocity' is measured between fixes, it will be an amalgam of the true flow velocity, the heading errors, leeway or sideslip and the errors in the water or air speed. All of these errors may contribute materially to the 'flow velocity'.

14. Flow velocity can also be found from direct measurement on the spot rather than inferred from past fixes. This method is, in practice, only used in aircraft and depends on measurement of drift (page 259, para 26). Today, drift is seldom measured in aircraft except those fitted with doppler.

15. If drift is available and course and speed are known, a spot wind may be measured by:

(a) *Drift and ground speed.* This may be achieved by doppler, which records both elements.

(b) *Multiple drift.* Drift is a measure of the wind effect at right angles to the craft compared to the ground speed. If drift is measured on two or more headings in quick succession, the wind effect in various directions may be measured and the total wind velocity found.

(c) *Drift and wind direction.* Wind direction may be inferred by cloud shadows, by smoke or by wind lanes, long streaks on the water, when flying low. If the wind direction is at a large angle to the heading, by combining with drift it is possible to measure the wind velocity approximately.

16. It is worth noting that, in the instance of a spot wind found by drift, the heading error will only lead to a corresponding error in the direction of the wind. Thus a heading error of 2° will lead to an error of only 1 knot in the measurement of a 30-knot wind. In the instance of a wind found from fixes, a heading error of 2° in a 300-knot aircraft will lead to a 10-knot wind error.

17. *Fix Monitored Azimuth.* The measurement of drift makes it

possible to find the wind effect at right angles to heading, and thus the future course line of the craft may be plotted. If this course line does not agree with the actual track of the aircraft as found by fixes, it follows that, provided that the fixes and the drift measurement are not in error, the heading must be wrong. Hence drift and fixes may be used to check heading. A similar system may be used during the take-off run of an aircraft along a runway of known direction as a means of aligning the heading of an inertial navigation system.

AUTOMATIC PLOTTING

18. It has been shown that, when a craft is continually turning, it is difficult to plot its path. In addition, allowances for the cutting of corners have to be made. As a result of these difficulties, automatic plotting devices have been introduced in craft that are continually changing course.

19. Automatic plotters generally work on the principle shown in Fig. 136. One cross-pointer is driven at a speed according to the

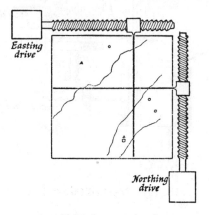

FIG. 136   Automatic plotter

speed of the craft in a north–south direction, known as northing. The other cross-pointer is driven at a speed according to the speed of the craft in an east-west direction, known as easting. Such a device may be fitted with a pen to record the track of the craft and may be known as a plotting table. Alternatively the map may be moved below a fixed pen, or a large area of country can be filmed and projected on to a screen and so moved that the position of the craft is always shown by the centre of the moving map display.

20. In order to record the progress of the craft in northing and easting, course made good and ground speed have to be converted thus:

Northing = ground speed × cos (course)
Easting = ground speed × sin (course)

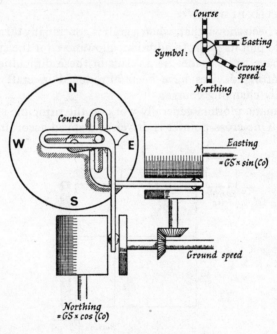

FIG. 137   Mechanical resolver

If the course is more that 090T but less than 270T, cos (course) will be negative and northing will be recorded in a southerly direction and may be called southing. If the course is more than 180T but less than 360T, sin (course) will be negative and easting will be recorded in a westerly direction and may be called westing.

21. *Resolvers.* To multiply by sines and cosines a resolver is used. Fig. 137 illustrates a simple mechanical resolver. The pointer

on the compass repeater has a pin that works in the grooves of two arms. The pointer is aligned to the course made good, which in the illustration is 080, and the pin positions the two arms. Each arm holds a ball which transmits rotation from a circular plate to a roller. Each circular plate is driven at a rate proportional to the ground speed of the craft.

22. The mechanical resolver acts as a multiplier. According to the distance that the ball is positioned away from the centre of the plate, so the rate at which the roller will rotate is increased. In the figure, the northing roller will hardly rotate at all, which is to be expected since the course is nearly due east. The easting roller, on the other hand, will rotate at almost the same speed as the plate.

23. In place of the mechanical multipliers, the arms may be made to operate electrical multipliers in the form of sliders that move along resistance wires. The inputs to these resistance wires will be electrical signals proportional to the ground speed. The outputs will be electrical signals proportional to sine and cosine. Such a device is known as a sin-cos potential divider or a sin-cos pot.

CALCULATION OF POSITION

24. The navigator may wish to calculate position rather than to plot. By multiplying the distance run by cos (course), the distance travelled in a northerly direction can be found. If the course is between 090T and 270T, cos (course) will be negative and the distance will, therefore, be southward. Similarly, by multiplying the distance run by sin (course), the distance travelled in an easterly direction can be found. If the course is between 180T and 360T, sin (course) will be negative and the distance will, therefore, be westward.

25. In a north–south direction, a nautical mile is approximately a minute of latitude. In an east–west direction a nautical mile is similarly a minute of departure (dep.). Instead of multiplying distance run by cos (course) and sin (course) the navigator may enter a traverse table with distance and course and extract difference of latitude and departure.

26. The next step will be to convert departure into difference of longitude. On the equator, a minute of departure will equal a minute of longitude but further north or south, a minute of

departure will equal more than a minute of longitude owing to the increasing reduction in the circumference of a parallel of latitude.

Fig. 138 shows that:

(Circumference of equator)/(circumference at lat. A)
$$= EQ/LA = EA/LA = \sec \theta = \sec (\text{lat. A})$$

Hence

(1′ of departure)/(1′ of longitude at lat. A) = sec (lat. A)

∴ (1′ of departure) = (1′ of longitude) × sec (lat.)

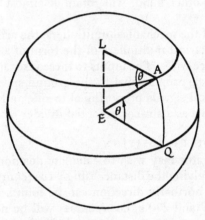

FIG. 138 Departure and longitude

To convert departure into change of longitude it is therefore necessary to multiply by sec (latitude) and this may be arranged by special tables in which the entries are departure and middle latitude, that is, the latitude half-way between the start and the finish of the distance run.

27. The process of calculating position from course made good and distance run may therefore be summarized as follows:

(a) Convert course and distance into change of latitude and departure.

(b) Change of latitude is added to starting latitude to find actual latitude.

(c) Convert departure into difference of longitude using secant of the latitude half-way between starting and actual latitudes.

(d) Difference of longitude is added to starting longitude to find actual longitude.

D.R. COMPUTER

28. It is possible to produce a computer that will automatically display D.R. positions in the form of latitude and longitude on counters. The first step is to convert course and ground speed into northing and easting by means of a resolver. The second step is to add the change of latitude to the starting latitude. This may be arranged by means of an adding device as shown in Fig. 139. The device is similar to the differential used in the back

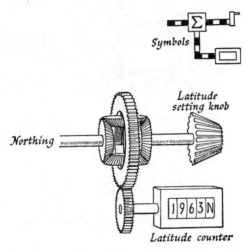

FIG. 139   Mechanical adder (or subtracter)

axle of a motor vehicle and, by reversing one of the input drives, can be made to subtract instead of to add. Adding and subtracting can also be achieved electrically by special adding circuits or by feeding two signals into a common summing amplifier.

29. The next stage will be to multiply easting by secant latitude. This is arranged by a secant gear which may be a resolver

as already described (page 284, para 21) but with the inputs reversed. Thus, in Fig. 137, if the arm is controlled in terms of latitude instead of course, and easting is fed into the lower roller, rate of change of longitude will emerge on the lower of the two plates. Indeed, Fig. 137 illustrates a secant gear multiplying by sec 80°. It will be noted that multiplying by sec 80° means gearing up by a ratio of about 6 to 1, at which point a mechanical resolver will generally start to slip. Similarly, at 80° a secant potential divider begins to become very sensitive to slight changes of angle and will be noisy. Fortunately, above 80° of latitude, latitude and longitude will generally be discarded in favour of a grid system.

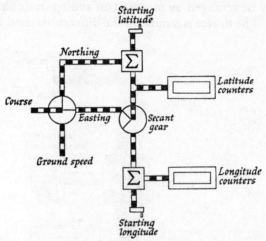

FIG. 140   Mechanical D.R. computer

30. The change of longitude can be added to the starting longitude and the resulting output will be actual longitude. There will of course be no need to multiply departure by middle latitude because, although in a calculation one value of sec (lat.) has to be used, in an automatic computer the value of sec (lat.) is continually adjusted as the craft moves north or south.

31. Fig. 140 shows the complete D.R. computer in a mechanical form. It is worth noting that, although counters can be designed quite simply to register distance gone, counters that register

latitude and longitude have to have their movements reversed on passing latitude 0000 or longitude 0000. One simple solution is to use two separate sets of counters, one for east and one for west, and one for north and one for south, blanking off the counters not being used. It is also worth noting that counters registering course have to be specially made to jump from 359 back to 000.

32. Inputs of course and ground speed may not be available. The simple computer may have to use heading and measured speed and therefore will maintain a water or air plot. In the air such a device is known as an air position indicator (API). To the plot, current or wind vectors may be added when a D.R. position is required. Unfortunately, in high latitudes, a long water or air plot can lead to a dead-reckoning longitude error. Fig. 141 shows the same position plotted twice in a high northerly

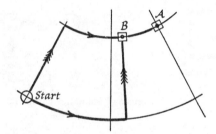

FIG. 141   Water or air plot in high latitudes

latitude, A with the flow vector plotted before the water or air plot and B with the flow vector plotted on the end of the water or air plot. The correct position should, of course, be somewhere between the two.

33. This longitude error can be avoided by feeding flow velocities into the computer so that D.R. positions are continually displayed. Fig. 142 shows a schematic diagram of a system into which flow velocity can be fed manually in the form of a direction and a speed. Resolvers convert the water or air velocities and the flow velocities into northings and eastings. An equipment of this type may be known as a ground position computer or indicator (GPI).

34. The allowance for the reduction in the length of a minute of

longitude according to the latitude is achieved in Fig. 142 by passing the rate feed-back into a cosine pot driven by the latitude shaft. This reduces the amount of feed-back according to the cosine of the latitude and thus makes the motor run faster in proportion and clock up more minutes of longitude than there are miles of easting.

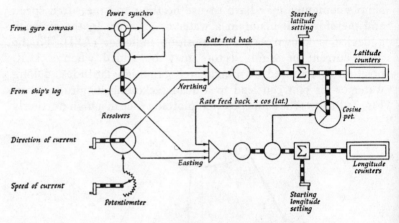

FIG. 142   Triangle of velocities computer

35. It is worth noting that the ability to feed flow velocities into a D.R. computer is not altogether an unmixed blessing. Certainly it saves time for the navigator and avoids longitude error, but if the wrong flow velocity be applied, it may be difficult to unscramble what has happened.

GRID COMPUTER

36. In many instances, vehicles will operate on a military or civil grid overprinted on a map or chart. One set of parallel grid lines will provide a reference of direction as well as position, and the other set of lines, which will be equally spaced at right angles, will provide a reference of position only. Position will be recorded from the bottom left-hand corner of the grid, first counting to the right across the grid lines that refer to direction, and then counting up the grid lines that refer to direction.

37. It might be imagined that owing to the absence of a secant gear, a grid computer would be much simpler than a latitude and longitude computer. However, certain complications are inevitable. They include:

(a) Arrangements to feed in the grid direction. A magnetic compass measures magnetic directions and a gyro compass as shown in Fig. 143 will measure true directions. Not only must the grid direction be set in initially, but it must also be altered as the vehicle moves east or west except on the equator where the meridians do not converge.

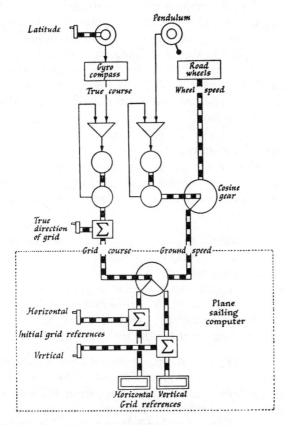

FIG. 143   Land vehicle D.R. computer

(b) Latitude will generally have to be fed into the heading system, particularly in the instance of a gyro compass, which may be essential in an armoured vehicle. The setting will have to be changed if the vehicle moves north or south.

(c) The ground speed in the instance of a land vehicle will depend on the cosine of the mean slope. This correction is often insignificant.

38. In a land vehicle, longitude and latitude are generally changing sufficiently slowly for the necessary convergency and latitude corrections to be fed in at intervals by hand, but in a high-speed craft it may be preferable to use automatic corrections which will involve a latitude and longitude computer. Fig. 143, which illustrates a mechanical grid computer for an armoured vehicle, has direction of grid and latitude fed in manually, but any correction for ground speed according to slope must obviously be provided automatically by a resolver which may be driven from indications provided by a pendulum damped in oil and operating through a power synchro system.

ADDITIONAL FACILITIES

39. In addition to providing a continuous measure of position either in the form of counters or of a plotting table or moving map display, a D.R. computer can provide inputs for heading reference systems:

(a) A gyro compass needs inputs of 15° sin latitude for the Earth's rate correction, and cos latitude is also required for speed correction.

(b) A gyro-heading reference or a gyro-magnetic compass may need inputs of 15° sin latitude and, if either system includes a stabilized gyroscope, cos latitude will be required to correct for the tilt of the Earth.

40. It is evident that an automatic plotter combined with a fixing system can not only check the fixing system but can also find the errors in the flow velocities that have been fed into the D.R. equipment. If the equipment is a simple water or air position computer, it can be used to find flow velocities directly from fixes.

2. D.R. ERRORS

CIRCLE OF UNCERTAINTY

1. The errors in a D.R. position may be divided into:

(a) *Cross-track errors* at right angles to the intended track of the craft. Heading references introduce cross-track errors.

(b) *Along-track errors*. Ground-speed errors act along track.

2. The probability area of a D.R. position will generally be an ellipse. However, with certain exceptions, the cross-track errors and the along-track errors will be of the same order. Since the cross-track errors will be at right angles to the along-track errors, the ellipse will not depart unduly from a circular shape and therefore D.R. errors are generally expressed by the radial error. The circle within which a D.R. position is expected to fall is generally known as the circle of uncertainty.

3. From page 59, para 9:

Radius of 95 per cent circle of uncertainty
= √(sum of squares of along-track and cross-track 95 per cent errors)

and, from page 59, para 10, this can be translated into:

Radius of 95 per cent circle of uncertainty
≃ √(sum of squares of 95 per cent D.R. errors)

The D.R. errors include not only across-track heading error and and along-track speed error but also the radial error of the flow velocity.

Example. Find the radius of the 95 per cent circle of uncertainty if the 95 per cent cross-track error due to heading is 3 n. miles, the 95 per cent along-track error due to speed is 2 n. miles, and the flow velocity error has a 95 per cent radius of 6 n. miles.

95 per cent circle of uncertainty = √(9 + 4 + 36) = 7 n. miles

4. The radius of the circle of uncertainty is often expressed as a proportion of the time since the D.R. was started or of the distance run since the D.R. was started. The actual units used are generally as follows:

(a) n. miles per hour of time since the D.R. was started.

(b) Percentage of distance run since the D.R. was started.

5. In order to convert a heading error into a cross-track error so that it may be applied to find the circle of uncertainty, either one of two formulae may be used:

(a) Cross-track error (n. miles per hour)
$$= \text{(heading error}^\circ) \text{ (speed (knots))}/60.$$
(b) Cross-track error (percentage of distance)
$$= 1\tfrac{2}{3}(\text{heading error}^\circ).$$

In both these formulae, the heading error will be the mean error over the period of the D.R. run.

6. These formulae will apply only if the D.R. run is roughly in a straight line. If it is an out-and-home run, the heading error will be less than if it is a straight run. For example, if the heading reference is magnetically monitored, the major error, that due to variation, will tend to cancel out on opposite headings so that, though the craft may be some distance in error at the extreme end of the journey out, the error will largely have disappeared by the time that the craft has returned to its starting point. The A errors of a magnetic compass will also cancel out, but the B and C errors, being opposite on opposite headings, will accumulate.

7. In the instance of a gyro compass, the error at the end of the run will be reduced if it is an out-and-home journey but probably less than with a magnetic compass. The same will apply to the gyro heading reference. For example, a drift rate of 1° per hour will average $\tfrac{1}{2}$° on an hour's run out and $1\tfrac{1}{2}$° in the opposite direction on an hour's run home, thus averaging $\tfrac{1}{2}$° of error over the whole of the 2 hours. On a straight run, the gyro would average 1° of error over the whole of the 2 hours.

8. Measured speed errors have already been expressed as a percentage of distance run. If measured speed is consistently short, a journey out and home will tend to cancel out the errors. It is perhaps worth noting that if course is changed through 90°, a heading error on the first course will be an along-track error on the second course and a ground-speed error on the first course will be a cross-track error on the second course.

9. Flow-velocity errors have already been expressed as radial errors. Since the direction and speed of the flow-velocity error will be unchanged by the changing heading of the craft, it will not be reduced as the result of an out-and-home or any other type of

journey. It will exist even if the craft is stationary in the water or the air and will be entirely dependent on time.

10. The radius of the circle of uncertainty will depend on the distance and duration of the D.R. run, the speed of the craft, the type of equipment used to measure heading and speed and the pattern of the route over the surface of the Earth. However, the major factor that affects the accuracy of D.R. in practice is whether the calculations can be assisted by information gathered during the journey itself or whether it is entirely unsupported by such information, and based entirely on forecasts.

D.R. UNSUPPORTED

11. It will be useful first to consider the accuracy of dead reckoning without any assistance in the form of past position or past flow velocities. In a land craft, this unsupported D.R. accuracy depends on the heading error and on the measured-speed error and the accuracy of any correction for the slope of the ground. The heading reference may have an error 95 per cent within $1\frac{1}{2}°$, giving a 95 per cent cross-track error of 2 per cent of distance run. The measured speed could have an accuracy, if the surface is not slippery, of less than 1 per cent. The overall 95 per cent circle of uncertainty might therefore have a radius of the order of 4 per cent of distance run.

12. In the instance of marine craft and aircraft, flow velocity has to be taken into consideration. Table X on page 296 gives examples of the radius of the 95 per cent circle of uncertainty using the formulae of paras 3–5.

13. It would, of course, be wrong to take this table as anything but an extremely broad and general example of the order of errors since so many factors are inevitably involved in each particular instance. However, the table may suggest why the navigator often takes a figure of 10 per cent of distance run for the circle of uncertainty. The table also shows that, in all instances, the overriding error is the flow-velocity error. From this, two conclusions follow:

(a) That a figure of 1 n. mile per hour for a marine craft and 30 n. miles per hour for an aircraft is not a bad approximation to the 95 per cent D.R. error.

(b) That, where the error is mostly due to flow-velocity errors, it will not be greatly reduced by an out-and-home journey.

TABLE X. 95 PER CENT D.R. ERRORS

Type of craft	Source of error	Item error	Percentage of run	
			Item	Total
10-knot ship	Magnetic compass	2°	3	
	Measured speed	$\frac{1}{4}$ knot	$2\frac{1}{2}$	
	Forecast flow velocity	1 knot	10	$10\frac{1}{2}$
20-knot ship	Gyro compass	1°	$1\frac{1}{2}$	
	Measured speed	$\frac{1}{4}$ knot	$1\frac{1}{4}$	
	Forecast flow velocity	1 knot	5	$5\frac{1}{4}$
200-knot aircraft	Gyro-magnetic compass	2°	3	
	True air speed		1	
	Forecast flow velocity	25 knots	$12\frac{1}{2}$	13
400-knot aircraft	Gyro-magnetic compass	3°	$4\frac{1}{2}$	
	True air speed		7	
	Forecast flow velocity	30 knots	$7\frac{1}{2}$	9

14. In these broad estimates, the inaccuracy of computing, the errors due to the shape of the Earth and other such minor errors have not been included in the calculations since the errors are small compared with heading, measured speed and flow velocity. Also, the errors have been assumed to be over a relatively short distance. Over 2000 miles, the forecast errors, the heading errors and the measured-speed errors will to a certain extent have cancelled out so that the overall error may not be much more than half the errors over a short distance.

D.R. SUPPORTED

15. Fig. 144 is a reminder that the forecast error tends to decrease with time but starts with a large value. It also shows that if the velocity of a craft can be checked after the start of the journey, the D.R. error will start at a low value, depending on the accuracy of the velocity check and that the error will take some time to build up to the forecast value.

16. The time interval after the start of a journey at which a check of velocity will be useful will depend on the accuracy of the

check. In a ship, a position at 2 hours' interval which has a radius of error of 5 n. miles may confirm but cannot improve on a D.R. circle of uncertainty with a radius of only 2 n. miles. It can, however, enable the dead reckoning of an aircraft, which may have a circle of uncertainty of 60 miles in 2 hours, to be virtually restarted. Unfortunately, in the instance of an aircraft, a velocity measured over the past 2 hours may not apply to the next 2 hours.

17. The lower curve of Fig. 144 assumes that the conditions in

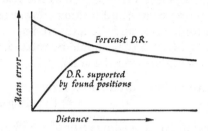

FIG. 144 Characteristics of D.R. errors

the future do not differ greatly from the conditions in the past. A change in conditions can be caused not only by a change in flow velocities but, more immediately, by a change in heading of the craft. If no allowance is made for flow velocities, and it is assumed that a change of heading will lead to an equal change of course and no change of ground speed, the assumption will be equivalent to rotating the flow velocity through an angle equal to the change of heading. The resultant error in D.R. position will be twice that of the flow velocity for a heading change through 180° and equal to the flow velocity for a heading change of 90°. For a heading change of less than about 60°, the error will only be about:

$$\text{(flow speed)} \times \text{(heading change °)}/60$$

Example (*a*). A ship in an average current flow of about 1 knot changes heading 20°, and makes no allowances for flow velocity.

Subsequent D.R. error $= 20 \times 1/60 = \frac{1}{3}$ n. mile per hour

It is not surprising that the seaman tends to use the term 'alter course' as if it had the same meaning as 'alter heading'.

Example (b). An aircraft flying in a wind of 45 knots changes heading by 20° and makes no allowance for the wind.

Subsequent D.R. error $= 45 \times 20/60 = 15$ knots

18. It now appears that, in aircraft at least, it will assist accuracy if flow velocity is taken into account when altering heading. However, on page 282, para 13, it was explained that the 'flow velocity' obtained from fixes would be compounded of heading error and measured-speed error as well as the real flow velocity. Hence, when altering course and making allowance for the 'flow velocity', the heading error and the measured-speed error will be maintained steady whereas they should be rotated. The resulting percentage error will, however, be small:

$$\sqrt{(\text{heading error}^2 + \text{measured speed error}^2)} \times (\text{heading change}°)/60$$

Example. An aircraft has a heading error of 2° (3% distance) and a measured-speed error of 2 per cent. Heading is changed through 20°, making allowance for wind.

D.R. error $= (\sqrt{(3^2 + 2^2)} \times 20/60) = 1$ per cent of distance

19. It is now evident that, particularly when there are no large alterations of heading, supported D.R. can be temporarily a great improvement on forecast D.R. It is partly for this reason that the navigator avoids large alterations of heading where possible. For example, if he finds that his craft has drifted a few miles to one side of his intended track, he will probably alter heading so as to parallel his intended track. This policy of paralleling track also tends to reduce subsequent alterations of heading particularly in instances where the original heading was an attempt to average out a changing flow velocity.

20. Although small alterations of heading assist the navigator to find the way, large alterations of heading may be necessary to avoid collision and for other tactical reasons. In these circumstances, the navigator may find it worth-while to take account of the flow velocity. On a long straight run, however, he could navigate without flow velocity were it not for the fact that he can never be certain that some sudden change of plan may not demand an alteration of heading on to a completely different

course. Hence navigating from one fix to another along a straight run without regard to flow velocity may be considered imprudent. It is sometimes referred to slightingly as 'track crawling'.

21. The real strength of the navigator probably lies in his ability to detect changes in the flow pattern. A slight alteration in the motion of the ship, a change in the pattern of clouds, such signs may be interpreted by the experienced navigator in terms of a feeling in his bones that he is to one side or other of his intended track. However, only a very experienced navigator can weigh subconsciously the forecast and the actual and arrive at the correct interpretation.

22. It is inevitable that the navigator will remember those instances in which his skill has bettered the forecast and will less readily take into account those occasions on which the forecast would have led him more quickly to his destination. The navigator may also be deceived by the accuracy of the final D.R. position in an out-and-home run.

3. AUTOMATIC D.R.

1. The use of airborne doppler to measure drift and ground speed in knots from an aircraft and the ability of inertial platforms to measure speeds in minutes of arc per hour in a north–south and in an east–west direction have already been described in Chapter VI. The heading references have been described in Chapter V. The main items to be dealt with under the heading of automatic D.R. will therefore be the computers used to find the doppler position and the inertial position.

AIRBORNE DOPPLER COMPUTER

2. A doppler computer will have inputs in the form of course, obtained by adding doppler drift to heading, and of ground speed. In practice, the resultant doppler velocity may be compared with the air velocity obtained from heading and true air speed and a 'doppler wind' velocity extracted. The 'doppler wind' may be reapplied to the air velocity to reproduce the original doppler velocity. This roundabout system is used so that, should doppler

temporarily fail to work or unlock over the sea, the 'doppler wind' for the time of unlocking may continue to be combined with the air velocity to give a good measure of the true velocity of the aircraft. The process is known as 'going on to memory'.

3. A doppler computer is sometimes made so that the distances are displayed not in terms of north and south or east and west but in terms of miles along a required track and miles across a required track as shown in Fig. 145. The counters are set to the

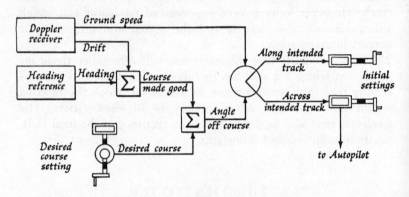

FIG. 145   Simplified layout of doppler computer (without memory)

correct position for the start of a run and the distances to left or right of track may be fed into the autopilot so that the aircraft is guided along the required track to the destination.

4. A problem can arise at a turning point. As a result of cutting the corner, the aircraft will complete the intended track to one side of the destination and start the next intended track not only to one side of the new required track but also a certain distance along it. It is possible for the computer to allow for this or, alternatively, the aircraft may overfly the destination before turning on to the new required track.

5. A doppler computer may provide the following refinements:

   (a) Allowance may be made according to the cosine of the angle that the path of the aircraft makes with the surface of the ground so that ground speed is reduced to allow for a climb or a descent.

(b) Allowance may be made for the greater distance that the aircraft has to travel at height. The amount is small, $\frac{1}{4}$ per cent even at 50,000 feet.

(c) Sin latitude signal can be fed into the heading reference system to offset the rotation of the Earth.

(d) Position can be made to operate a variation cam of the type described on page 202, para 41, so as to feed variation automatically into a gyro-magnetic compass.

AIRBORNE DOPPLER ERRORS

6. Over the land, where doppler speeds have been integrated into distances, the errors that can result may be of the order of 95 per cent within $\frac{1}{4}$ per cent of distance or less if allowance is made for height and for the shape of the Earth in the doppler computer. The only major error will be the heading. Since airborne doppler is seldom fitted to craft that travel at less than 300 knots, a 95 per cent compass error of 2° can represent an error of 10 n. miles in an hour, whereas the doppler errors are only of the order of 1 n. mile per hour over land.

7. Over the sea, the doppler errors have been shown to be greater, due to ocean currents, long-term surface winds, immediate surface winds and the state of the sea. The resultant error is 95 per cent within 5 n. miles per hour as explained in Chapter VI. Once again, this error is small compared with the compass error particularly when it is realized that the two have to be combined by the golden rule of squares.

8. In a very high speed aircraft, a gyro heading reference may be preferred. For a 600-knot aircraft travelling a distance of 2000 miles, the airborne doppler error over the sea may be only of the order of 3 n. miles per hour or nearly 10 n. miles for the duration of the trip. This will represent a mean heading error of about $\frac{1}{3}$° which, in terms of gyro drift over the period of 3 or 4 hours, means a rate of the order of $\frac{1}{4}$° per hour. This implies the use of a precision gyroscope possibly mounted on an inertial platform.

9. Just as classical D.R. may be supported by position finding and the errors substantially reduced, so also may doppler be supported. Since the major error is generally heading, at least over the land, a fix may be used in comparison with the position

found by doppler to measure the heading error and the heading subsequently corrected.

INERTIAL NAVIGATION COMPUTER

10. An inertial computer will have inputs of easting and northing velocities from the inertial platform, these velocities possibly being smoothed by water speed or by airborne doppler. The computer will clock up latitude and longitude and, as with all D.R. computers, will feed a correction in the form of 15° sin latitude to precess the azimuth gyro and a correction in the form of 15° cos latitude to precess the east–west gyro. Thus Earth's rotation and Earth's tilt will be compensated.

11. If the craft travels at high speed, the computer may allow for coriolis which will introduce an error in the apparent direction of gravity of $0.026 \times$ speed (knots) $\times$ sin (latitude) minutes of arc (page 70, para 23). Since coriolis acceleration operates at right angles to the speed, the correction due to easting will be fed into the north–south accelerometers and the correction due to northing into the east–west accelerometers.

12. *Ballistic Missile Computer*. A special type of computer is used in ballistic missiles in which the platform maintains its alignment in space for the few minutes during which the inertial system is operating to launch the warhead. Into the computer is fed the speed and the position that the warhead ought to achieve when the motors are cut off. The actual positions and speeds are recorded from information taken from the inertial platform and, by comparing the two, a correction may be passed to the control system of the missile. The correction ensures that the motors are cut off when the warhead is travelling at a speed and from a position which will enable it to strike the same target as if it had followed exactly the pre-planned path.

13. The pre-planned path takes into account the change of the direction of gravity due to the forward movement of the missile, the change in the strength of gravity due to the upward movement of the missile, Earth's tilt, Earth's rotation and coriolis. The pre-planned path may therefore involve a good deal of calculation and as a result it may not be easy to alter the aiming point by more than a small amount without a completely fresh pre-planning. The computer may be able to pre-plan a certain

number of targets but, evidently, in order to limit the size and complexity, the number of targets will be limited. Alternatively, it will be necessary to plug in a computer element for each block of targets.

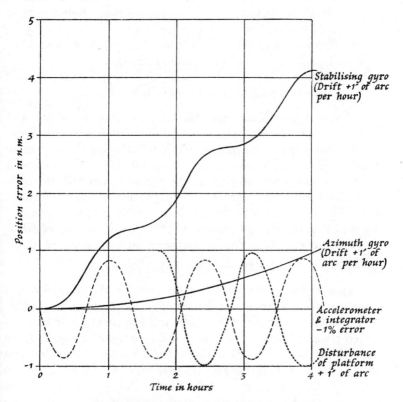

FIG. 146 Theoretical inertial navigation errors

INERTIAL NAVIGATION ERRORS

14. Fig. 110 on page 233 showed the types of errors that could arise in the measurement of speed by an undamped inertial platform. These errors, together with the errors due to the drift of the azimuth gyroscope, will lead to position errors which will follow a pattern shown in Fig. 146. Added to these errors will be errors in position due to the second integrators.

15. The curves of Fig. 146 were derived from the formulae:

(a) *Stabilizing gyro error.* Error in n. miles $\simeq$ gyro drift
($°$/hour) $\times$ [time (mins) $- 13 \times \sin (4\cdot3 \times$ time (mins))].

(b) *Accelerometer and 1st integrator error.* Error in n. miles $\simeq$
$0\cdot0022 \times$ (acc. and int. error (percentage of distance)) $\times$
(speed (knots)) $\times \sin (4\cdot3 \times$ time (mins)).

(c) *Disturbance of platform.* Error in n. miles$\simeq$(disturbance
(mins of arc)) $\times \cos (4\cdot3 \times$ time (mins)).

(d) *Azimuth gyro error.* Error in n. miles$\simeq$(gyro drift ($°$/hour))
$\times$ speed (knots) $\times$ (time (mins))^2/400,000.

16. These basic errors are modified by cross-coupling. For
example, although according to the basic formulae the craft will
have to cover the major part of 10,000 miles before the drift of an
azimuth gyroscope causes an error as great as the same drift of a
stabilizing gyroscope, in practice the azimuth gyro drift interacts
with the stabilizing gyros. The misalignment of the platform in
azimuth will cause the north–south stabilizing gyro to be affected
by the tilt of the Earth's surface, so that for each minute of arc of
misalignment a tilt of the stabilizing gyro will occur equal to:

$$\tfrac{1}{4} \cos (\text{lat}) \text{ minutes of arc per hour}$$

17. This formula shows that a heading error of 10 minutes of arc
can introduce a tilt of 2 minutes of arc an hour in the north–
south stabilizing gyroscopes which will represent a north–south
speed error of 2 knots. This error will be integrated into an error
in latitude. As a result, the wrong value of latitude will be fed into
the computer that arranges for the east–west tilt of the platform in
order to offset the rotation of the Earth. Also, the wrong value of
latitude will be fed into the computer that arranges for the
azimuth gyro to be precessed according to the Earth's rotation.
18. Fortunately, the cross-coupling between the north–south
accelerometer and the azimuth gyro tends to cancel the errors out
so that the system, over a long period, tends to oscillate about the
correct heading and latitude although errors in longitude will
accumulate. Also, if a gyroscope drifts clockwise on one side of
the globe, it will be drifting anticlockwise to the other side of the
globe so that, 12 hours later, its drift will be reversed. Again, as the
platform travels round the Earth, drifts due to gravity acting on

unbalance in a gyro will act in the opposite direction after 12 hours if the gyro is maintained steady in space as in the normal marine system. Hence a 24-hour period oscillation will tend to develop about the correct latitude in a very high quality inertial navigator. An accurate fixing system seems to be the only way in which this oscillation may be reduced. It is certainly the only way in which longitude error may be reduced.

19. An inertial navigation system depends for its accuracy entirely on the way it is engineered. The system is governed by the direction of the force of gravity so that, apart from second-order fluctuations in the 84-minute period, the shape of the Earth introduces no major errors. It is this complete independence of nature which makes the inertial system so attractive a proposition for navigation in the future not only for military but also for civil applications. Also, the platform itself can act as the sensor for control of the craft.

20. It may be worth noting that 1 n. mile an hour is a target for an airborne system weighing a few tens of pounds. For a marine inertial navigator, the requirements may be a couple of orders higher, but the weight may be at least an order greater.

21. For the ballistic missile system, which has to work only for the first few minutes of flight, the gyroscope error, as shown in Fig. 146, will be low. However, a 1 per cent error in first and second integrators will obviously be quite unacceptable for a missile travelling several thousand miles. The requirement will be certainly better than 0·1 per cent and probably approaching 0·01 per cent or 1 in 10^4, a figure which can only be achieved with difficulty.

4. TIMING

1. Provided that the navigator is concerned only with the progress of a single craft along its ways, position may satisfy his navigational requirement. However, when he has to operate with another craft, or with a ground organization, or with another system within his craft, time generally becomes the essential link. Thus it will be necessary to know the time at which a ship will arrive in port so that arrangements may be made to disembark

passengers or unload cargo. It will be necessary to convert distances and speeds into time for an accurate measure of fuel
requirements to be obtained.

E.T.A. CALCULATION

2. The time at which a craft expects to arrive at a future point is
known as the E.T.A. (estimated time of arrival). If the craft
travels at a constant ground speed, it will be a simple matter to
divide distance to go by speed to find time to go and to add this to
the present time. The actual time at which a craft arrives is
known as the A.T.A.

3. Finding time to go by dividing distance to go by present speed
assumes that the measured speed of the craft will be held
constant and that the present flow velocity will remain unchanged.
In aircraft, this assumption may be modified by assuming a
decrease in ground speed depending on the decrease in height, but
the simple principle will remain unchanged. The error in the
time to go will be large if the final flow velocity differs greatly
from the present flow velocity but, as the distance to go shortens,
the present speed will progressively approach the speed at the
end of the run until the two finally coincide. On the other hand,
although it will be more accurate to assume a forecast flow
velocity for the end of the run if the distance to go is long, the
mean error will depend mainly on half the error of the forecast
flow velocity and this error will persist right up to the end of the
run. Hence there will be a point at which the simple time to go
calculation becomes more accurate than the more sophisticated
system based on forecast flow velocities. At sea, this distance will
vary very greatly, but will be a matter of hours in most instances.
In the air, a typical value will be half an hour in the cruise and a
quarter of an hour in the descent.

4. Time to go is not convenient because it is continually changing.
E.T.A., on the other hand, will only change as ground speed
changes and will only drift slowly as flow velocity alters. The
way in which E.T.A. is changing can itself be used as a means to
improve a final E.T.A.

5. If the craft should deviate to one side or other of its course, the
ground that it will cover on its journey will be greater than the
distance to go and the E.T.A. will consequently be later. In

practice, the difference between the two is slight. A deviation of as much as 5° from the correct course, if not corrected until the middle of a run, will only increase the distance by secant 5°, about ¼ per cent. However, if the craft should drift off to one side of track and course is then changed, the distance to go can be affected as shown in Fig. 147. For a 5° deviation from the correct

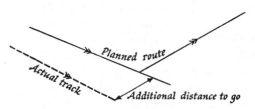

FIG. 147   Cross-track error and E.T.A.

course and an alteration of heading in the middle of the run, the error will be 4 per cent if the alteration of course is 90°.

6. In the instance of a marine craft or an aircraft, an alteration of course will generally mean a recalculation of the triangle of velocities if the alteration is more than a few degrees and the flow velocity is large compared to the speed of the craft. In addition, even if there is no alteration of course, it may be necessary to split the run into a number of sectors, known as legs, so that for each leg a flow velocity may be used that will be sensibly constant over that leg. From each of these triangles of velocity, a time to go for each leg can be calculated and the times to go can be combined if necessary to find the E.T.A. for the end of the run.

MAINTAINING E.T.A.

7. It may be essential for a craft to reach a point, such as the entrance to a dockyard or the end of a descent path, at a pre-determined E.T.A. The speed may have to be adjusted, and in theory this can be achieved by constructing a triangle of velocities to find the correct water or air speed that has to be maintained.

8. In practice, an E.T.A. can generally be achieved by increasing or decreasing the water or air speed by the same amount as the

increase or decrease of ground speed required. In theory, this may not give the correct answer and, if the current or wind is from the beam, this simple method can lead to a slight over-estimate of the correction. Nevertheless, the error can generally be neglected in practice.

9. It may not be possible for a craft to increase speed through the water or the air to any extent without incurring a disproportionate fuel penalty. This will be particularly true in the instance of the ship. Therefore the navigator will tend to allow a margin in his forecast of an E.T.A. if he knows that it is important that the E.T.A. shall be met and he will lose the margin of time by slowing down as necessary.

10. A subsonic aircraft tends to be inflexible with regard to speed. The only way in which to achieve an E.T.A. will be to allow for a considerable margin and to fly a time-wasting pattern if this margin is not required. This will inevitably lead to a demand for additional fuel reserves and less economical operation.

11. It follows that, in general, a subsonic civil aircraft cannot maintain an E.T.A. It must be accepted that arrival at an airport will have large random errors in timing compared to the original flight plan. However the supersonic aircraft will have a margin of speed to enable it to maintain a time schedule.

12. The military aircraft may have to achieve an exact E.T.A. irrespective of fuel economy. The navigator will ensure that there is ample margin in the E.T.A. and will absorb the margin as necessary by flying time-wasting patterns. Time-wasting patterns may be dog-legs (page 348, para 38) or orbits (page 351, para 8).

FUEL IN TANKS

13. From the speed and the weight of a craft along a leg, the rate of consumption of fuel is found and multiplied by the time taken by the craft to travel along the leg. This gives fuel consumed on the leg. If the fuel consumed is subtracted from the fuel in tanks at the start of the leg, the fuel in tanks at the end of the leg will appear.

14. In a high-speed aircraft the problem is complicated by a number of factors. For example, owing to the fuel consumed, the all-up weight at the end of the leg will differ from the all-up weight at the start of the leg, and the average all-up weight will

accordingly depend also on the all-up weight at the end of the leg. However, the all-up weight at the end of the leg will depend on the time taken to travel along the leg. But, until the all-up weight for the leg is known, the correct speed for the craft cannot be known so that the time cannot be determined. Hence the calculation of fuel consumption may involve a succession of approximations until the correct compromise of speed is found. In addition, speed will depend on air density and air temperature both of which, in a jet aircraft, react on fuel consumption.

15. Over a short distance, the fuel consumed may be computed directly from a flow meter and the time to go. This computation will always be pessimistic as it will fail to allow for the improvement in consumption that must occur with the reduction of weight as fuel is consumed.

16. The calculation of fuel in tanks in a high-speed craft could be managed by a digital computer. The alternative will be to prepare beforehand a complete schedule of expected fuel in tanks at various points along the route and to compare the actual fuel with the expected fuel. From this the drift of the actual from the expected can be found and extrapolated to forecast the final fuel in tanks on arrival at the destination.

17. It will be noted that the calculation of fuel in tanks has been linked with time rather than with distance. In a ship or an aircraft, fuel cannot be linked with distance without taking into account the effects of ocean currents or winds. The use of time enables fuel consumption to be worked out taking account of flow velocities.

GRAPHICAL D.R.

18. Time and fuel may be estimated by graphical methods. The horizontal scale of a graph could be in distance, as shown in Fig. 148, in such a way that it could be reconciled with the track drawn on the map or chart covering the journey. At certain intervals, time and fuel in tanks may be marked on the vertical scale, in this particular instance fuel appearing in the form of food for men and dogs. A profile of the journey might also be shown and this may be particularly valuable in the instance of an aircraft.

19. A graphical representation of time and fuel in this form is

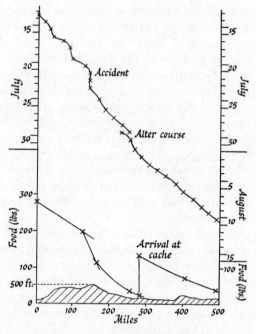

FIG. 148   Howgozit

generally known as a howgozit. If the craft should deviate from the planned path, a discontinuity in the graph will appear on the howgozit when course is changed, and this is illustrated on midday, 29th July, in Fig. 148. The graph shows very clearly the general trend of the navigation.

5. PLOTTING EQUIPMENT

1. For dead reckoning on a chart and, as will be shown in Chapter X, for plotting navigational aid information, the navigator will need a chart table or, in a small craft, a plotting board, the size depending partly on the size of the area on the chart with which the navigator is concerned. A plotting arm similar to that used on a draughtsman's drawing board may be fitted, complete with parallel motion and protractor. In certain instances, the arm may include a mechanical triangle of velocities linkage.

However, the use of a plotting arm implies that the chart will be fixed to the table and will be on a mercator projection (see page 320, para 7).

2. For dead reckoning and for plotting navigational aid information, parallel rules will be useful. On the chart, compass cards, known as compass roses, will often be printed so that the navigator can draw a direction from any point by transferring the direction from the nearest compass rose. Particularly at sea, parallel rules are used and these may be in the form either of two rules connected by a linkage or a single rule with a long roller just proud of the surface on the underneath.

3. In the air, parallel rules are not generally used owing partly to vibration. Instead, directions will be measured by a protractor placed on the nearest meridian. These protractors will generally have a grid of parallel lines marked on the surface so that the centre of the protractor may be placed on the point from which the direction is to be drawn, and the protractor aligned by means of the grid with the nearest meridian as shown in Fig. 149(a).

4. Certain types of protractor have the scale reversed. Using a protractor of this type, the pencil is placed on the point from which direction has to be drawn, and the protractor is rotated and slid until the centre is on a meridian as shown in Fig. 149(b). The direction can then be drawn with one movement. When drawing directions close to north or south, it is necessary to align the protractor on a parallel of latitude and a second reversed scale may be provided for this purpose. The use of a reversed scale can lead to mistakes, even if the figures and markings be specially arranged as suggested in Fig. 149(c). Hence this method is not recommended by experienced navigators, although many of them may use it in practice.

5. The grid of lines on the protractor enables the navigator to draw parallel lines. In certain instances, where the navigator works on charts which are roughly constant in scale, a distance scale may be marked on the protractor. However, generally, distances are stepped off by dividers and transferred to the nearest latitude scale since 1' of latitude is roughly a nautical mile.

6. In many instances, a navigator measures distance only so that he may translate it into time according to the speed of his craft.

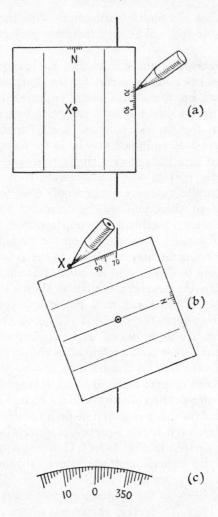

FIG. 149   Navigational protractor

On a constant scale chart, a time–speed scale may be used as shown in Fig. 150(a). The scale may be drawn separately or engraved on perspex to be placed directly on the chart. On a mercator chart, since the scale is not constant, devices such as time–speed dividers may be used as shown in Fig. 150(b). The dividers are set to the speed and the distance stepped off on the longer arms. The dividers are then transferred to the latitude scale, but the shorter arms are used and the interval recorded by the minutes of latitude will be the time in minutes.

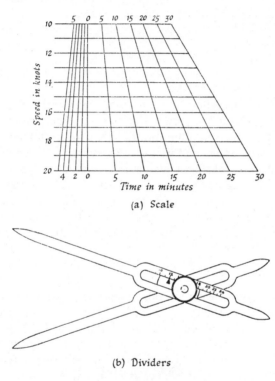

(a) Scale

(b) Dividers

FIG. 150   Time–speed devices

NAVIGATOR'S LOG

7. In addition to plotting on his chart, the navigator generally maintains a record of courses and measured speeds known as a log. This log may also include information regarding navigational observations and other items concerned with the navigation of the craft including fuel readings and engine readings, and will generally record important happenings. Such a log is

known as a deck log by mariners, or as a flight log by airmen.
8. The log may be maintained in a book, and this is common practice at sea, or on a form, which is normal in aircraft. The log is of importance for two main reasons:

(a) It acts as a record of the past to provide basic dead-reckoning information for the future.
(b) It provides evidence in case of accident or other eventuality.

FLIGHT PROGRESS STRIPS

9. Air-traffic controllers operate basically on the flight plans prepared by aircraft but, since numbers of aircraft are involved, these flight plans are split up into E.T.A.'s for a number of points such as turning points and points of entry into airfields. For each aircraft, a series of flight strips is prepared which show the identity, the height, the speed and the E.T.A. at the various points. The flight strips are mounted on metal frames and slid into a large board one above the other, each board representing a point on the route. Thus the controller supervising that part of the route has a display that shows him which aircraft will be arriving, when they will be arriving and at what heights.

10. As the flight of each aircraft progresses, position reports are received either in the form of an A.T.A. sent by the aircraft on arrival at a certain point or in the form of a revised E.T.A. sent by the aircraft. By such means, the flight strips are continually updated. It is by the dead-reckoning presentation afforded by flight strips that the air-traffic controller is able to ensure that the separation between aircraft is adequate. Flight strips also assist him to take the necessary correcting action in the form of instructions to aircraft.

11. The manual preparation of flight strips is extremely time-consuming. Automatic flight-strip printers have been built which up-date flight strips quickly and accurately. A printer runs up and down the board and prints amendments to the flight strips or the strips are replaced by counters, which display appropriate letters or numerals in rows of windows.

6. SUMMARY

D.R. TECHNIQUES

A position ahead may be plotted by:

(a) Simple extrapolation according to the mean ground speed measured between past positions. The method is accurate if there are no changes of heading or speed of the craft and if the flow velocity remains constant.

(b) Calculation of positions ahead by means of the triangle of velocities. Heading and measured speed errors reduce the accuracy if heading is changed, but the reduction is generally very small. This is known as a track plot.

(c) Calculation of positions ahead as if there was no flow velocity and subsequent addition of a flow velocity vector. The method is convenient if heading is continually being changed, but errors can arise if the craft is covering a wide band of latitudes. This is known as a water or air plot.

A track plot or water or air plot may be used to measure the past flow velocity and to amend the forecast flow velocity for the future. In the air, drifts may be measured directly, and combined with other measurements to find a spot wind velocity. Alternatively drifts compared with found positions may be used to check heading accuracy.

D.R. COMPUTERS

D.R. computers can be connected with automatic plotters that continually display the track of the craft or its water or air path. If the eastings are multiplied by sec (latitude) and the starting latitude and longitude is fed in, the computer can continually display in latitude and longitude either the ground position based on the flow velocities that have been fed in, or the water or air position.

AIRBORNE DOPPLER COMPUTERS

Airborne doppler computers may measure positions either in latitude and longitude or as so many miles along and across the intended track of the craft. The computer can be arranged to operate for a time on the wind measured by doppler so that the dead reckoning may be continued during a period of unlocking over the sea.

INERTIAL NAVIGATION COMPUTERS

Inertial computers need accurate integrators to convert the inertial platform speeds into distances. The computers will need to feed corrections for Earth's rotation and tilt into the platform gyroscopes and, possibly, corrections for coriolis.

A ballistic missile may use a flight plan computer. Actual speeds and positions may be compared with the ideal values and corrections sent to the control system.

ERRORS

Errors are generally expressed according to the radius of the 95 per cent circle of uncertainty.

The following are approximations for equipment errors:

(a) *Marine D.R. using forecast flow velocity*. Probably rather greater than 1 n. mile per hour over short distances and $\frac{1}{2}$ n. mile per hour over very long distances (95 per cent).

(b) *Aircraft D.R. for aircraft with speeds of only a few hundred knots*. Probably rather greater than 30 n. miles per hour over short distances and 15 n. miles per hour over long distances (95 per cent).

(c) *High-speed aircraft using airborne doppler*. Errors depend mainly on the errors of the heading reference system over the land. Over the sea probably 95 per cent within 7 n. miles per hour is a reasonable average.

(d) *Inertial navigation system* accuracy is limited by engineering capability. 1 n. mile per hour is a good target for a miniature airborne system with doppler damping. One or two orders better may be required for marine applications. Ballistic missile limitations may be between 0·1 per cent and 0·01 per cent of distance to the target.

TIMING

Time is essential if a craft has to link its passage with the activities of the world outside. Since craft may not be able to increase speed, a timing margin is essential if a schedule has to be maintained and reductions in speed can be arranged or time-wasting diversions made from the planned route.

Time is a link between positional navigation and fuel consumption which is particularly important in a high-speed craft.

Timing accuracy may be expressed by the error of an E.T.A. as a percentage of the time taken to complete the run or as so many minutes per hour.

PLOTTING EQUIPMENT

Navigators tend to use simple plotting equipment. Time–speed devices and howgozit graphs may be helpful.

Air-traffic controllers operate by means of flight strips.

CHAPTER IX

The Route

DEFINITIONS

1. *Rhumb Line.* A rhumb line on the surface of the Earth is a line that cuts all the meridians that it crosses at the same angle. A rhumb line of 000T or 180T will lie along a line of longitude, and a rhumb line of 090T or 270T will lie along a parallel of latitude. Any other rhumb line will follow a spiral as suggested in Fig. 151,

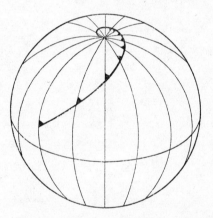

FIG. 151   Rhumb line 045T on globe

the spiral being known as a loxodrome. A craft that is steering a steady course by gyro compass or by a magnetic compass with variation corrected will follow a rhumb line.

2. *Great Circle.* A great circle (G.C.) on the surface of a spherical globe is a path traced out by a plane that passes through the centre of the globe. A path traced out by a plane that does not pass through the centre is known as a small circle. The shortest distance between two points on a globe and the longest distance both lie on the great circle joining the two points.

3. If the great circle on a spherical globe were transferred to a map of the surface of the Earth, the line would be known as a great circle. Owing to the shape of the Earth, the line will generally not lie on a plane passing through the centre of the ellipsoid.

1. CHARTS

1. A chart was originally a delineation of a portion of the sea which might have coastlines marked on it. It was used for plotting and for dead reckoning. When air navigation began, the word chart was extended to cover areas of the Earth previously only covered by maps. The air chart therefore included features of the surface such as towns, high ground and political boundaries, and, more recently, radio aids and airways have been added. Nevertheless, an essential distinction has remained. A chart is used for navigating, a map for finding position.

2. It may be noted that the methods used to depict the curved surface of the Earth on a flat chart are used likewise to depict the positions of the stars as seen from the Earth, and could be used to show the surface of the Moon or of a planet. Space navigation is unlikely to demand the use of a chart, but it may be convenient to use the plane of the ecliptic as a foundation for diagrams.

3. Originally, the features of a globe were imagined as being projected on to a flat chart as from a point source of light within the globe. Today, the navigator generally uses the term projection to describe the mathematical system whereby the curved surface of the globe is drawn on a sheet of flat paper. Inevitably, all projections will introduce some distortion.

PROJECTION REQUIREMENTS

4. *Orthomorphism.* Since a chart is to be used for plotting the course of the craft, it will be essential that directions are correctly represented all over the surface. A chart must therefore be free from angular distortion so that a protractor can be used anywhere over its surface. A chart with this characteristic is said to be 'orthomorphic' or 'conformal'.

5. In order that angles shall be represented correctly, the chart must have two features:

(a) The meridians and parallels must cross at right angles.

(b) The scale along a meridian at any point must be equal to the scale along the parallel at the same point. This does not imply that the scale must be constant all over the chart, which is impossible. It implies only that, at any point, the scale must be constant in all directions.

6. In addition to orthomorphism, there are four other desirable features in a projection:

(a) *Constancy of scale.* This enables a rule to be used to measure distance and simplifies automatic plotting devices. Absolute constancy is not possible but, over a small area, most projections are reasonably constant.

(b) *Rhumb line as straight line.* This will greatly assist plotting if a craft is fitted with a gyro compass or with a magnetic compass which is corrected for variation.

(c) *Great circle as straight line.* This will be convenient in a chart that is used to draw long-range radio bearings which travel in great circles or if the craft is steered by a directional gyro not corrected for convergency.

(d) *Fit of adjacent sheets.* This will simplify passing from one chart to the adjacent chart whether the plotting be manual or automatic. Unless sheets fit, a grid cannot be transferred from one chart to the next. Fit is also necessary for a wall map covering a large area.

MERCATOR

7. Until recently, all craft navigated by means of compasses so that their courses followed rhumb lines. Since a rhumb line cuts all meridians at the same angle, it is necessary that all meridians on a chart should be parallel and that the chart should be orthomorphic if the rhumb line is to appear as a straight line. The mercator is the only projection that achieves this.

8. Fig. 152(a) shows the way in which, by fitting a chart as a cylinder around the equator, the meridians on a globe can be projected on the chart as a series of parallel lines. Fig. 152(b)

shows that, to maintain orthomorphism, the intervals between the parallels of latitude have to be expanded to keep pace with the expansion resulting from parallel meridians on the chart compared to the converging meridians on the globe. On page 285, para 26, it was shown that to convert minutes of departure into longitude it was necessary to multiply by sec (latitude). Hence the scale of the mercator chart and the intervals between parallels of latitude will increase according to sec (latitude) approximately. The correct distribution of parallels is shown in tables of meridional parts (mer. parts), which not only give the distances from the equator of the parallels of latitude on a mercator chart measured in minutes of longitude, but also allow for the ellipticity of the Earth.

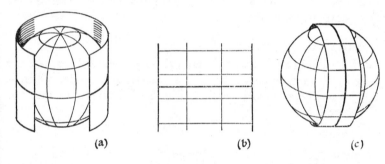

(a)   (b)   (c)

FIG. 152   Mercator chart

9. It is impossible to measure distances over a large area by means of a constant rule except near to the equator, owing to the expanding scale. However, it is possible to measure the distance between two points on a mercator by picking off the interval on a pair of dividers and transferring it to a meridian at the same latitude. Along this meridian a scale will be marked in the form of minutes of latitude. By this means it will be possible to measure distances in nautical miles along rhumb lines with an accuracy of better than 1 per cent so long as the latitude scale does not change too greatly over the interval to be measured.

10. If the mercator chart is based not on the equator but on some other great circle, it is known as an oblique mercator. The chart will be orthomorphic, but the meridians will no longer appear as

straight lines. Such a projection may be suitable for a craft using a grid system of steering with a gyro heading reference. A special example is the transverse mercator sometimes known as a Gauss conformal that uses a meridian as the basic great circle and is illustrated in Fig. 152(c). The meridians, apart from the central meridians, will appear as curves and the parallels as parts of ellipses. The scale is obviously not constant but scales of nautical miles can be marked along the parallels.

11. A number of mercator charts may be fitted together to cover as wide an area as is desired. Inevitably, as the equator is left, the increase of scale becomes more exaggerated, producing the polar distortion that is so obvious on world maps that use the mercator projection. However, a true direction is constant all over the chart so that a plotting arm set to a direction can be used anywhere on its surface.

CONICAL ORTHOMORPHIC

12. Instead of forming a chart as a cylinder around the equator, it may be formed as a cone around a parallel of latitude, which is known as the standard parallel. Fig. 153(a) illustrates that the

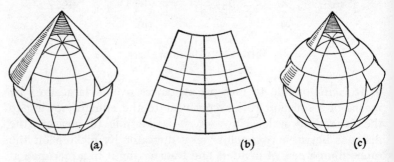

FIG. 153 Conical orthomorphic and Lambert's conformal

meridians will be straight converging lines, but the intervals between the parallels will have to be adjusted according to the expansion of the meridians north and south of the standard parallel, as shown in Fig. 153(b).

13. Constancy of scale can be improved by using two standard parallels so that the chart will now cut the globe rather than

touching it, as shown in Fig. 153(c). This secant conical orthomorphic is generally known as the Lambert conformal. The scale
between the parallels will have to be slightly collapsed, but
outside the parallels the expansion will increase rapidly. Hence
the standard parallels will have to be widely spread, generally
about five-sixths of the band of latitude covered by the
particular chart.

14. Because the Lambert conformal fits more closely to the
contours of the Earth at high latitudes than does the mercator, the
scale over the surface will be much more constant. It also happens
that a great circle will be close to a straight line. However,
because the meridians converge, a rhumb line will appear as a
curve. In spite of this, the chart is commonly used in air navigation because the air navigator tends to use his chart also as a map
and in particular as a map on which to mark radio aids, which
transmit along great circles.

15. A conical orthomorphic chart will fit exactly a chart covering
an area to the east or to the west because the meridians are
straight. However, since each band of latitude will be based on
different standard parallels with different curvatures, a conical
orthomorphic chart will only be a rolling fit with a similar chart
for a higher or lower latitude, as shown in Fig. 155(a). Hence the
tendency to use the oblique mercator for grid navigation except
for journeys that run east or west.

STEREOGRAPHIC

16. If the standard parallel of a conical orthomorphic chart were
to be moved further away from the equator until it collapsed into
a point at the pole, the cone would become a flat sheet and the
projection would be a polar stereographic as shown in Fig. 154(a).
The meridians would appear as a sheaf of straight lines radiating
from the pole and the intervals between the parallels would be
expanded according to the expansion of the meridians as the
distance from the pole is increased. The resulting projection is
shown in Fig. 154(b). The Greenwich grid is always drawn on a
polar stereographic chart.

17. The properties of the stereographic will be similar to those of
the conical orthomorphic but, because the former is based on a
point whereas the latter is based on a parallel of latitude, the

constancy of scale will be less. It is possible to devise a polar chart based on two parallels of latitude, the higher parallel being practically at the pole, and this will have a slightly better constancy than the stereographic, but angular distortion occurs close to the pole itself. Such a projection is illustrated in Fig. 154(c). In general, however, the polar stereographic will probably be preferred on the grounds that it is easy to construct.

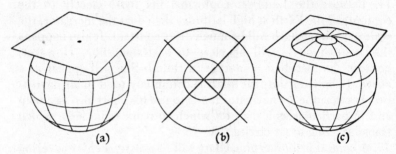

FIG. 154   Polar stereographic

18. It is interesting to note that the stereographic chart is a 'true' projection in the sense that, if the pattern of a polar area were projected on to a polar chart from the opposite pole, the projection would be stereographic. As a result of this peculiarity, a circle on the surface of the Earth appears as a circle on a stereographic chart although the centre will be displaced. For this reason stereographic projections have been used for plotting range circles obtained by astronomical observations (see page 457, para 19).

SPECIAL PROJECTIONS

19. Although orthomorphism is important, it may be possible to relax the requirement slightly where it is particularly required to improve the constancy of scale over a small area, or to improve the correspondence between a great circle on the surface of the Earth and a straight line on the chart.

20. *Polyconic*. The polyconic is an example of a compromise projection. If a series of conical orthomorphic charts covering a narrow band of different latitudes be formed into one large chart, exact correspondence can be achieved down the central meridian.

However, since the standard parallel of the conical orthomorphic chart for each parallel of latitude will be different, there will be gaps at the edges of the charts. If the charts are distorted so that these gaps are made good, the result will be a chart with a straight central meridian and curved outer meridians as shown in Fig. 155(b). As the distance from the central meridian is increased, so

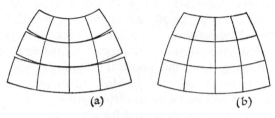

(a)   (b)

FIG. 155   Polyconic

the scale will become less constant and angular distortion will be introduced. At distances of 1000 miles from the central meridian, the scale errors may be of the order of 3 per cent and the angular distortion around 2°. Hence polyconic projections are not used for navigation over large areas.

21. *Gnomonic.* Although absolute constancy of scale is quite impossible, complete correspondence between the great circle on the surface of the Earth and a straight line on the chart can be achieved by the gnomonic projection. This is a 'true' projection which could be produced by placing a flat chart at a point on the surface of the globe and projecting the pattern of the surface from the centre of the globe. Since all great circles lie on planes that pass through the centre of the globe, they will appear as straight lines when projected on the gnomonic chart. Unfortunately, the projection suffers from considerable distortion as distance from the central point is increased. At 1000 miles, the distortion of scale may be of the order of 5 per cent compared to the centre and the angular distortion may be around 2°. However, a gnomonic chart is convenient for finding quickly the points at which a great-circle route from one point to another cuts various meridians. It is also convenient for maps which display long-range directional radio information since radio bearings appear

as great circles on the surface of the Earth, if the oblateness of the Earth is ignored.

22. In addition, the following projections, though not used for navigation, may be encountered:

(a) *Cassini's.* A standard meridian is chosen and points are plotted according to their distances at right angles to this meridian. The projection is accordingly comparable to the transverse mercator and is used sometimes for mapping narrow strips of the globe that run up a meridian.

(b) *Zenithal equidistant.* A point is chosen instead of a meridian and positions are plotted according to distances and bearings from this point. The scale at right angles to these bearings will be far from constant so that the projection will be far from orthomorphic. This projection is, however, sometimes used for star maps.

(c) *Orthometric.* Just as the zenithal equidistant projection shows great-circle bearings and distances from a central point, so the orthometric projection shows rhumb-line distances and directions from a central point. It obviously has less application to navigation even than the zenithal equidistant.

23. There are also certain projections that show deliberate distortions for specific purposes. Typical examples are:

(a) Equal area or authalic projections that show areas correctly. Bonne's has a scale correct along a central meridian and along all the parallels, the parallels being equally spaced about the equator. Molleweide's has a straight central meridian, but the other meridians appear as ellipses and the distance between the parallels is adjusted to make an equal area projection.

(b) Iso-azimuthal and Lettrow projections show the bearing of a point accurately from any two fixed points and have therefore been used for radio-bearing maps.

(c) The orthographic projection shows a side view of the globe or of the sky and has been used for star maps.

(d) Inverted lattice projections will be described on page 523, para 9.

(e) Weir's diagram will be described on page 447, para 21.

COMPARISON OF PROJECTIONS

24. For normal chart work, the only projections to be considered are the three orthomorphic projections, the mercator, the conical orthomorphic or Lambert's conformal, and the stereographic. Of the three, the mercator alone shows rhumb lines as straight lines and therefore, in spite of its changes of scale with latitude, is widely accepted for marine craft and aircraft that use gyro compasses or magnetic compasses. The only major drawback is that the projection becomes unwieldy at latitudes much greater than 80°. However, above such latitudes, compasses are virtually useless and a polar stereographic chart with a grid superimposed will probably be used.

25. For aircraft that operate along great-circle radio tramlines, a conical orthomorphic chart or Lambert conformal is extremely convenient. For aircraft that use heading reference gyroscopes, there is a strong case for grid navigation based on the use of an oblique mercator.

26. Where the area to be covered by a craft is small, the difference between projections decreases. As a general rule, it may be stated that the errors of any projection increase as the square of the distance from the central point or the central line. Thus for an area of only a few hundred miles each way, almost any projection will have small errors. Where the distances stretch for 1000 miles from the central point or line, the errors will be of the order of a hundred times as great.

27. Table XI on page 328 gives a comparison of the accuracies of the various types of orthomorphic chart projection. In each instance, the chart is covering a distance of 600 n. miles from the central point.

CHART DESIGN

28. The size of a chart depends on the size of the table that is likely to be available to the navigator. Generally, a chart is not greater than 40 inches by 27 inches and more usually the size is closer to 30 inches by 23 inches. Maps may be much smaller and those intended to be held in the hand of the pilot of an aircraft or the helmsman of a small boat may be only the size of the page of a book.

29. The paper has to stand up to wear and not be unduly affected

TABLE XI.　CHART ERRORS

Type of error	Projection	Maximum errors Range of latitudes (deg.)				
		0–20	20–40	40–60	60–80	80–90
Error in nautical miles caused by drawing a 200 n.m. rhumb line as a straight line	Mercator	0	0	0	0	
	Conical orthomorphic	½	1	3	10	Very great
	Polar stereographic					
Error in nautical miles caused by drawing a 200 n.m. great circle as a straight line	Mercator	½	1	3	10	
	Conical orthomorphic		very small			
	Polar stereographic					small
Percentage errors in assuming a constant scale	Mercator	3	13	23	70	
	Conical orthomorphic	¾	½	½	½	¾
	Polar stereographic					

by water. Water-proofing generally makes writing difficult, particularly the marking of corrections. Unfortunately the paper may tend to stretch with time and with extremes of atmospheric conditions so that errors of the order of 1 per cent of distance can be expected which, except in the instance of the mercator chart, may be greater than those due to the measurement of distances by a simple rule.

30. *Scale of Chart.* The scale of a chart is defined as the ratio of the size of the chart to the particular portion of the Earth that it represents. Thus a large-scale chart covers a small area and a small-scale chart a large area. Scale is measured generally along the standard parallel of the chart, but in the instance of a mercator, the equator may not be used as the standard for scale but the middle latitude of the individual chart. This will cause inconvenience when going from one chart to another of a different latitude, but it will effect economies in the numbers of charts needed to cover an area in high latitudes.

31. The scale of charts may vary from 1:5 million to 1:20,000 or even less. A common size for planning marine operations or for air operations is 1:1M (about 14 n. miles to the inch) or 1:2M (about 27 n. miles to the inch). Hence a chart on a large sheet of paper will cover about 500 n.m. on a 1:1M scale or about 1000 n.m. on a 1:2M scale.

32. Although a small-scale chart is necessary for planning, for navigating a larger-scale chart may be preferred. The larger the scale, the shorter the distances that can be plotted accurately. If plotting is necessary at, say, half-hourly intervals, the scale of the chart will be according to the speed. In half an hour an aircraft may travel 200 n.m., over 7 inches on a 1:2M scale, which is a comfortable distance. In a ship, the distance travelled may be only 10 n.m., and this will represent less than $\frac{1}{2}$ inch on the same scale. On a scale of 1:200,000, however, it will represent nearly 4 inches.

33. A large scale has, however, a special disadvantage. In order to transfer a plot from one chart to another, the navigator has to reproduce certain parts of the plot. In an aircraft travelling at 400 knots he will only be able to travel 2 hours on a normal 1:2M chart without having to change to the next chart. In a ship travelling at 10 knots, even a 1:1M chart should cover enough distance for two days' sailing, and a chart of 1:200,000 will last for the best part of 12 hours.

34. It now appears that the size of a chart will be closely allied to the room available in a craft, and the scale of a chart will be closely allied to the speed of the craft. Where craft travel slowly or follow complicated patterns, a large-scale chart may be used temporarily because not only will it present the necessary information more clearly but also it will suffice for a longer period of time.

35. At sea, small-scale general or sailing charts are used for en-route navigation with larger-scale coast charts and still larger-scale harbour charts for terminal navigation. In the air, small-scale aeronautical or air charts are used for en-route navigation, often including a great deal of radio navigational information so that they may be known as radio facility charts. Larger-scale approach charts are used for terminal navigation, these charts showing radio aids and runways and giving height information.

2. CALCULATION OF COURSE AND DISTANCE

1. The navigator generally calculates courses and distances from one point to another as if the Earth were a perfect sphere. Except

when the distances approach the limit of a little over 10,000 nautical miles, the errors in calculation of a course on this assumption are negligible. The calculation of distances will, however, be absolutely correct if distances are measured in minutes of arc. These distances will have to be modified to produce answers in nautical miles (see page 16, para 4).

2. To illustrate the calculation of courses and distances, an example will be taken of a journey from a point in New York, 40° 43′ N. 74° 00′ W. to a point in Moscow, 55° 45′ N. 37° 37′ E. The difference of latitude (d. lat.) between New York and Moscow will be 15° 02′ N. which can be converted into 902′ of latitude. The difference of longitude (d. long.) between New York and Moscow will be 111° 37′ E. which can be converted into 6697′ of longitude.

3. In order to find course and distance, the cartesian coordinates of d. lat. and d. long. will have to be converted into polar coordinates. The formulae that will be used will be based on the assumption that d. lat. will be considered as measured in northing and will be negative if measured in southing and that d. long. will be measured in easting and will be considered as negative if measured in westing.

RHUMB-LINE COURSE AND DISTANCE

4. *Course.* From page 285, para 26,

$$\text{departure} = \text{d. long} \times \cos(\text{lat.})$$

In the instance of the journey from New York to Moscow, the latitude of New York is 40° 43′ N. and the latitude of Moscow is 55° 45′ N. The middle latitude (mid. lat.) is 48° 14′ N. and this value may be used to calculate the departure approximately:

dep. = d. long. × cos (mid. lat.)
     = 6697′ × cos 48° 14′   log 6697   = 3·82588
                        + log cos 48° 14′ = 9·82354
     = 4461′   = log dep.   3·64942

5. Because the rate of decrease of longitude with latitude accelerates as the equator is left, departure cannot be calculated accurately from mid. latitude. To mid. latitude has to be added an

increment known as the mid. latitude correction which is extracted from books of navigational tables according to approximate mid. latitude and difference of latitude. In the particular instance being considered, the mid. latitude correction will be 32'. Hence:

dep. = d. long. × cos (mid. lat. + correction)

$$= 6697' \times \cos (48° \ 14' + 32') \qquad \log 6697 \qquad = 3 \cdot 82588$$
$$+ \log \cos 48° \ 46' = 9 \cdot 81897$$

$$= 4414' \qquad\qquad\qquad\qquad = \log dep. \qquad 3 \cdot 64485$$

6. The rhumb line can now be calculated from departure and d. lat. as shown in Fig. 156(a):

Co. T = tan⁻¹ dep./d. lat.
= tan⁻¹ 4414/902

$$\log 4414 \qquad = 3 \cdot 64485$$
$$- \log 902 \qquad = 2 \cdot 95521$$

$$= 079T \qquad\qquad = \log \tan (Co.T) \quad 0 \cdot 68964$$
(actually 078° 37')

7. *Mercator Sailing.* An alternative method of measuring the course is based on the use of tables of meridional parts (page 320, para 8) which show the distance of any parallel of latitude from the equator on a mercator chart measured in minutes of longitude. As shown in Fig. 156(b), course can be found from the ratio of d. long. to the difference of meridional parts (d. mer. parts). In the particular example chosen:

Mer. parts 55° 45' = 4047
Mer. parts 40° 43' = 2679

d. mer. parts   = 1368

The course can now be found as follows:

Co. T = tan⁻¹ d. long/d. mer. parts
= tan⁻¹ 6697/1368

$$\log 6697 \qquad = 3 \cdot 82588$$
$$- \log 1368 \qquad = 3 \cdot 13609$$

$$= 078T \qquad\qquad = \log \tan (Co. \ T) = 0 \cdot 68979$$
(actually 078° 27')

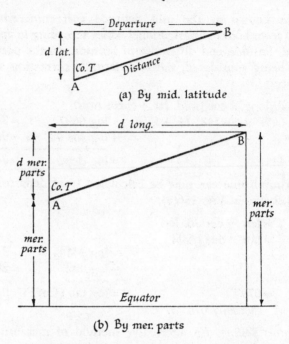

(a) By mid. latitude

(b) By mer. parts

FIG. 156   Rhumb-line course and distance

8. *Distance.* Fig. 156(a) shows that Cos (Co. T.) is d. lat. divided by distance so that:

$$\begin{aligned}
\text{Dist.} &= \text{d. lat.}/\cos(\text{Co. T.}) \\
&= \text{d. lat.} \times \sec(\text{Co. T}) \\
&= 902' \times \sec 78°\ 27' \\
&= 4505'
\end{aligned}$$

$$\begin{aligned}
\log 902 &= 2\cdot95521 \\
+\log \sec 78°\ 27' &= 0\cdot69849 \\
\hline
= \log \text{distance} &= 2\cdot65370
\end{aligned}$$

If the course is nearly 090T or 270T, a small rounding-off error in the course will be magnified when multiplying by sec (Co. T). However:

$$\begin{aligned}
\text{secant} &= \text{adjacent/hypotenuse} \\
&= (\text{adjacent/opposite}) \times (\text{opposite/hypotenuse}) \\
&= \text{tangent} \times \text{cosecant}
\end{aligned}$$

Hence:

$$\text{Dist.} = \text{d. lat.} \times \tan (\text{Co. T}) \times \text{cosec} (\text{Co. T})$$
$$= 902' \times \tan (\text{Co. T}) \times \text{cosec } 78° 27'$$

	log 902	$= 8 \cdot 95521$
(from para 7)	$+ \log \tan (\text{Co.T})$	$= 0 \cdot 68979$
	$+ \log \text{cosec } 78° 27'$	$= 0 \cdot 00888$
$= 4507'$	$= \log \text{distance}$	$= 2 \cdot 65388$

The method is particularly accurate because the exact value of tan (Co. T) is given in the calculation of course, and cosec (Co. T) only changes slowly when the course is close to 090T or 270T.

9. An alternative method, if departure is known, is to apply it instead of d. lat. in order to measure distance where the course is close to 090T or 270T. Thus:

$$\text{Dist.} = \text{dep.} \times \text{cosec} (\text{Co.T})$$
$$= 4414' \times \text{cosec } 78° 27'$$

	log 4414	$= 3 \cdot 64483$
	$+ \log \text{cosec } 78° 27'$	$= 0 \cdot 00888$
$= 4505'$	$= \log \text{distance}$	$= 3 \cdot 65371$

10. *Rhumb-Line Computers.* Rhumb-line computers are seldom used in practice since, unless the distances are short, the rhumb line is a curve on the surface of the Earth. However, if a rhumb-line computer should be a requirement, it could be very similar to that shown on page 288, Fig. 140, which illustrates a D.R. computer. The actual and destination latitudes, the latter perhaps being set by hand, would be differenced to find the d. lat. and d. long. The d. long. would be multiplied by cos (lat.) to convert it to departure and, since the distances would be short, latitude of destination might be sufficiently accurate. Departure and d. lat. would then be fed into a resolver whose outputs would be rhumb-line course and distance.

GREAT-CIRCLE DISTANCE AND COURSE

11. *Distance.* A great-circle distance may be as much as 180° of arc. Sin 89° = sin 91°, tan 89° = tan 91° and cos 89° = − cos 91°

or cos 271°. To avoid these ambiguities, the haversine (hav) is used which goes from 0 at 0° to 1 at 180° and is derived thus:

$$\text{hav} = \tfrac{1}{2}\,(1 - \cos)$$

12. It can be shown that for a journey from A to Z:

hav (dist.) = cos (lat. A) × cos (lat. Z) × hav (d. long.) + hav (d. lat.)

This is known as the cosine haversine formula.
We can use this formula to find the great-circle distance from New York 40° 43′ N. 74° 00′ W. to Moscow 55° 45′ N. 37° 37′ E.

lat. A	= 40° 43′N.	log cos lat. A	= 9·87964
lat. Z	= 55° 45′N.	+ log cos lat. Z	= 9·75036
d. long.	= 111° 37′	+ log hav (d. long).	= 9·83518
			9·46518

	Cos (lat. A) cos (lat. Z) hav (d. long.)	= 0·29186
d. lat. = 15° 02′	+ hav (d. lat.)	= 0·01711
	= hav (dist.)	= 0·30897
	distance	= 67° 32′
		= 4052′

13. The calculation need only involve entries in two tables. The first two entries come from log cos tables. All the remaining work can be confined within haversine tables which are specially made to include log haversines as well as natural haversines so that they can also be used to convert logs back into ordinary numbers. It will be noticed that the great-circle distance is more than 10 per cent shorter than the rhumb-line distance.

14. *Course.* A great circle is continually changing true direction unless it is the equator or a line of longitude. Therefore the course for a great circle cannot be calculated. All that can be done is to calculate the course for the start of the great circle, known as the initial course (I. Co.), or for the finish of the great circle.

15. The initial course from A to Z can be found from the formula:

sin (I. Co.) = cosec (dist.) × sin (d. long.) × cos (lat. Z)

To continue with the example of the great circle from New York to Moscow:

dist.　= 67° 32′	log cosec (dist.) = 0·03533
d. long = 111° 37′	
= 180°–68° 23′	+ log sin (d. long) = 9·96833
lat. Z　= 55° 45′	+ log cos (lat. Z) = 9·75017
	log sin (I.Co.)　= 9·75383
	I.Co.　　= 034½T
	(034° 34′T)

16. It so happens that the initial course is not close to 090T nor to 270T. Had it been, it would have not been possible to distinguish whether it was greater or less by using sines. Once more, it is necessary to return to haversines. The formula would be:

$$\text{hav (I. Co.)} = \text{cosec (dist.)} \times \text{sec (lat. } A) \times [\text{hav } (90° - \text{lat. } Z)$$
$$- \text{hav } (90° \sim (\text{lat. } A + \text{dist.}))]$$

	90° 00′	lat. A	= 40° 43′
− lat. Z	= 55° 45′	dist.	= 67° 32′
90° − lat. Z	= 34° 15′	lat. A + dist.	= 108° 15′
		90° ∼ (lat. A + dist.) =	18° 15′

hav (90° − lat. Z) = 0·08671			
− hav (90° ∼		log cosec (dist.)	= 0·03428
(lat. A + dist.)) = 0·02515		+ log sec (lat. A)	= 0·12036
DIFF	0·06156	+ log DIFF	= 8·78930
		log hav (I. Co.)	= 8·94394
		I. Co.	= 034½T
		(034° 30′T)	

17. An alternative formula, which may be quicker for those who are accustomed to it, uses tables that give the logarithms of the square roots of haversines, known as half-log haversines. The formula in terms of the route from A to Z is:

$$\text{hav (I. Co)} = \sqrt{\text{hav } (180° - (\text{lat. } A + \text{dist.} + \text{lat. } Z)}$$
$$\times \sqrt{\text{hav (lat. } A + \text{dist.} - \text{lat. } Z)}$$
$$\times \text{cosec (dist.)} \times \text{sec (lat. } Z)$$

GREAT-CIRCLE COMPUTER

18. The formulae mentioned so far have been intended for use with tables. In each instance, the solution demands making entries in only two tables. For computing, the requirement is different since resolving into sines and cosines can be achieved with a resolver. Accordingly, the great circle will generally be computed from a derivation of the 'four parts' formula which, in terms of the route from A to Z, reads:

cot (I. Co.) =
    cos (lat. A) × tan (lat. Z) × cosec (d. long.)
        − sin (lat. A) × cot (d. long)

This formula is useful if the initial course has to be found but distance is not already known. In a computer, it may be amended to:

cot (I. Co.) =
[cos (lat. A) sin (lat. Z) − sin (lat. A) × cos (lat. Z) × cos (d. long.)]
                cos (lat. Z) × sin (d. long.)

19. Fig. 157 shows how this formula can be computed using four sine-cosine potentiometer resolvers. Destination latitude (lat. Z)

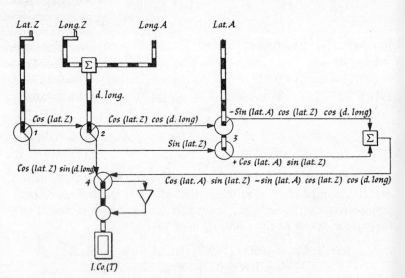

FIG. 157   Great-circle analogue computer

is set into a resolver and cos (lat. Z) and sin (lat. Z) produced as voltages. Cos (lat. Z) is fed into a second resolver set according to d. long. so that the outputs are cos (lat. Z) × sin (d. long.) and cos (lat. Z) × cos (d. long.). The former is the voltage required by the denominator in the formula and the latter, together with sin (lat. Z), can be fed into a third resolver, set according to (lat. A), and shown for convenience as split into two parts, one being a cosine resolver and the other a sine resolver. The two outputs are subtracted to produce the numerator of the formula as a voltage. Numerator and denominator are then fed into a fourth resolver and any unbalance is amplified and used to drive a motor until the resolver is set to the correct ratio. It will then be reading the initial course. An additional resolver will be needed if the distance is also to be calculated.

20. An analogue great-circle computer has been illustrated to emphasize that the problem is not very complex. A computer such as has been illustrated when fed with inputs from a dead-reckoning position computer could indicate continuously the shortest distance to destination and the course to steer for this shortest distance.

SHORTEST DISTANCE

21. On page 318, para 2, it was stated that the great circle is the shortest distance between two points on a globe. It is not the shortest distance between two points on the Earth because the Earth is not a perfect sphere. However, the distances will not differ by as much as $\frac{1}{2}$ per cent.

22. The development of craft that can travel outside the Earth's atmosphere has emphasized that the shortest distance between two points also depends on the speed of the craft. For example, suppose that a craft were to travel from a point on the Greenwich meridian at 80° north to a point at Longitude 180° east or west also at 80° north. If the craft were to travel outside the Earth's atmosphere at 150 knots, it would best travel due eastwards where it would remain hovering in the sky for 12 hours until the opposite point, travelling at 150 knots due to the rotation of the Earth, arrived below 12 hours later. If the craft were to travel at 300 knots, it would best set course 300T and meet the destination 5 hours later as it travelled round the Earth. At 600 knots, it

would set course 330T and meet the destination 2 hours later, and at 1200 knots it would set course 345T and meet the destination 1 hour later. Only if it travelled infinitely fast compared to the rotation of the Earth would the craft head 360T along the great circle. Hence light and radio waves travel along great circles for all practical purposes.

23. The land, the sea and the atmosphere will rotate with the rotation of the Earth. Hence a land craft, marine craft or aircraft will be constrained to follow a great circle, but in so doing they will be accelerated sideways, this acceleration being coriolis. A craft that travels outside the Earth's atmosphere will, however, travel along a path not above a great circle on the surface of the Earth and will not be affected by coriolis.

24. A satellite or space rocket will be launched eastwards to take advantage of the rotation of the Earth. A ballistic missile will likewise travel further if fired eastward, the difference in range being expressed in hundreds of miles for flights of thousands of miles.

3. ROUTING

1. The navigation of a craft during a journey may be greatly assisted by sound strategic planning including the choice of a suitable route. The route is chosen generally with two main points in view:

> (a) *Avoidance of collision* either with other craft or with the ground.
> (b) *Economy of operation*.

COLLISION WITH OTHER CRAFT

2. If no precautions were taken, the risk of collision between craft would depend mainly on three factors:

> (a) The size of the craft. The greater the size, the greater the space filled by each craft.
> (b) The numbers of craft. The greater the traffic density, the smaller the area within which a given number of craft will be packed.

(c) The speed of the craft. The faster the craft, the more collisions will be packed into a given period of time.

3. The navigator cannot alter the size of his craft nor the numbers of craft. In order to reduce the difficulties involved in deciding action in the presence of multiple targets, he can only reduce speed and, in the air, he cannot even take this action. It follows that there will come a point at which tactical avoidance becomes virtually impossible.

4. A very early example of strategic collision avoidance is the 'keep to the right' rule which obtains in rivers and channels and on most roadways. When craft have thus been formed into streams all moving the same way, the relative speeds of craft within each stream will be greatly reduced and tactical avoidance may then become relatively simple.

5. On the roads, one-way streets have been introduced to help the safe flow of traffic. Similar systems have been introduced at sea in special areas where the convergence of traffic is such that tactical avoidance becomes too difficult. Typical examples are narrow channels and headlands that are rounded by ships coming from several directions.

6. In air navigation, civil aircraft are channelled into lanes known as airways in order to simplify the task of the air-traffic control authority. In addition, aircraft can be separated into height bands provided certain precautions are taken, as described on page 74, para 31, so that all aircraft are operating to a common datum. The great advantage of height separation is that, although an aircraft may not remain still in the air geographically, it can maintain a given altitude as recorded by pressure altimeter.

7. In areas where no air-traffic control of height is exercised, a procedure known as quadrantal height separation is commonly accepted. According to this procedure:

(a) On headings from 000T to 089T, the aircraft flies at an odd thousand of feet of altimeter reading with standard pressure set.

(b) On headings from 090T to 179T, the aircraft flies at an odd thousand of feet plus 500 feet with standard pressure set.

(c) On headings from 180T to 269T, the aircraft flies at an even thousand of feet with standard pressure set.

(d) On headings from 270T to 359T, the aircraft flies at an even thousand of feet plus 500 feet with standard pressure set.

COLLISION WITH GROUND

8. Stranding at sea and flying into high ground are major navigational hazards. The route itself will naturally be chosen to avoid such hazards by a reasonable margin. Accidents of this type generally occur from two causes, provided the route has been adequately planned:

(a) Lack of accurate knowledge of position. This is probably the major cause.
(b) Change of route and consequent inadequate knowledge of heights and depths.

9. On marine charts, depth of water is recorded in 6-foot or fathom intervals. Ample spot depths are marked and a few contours, generally at 5, 10, 20 and 100 fathoms. The depth of water is generally measured according to the depth at mean low water spring tides and only under exceptional conditions will there be less water under the hull. It is worth noting that should feet or metres be used for depths, the navigator might run into danger by imagining that the water was six times or twice as deep as it is.

10. On aeronautical or air charts, height of ground above sea-level is generally recorded in feet. Occasionally, metres may appear on maps which can lead the navigator to assume that ground is three times as low as it is. Heights on charts are generally shown in the form of spot figures, and in charts used for radio navigation there is seldom enough room for any but a very few spot heights to be marked. On maps, including those of airfields, contours may appear provided that the radio information is limited and the charts are of a sufficiently large scale.

11. It has been shown that as a result of differences between the atmosphere and the ICAO atmosphere by which the altimeter will be calibrated, the altitude given by the pressure altimeter may differ considerably from that of true height above sea-level, but that the altimeter has to be used as a standard in order to ensure traffic separation. Hence operators of aircraft tend to lay down

allowances to be made for clearing high ground, and this may lead to a definition of the minimum altimeter reading or safety 'height' along each portion of the route. This altimeter reading will take into account the height of ground a number of miles each side of the route in order to allow for navigational inaccuracies. Where possible, minimum altitudes will be specified on alternative routes but, nevertheless, an emergency change of route can introduce particular problems in allowing for adequate high-ground clearance.

GREAT-CIRCLE ROUTE

12. Section 2 of this chapter explained that a great circle is nearly the shortest distance between two points over the surface of the Earth. The great-circle distance from New York to Moscow was calculated as 4052 miles whereas the rhumb-line distance was calculated as 4505 miles, about 12 per cent longer.

13. The difference in distance between a great circle and a rhumb line depends on the distance travelled in an east–west direction and on the latitude, and the following table gives a rough guide:

TABLE XII. SAVINGS EFFECTED BY GREAT CIRCLES

Distance travelled east–west (n. miles)	Latitude (degrees)	Percentage saving effected by great circle
2000	up to 20	less than $\frac{1}{4}$
2000	up to 40	about 1
2000	up to 60	about 5
500	up to 60	less than $\frac{1}{4}$

14. Since the distance saved by using a great circle depends on east–west distance as well as on latitude, a great circle is commonly split into intervals or legs at the points where it crosses certain longitudes. For example, the New York to Moscow route could be split into intervals according to the crossing of each whole 15° of longitude. Rhumb-line legs between these intervals would be insignificantly longer than the great-circle distance and, indeed, in this particular instance, the difference is less than 1 n. mile.

15. *Calculation of points along a great circle.* The simplest way to find the points at which a great circle would cut successive 15° lines of longitude would be to draw the route as a straight line on a gnomonic chart and to note the points at which the straight line crosses the lines of longitude. These points could then be transferred to a mercator chart and the rhumb lines drawn as straight lines between them. If a gnomonic chart is not available it is possible to calculate the positions of these points.

16. The first step in the calculation is to find the most northerly point of the great circle, known as the vertex, for which the letter V may be used. This will be the first step even though the vertex may not lie on the route itself but may be on an extension to the route. To find the latitude and longitude of the vertex, the following formulae can be used:

$$\cos (\text{lat. } V) = \cos (\text{lat. } A) \times \sin (\text{I. Co.})$$
$$\cot (\text{long. } V \sim \text{long. } A) = \sin (\text{lat. } A) \times \tan (\text{I. Co.})$$

the terms A and I. Co. referring to the starting point and the initial great-circle course. For the New York to Moscow great circle, I. Co. was calculated on page 334, para 15, so that the calculation of the latitude and longitude of the vertex becomes:

lat. $A = 40°\ 43'$ log cos (lat. A) $= 9{\cdot}87964$
I. Co. $= 34°\ 34'$ log sin (I. Co.) $= 9{\cdot}75386$

$$= 9{\cdot}63350$$
$$\text{lat. } V = 64°\ 32'$$

log sin (lat. A) $= 9{\cdot}81446$
log tan (I. Co.) $= 9{\cdot}83822$

$$= 9{\cdot}65268$$
long. $V \sim$ long. $A = 65°\ 48'$
long. $A = 74°\ 00'$

$$\text{long. } V = \ \ 8°\ 12'$$

17. When the position of the vertex has been found, the latitude at which the great circle cuts any line of longitude X can be calculated from the following formula:

$$\tan (\text{lat. } X) = \cos (\text{long. } V \sim \text{long. } X) \times \tan (\text{lat. } V)$$

The calculation may be arranged in a tabular form thus:

long. X	60° 00′ W	45° 00′ W	30° 00′ W	15° 00′ W	00° 00′ W	15° 00′ E
long. V	8° 12′ W	8° 12′ W	8° 12′ W	8° 12′ W	8° 12′ W	8° 12′ W
d. long.	51° 48′	36° 48′	21° 48′	06° 48′	08° 12′	23° 12′
log cos (d. long.)	9·79128	9·90349	9·96778	9·99693	9·99554	9·96338
log tan (lat. V)	0·32215	0·32215	0·32215	0·32215	0·32215	0·32215
log tan (lat. X)	0·11343	0·22564	0·28993	0·31908	0·31769	0·28553
lat. X	52° 24′ N	59° 15′ N	62° 51′ N	64° 23′ N	64° 18′ N	62° 36′ N

18. *Composite Course.* It may be necessary to arrange for a great-circle course to be limited to a certain latitude. In this event, the great circle has to be constructed from the starting point to touch the limiting latitude and this limiting latitude is then followed until a great circle can be drawn to lead smoothly on to the destination. Such a route is known as a composite course. It can be drawn on a gnomonic chart or calculated from the formulae in para 16, the point at which the great circle touches the latitude being the vertex. By knowing lat. V, I. Co. can be found and, subsequently, long. V.

OPTIMUM ROUTE

19. The progress of a ship may be impeded by heavy seas and, in particular, by heavy head seas, as described on page 105, para 14. These conditions will make it necessary to reduce speed. Similarly, an aircraft may suffer a reduction of ground speed as a result of a head wind, or it may be able to take advantage of a tail wind. In either instance, the ground speed of a craft travelling along a particular course may be forecast at any point with the help of the meteorologist and the wave forecaster. The wave forecaster may on a chart plot isopleths, lines along which waves of a certain height are anticipated. The meteorologist may plot isotachs, lines along which winds will be of a certain strength. In addition, the forecasters will plot the directions of motion of the seas or the winds.

20. Suppose that a craft has to travel from a point A to a point B. From the starting point A, the distances that can be covered in various directions according to the ground speed in those directions can be established for a day in the instance of a slow

marine craft or an hour in the instance of a subsonic aircraft. Assuming that a wave of identical craft leave A simultaneously but in directions that differ slightly, the positions that these will reach after the interval of time can be plotted as a wave front. From the various points on the wave front, ground speeds for the next interval of time can be calculated in various directions and a second wave front produced. The process may be continued, certain directions being discontinued as it becomes evident that progress along these lines would be unprofitable. Certain additional lines of progress may be added as the separation between the tracks becomes too great. Eventually, as shown in Fig. 158,

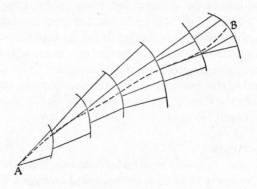

FIG. 158   Minimum time path, by 'Wave Front' method

the complete route from A to B can be covered by wave fronts and the minimum time route evolved as shown by the dotted line.

21. The process of finding the shortest route by means of wave fronts is somewhat cumbersome. However, if the forecast charts are reasonably constant in scale, a simple rule or a template can be prepared for each type of craft so that the wave fronts can be plotted directly. The errors in choice of route due to errors in assuming a constant distance on the chart for speed will be insignificant. In any event, when the route has been chosen, it will generally be approximated by a series of straight line legs, which in the instance of a craft fitted with a compass may well be in the form of rhumb lines.

22. Isopleths have to be calculated according to complex formulae involving wind speeds, directions and fetch. It has been estimated that an effort of the order of one man/day or 24 man/hours is needed to work out figures for crossing a major ocean. Accordingly, the use of a computer not only for wave-front calculations but also for isopleth calculations has particular attractions.

23. In addition to the saving of time and fuel, there will be other factors. Hurricanes can damage ships. Icing can endanger aircraft. A route that avoids heavy weather at sea or storms in the air may avoid damage to fragile cargo or distress to nervous passengers, and as such may have a special economic value quite apart from the question of possible loss or damage to the craft itself.

24. It is of interest to note that very complete route planning involving an accurate knowledge not only of tides but also of the speed in still water is required by long-distance swimmers. In particular, the swimmer avoids fighting the tides when crossing a channel. He seeks to allow the tides to drift him one way at one stage of his swim so that it will return him to the desired point of arrival in the final stage. The same considerations apply in ocean yacht racing.

25. A parallel solution has been applied to aircraft planning. It was explained on page 260, para 26(c), that drift could be found from the pressure difference at each end of an intended track. Similarly, by applying the pressure difference for each end of a complete route, a mean drift can be found which will avoid the necessity for the aircraft having to oppose the wind at one stage and oppose the opposite wind at a later stage. In general, the single heading route will lead an aircraft to follow a favourable wind pattern, but not always and, therefore, the method is generally replaced by a more complex system based on the over-all flow of winds and perhaps supported by a wave-front analysis.

NAVIGATIONAL AID ROUTING

26. It will be useless to choose a route that will avoid collision with other craft and that will avoid collision with solid earth if the craft is not able to follow that route. Where traffic densities are high, ample navigational aids are invariably provided which tend to determine the routes.

27. Where traffic densities are low, aids may be few and far between, but the routes may still be chosen to simplify navigation. The small-boat sailor may deliberately divert so as to follow a coastline to assist him during a voyage. The camel train crossing the desert may zigzag across it from one distinctive point to another. The military navigator may use a similar procedure to find a point not readily distinguished by navigation aids. He may first locate an adjacent unmistakable landmark and make a short run from thence to his objective.

ROUTE PREPARATION

28. The detailed planning of the route will be necessary so that it may be possible to calculate the timing and fuel requirements. This will enable arrangements to be made in advance to turn round the craft on arrival so that it can continue to operate with the minimum of delay, turn-round being a crucial factor in both civil and military operations. The calculations will also ensure that adequate fuel is available for the journey, which is particularly important in craft in which fuel is a large proportion of the weight.

29. The detailed dead-reckoning calculations for the journey can act as a basis for the subsequent navigation. In aircraft, navigation en-route is invariably based on a flight plan in which the fuel requirements have been worked out in detail, so that the safe take-off weight is not exceeded, taking into account length of runway, head wind, temperature (which may affect engines) and height above sea-level (which will affect lift).

30. In addition to the preparatory calculations, the navigator may have to amend his charted information to allow for chart inaccuracies, or changes such as shifting sand-banks, sunken wrecks at sea or high pylons over land. Inevitably, navigational aid siting may change, aids may become temporarily unserviceable, traffic patterns may be altered or modified and areas may be forbidden to craft for military reasons.

31. The navigator may have to contend with a great deal of information either marked on the chart or made available elsewhere. This information may be circulated in the form of Notices to Mariners or to airmen (NOTAMS) or may be published in the form of 'sailing directions' or 'coast pilot' at sea, or 'route

manual' or 'air pilot' in the air. The arrangements for making sure that all the relevant information is available can represent a major problem, and its presentation in the craft can lead to cluttering of the chart or excessive documentation.

32. The navigator may prepare certain observations beforehand. For example, he may draw in radio bearings that he will subsequently observe, or prepare astronomical observations. Preparations such as these are a particular feature of high-speed operations or for voyages under difficult conditions, such as single-handed navigation.

EMERGENCY PLANNING

33. In addition to the normal planning for the chosen route, special planning may be advisable to take account of emergencies. For example, it may be necessary to plan alternative routes in case the main route has to be changed. In addition, two special calculations are commonly made:

(a) Critical point.
(b) Point of no return.

34. *Critical Point*. The critical point of a journey is the point at which the same amount of fuel will be required to complete the journey as to turn back to the starting point. This critical point may be of importance in land exploration, particularly in polar crossings, where food may be an over-riding factor. The critical point is generally calculated on the average ground speed out and the average ground speed on a return journey, taking into account the mean flow velocity expected on the route. The critical point will then be the following fraction of either the time out or of the distance:

(return ground speed)/(ground speed out + return ground speed).

35. *Point of No Return*. The point of no return is that point at which there will be insufficient fuel to turn back to the start of the journey. After passing this point, there may be no turning back. If the total time taken for the journey out and the total time that would be taken for the return journey are calculated, the point of

no return will be the following fraction of either the time out or of the distance out:

(Maximum time in cruise)/(time out + time for return).

36. Both these calculations assume constant flow velocity and constant fuel consumption. In many instances, neither will obtain. In these circumstances, it will generally be advisable to plan an imaginary route backwards to the starting point so as to discover:

(a) When the fuel available on the reversed route is the same as the fuel available on the planned route assuming in both instances the minimum fuel. This will be the critical point.

(b) When the fuel available on the reversed route is the same as the fuel available on the planned route assuming the minimum fuel on the reversed route but the planned fuel on the planned route. This will be the point of no return.

37. It is an unfortunate feature of navigation, particularly of air navigation, that, while the normal planning may be simple and involve little documentation, emergency planning, which may not be required, entails the provision of a great deal of additional documentation and information.

TACTICAL ROUTING

38. In order to achieve an exact E.T.A., the air navigator may waste time by flying a dog-leg. If 3 minutes are to be wasted, he may alter course for 3 minutes by 60° to port or starboard and return to track by a subsequent alteration through 120° to starboard or port. Alternatively, time may be wasted by orbits, a rate 1 orbit wasting 2 minutes, and a rate $\frac{1}{2}$ orbit, 4 minutes. These time-wasting manœuvres are, of course, not acceptable on airways except at chosen points. (See page 351, para 8.)

39. Special routing is used for searching areas. There are two common methods:

(a) *Square search.* Used when the object was last located at a certain point. The craft starts at this point and travels in a

series of expanding squares, the distances between successive tracks being twice the distance at which it can expect to
detect the object.

(b) *Creeping line ahead.* The craft covers an area by a series of
parallel tracks travelling to and fro but advancing each
time so that each track is separated from the previous track
by twice the distance at which it can expect to detect the
object of the search. The method is used when it is not
known whether there is an object in an area.

40. Special routing, particularly in the vertical plane, is also
needed for jet aircraft and particularly for supersonic jet aircraft
in order to reduce noise at take-off and noise due to supersonic
bangs (see page 108, para 26).

4. TERMINAL ROUTING

QUEUES

1. In terminal areas, queues may build up. The reason is the
limited rate at which craft may be accepted. The maximum rate
over a period of time at which craft may be accepted is known as
the acceptance rate of the port. If the mean arrival rate over a
period of time is low compared to the acceptance rate, it will on
occasions exceed the acceptance rate and queues will occasionally
occur. If the mean arrival rate over a period of time is close to the
acceptance rate, queueing will become chronic.

2. It is convenient to define the ratio of the arrival rate over a
period of time to the acceptance rate over the same period of time
as the 'acceptance ratio'. If, on the average, one ship arrives at a
port each day and the port can handle one ship an hour, the
acceptance ratio will be 1/24. It is possible to show that, if the
arrivals are absolutely random:

Average number in queue
$$= (\text{acceptance ratio})/(1 - \text{acceptance ratio})$$
Proportion of time that a queue of N craft will build up
$$= (1 - \text{acceptance ratio}) \times (\text{acceptance ratio})^N$$

Example. Craft arrive at a port at half the rate that the port can tackle.

> Acceptance ratio $= \frac{1}{2}$
> Average number in queue $= \frac{1}{2}/(1-\frac{1}{2}) = 1$ craft.
> Proportion of times that a queue of five craft will build up
> $$= (1-\frac{1}{2}) \times (\frac{1}{2})^5 = 1/64 = 1\frac{1}{2} \text{ per cent of time.}$$

3. The figures indicated by the formulae are not accurate partly because arrivals are seldom purely random and partly because, when congestion builds up, craft may be diverted to other ports. Also, a period of congestion caused by bad weather may lead to the acceptance rate being speeded up due to the port facilities having been rested. Nevertheless, the formulae give an idea of the extent of the problem and stress the difficulties that must arise when the arrival rate approaches the acceptance rate.

4. In marine operations, queueing is seldom serious mainly because arrivals are not random but are planned and generally ships are able to arrive at their berths on schedule or delayed in a regular pattern. However, the situation is very different at an airport where the runways act as a bottleneck that produces a limited acceptance ratio. The problem is handled by air-traffic control authorities.

5. The landing rate on a runway is limited by the need to allow the pilot to complete the landing manœuvre without being harassed by the presence of other aircraft. This generally limits the landing rate to about one aircraft every 2 minutes. Take-offs may be fitted into gaps between landings and, if the operations are closely controlled, the rate of movements, which includes take-offs as well as landings, may be around forty an hour. If a higher rate of movements is needed, twin runways may have to be built.

6. The difficulties that subsonic aircraft encounter in attempts to keep to time schedules have already been stressed (page 308, para 10). Even if an aircraft were able to arrive on schedule and could therefore book an arrival 'slot' time for landing, there might be another aircraft short of fuel or one that had taken overshoot action and needed to be fitted into the pattern unexpectedly. For these reasons, it has been the practice of controllers to feed aircraft into runways on a first-come first-served basis, although some preference may be given to the big jet aircraft with a high

fuel consumption and therefore limited reserves in terms of minutes of time.

ATC ROUTING

7. In order to feed aircraft regularly into a landing stream, it is necessary for air-traffic controllers to introduce time-wasting patterns known as holding patterns or holds. Since emergencies may upset long-range timing, these patterns are usually flown close to the terminal airfield and the aircraft is normally fed straight from the pattern into the landing.

8. *Holding patterns.* The simplest holding pattern is a circular orbit starting and finishing at a point marked by a navigational aid, the orbit being generally to the left so that the captain, who sits in the left-hand seat, can watch for overtaking traffic during the turn. However, in place of a circular orbit, a race-track pattern is commonly flown which is two semicircular arcs joined by straight parallel tracks.

9. The aircraft approaching the airfield makes a turn through 180° generally to the left, starting at a point preferably marked by a navigational aid. The aircraft then flies on a reciprocal for a number of minutes specified by the controller and a second turn through 180° in the same direction brings the original starting point ahead. The aircraft then flies back to the starting point ready either to approach the airfield or, if so instructed by the controller, to complete a second pattern.

10. *Procedure turn.* An aircraft may approach an airfield from the reciprocal direction to that for landing. A procedure turn may be made consisting of a turn generally through about 45° to port, followed by a steady run of 1 or 2 minutes on this heading and a turn through 180° to starboard to bring the aircraft back on a line approaching the track guide into the airfield at a convenient angle. Procedure turns and holding patterns may be printed on approach charts.

11. *Stack.* If there is more than one aircraft in the queue, it will be preferable not to set up a second holding pattern at a point further from the airfield owing to the need to correct timing as late as possible. Generally, a number of aircraft can be fitted into the same holding pattern one above the other separated at low levels by 1000 or 2000 feet. Such an arrangement is known

as a stack. Aircraft may be directed off the lowest level on to the approach to the runway while those above are moved down to lower levels.

12. *Path stretching.* To feed aircraft of different speeds off the stack into a regularly spaced stream approaching the runway, path stretching may be used. For example, the controller may direct the aircraft off the stack on to the reciprocal of the approach path and then instruct the pilot when to turn on to the approach path so as to ensure safe separation from other aircraft coming in to land.

5. SUMMARY

CHARTS

A chart used for navigation has to be orthomorphic or conformal in order that directions shall be measured by a protractor. Approximate constancy of scale is also useful.

Over a small area, the projection is immaterial. Over a large area, four types of chart are commonly used:

(a) *Mercator.* Orthomorphic. A rhumb line appears straight, so this chart is used with a magnetic, gyro-magnetic or gyro compass. Scale is not constant. Adjacent sheets on the same equatorial scale will fit.

(b) *Conical orthomorphic or Lambert's conformal.* Orthomorphic. Great circle appears as a straight line approximately so that the projection is convenient for radio presentation and for steering with a gyro heading reference. Approximates to constant scale.

(c) *Polar stereographic.* Orthomorphic. Used for polar grid navigation using a gyro heading reference.

(d) *Transverse mercator.* For craft with limited range operating over a wide range of latitudes including the poles.

A gnomonic chart can be used for great-circle planning.

Marine charts show ample spot depths in fathoms and a few contours. Air charts may show simplified contours or hachures and a few spot heights.

Charts are continually corrected and other information supplied through Notices to Mariners and NOTAMS, etc.

ROUTING

Routing depends on:

 (a) Avoidance of stranding or flying into high ground.

 (b) Following of prescribed routes, at prescribed heights in the instance of aircraft, in order to reduce the chances of collision.

 (c) Avoidance of head winds and bad weather, which affect speeds of ships at sea and speeds of aircraft over the ground. Route must also avoid dangerous storms and icing.

 (d) Selection to make best use of navigational aids.

In civil aviation, routing is generally determined by the requirements of air-traffic control authorities. Routes may include the flying of patterns to waste time so that aircraft may be fed at the correct intervals into airfields for landing.

PLANNING

The navigator may complete a dead-reckoning plan of his journey before the start, including emergency plans such as critical point and point of no return.

In airways operations, air-traffic controllers may instruct aircraft to fly holding patterns in order to fit into landing sequences.

BIBLIOGRAPHY: TECHNIQUES

This part of the book is so fundamental to navigation that most of the information will be found in general books on navigation appropriate to the particular craft and listed on page 613. In addition, there have been a few specialized papers written:

COURSE AND DEAD RECKONING

Calvert, E. S., A comparison of two systems for avoiding collision, *J. Inst. Navig.*, **14**, 379.

Calvert, E. S., Manœuvres to ensure the avoidance of collision, *J. Inst. Navig.*, **13**, 127.

Durst, C. S., The accuracy of dead reckoning in the air, *J. Inst Navig.*, **8**, 91.

Hollingdale, S. H., The mathematics of collision avoidance in two dimensions, *J. Inst. Navig.*, **14**, 243.

Morrel, J. S., The mathematics of collision avoidance in the air, *J. Inst. Navig.*, **11**, 18.

Morrel, J. S., The physics of collision at sea, *J. Inst. Navig.*, **14**, 163.

Oudet, L., *Radar and Collision*, Hollis & Carter, London.

Sawyer, J. S., *Theoretical aspects of pressure pattern flying*, H.M.S.O.

CHARTS AND ROUTING

Adams, O. S., see Deetz, C. H., and O. S. Adams.

Anon, The modified Lambert conformal projection for polar areas, *Canad. J. Res.*, Vol. 27.

Clough-Smith, J. H., *Applied D.R. navigation and flight planning*, Pitman, London.

Deetz, C. H., and O. S. Adams, *Elements of map projection*, U.S. Coast and Geodetic Survey, Dept. of Commerce, Washington, D.C.

Fraser, D. O., Optimum flight paths, *J. Inst. Navig.*, **4**, 178.

Greenhood, D., *Mapping*, University of Chicago Press.

Hanssen, G. L., The U.S. Navy hydrographic office ship routing programme, *Navigation (U.S.A.)*, **6**, 157.

James, R. W., *Application of wave forecasting to marine navigation*, H.O.

Katz, R., Flight path of shortest time, *Navigation (U.S.A.)*, **2**, 41.

Myerscough, W., *Maps and elementary meteorology*, Pitman, London.

Ney, C. H., The modified Lambert conformal projection for polar areas, *Canad. J. Res.*, Vol. 27.

Wepster, A., Weather routing of merchant ships, *J. Inst. Navig.*, **16**, 389.

Worthington, G. D. P., *Flight planning*, Pitman, London.

PART FOUR

BASIC AIDS

CHAPTER X. POSITION FINDING. The procedures by which information from aids is translated into position lines and fixes form the substance of this chapter. The various types of position line are first described and then the methods adopted to plot position lines at long ranges from the origins. The use of the D.R. position for plotting is explained and also the accuracy of a position found by combining a position line with a D.R. position. Automatic homing is described together with the principles of lock-follow devices. Fixing accuracies from bearings and distances are given in terms of accuracy contours, but fixes from differences of bearings or distances are deferred until later chapters in which they have particular applications. Finally the value of the D.R. position as a check on the reliability of the fix is emphasized.

CHAPTER XI. GENERAL AND VISUAL AIDS. The first section deals with the general principles by which positional information is conveyed to a craft. The use of waves and their propagation characteristics, the need for band-width, and the problems of signal-to-noise ratio are discussed briefly. The particular problems of military navigation and the importance of identification are also explained. The remaining parts of the chapter deal with sensory aids in the form of light, heat and touch. The basic properties of light waves and of optical instruments are first described. The over-riding problem of identification in visual navigation continually recurs in the third section of the chapter and the way in which the accuracy of line of sight measurement are used in the form of differences of bearings is explained. The value of visual systems for collision avoidance, for aiming systems and for berthing ships or landing of aircraft is emphasized together with the difficulty of visual measurement of distance, a difficulty that may eventually be resolved by the laser. A brief mention is then made of the use of infra-red in military systems and of the sense of feel in swinging the lead.

CHAPTER XII. ASTRO-NAVIGATION. This highly compressed survey of astro techniques first explains the problems of sight taking, using the marine and the bubble sextant, the errors that arise, and the limitations which may partly be mitigated in aircraft by star trackers but which cannot readily be solved by radio astronomy. The positions of stars and the movements of bodies over the celestial sphere are next described and their effects on tabulation in almanacs. This leads naturally on to sight reduction, star curves providing the illustration of the basic methods. The various systems of sight reduction can only be dealt with in outline, but some simple comparisons between types of system have been included. Finally a section on special procedures describes the use of astro as a heading reference, special methods of sight reduction, and the possibilities of artificial satellites as sources of astro positions.

CONTENTS

CHAPTER X

Position Finding

1. POSITION LINES

1. A position line (P.L.) or line of position (L.O.P.) defines the position of a craft as being along, below, or above a line on the suface of the Earth. A position line may be marked on a chart by a line with a single-feathered arrow at each end. The time at which the craft was known to be on that line is generally recorded on the chart beside the position line.

2. A position line may be of one of four types:

    (a) Bearing (directional measurement).
    (b) Distance measurement.
    (c) Difference of distances.
    (d) Difference of bearings.

PLOTTING BEARINGS

3. A bearing (brng) is the direction of a craft from a point measured along a great circle. The point may be either a fixed point or a moving point such as another craft. The measurement is expressed in degrees clockwise through 360° from the true or magnetic meridian at the point and is suffixed T or M accordingly. A bearing from a point is unlikely to be expressed in grid directions since grid directions are only used by moving craft.

4. A bearing may be measured from the craft. In this event, it will generally be recorded relative to the heading of the craft and should be known as a relative bearing (brng rel.). Such a bearing may be measured clockwise from ahead through 360° and suffixed R. Alternatively, it may be measured from ahead through 180° either to port or starboard and named red or green.

5. A true or magnetic bearing may be measured from a craft by means of an instrument oriented true north or magnetic north. Alternatively, a relative bearing may be converted into a true or

magnetic bearing by the addition of the true or magnetic heading of the craft, subtracting 360° if the total is more than 360°. It is essential that a bearing taken *to* a point from a craft be clearly distinguished from a bearing that is taken *from* a point. It may, therefore, be known as a bearing *of a point*, a bearing *to a point*, or a bearing *from the craft*.

6. *Conversion Angle.* Long-range bearings may be printed on a special chart, either as straight lines on a gnomonic chart or as slight curves on a conical orthormorphic or a stereographic chart. However, a long-range bearing will often have to be plotted on a mercator chart. Owing to the convergency of the meridians (page 184, para 5) the great circle will appear as a curve on the mercator chart, the curvature being towards the equator. Hence the rhumb line between the point and the craft will always lie on that side of the great circle which is towards the equator.

7. The angle between the rhumb-line and the great-circle bearing is roughly equal each end and is known as the conversion angle. It can be calculated from the formula:

$$\tan (\text{conversion angle}) = \sin (\text{mid. lat.}) \times \sec (\tfrac{1}{2}\text{d. lat}) \times \tan (\tfrac{1}{2}\text{d. long.})$$

If d. lat. and d. long. are not too great, the formula becomes:

$$\text{conversion angle} = \tfrac{1}{2} \sin (\text{mid. lat.}) \times (\text{d. long.})$$

A simple conversion angle table can be constructed from which the difference of longitude between two points in degrees may be multiplied by a factor to give conversion angle:

Mid. Lat.°	Conversion angle factor
0	
	0·0
6	
	0·1
18	
	0·2
30	
	0·3
45	
	0·4
65	
	0·5
90	

It is evident that the conversion angle between two points will be half the convergency of the meridians at those two points.

8. Fig. 159 shows the plotting of a long-range bearing on a mercator chart. The bearing from a radio station R to a craft

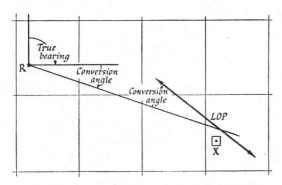

FIG. 159   Long-range bearing on mercator chart

whose D.R. position is X is assumed to be 090T. The process of drawing the position line will be as follows:

(a) Calculate the conversion angle between R and X.

(b) Since the great circle curves towards the equator, add the conversion angle to 090T in this particular instance, and draw a straight line from R in this direction.

(c) From the point where the straight line crosses the longitude of X draw a position line at an angle to the straight line equal to the conversion angle but such that, if extended, it would pass the ground station on that side which is away from the equator.

9. *Curve of Equal Bearing.* The process will be complicated if the bearing is taken from the craft to the station. Fig. 160(a) shows that on a mercator in high latitudes, if a craft records the bearing of a radio station R as being 090T, it may be anywhere along a curve XYZ. This is known as a curve of equal bearing and is roughly as far toward the equator compared to the rhumb line from X to R as the great circle is away from the equator compared to the rhumb line from X to R.

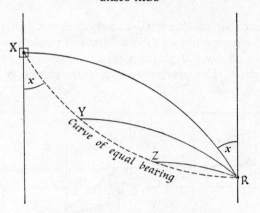

(a) Curves of equal bearing on a
Mercator chart

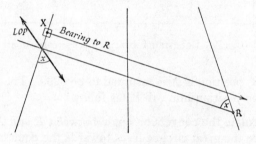

(b) Plotting on Conical Orthomorphic chart

FIG. 160   Long-range bearings from the craft

10. If the bearing has to be plotted on a conical orthomorphic
chart it will evidently be necessary first to draw a trial bearing
from the D.R. position of the craft towards the radio station and
then to draw a line parallel to this trial bearing to represent the
actual bearing as shown in Fig. 160(b). A position line to represent the curve of equal bearing can then be drawn through
the point where the bearing crosses the D.R. longitude of the
craft and in a true direction equal to the true direction of the
bearing at the radio station.

PLOTTING DISTANCES

11. If the distance measured from an object is only a few tens of
miles, the navigator may plot it on his chart by drawing a circle

round the object with a pair of compasses. As the distance increases, so the distortion of the circle will increase. This will be particularly noticeable on a mercator chart in high latitudes, the circle becoming pear-shaped with the bigger end towards the pole. On a stereographic projection, on the other hand, the circle will remain a circle but the centre will be offset.

12. In practice, the navigator does not use a pair of compasses, largely as a result of the difficulty of drawing a circular shape on a distorted chart. It is more usual for him to draw a straight line close to the D.R. position to represent the arc. If the craft is not at the D.R. position but at a distance at right angles to the bearing

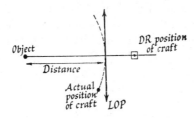

FIG. 161   Short-distance measurement plotting

of the object, as is the actual position in Fig. 161, an error will arise. This error will depend not only on the distance that the craft is at right angles to the bearing but also on the distance that the craft is from the object. Thus:

Error in distance plotted (n. miles)
  = (distance at right angles to bearing (n. miles))^2/
      (2 × distance to object (n. miles))

13. As the distance from the craft to the object increases, the errors in the plotting of the position line tend to increase. The latitude scale may be in error by up to one-half per cent when used to measure distances in nautical miles. In addition, if distance is being plotted on a mercator chart:

  (a) The distance from the object to the D.R. position ought to be measured along the great circle whereas the straight line on the chart is a rhumb line.

  (b) Any bearing will be in error according to the conversion angle and therefore the position line drawn at right angles to the bearing to the object will be at a finer angle to the meridian than it should be.

(c) The straight position line on the chart will not represent a great circle. Therefore, in addition to the error that will arise because the position line should be drawn as a small circle, an error will arise according to how far the craft happens to be from the meridian that passes through the D.R. position. The error in n. miles will be:

$$(\text{Distance to D.R. meridian (n. miles)})^2/(115 \times \tan (\text{lat.}))$$

14. If the distance to the object is measured in hundreds or thousands of miles, or if the object is not on the chart that the navigator is using, it will be necessary to calculate the distance and the bearing of the object from the D.R. position. It will then be possible to draw a line from the D.R. position towards the object, as shown in Fig. 162, and to cut off, along this line, an

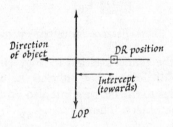

FIG. 162   Long-distance measurement plotting

interval known as the intercept, which is the difference between the measured distance and the calculated distance between the craft and the object.

15. In order to calculate a distance to an object, it may be convenient to choose a point a little distance from the D.R. position. In this event, the distance that the craft is at right angles to the bearing from this chosen or assumed position may be large so that the error mentioned in para 12 will arise even though the distance involved may be much greater. The error in n. miles will be:

$$\frac{(\text{Distance at right angles to bearing (n. miles)})^2}{(115 \times \tan (\text{distance}'))}$$

the term (distance') referring to the distance to the object in minutes of arc.

16. An additional problem arises if the object is not at the same height as the craft and distance has to be measured in the horizontal plane. For example, the distance measured from an aircraft to the ground will be a slant distance and the map distance will be shorter. Except close to the object, the difference between slant and map distances in n. miles will be approximately:

$$\text{height (thousands of feet)}^2/(72 \times \text{distance (n. miles)})$$

Example. An aircraft measures a slant distance in n. miles which is equal to its height in thousands of feet:

$$\text{error} = \text{distance}^2/(72 \times \text{distance}) = \text{distance}/72$$
$$= 1\tfrac{1}{3} \text{ per cent of distance}$$

17. *Range.* To use the term 'range' for measured distance can cause confusion if 'range' is also used for limits of distance such as the maximum range of a craft or the range at which signals from a radio station can be received. Hence there will be a good reason for restricting the use of the term 'range' to a limit of distance. Nevertheless, range is often used by navigators to mean distance. For example, slant distance mentioned in the previous paragraph is generally known as slant range.

DIFFERENCE OF DISTANCES

18. In radio equipments, it is often arranged that differences of distance between two ground stations shall be measured. The position line so produced will be a hyperbola as shown by the solid line in Fig. 163. In practice, two ground stations may be regarded as developing a sheaf of hyperbolae shown by the dotted lines in the figure and, since the plotting of hyperbolae would be beyond the capability of the navigator, these sheafs of hyperbolic position lines are invariably printed either on normal plotting charts or on special charts from which positions may be transferred to the plotting chart.

19. If the two stations in Fig. 163 had been very close together, the hyperbolae would have appeared as a sheaf of lines radiating

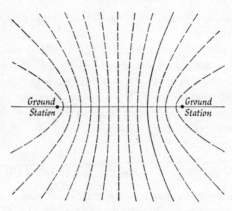

FIG. 163   Hyperbolae produced by
differences of distances

as shown in Fig. 164. A system of this type is generally known as a
collapsed hyperbolic system and, in effect, gives bearing information. However, as the bearings are not equally spaced in all
directions, they will be tabulated or may be plotted on a gnomonic
chart for transference to the normal plotting chart.

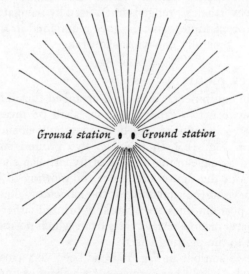

FIG. 164   Collapsed hyperbolae

DIFFERENCE OF BEARINGS

20. Difference of bearings can be measured from a craft when the heading information is greatly inferior in accuracy to the measurement of direction. This situation commonly arises with visual bearings. The difference between two visual bearings can be measured with great accuracy but the compass will generally have an error which may be two orders greater. A position line is shown plotted in Fig. 165 and is obviously an arc of a circle.

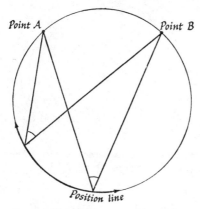

FIG. 165   Difference of bearings

21. A difference of bearings is seldom plotted as a position line. However, provided that the craft is roughly equidistant from the two points on which bearings are being taken, the difference of bearings will give a measurement of distance, a rule of thumb approximation being:

Distance in nautical miles from mid-point of two objects
$= 25 \times$ distance between objects (n. miles)/difference in bearings°

it is perhaps interesting to note that, at long-range, differences of distances provide a measurement of bearing and differences of bearings provide a measurement of distance.

ACCURACY DIAGRAMS

22. A position line is a band of probabilities as explained on page 55, para 1. The probability will be expressed in terms of the band

within which 95 per cent of the observations can be expected to fall. The width of the band will naturally depend on the aid that is used. However, each type of position line has its own characteristics.

23. *Bearings.* The errors depend on the angular errors of the bearings. In terms of distance, the errors will therefore increase with the distance from the station. Hence the pattern of accuracy as shown in Fig. 166(a) will be a series of concentric circles which

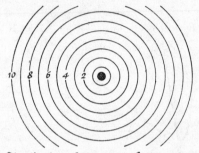

(a) Distribution of accuracy of measurement
of bearing or distance

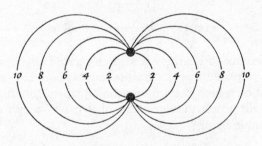

(b) Distribution of accuracy of position line
from hyperbolic pair

FIG. 166   Accuracy diagrams

should in theory be equally spaced but which in practice tend to lose accuracy with increasing distance at a rate greater than the linear relationship.

24. *Distances.* Distances will generally have errors which may be expressed as a percentage of distance. Hence the distribution of

accuracies about the station or object will be similar to that of bearings except that the percentage error may lessen with distance.

25. *Hyperbolic Lines.* The way in which the accuracy of a hyperbolic pair of ground stations decreases with distance is apparent from Fig. 163 but is shown as an accuracy diagram in Fig. 166(b). The accuracy depends on the direction compared to the line at right angles to the two ground stations.

26. *Differences of Bearings.* The pattern of the distribution of accuracy of position lines evolved from differences of bearings is very similar to that shown in Fig. 166(b) except close to the origins. Here the contours become ellipses, then change to a dumb-bell shape, and eventually to pear shapes about the origins of the bearings.

2. POSITION-LINE NAVIGATION

HOMING

1. The driver of a road vehicle can find the way by sign-posts that tell which way to turn. Navigation can likewise be conducted by position lines. In particular, if the relative bearing of a point can be measured from the craft, the point can be reached by turning until the relative bearing is nil. The navigator need not even know the heading of his craft.

2. This simple type of homing will be less satisfactory if there is a component of flow velocity across the course. The cross-track component will cause the craft to drift sideways from the original line. A continual alteration of heading will be necessary to keep the destination ahead and the craft will approach along a curve of pursuit finishing with a tendency to turn into the flow of the water or into the wind.

3. The curve of pursuit may be countered in one of two ways:

(a) An estimate of flow velocity may be used to find the course to reach the destination directly.

(b) As soon as a change in the relative bearing is noticed, an alteration of heading can be made not only to correct for this change of bearing but also to counteract the drift. If the line of sight is drifting at a degree in so many minutes,

25—P.N.

the additional alteration to correct for drift can be found by dividing this period into the time taken to reach destination, the time again being calculated by dead reckoning.

Example. A craft heads directly towards an object which, 20 minutes later, has changed its bearing 2° to starboard. It is reckoned that the craft will reach the destination in 1 hour.

Alteration to head craft at object	2° Green
Alteration to offset drifting	
2° in 20 min. = 1° in 10 min. = 6° in 60 min.	6° Green
TOTAL ALTERATION	8° Green

4. It may be necessary to rely on a single position line to lead the craft to the destination. This single position line may be a coast-line and the navigator will need to know which way to turn when he arrives. He may set course to strike the position line sufficiently far to one side of the destination to be confident which way to turn. If the distance is more than twice the 95 per cent radius of uncertainty, he should know which way to turn with some confidence.

5. It may happen that the single position line does not pass through the destination. In this event, the navigator may plot on his chart a line through his destination parallel to the position line and calculate the time at which his craft will arrive at this future line according to his D.R. ground speed, as shown in Fig. 167. A position line thus extrapolated into the future is said to be 'advanced' (see page 278, para 3). It will be noticed that the

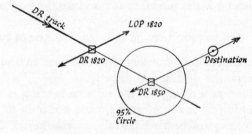

FIG. 167   Finding the island

advanced position line has been marked with a double-barbed arrow at each end, and this is common practice. On arrival at the advanced position line, the navigator may alter course towards the destination. This procedure is sometimes known as 'finding the island'.

MOST PROBABLE POSITION

6. The circle drawn round the D.R. position in Fig. 167 is not meaningful. The position line at 1820 has established the position of the craft along that axis so that the area of uncertainty at 1850 hours will be a long narrow strip in the direction of the advanced position line but limited by the circle of uncertainty. The combinations of D.R. positions with lines of position may thus lead to an error pattern differing greatly from the radial error.

7. A most probable position (M.P.P.) may be calculated from a D.R. position and a position line. Three main configurations of the 95 per cent band of probability of a position line and the 95 per cent circle of uncertainty are shown in Fig. 168:

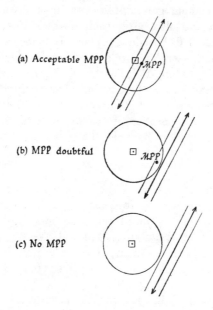

(a) Acceptable MPP

(b) MPP doubtful

(c) No MPP

FIG. 168   D.R. position and position line

(a) The band of probability and the circle of uncertainty overlap. The navigator may choose as the M.P.P. either the point on the position line closest to the D.R. position or, if the position line has the greater error, he may accept his original D.R. position.

(b) The band of probability and the circle of uncertainty overlap, but the position line is outside the circle of uncertainty and the D.R. position is outside the band of probability. With such a configuration, it is likely that a mistake has been made.

(c) The band of probability and the circle of uncertainty do not overlap at all. A mistake is most likely.

8. Although 95 per cent bands have been used in this illustration, the normal practice has been to use 50 per cent bands with 50 per cent circles of uncertainty and different criteria. However, it happens that the results are similar to those obtained by the methods of para 7.

9. The formal plotting of an M.P.P. is of value in training. The experienced navigator applies similar procedures by a process of estimation and also, after each position line, reassesses the accuracy of his D.R. based on a relatively inaccurate M.P.P. If an M.P.P. can be drawn, the circle of uncertainty will be reduced in size. However, if an M.P.P. cannot be drawn, the circle of uncertainty may have to be extended, mentally at least, to cover the possibility that the craft may be anywhere in the circle of uncertainty, in the probability band close to the circle of uncertainty, or anywhere between the two areas.

TRACK GUIDE

10. A path over the surface of the Earth which the craft is required to follow may be defined, for example, by means of radio signals transmitted from a ground radio station. The craft may be equipped so that the signals will tell the navigator not only when the craft is on the centre line but, if not, to which side and roughly by how much. A system of this type may be known as a track guide.

11. The position of the craft as compared to the centre line may be given by aural signals but more generally a left–right meter

will be provided. A typical example is the flight compass illustrated in the lower half of Fig. 169. The track guide appears as a
bar oriented manually by the pilot according to the direction of
the track guide and moving to left or right of the fixed aircraft in

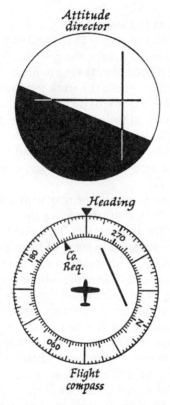

FIG. 169   Basic aircraft control instruments

the centre of the situation display to show which way the aircraft
ought to turn. The orientation is controlled by the aircraft compass and the display has a compass rose round the perimeter.
12. The track guidance signals from the ground station may
radiate in a pattern which becomes broader as the station is left.
Hence the extent of the left-right indications may not show the
distance that the craft is to one side of the centre line but the

angular deviation of the craft from the centre line as measured from the radio station. The closer that the craft approaches the ground station, the greater may be the reaction of the track guide display to any divergence of the craft from the centre line.

COUPLING

13. A craft being guided automatically is said to be coupled to a track guide. Fig. 54(a) on page 138 showed that if a position term alone were used to guide a craft, the craft would weave from side to side about the required line. Owing to noise, it will generally be unsatisfactory to differentiate the track guide signal to produce a rate signal. However, Fig. 54(b) on page 138 also showed that the rate term used alone will cause the ship to head down the line of the canal. A simple heading term, produced by the difference between heading down the track guide and the actual heading, will produce the same effect and, likewise, can be used to damp the track guide signal.

14. The craft may make leeway or may drift sideways so that the heading when travelling along the track guide may not be the same as the direction of the track guide. The result will be a hang-off error which may be sufficiently small to be ignored. If not, it may be reduced by adding an integral term or may be eliminated by feeding in course instead of heading. Other terms may be added by rate gyroscope or stabilized accelerometer signals and the whole combined to produce a directing signal.

15. To make it possible for the helmsman or pilot to take over should the automatic controls fail, the directing signal may be fed into a left–right meter known as a director or a quickening display. In aircraft, the left–right pointer may be combined with an up–down pointer to give guidance in the vertical as well as the horizontal plane. In aircraft such an instrument is commonly combined with the artificial horizon. The combined attitude director or director horizon is shown in the upper half of Fig. 169.

16. Certain special problems arise when a craft is being coupled initially. If the angle at which the craft approaches the guide is too coarse, the craft may over-shoot and fail to capture. If the angle is too fine, the craft may fail to intercept the guide as an adequate distance from the origin to enable it to settle down before arrival. Also, as the craft approaches the origin of the guide, the pattern of

signals radiated will become narrower. The position term will therefore become unduly sensitive and the damping may consequently be inadequate.

VERTICAL NAVIGATION

17. The examples quoted so far have largely been concerned with position lines that define position in the azimuth plane. Position lines may also define position in elevation, and may likewise provide guidance in elevation. Guides of this type may be known as slope guides. Slope guides may use position-finding aids or may depend on dead reckoning such as doppler (page 222, para 8) or inertia (page 239, para 43).

18. In certain instances, a slope may best be defined by cartesian coordinates of height or depth, and distance. For example, the slope of the descent path of an aircraft may be defined by the ratio of the altitude above a certain point and the distance to go to that point. Similar methods may be used to define the path in elevation of a submarine.

19. Systems that provide signals in elevation are used by aircraft for approach and landing. A guidance in elevation of this type is known generally as a glide slope. Combined with the appropriate track guide, a glide slope defines the glide path of the aircraft.

LOCK-FOLLOW

20. Two-dimensional guidance may be provided by a system that automatically aligns itself towards a transmission. For example, a space craft may have to align itself towards the Sun or a missile may need to be guided by a radar transmission. A device that automatically aligns itself is known as a lock-follow device. It may be one of two types:

(a) *Cartesian*. The equipment may measure whether the object is aligned to left or right and up or down.
(b) *Polar*. The equipment may measure in which direction the object is misaligned and by how much.

21. *Cartesian Lock-Follow*. Fig. 170(a) shows the way in which a space craft equipment may align itself with the Sun. A plate masks a pair of light sensitive or photo-electric cells equally when

the device is aligned correctly. Any deviation, as shown in the figure, causes the shadow to obscure one cell more than the other and this drives the space craft through an angle until the device is once more aligned. A second pair of sensitive cells placed at right angles will enable alignment to be maintained in a second plane at right angles. In theory, three cells may be used instead of four cells.

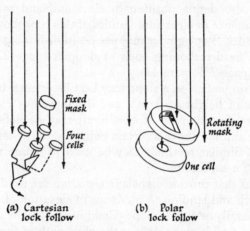

(a) Cartesian lock follow

(b) Polar lock follow

FIG. 170   Lock-follow devices

22. Polar Lock-Follow. Fig. 170(b) shows the way in which a rotating plate and a single cell may cause a device to align itself towards a star. As the plate rotates, the light from the star falls along the circumference of a circle. If the cell is exactly aligned towards the star, this will produce a steady signal, but if the cell is at an angle, the rotation will produce a sine wave signal, the amount of the sine wave showing the amount of misalignment and the phase of the sine wave showing the direction of misalignment.

3. FIXING

1. A fix defines the position of a craft as being on, below or above a point on the surface of the Earth. A fix is generally marked on a chart as a point surrounded by a circle. The time at which the craft was at that point will be marked alongside.

TWO POSITION LINES

2. A fix may be derived directly, for example, when a vehicle arrives at a landmark, and this is known as a pin-point. However, a fix is more generally the intersection of two position lines. On page 359, para 2, four types of position line were described and, although a fix may be derived from any combination of these, the most usual will be:

(a) Two bearings.
(b) Bearing and distance.
(c) Two distances.
(d) Two differences of distances.
(e) Two differences of bearings.

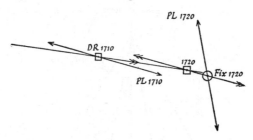

FIG. 171   Running fix

3. It may be possible to fix position by two position lines obtained simultaneously, but often the two position lines will be separated by an interval of time. The first position line will be advanced (page 370, para 5) so that it will be as if it were taken at the time of the second observation. This is managed by moving the line along the D.R. track a distance according to the D.R. ground speed and the time interval as shown in Fig. 171. Many navigators arrange that the time interval between the position lines shall be a convenient fraction of an hour, preferably 6 minutes. A fix found in this way is known as a running fix.

4. In Fig. 171, although the first position line has been advanced for a considerable distance, it has not been shifted far because it is practically parallel to track. For this reason, the navigator may try to ensure that the first position line is more nearly parallel to track than the second. If not, he may retard the second instead of advancing the first.

5. Had the two position lines in Fig. 171 cut at a fine angle, a slight error in the plotting of either or in the advancing of one to cut the other would have shifted the position by a large distance. Angle of cut is therefore important in fixing systems. This was shown by the formula for radial error on page 59, para 9. The radial error varies as 1/sin (cut) and therefore a cut of 30° will double the error and a cut of 20° will treble the error. In practice the navigator avoids a cut of less than 30°.

6. The angle of cut depends on the position of the craft compared to the line joining the extremities of the system which provides the fix. This line is known as the base line. In the instance of two bearings as shown in Fig. 172:

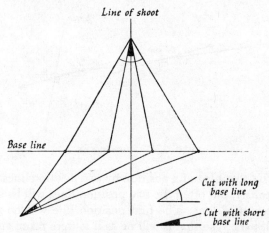

FIG. 172   Cut, line of shoot and base line

    (a) The longer the base line, the greater the angle of cut, provided the craft is not too close to the base line.

    (b) The closer the craft to the perpendicular bisector of the base line, known as the line of shoot, the greater the angle of cut, except close to the base line.

These rules apply generally to fixing systems.

FIXING FROM ONE OBJECT

7. A position may be obtained from one object by simultaneous bearing and distance or by a running fix from two bearings or

two distances taken at different times. The time interval between the latter position lines has to be sufficient to make a good cut.

8. A development of the latter method is to take a relative bearing and note the time. The time is then noted at which this relative bearing has doubled. This is known as 'doubling the angle at the bow'. The distance of the object at the time of the second relative bearing is taken to be equal to the D.R. distance run between the two relative bearings. A similar technique is used when the navigator needs to know how far his craft has passed by an object. He notes when the object bears 045° from dead ahead and when it is abeam. The D.R. distance run between the two observations is his distance off the object.

9. These simple rules of thumb will have errors if there is a cross-track component of the flow velocity acting on the craft or if the craft is making leeway or drifting. The bearings ought in these instances to be corrected for this drift angle, otherwise the calculated distance of the object will be too large or too small according to whether the drift is away from or towards the object. The proportional error will be the proportion of sin (drift) to tan (original bearing) or, if the original bearing is small, the proportion of drift to original bearing.

DIFFERENCES OF DISTANCES AND BEARINGS

10. *Differences of Distances* are obtained by hyperbolic systems using radio (page 519, para 1) and special hyperbolic charts are used for plotting fixes. An exception is the collapsed hyperbolic system which is used exactly as if it were a bearing.

11. *Differences of Bearings* are plotted as fixes using one of two techniques:

(a) The two differences of bearings are drawn on a sheet of transparent paper and the sheet is moved about the chart until the bearings pass through the objects on which they were taken. The origin of these bearings on the sheet of transparent paper shows the position of the craft.

(b) A station pointer is used. This is a protractor with three arms that can be set to the necessary angles. The station pointer is then moved about over the chart until the three arms are aligned with the three objects and the position of the craft will then be at the centre of the protractor.

FIXING COVERAGE

12. It was shown in section 5 of Chapter 1 that, if two 95 per cent bands of probability cut, the 95 per cent area will be an ellipse that would fit into bands $1\frac{1}{4}$ times as wide as the probability bands. It was also shown that the radius of the circle within which the fix can be expected to fall on 95 per cent of occasions, known as the radial error, is approximately equal to:

$$\sqrt{(A^2 + B^2)}/\sin(\text{cut})$$

where A and B are the 95 per cent errors of the two position lines.
13. Fixing accuracies are generally expressed in terms of radial errors, but if the cut is fine and the position lines of very different accuracies, the ellipse will be considerably elongated. In order to emphasize this point, any diagrams showing fixing accuracies may include sketches of ellipse shapes at various points.
14. A chart showing the accuracy of a fixing system over an area may be known as a fixing coverage diagram. Fig. 173 shows the

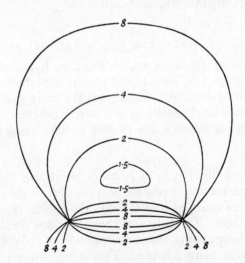

FIG. 173   Accuracy contours for two bearings. (95 per cent radial errors in n. miles assuming (i) base line = 100 n. miles; (ii) 95 per cent error of each bearing = 1°)

fixing coverage resulting from bearings on two objects. If the objects were 10 n. miles apart, the radial errors would be decreased by a factor of 10. If the bearing accuracies were improved by a factor of 2, the 95 per cent radial errors would be reduced by a factor of 2.

15. The fixing accuracy for a bearing and distance from a point can be shown to be approximately:

$$0.01 \times \text{distance} \times \sqrt{(3 \times (\text{bearing error}°)^2 + (\text{percentage distance error})^2)}$$

Hence, the error depends on distance, and the coverage diagram would appear as a series of concentric circles equally spaced.

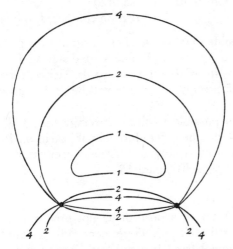

FIG. 174   Accuracy contours for two distances. (95 per cent radial errors in n. miles assuming (i) base line = 100 n. miles; (ii) 95 per cent error of distance measurement = 1 per cent)

16. Fig. 174 shows the fixing coverage resulting from measurements of distances from two objects. It will be seen that the contours have the same shape as those in Fig. 173 except that, being expressed in percentage of distance instead of in degrees, the accuracy over the area will be higher in the proportion that 1 in 100 is smaller than 1 in 60. Also, although the ellipses in Fig. 173 will generally lie with their greatest lengths at right angles to

the accuracy contours, in Fig. 174 the ellipses will lie with their greatest axes roughly along the lines of the accuracy contours.

17. In both figures the accuracy diagrams approximate at long ranges to figures of eight. This can be expressed by saying that the radial error will vary approximately as the secant of the direction of the craft compared to the line of shoot. In addition, as distance is doubled, so the area of the fix tends to be multiplied by four because the errors due to distance tend to be doubled and the angle of cut halved. Hence the radial error tends to increase with the square of the distance. Taking the two effects together, radial error (2 distances or 2 bearings) is proportional at long ranges to:

(distance from centre of base line)²
× sec (direction compared to line of shoot)

18. It is possible to draw coverage diagrams for pairs of position lines obtained by two differences of distance. However, these fixing systems invariably use radio aids. Hence, for convenience, the details of coverage diagrams will be dealt with on page 520, para 4.

19. It is also possible to draw coverage diagrams for pairs of position lines obtained by differences of bearings. However, these fixing systems invariably use visual observations and will be dealt with on page 407, para 15.

MULTI-POSITION LINES

20. The accuracy of a position is not greatly improved by an additional position line. A 95 per cent radial error of 1·4 n. miles can be developed from two position lines at right angles, each with a 95 per cent error of 1 n. mile. Adding to one of these a third position line of 1 n. mile will reduce the error in that axis to 0·7 n. miles. The radial error will then be $\sqrt{(1+0·7)^2}$ or approximately 1·2, representing a reduction of considerably less than 20 per cent. By the same reasoning, six position lines would have to be added to the original pair in order to halve the radial error.

21. The main reason for using additional position lines is not to increase accuracy but to increase certainty. Three position lines meeting at a point may give greatly increased confidence. Gener-

ally the three will form a small triangle known as a 'cocked hat'. If one of the three position lines was markedly inaccurate, the fix might be taken to be in the intersection of the other two lines. If all are equally accurate, the navigator generally chooses as his position the centre of the circle that would fit inside the cocked hat.

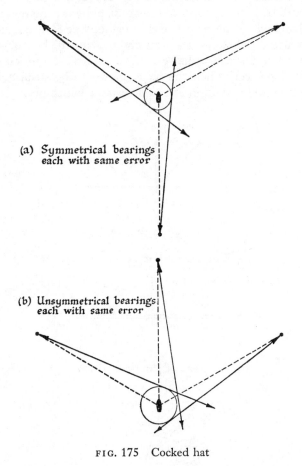

(a) Symmetrical bearings each with same error

(b) Unsymmetrical bearings each with same error

FIG. 175   Cocked hat

22. Fig. 175(a) shows that the centre of the circle inside the cocked hat will give the correct answer if three bearings each with the same error are taken on three symmetrical objects. However,

Fig. 175(b) shows that, if the objects are not symmetrically distributed, the true position will be the centre of a circle touching the three lines but outside the cocked hat. The situation is disguised by the fact that the cocked hat which gave the accurate indication in Fig. 175(a) is large whereas the cocked hat which gave the inaccurate indication in Fig. 175(b) is small.

23. It will be possible to solve the problem by the method used to combine the D.R. position and the position line. The two position lines which are the most accurate and provide the best cut can be combined to form a radial error and the third line compared with it. However, when the fix is shown to be suspect, it will need yet another position line to determine which position line is in error.

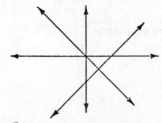

(a) Four symmetrical position lines

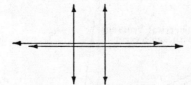

(b) Two pairs of parallel position lines

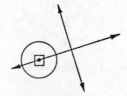

(c) Two position lines and a D.R. position with a circle of uncertainty

FIG. 176   Multi-position line fixes

24. Fig. 176(a) shows a fix found from position lines distributed symmetrically. From these four lines, it is evident which position line is in error. Fig. 176(b) shows four position lines in parallel pairs. The fact that there is an error is still evident, but which of two lines is in error can only be determined by a fifth position line.

FIXING AND D.R.

25. In practice, the navigator may use his D.R. circle of uncertainty to check his fix. This will inevitably show up a large blunder as shown in Fig. 176(c). The great advantage of the D.R. position is that, being approximately a circular error, it may be regarded as comprising two position lines symmetrically disposed about the actual position lines. It is this that makes the D.R. position an excellent guard against a blunder.

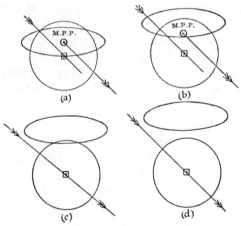

FIG. 177 Combining a fix and D.R. position

26. It would be possible to compare a fix with a D.R. position on lines similar to those described on page 371, para 7, working in 95 per cent errors. There may be four particular cases all of which are illustrated in Fig. 177:

(a) When the overlap is very large, the more accurate position
26—P.N.

may be chosen, possibly with a slight bias towards the less accurate position.

(b) When the overlap is small, the centre of the common chord may be taken as the M.P.P.

(c) When there is an overlap but the fix is outside the circle of uncertainty and the D.R. position is outside the radial error of the fix, it is likely that a mistake has occurred.

(d) When there is no overlap, a mistake is extremely likely.

27. In practice, the navigator may not use an M.P.P. but may rely on methods based on the way that he tends to take decisions. At sea and in the air, when a decision has to be made quickly, the navigator tends to search for the over-riding factor and to make a decision on that alone. Thus he may continue his D.R. plot until he obtains a fix that he considers is more accurate and reliable. He then restarts his D.R. plot from that fix. He will, if experienced, mentally carry forward an estimate of the accuracy of that fix.

28. If the navigator considers that a position biased in one direction may run him into danger, he may start his D.R. not at the fix but at a point biased towards the danger. This treatment of radial errors and circles of uncertainty is a feature of practical navigation.

FIXING IN THREE AXES

29. Navigation grew up on the surface of the sea and this has tended to obscure the fact that a position line is really a surface and is only a line when it cuts the surface of the Earth. The shape of the surface defined by a position line will vary as follows:

(a) A bearing is a plane.

(b) A distance is the surface of a sphere. A depth or a height is likewise the surface of a sphere but one that is concentric with the surface of the Earth.

(c) A difference of distances is a hyperbolic surface known as a hyperboloid.

(d) A difference of bearings is the surface of a toroid.

30. Two surfaces intersect along a line. Thus in surface navigation, the intersection of a position surface and the surface of the Earth is truly a position line. However, in more general terms, for a craft travelling above the Earth:

(a) When two bearings cut, the craft is on a line.
(b) When a distance and a bearing cut, or two distances, or a bearing and a difference of bearings or two differences of bearings, the craft is on an arc of a circle.
(c) When a bearing and a hyperboloid cut, the craft is on a hyperbola.

31. It is now obvious that only when two bearings intersect is a line formed which runs vertically up from the surface and can therefore fairly be represented by a fix marked on the surface of the Earth. In all other instances, the line is curved. For example, a distance and bearing or two distances measured by a high-flying aircraft will cut along an arc so that the position of an aircraft above the surface of the Earth can only be found if its height is known. Again, if an hyperboloid is cut by a sphere, the intersection will be a distorted hyperbola so that hyperbolic systems on the surface of the Earth produce patterns that progressively diverge from the truly hyperbolic pattern as their origin is left.

32 In order to fix a craft absolutely, two sources of information are inadequate. For example, two bearings, one in azimuth and the other in elevation, produce a sloping path without giving a fix unless there is additional information. To produce a fix, three sources of information must be provided, one of which may be that the craft is on the surface of the sea or some distance above or below.

4. NAVIGATIONAL AID REQUIREMENTS

1. *Marine Navigation.* The International Meeting on Radio Aids to Marine Navigation (I.M.R.A.M.N.) has established requirements for radio navigation aids which may be regarded as having a general application to non-radio aids as well. The following table shows these requirements tabulated in a form so that they can readily be compared to those for air navigation aids.

TABLE XIII. MARINE NAVIGATIONAL AID
REQUIREMENTS

Range	Function	Accuracy required	Order of time to establish position
Long	Transoceanic navigation. More than 50 n. miles to nearest danger	± 1 per cent of distance to danger	15 min
Medium	Aid to approaching land, to coasting and general port approach. 50 to 3 n. miles to nearest danger	$\pm \frac{1}{2}$ n. mile down to 200 metres	5 min to $\frac{1}{2}$ min
Short	Aid to harbours and entrances. Less than 3 n. miles to nearest danger	± 50 metres	Instantaneous

2. *Air Navigation.* The requirements for air navigation have been recommended by the International Civil Aviation Organization (ICAO). These requirements may be summarized as follows:

TABLE XIV. AIR NAVIGATIONAL AID
REQUIREMENTS

Range	Function	Accuracy required	Order of time to establish position
Long	More than 250 n. miles and up to at least 1500 n. miles	10 n. miles	5 min
Short	Less than 250 n. miles	$\frac{1}{2}$ n. mile	5 sec
Airfield approach	Position and path in plan and in height	50 ft 10 ft	Instantaneous
Airfield	Position and path in plan and in height	15 ft 2 ft	Instantaneous

3. As with all operational requirements, the formulation is affected by what can be achieved. For example, the demarcation in air navigation between long-range and short-range aids is connected with the performance of those systems in which air-

craft operate outside direct 'line of sight' contact with the fixing aid, and those systems in which the aircraft may be in direct 'line of sight' contact with the fixing aid.

4. It is also evident that only at long and medium ranges at sea and at long range in the air can there be time for the plotting of position lines and fixes by the navigator if the requirements for time to establish position are to be met. In practice, by means of dead reckoning, a navigator not concerned also with the control of the craft may well be able to provide adequate steering information to enable a ship or an aircraft to operate safely even when the aids available take much longer than the standard time to establish position. Nevertheless there is a growing tendency in air navigation to seek for instantaneous fixing at all ranges in order to provide coupling to the aircraft automatics.

5. SUMMARY

POSITION SYSTEMS

Positions are measured by:

(a) Landmarks.
(b) Bearings which are directions from ground stations, or relative bearings which may be converted into bearings from the craft.
(c) Bearing and distance from one station on the ground or from the craft on to one object.
(d) Distances measured between the craft and objects such as ground stations.
(e) Hyperbolic systems composed of various configurations of hyperbolic pairs.
(f) Differences of bearings.

The accuracy of a position within a fixing system depends generally on:

(a) Distance between the craft and the base line. This affects accuracy of measurements and also the angle of cut of these position lines.

(b) Direction of craft compared to line of shoot of system. This affects the cut in the instance of bearings and distances but also affects the accuracy of the position lines in the instance of hyperbolic pairs.

(c) The base line of the system. At very short ranges, a long base line may increase errors, but at long distances it will increase the cut and reduce errors.

USE OF D.R.

D.R. may be used:

(a) To plot a position line. Long-range bearings and distances are plotted with the help of the D.R. position.

(b) To check a position line or a fix. If a position line or a fix falls outside the 95 per cent circle of uncertainty, an error may be suspected.

(c) To combine with a position line or with a fix to produce an M.P.P.

HOMING

A position line may be used to home to destination. If the position line is obtained from destination, it can bring the craft to the destination by a process of continual correction. Alternatively, a single line of position may be used as a leading line.

A craft may be coupled to a position line aid. The ability of the craft to follow the line may depend on heading damping and on an integration term to back off the cross-track component of the flow velocity.

Lock-follow systems enable a craft to follow guidance signals in two dimensions.

MULTI-POSITION-LINE FIXES

If more than two position lines are used, the resultant position can be more reliable but will be little more accurate. Symmetry of position lines is most important in multi-position-line fixes.

A bearing is a plane surface and a distance is the surface of a sphere. A difference of distance is a hyperboloid and a difference of bearing is a sphere. Only in the instance of two bearings will the craft be on a vertical line passing through the intersection of the bearings on the surface of the Earth.

CHAPTER XI

General and Visual Aids

1. INFORMATION

WAVES

1. Positional information is necessarily relative to some known point or points generally on the surface of the Earth. The information has therefore to be carried to the craft by some means. Invariably the information is carried to the craft by waves whose frequency may be measured in:

(a) Cycles per second (c/s).
(b) Kilocycles per second (kc/s) or thousands of cycles per second.
(c) Megacycles per second (Mc/s) or millions of cycles per second.
(d) Gigacycles per second (kMc/s) or thousands of millions of cycles per second.

2. Waves that carry information may be of two types:

(a) Sound waves, which are compression waves that travel at approximately 1100 feet or 300 metres per second in air.
(b) Electro-magnetic waves which are lateral waves that oscillate up and down or sideways or at an angle in a direction known as the plane of polarization or may oscillate with a circular motion known as circular polarization. They travel at roughly 160,000 n. miles or 300 million metres per second.

3. The interval between crests of waves of a certain frequency will depend on how fast the waves are travelling. If waves are travelling fast, the intervals between the crests will have to be greater than if the waves are travelling slowly. Since the speed at which both sound and radio will travel depends on the medium through

which the waves are moving, the wavelength will vary. Hence the radio engineer always works in frequencies. It will, however, be found convenient in many instances for the navigator to work in wavelengths, particularly when using waves to measure distances.

4. The connection between wavelength and frequency for signals that travel though the air is approximately:

   (a) *Sound waves.*
   Frequency (c/s) = 300/wavelength (m)
   (b) *Electro-magnetic waves.*
   Frequency (c/s) = 300,000,000/wavelength (m)

5. Fig. 178 shows the spectrum of sound waves and electro-magnetic waves in the air which includes:

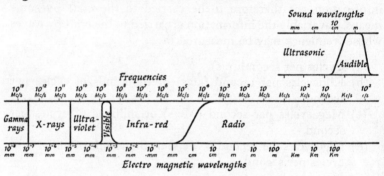

FIG. 178   Frequencies and wavelengths

   (a) Sound waves used for aural communication.
   (b) Ultrasonic waves of a frequency higher than audible sound.
   (c) Radio waves.
   (d) Infra-red or heat waves whose frequency is higher than radio.
   (e) Light waves whose frequency is higher than infra-red.

WAVE PROPAGATION

6. When waves spread out from a source, they appear as an ever-expanding sphere centred about that source. Therefore, in the absence of any interruption, the strength of a wave will decrease in the same way that the area of a sphere increases, as the square of the distance from the centre. However, in practice, the waves

transfer some of their energy to the medium through which they are travelling and therefore become weakened or attenuated.

7. Waves of all types may be reflected. The process is as shown in Fig. 179(a). If the path of a small portion of the wave front is followed, it will travel as shown in Fig. 179(b). This is a more convenient way in which to show what happens to a wave.

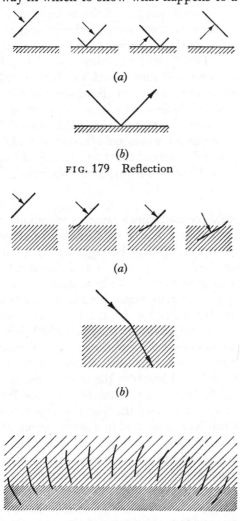

(a)

(b)

FIG. 179 Reflection

(a)

(b)

(c)

FIG. 180 Refraction

8. Waves of all types may be bent or refracted if they pass into a medium which causes them to slow down or to speed up. Fig. 180 (a) shows a wave front which enters a medium through which its speed is decreased. The direction of motion of the wave is modified or refracted so that it is bent towards the medium through which it travels the more slowly. Once again, this may be illustrated by a small portion of the wave front as shown in Fig. 180(b). If the wave front should enter a layer of a medium so that its speed is gradually increased, it may be bent right back until it emerges. This type of reflection is shown in Fig. 180(c).

9. Waves of all sizes will flow round an obstacle. However, as might be expected, short waves will be obstructed more than long waves because the obstacle will be larger in proportion. Thus, in the electro-magnetic spectrum, long radio waves flow round obstacles but centimetric waves are obstructed, and light waves, which are a hundred thousand times shorter, cast sharp shadows, although they too bend round very small obstacles.

BAND WIDTH

10. The human voice transmits a range of vibrations, the highest being about 5 kc/s. 5 kc/s may be regarded as a number of ups and downs. An up or a down may be regarded as a 'bit' (page 27, para 6). Hence the human voice has an information rate which may be regarded as so many bits per second.

11. The range of vibrations transmitted by a system is known as the band width. If the band width is 5 kc/s, a certain number of bits per second can be passed. If the band width is reduced, less bits per second will be passed and the rate of information will be reduced. In the instance of a human voice, reducing the band width progressively will first blur the characteristics of the voice and finally render the voice indistinct. In the instance of a navigation system, reducing the band width will reduce the accuracy that can be transmitted in a given period of time.

12. It might be imagined that accuracy could be obtained by switching a signal on and off suddenly. However, as shown in Fig. 181, the basic signal of curve A represents only a very gradual rise of signal. By mixing two other signals of different frequencies, the rise is greatly accelerated. If enough signals of different frequencies were added, any degree of sharpness of signal could

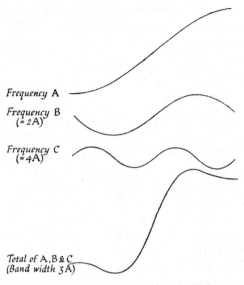

Frequency **A**

Frequency **B**
(= 2A)

Frequency **C**
(= 4A)

Total of A, B & C
(Band width 3A)

FIG. 181   Accuracy and band width

be achieved. This shows that a sharp signal demands a considerable band width.

13. Information is generally superimposed on basic waves known as carrier waves in the form of a modulation to those waves. This modulation may be one of three types:

(a) *Amplitude modulation* (AM). The strength of the waves may be varied.

(b) *Pulse modulation.* The waves may be transmitted in short bursts or pulses.

(c) *Frequency modulation* (FM). The frequency of the waves may be varied.

In order to carry a certain rate of information, a certain band width will be demanded either to distort the strength of the waves or to vary their frequency.

14. Certain systems may use simple continuous waves (CW). Such systems may not measure positions but can record changes of position so that the progress of the craft from a known point may be followed. If an initial position has to be found, it must

either be by other means or else the simple continuous waves must be modulated, the modulation demanding band width. It is also worth noting that a moving craft demands additional band width in order to cover the doppler spread of frequencies (page 572, para 1).

NOISE

15. The existence of noise in equipment has already been mentioned. Noise also appears from outside the craft. Bodies from space and storms in the atmosphere generate radio noise. Aural noise is present even in the best sound-proofed craft.

16. Noise generally covers a very broad wave band. A flash of lightning may cover most of the visual band and set up noise through a large part of the radio spectrum. When noise covers a very wide band it is known as 'white' noise because white light is compounded of frequencies of all the various colours of light.

17. A simple signal may be read through noise. The hooter of a motor vehicle which carries only one bit of information, a warning, can easily be distinguished against the background of the traffic noise. The voice of an opera singer, on the other hand, has a very wide range of vibrations in order to carry subtle feelings to the audience. This wide band width is easily upset by extraneous noise. This suggests that the more complex the signal, the more vulnerable it will be to noise.

18. A complex signal can only be transmitted through noise by some form of redundancy. Either the signal must be repeated a number of times or the signal itself must have enough redundancy to be received in spite of noise. For example, t*e mean**g o* * m*ssag* m*y b* obvi**s, even though one letter in three has been obscured. However, the need for redundancy or repetition means that more information has to be passed so that the rate is reduced.

19. More information cannot be passed by increasing the band width because, since noise generally covers a wide band, increasing the band width will merely open the door to still more noise. It is therefore necessary to pass the extra information by spreading the signal over a longer period of time. For example, the signal may be repeated a number of times and read through the noise by averaging the repetitions.

SIGNAL-TO-NOISE RATIO

20. The proportion of the strength of a signal to the strength of the noise is known as the signal-to-noise ratio. If the signal-to-noise ratio is too low, the equipment may not operate satisfactorily.

21. The signal-to-noise ratio can be improved by increasing the power of the transmitted signal, and this may allow the signal to travel a longer distance before the noise level becomes too great. Unfortunately, this solution is not readily available for a system in which signals have to be generated by the craft itself. It may, however, be possible to increase the signal-to-noise ratio by compressing the signal in two ways:

(a) *In space* by beaming.
(b) *In time* by concentrating the signals into pulses. Unfortunately the build-up of pulses will require a large band width, as explained in para 12, and this will let in more noise.

22. The use of pulses makes it easier for the receiver to detect the signal against a background of noise, particularly if the pulses follow a pattern that can be recognized. This is an example of coding signals not to avoid translation by an enemy but to ensure reception by a friend. The term coding is often used in this context.

MILITARY NAVIGATION

23. In war, an enemy may generate noise. The further he travels from his homeland, the greater the distance that an attacker's ground-based transmission has to travel, and the smaller the distance the defending noise has to travel. Hence, the signal-to-jamming ratio will become lower. The attacker can concentrate his signals in space and time and use the maximum amount of coding but, in enemy territory, they may still be vulnerable.

24. It is plain that a system based on transmissions from the craft will confer on the craft a favourable signal-to-noise ratio in its own vicinity. Hence, military navigation systems that have to navigate in hostile areas may depend on transmissions from the craft. Unfortunately these very transmissions can reveal the

position of the craft. Ideally, systems which need no transmissions, such as inertial navigation, will be used.

25. Not only may signals be jammed but also they may be faked.
The simpler the signal, the easier it will be to mislead by injecting
a false signal. This effect is perhaps even more dangerous than
jamming since wrong information is more likely to be disastrous
than no information at all. The solution is to code the signal so
that it can only be faked with great difficulty. In particular, signals
transmitted and echoed back to the originating equipment will be
difficult to fake.

26. It is now evident that military navigation aids have requirements that differ fundamentally from non-military aids. Immunity from enemy interference is an over-riding requirement. Apart
from aids, the problems of military navigation and non-
military navigation differ relatively little, except that the great
advantage of self-contained aids encourages the soldier, sailor,
submariner and air force navigator to rely much more on dead
reckoning.

IDENTIFICATION

27. In order to find geographical position on the surface of the
Earth it is necessary to link the craft with the ground and to
know the geographical position of the ground links. It follows
that the first stage in the use of any aid is identification of the
ground link. If the aid is visual, the landmark has to be recognized. If the aid is radio, the signal has to be identified.

28. In civil operations, the aids will be designed for ease of
identification. In war, the enemy may use camouflage or may try
deliberately to confuse recognition of the identity of navigational
aids.

REDUNDANCY

29. In control systems, or in inertial navigators, redundancy may
take the form of duplication or triplication because the inputs
will not depend on transmissions. However, in most guidance
systems, transmission will be a vital element. In certain instances,
duplication of equipment may be used but, more generally,
systems with different transmission characteristics will be
provided. This diversification is a feature of non-inertial

navigational aid systems. The craft will be provided with radio aids probably of several frequencies, supported by the eyes of the navigator and by the light from the Sun or from the stars above.

2. LIGHT

1. As shown in Fig. 178 on page 392, light waves cover a frequency band between 10^8 and 10^9 Mc/s so that the average wavelength is less than a micron (millionth of a metre). The polarization of light waves may be demonstrated by passing light though a special type of crystal, the emerging light thus being robbed of all vibrations except those in line with the axis of the crystal. This polarized light will not pass through a second similar crystal whose axis is at right angles to the first.

REFRACTION

2. When light from outer space passes through the atmosphere it becomes slowed and bends towards the Earth. Similarly, the light from the horizon tends to bend towards the Earth so that the visible horizon is further away than the real horizon, as shown in Fig. 182. The distance, in nautical miles, of the visible horizon seen from a height is:

$$1 \cdot 15 \sqrt{\text{height (feet)}}$$

If refraction is ignored, the factor 1·15 becomes 1·06.

3. Fig. 182 also shows that the angle through which the horizon appears to dip is less than the angle through which it would dip if there were no refraction. The angle of dip in minutes of arc allowing for normal refraction is:

$$0 \cdot 98 \sqrt{\text{height (feet)}}$$

If refraction is ignored, the factor 0·98 again becomes 1·06. Also, from the previous paragraph:

distance (n. miles) = 1·17 dip (minutes of arc)

or, if refraction is ignored,

distance (minutes of arc) = dip (minutes of arc)

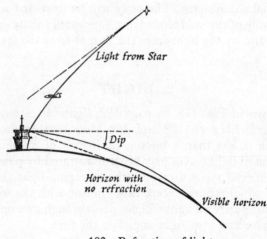

Light from Star

Dip

*Horizon with
no refraction*

Visible horizon

FIG. 182   Refraction of light

4. Dip and distance of the horizon may be given in nautical tables. However, close to the water, account should also be taken of the difference between the air temperature and the sea temperature. The importance of this correction increases greatly as the height of the eye decreases and, therefore, dip or horizon distance is not reliable when measured close to the water. Nor is it reliable from a height of more than a few thousand feet and at great heights the horizon is generally blurred.

5. When an object appears on the horizon, its distance may be measured. The sea navigator may change his height until a light just dips the horizon. He can then measure his distance to the light.

Example. A light 400 feet high is just visible on the horizon to a mariner whose eye is 25 feet above the water line.

Distance of ship to horizon $1 \cdot 15 \sqrt{25}$ $= 5\frac{3}{4}$ n. miles
,,   ,, horizon to light $1 \cdot 15 \sqrt{100} = 23$ n. miles
,,   ,, ship to light $= 29$ n. miles

6. Refraction must also be taken into account when sighting on the top of a mountain. As a general approximation, the curvature of the light in minutes is one-twelfth of the distance in nautical miles. A closer approximation can be found by adding to the angle

of elevation of the top of the mountain an angle equal to half the dip of the horizon.

7. Occasionally, abnormal refraction occurs, in particular when there is a very warm air mass over cold sea. In this event, the light from an object well below the visible horizon is so bent that the object may appear over the horizon, a phenomenon known as 'looming'. When the reverse happens and very cold air passes over warm water, or warm air over very hot sand, the light may be bent upwards so that the visible horizon is closer than the theoretical horizon and distant objects may appear inverted in the sky.

OPTICAL INSTRUMENTS

8. Refraction is applied in lenses to make objects appear closer. The light is collected by a convex lens, thicker at its centre than at its edges, and an image is formed at a point according to the focal length of the lens. Such a lens is known as a field lens, an object glass or an objective lens. Different wavelengths or colours of light are bent by different amounts by various types of glass and a simple lens will therefore have colour distortion known as chromatic aberration. However, a field lens may be built up from several lenses of different types of glass so as to reduce this aberration.

9. The image formed by a convex lens will be upside-down and, if viewed by a simple eyepiece, the object will appear inverted, that is upside-down and left to right. This inversion needs to be corrected to assist recognition, and so that the instrument can be aligned with the object by a movement which will be in the natural direction. Reinverting the object can be achieved by methods shown in Fig. 183:

(a) A concave lens, thinner in the centre than at the edges, is placed in front of the image. This is known as a Galileo's telescope.

(b) An inverting lens is placed between the image and the eyepiece. This method is used in good telescopes.

(c) Two prisms are used, one to turn the image upside-down, and the other to turn it from left to right. This method is used in prismatic binoculars.

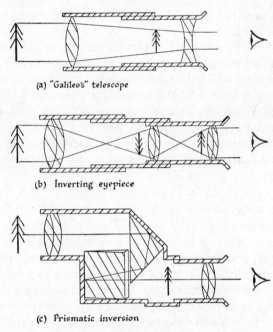

(a) "Galileo's" telescope

(b) Inverting eyepiece

(c) Prismatic inversion

FIG. 183   Typical optical systems

10. The angle through which an optical system will view the outside world is known as the field of view. The field of view is limited partly by the size of the field lens and partly by the design of the system, a Galileo's telescope always having a relatively poor field of view. It is also limited by the eye which has an angle of view of about 50°. If the object is magnified by a factor of ten, it will be equivalent to picking out the centre of the field of view and magnifying it so that the field of view in this instance will be reduced to 5°. The effect of magnification is to concentrate the light from the field lens into a small area. It may therefore be necessary to fit shades to reduce glare.

11. The use of a prism for reflection has already been mentioned in para 9(c). In addition, silvered glass sheets may be used as reflecting surfaces. If the amount of silvering is carefully adjusted light will partly pass through the glass and partly be reflected. Thus two images, one viewed directly and the other by reflection may be superimposed in order that the difference in direction

can be measured precisely. If one of the objects is a point, such as a distant light, it may be convenient to distort it so that it appears as a line. This is achieved by an astigmatizer, which is a glass plate curved in one plane so that the point source of light is stretched out in that plane.

3. VISUAL NAVIGATION

IDENTIFICATION

1. The eye has a wonderful ability to discriminate and to accept a vast amount of information. It can detect subtleties of shape, size, colour and movement, and it passes all this information to the brain which immediately recognizes what it has seen. This recognition is the result of accumulated experience of what things are really like. That this is true is evident from the behaviour of individuals who regain sight. They may have to feel shapes before they can recognize them.

2. The characteristic of the brain which enables it to see what it thinks is there is useful in ordinary life. Were the brain to work any other way, it would never handle the vast amount of impressions passed by the nerves of the eye. The existence of this characteristic can be demonstrated quite easily. If a man be given an ellipse and asked to memorize its shape and the ellipse be then replaced by a round plate which is tilted until the man sees it as the same shape, it will be found that the outline of the plate he chooses is far narrower than the ellipse. The brain knows that the plate is round and has distorted the image accordingly.

3. In everyday life, misrecognition may not be serious. The brain expects to see something and then 'sees' it. A moment later, something in the pattern is recognized by the brain as being inconsistent and the result is the well-known 'double-take'. However, in navigation, misrecognition may be very serious. The shadowy vagueness of a distant landfall can take on the exact pattern that the seaman expects and his brain may only reject this pattern when certain unmistakable features appear that make it quite incompatible. The shock of realization is well known to experienced navigators, and so are the serious consequences that

may follow. For this reason, navigators learn to identify landfalls and pin-points according to specific features and not from general appearances. It seems likely that the reliability of identification increases as the factorial of the number of features. Thus, compared to one feature:

2 features may have a reliability of $2 \times 1 = 2$
3   „   „   „ „   „   „ $3 \times 2 \times 1 = 6$
4   „   „   „ „   „   „ $4 \times 3 \times 2 \times 1 = 24$

MAPS

4. The essence of a navigational map is that it should portray those features which will assist in the identification of landmarks. Therefore distinctive features need to be depicted. On a marine chart, these distinctive features will be different from those of an air chart since the seaman is looking at the land from the surface. He will recognize contour shapes whereas the airman may not. The features will also depend on the terrain. A small river may be a distinctive feature flowing out from a dusty plain but quite indistinguishable in the maze of a tropical delta.

5. Maps are designed for purposes other than navigation. Place names, boundaries and other details may tend to clutter up the presentation from the position-finding point of view. The seaman is, however, particularly fortunate. He will not sail over his landmarks in the same way that an airman will fly over his. Therefore, on a marine chart, the necessary topographical detail can be printed without introducing a clutter of lines over which the navigator has to plot. In an air map, the detail is such that it is generally impossible to plot. Perhaps a line may be drawn on the map and the pilot of the light aircraft or the glider can thumb his way along from one landmark to another. More generally, however, the topographical map has to be separate from the chart. A position identified on the map has to be translated into latitude and longitude and transferred.

6. The air map is designed so that features that will be distinctive from the air are shown. For example, railway lines are particularly distinctive though roads tend to repeat patterns at intervals that are too frequent. Also, small dusty country tracks may show up better than tarmacadam. Towns are distinctive but tend to change

shapes as do woods. Rivers are of great value where they are combined with roads and railways. Lakes and reservoirs are generally good landmarks though in salt-pan areas the colours may change overnight with a change of wind.

7. The use of the map as a means of identification is based on the circle of uncertainty. The navigator will generally know within what area to search for a certain combination of features. Having found what seems a reasonable solution, he will look in adjacent areas to see whether this particular combination is repeated. In particular, he will check whether there is a similar combination of shapes even if the sizes are very different. It is extremely difficult to judge sizes when seen from a distance.

MARKS

8. A light will be used for a mark by night, for example a coastal light, light-vessel (L.V.), lighted buoy, aerial light or airfield light beacon. By day, a buoy will mark the surface of the water. To identify a light or a buoy, coding is essential. If the code be simple, it will be easily recognized, but if the marks are close together, there will be insufficient variations. The coding may have to be repeated at short intervals, and if the craft has a large circle of uncertainty, misidentification can result.

9. *Lights.* Aerial lights or airfield light beacons can use Morse coding. Marine lights, which may only be glimpsed briefly through the wave tops, tend to use simpler codes such as:

(a) Flashing (Fl.). A periodic flash.
(b) Group flashing (Gp. Fl.). A series of flashes followed by a period of darkness, the sequence recurring at regular intervals.
(c) Fixed and Flashing (F. Fl.). A steady light with brighter flashes.
(d) Occulting (Occ.). A steady light with, periodically, a short period of black-out.
(e) Group occulting (Gp. Occ.). A steady light with a series of short black-outs, the sequence recurring at regular intervals.
(f) Alternating (Alt.) A light that changes colour, generally from red to white.

10. Certain powerful landfall lights may be uncoded. Smaller uncoded lights are also used, known generally as fixed (F.) lights. It is also common for a light to change colour or coding in various sectors so that the seaman can know when his craft is on a dangerous bearing from the light.

11. *Buoys*. Buoys may be lighted by night but otherwise may be coded in three ways:

  (a) *Shape*. Typical shapes are a can, a cone (sometimes known as a nun buoy), a cask, a spar and a sphere. Some buoys have distinctive shapes at the top and may be known as topmark buoys.

  (b) *Colour*. A buoy may be any distinctive colour or may be checkered or striped.

  (c) *Sound*. The buoy may sound a bell, gong, horn, trumpet or whistle and is then known as a sound buoy.

POSITION FINDING

12. When a ship passes close to a buoy or an aircraft passes over a landmark, position to a high degree of accuracy may be established. In the instance of an aircraft, it is not generally possible to look straight downwards and the eye tends to underestimate divergence from the vertical. A landmark 30° to one side of the vertical will be four nautical miles away at 42,000 feet and pro-rata at lower heights.

13. *Bearings*. Generally visual positions are fixed by bearings either from a number of objects or by a running fix from one object, doubling the angle at the bow being a common method (page 379, para 8). These bearings may be measured by:

  (a) *Bearing plate*. A simple rotating sight that may measure relative bearings or be driven by a compass repeater and measure true or magnetic bearings according to the type of compass. A bearing plate is sometimes known as a pelorus or alidade.

  (b) *Bearing compass*. A hand-held instrument which combines a bearing plate and a simple magnetic compass so that magnetic bearings can be taken.

14. Visual bearings will have errors that depend on the instantaneous accuracy of the heading reference. The compass error at any instant may be several degrees. In addition, an error can arise if the instrument is not level or if the craft is accelerating. The compass errors can be reduced considerably by taking bearings on objects disposed symmetrically about the craft (page 383, para 22). Nevertheless, fixing accuracy will generally be relatively low in spite of the accuracy with which objects can be aligned visually.

DIFFERENCE OF BEARINGS

15. The extreme accuracy with which the human eye can measure alignment, coupled with the inevitable degradation that arises when the inaccurate heading of the craft has to be applied to this measurement, has led the mariner to use differences of bearings to find position lines. An important special instance is the transit, a position line obtained when two objects are in the same direction. Position lines of this type are particularly used as leading lines to help the seaman to guide his craft into narrow channels. Distinctive leading lines may be marked on charts of entrances to harbours.

16. Differences of bearings may be measured by tilting a sextant (page 419, para 1) sideways and plotting differences from three objects to provide a fix (page 379, para 11). It was shown that the position line resulting from a difference in bearing measurement will lie on a circle passing through the two objects and the craft. Hence if the three objects and the craft all lie on the one circle, there will be only a position line available. If four points lie on a circle, the opposite angles add up to 360°. Therefore, if the angle formed by the lines joining the objects on the chart, added to the angle between the two extreme objects measured from the craft, makes a total of 360°, a fix is impossible. Unless it is at least 30° away from 360°, the limiting angle of cut of 30° will not be achieved. In addition to this need to achieve a good cut, the errors in the individual position lines will increase with distance so that the radial error will be roughly proportional to distance from centre of gravity of the three objects and the secant of the angle of cut.

17. Another application of difference of bearings is the measurement of distance to an object on the surface of the sea by

comparing the dip with the dip of the horizon. The formula is:

distance n. miles $= 1\cdot17$ [dip$'$ $- \sqrt{(}$dip$'^2 - 0\cdot96 \times$ (horizon dip$'$)^2)]

The dip of the horizon may be calculated from the height of observation, as explained on page 399, para 2. Alternatively, the formula may be replaced by books of tables. In either event, standard refraction will be assumed and the formula only applied to a sight taken from a low height.

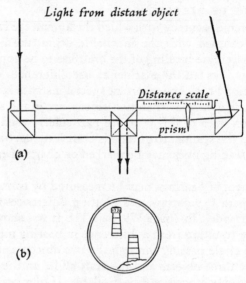

FIG. 184   Rangefinder

RANGEFINDER

18. The rangefinder measures distances by the same method that the human eye measures distances, that is, according to the angle that the 'eyes' at the ends of the rangefinder 'look' inwards. This inwards looking can be arranged by means of mirrors as in Fig. 184(a) so that a distant object appears in two halves as shown in Fig. 184(b). By turning one of the end mirrors through a small angle, the two halves of the image can be made to line up with each other. In practice, a prism is moved along the rangefinder so that the angle by which the light is reflected from one end of the rangefinder will be adjusted, this prism registering against a

scale of distance. The greater the separation of the end mirrors, the longer the baseline and therefore the more accurate the range measurement.

19. Generally, a telescope system is combined with the rangefinder. Also astigmatizers can be switched in so that a point source of light may be drawn out into a vertical line. It is perhaps unfortunate that the rangefinder is so named. In navigation, range should mean maximum distance rather than measured distance (page 365, para 17).

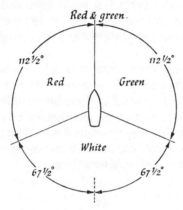

FIG. 185   Navigation lights

COLLISION AVOIDANCE

20. Interception requires the accurate measurement of line of sight. On land, provided that the target is kept in line with a distant object, the line of sight may be maintained constant and, indeed, it is by this means that collisions are anticipated on the roads. However, at sea there may be no object sufficiently distant and distinct. In the air, the problem is complicated by the need for two-dimensional references. At height, a target may appear to be well above owing to the dip of the horizon whereas, on approaching, it may suddenly appear to dip and may pass underneath.

21. The human eye has the ability to judge the aspect of the target. This is of great importance since it assists the navigator to decide whether to stand on or to give way. At night, as shown in Fig. 185, a craft will carry a red light on its port side and a green

light on its starboard, a ship's lights showing from ahead to $22\frac{1}{2}°$ (two points) abaft either beam. Thus if another craft sees both port and starboard lights, it has a meeting situation (page 265, para 14); if it sees a red light, it knows that the other ship will have it on its port side; if it sees neither light but only the white stern light, it knows that it must be overtaking or astern. The stern light covers the sector not covered by the side lights. In addition, two mast-head lights, the lower one ahead of the other, are visible on a ship over the sectors covered by the side lights. An aircraft carries similar lights but has a light underneath in place of masthead lights. All its lights are made to wink so that they can readily be distinguished from stars. These lights are known as navigation lights.

22. By visual means, the navigator is able to assess immediately when the target has altered its course. At sea, it may also be possible to estimate the speed of the other craft by its type and its wash, and in the air, by its type. All this information is available instantly. Nevertheless, the absence of a stable line of sight means that collisions can and do occur between two craft in broad daylight and with no other distractions.

AIMING

23. The aiming of a projectile is not a navigational problem in the strict sense but it may have navigational implications. If the target is moving, the projectile has to travel on an interception path that may have to allow for slowing down as it travels on its way. The velocity of the target relative to the platform from which the projectile is launched will have to be known and, if the projectile travels through the air, the time of travel will have to be known in order that gravity drop can be allowed for. Distance may be measured visually by a rangefinder or according to the apparent size of a target whose dimensions happen to be known.

24. In the particular instance of a bomb or supplies being dropped from an aircraft, the distance to the target can be calculated from the line of sight and the height, the height being found from atmospheric pressure compared to forecast atmospheric pressure at the target. There are two major variants of the problem:

(a) *Tachometric sight.* A well-shaped bomb will maintain its forward speed after it has been released and therefore it will strike the ground at a point directly below the aircraft. The aiming requirement is therefore track and ground speed as well as line of sight. A sight of this type is known as a tachometric sight.

(b) *Triangle of velocities sight.* A poorly shaped object will lag behind the aircraft so that the latter will forge ahead through the block of air. Hence the impact point will be behind the heading of the aircraft and to one side of the track by a distance known as the cross trail, as shown in Fig. 186. Hence, for a poorly shaped object, the triangle of

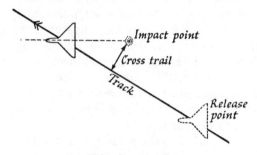

FIG. 186   Cross trail error

velocity will have to be calculated. In the extreme instance of parachuting, the release point will depend on the mean wind velocity between the aircraft and the ground and the time taken to reach the ground. The initial forward velocity will be lost almost immediately.

25. Certain missiles are steered visually, notably guided bombs which are controlled by radio and field of battle weapons used to destroy tanks and vehicles. These latter weapons may be controlled by a simple thumb joystick which is so connected that it alters the rate that the missile closes with the line of sight to the target. An interesting feature is that the human eye is so precise that vision alone can be used to navigate. The signals are sent to the missile along wires which are fed out from a bobbin within the missile so as to reduce air resistance and friction with the

ground. A mile of wire may only weigh 2lb or 3lb, which is hardly more than a very light radio receiver. This system guards against any interference with the signals but provides a leading line direct to the aimer.

BERTHING AND LANDING

26. The berthing of a ship and the landing of an aircraft are particular instances of a type of aiming in which the craft itself has to be aimed with extreme accuracy. For this purpose, the human eye can see immediately when the craft is changing its alignment. This is particularly important in the instance of a ship in which berthing involves judgment of factors such as wind and tide which may interact in a most delicate fashion.

27. Landing an aircraft involves the exact judgment of a flare-out. (page 125, para 7). Cine-recording suggests that the visual information at landing is obtained partly from the pattern streaming past the eyes and picked up by parafoveal vision, since the pilot tends to look steadily forwards. Take-off is a simpler operation except in certain jet aircraft in which the rotation at lift-off causes the ground to fall away below the nose so that the flare-up has to be on instruments.

28. By night, the lead in to the runway is marked by a funnel of lights and the approach to the threshold assisted by rows of approach lights whose relative positions give guidance. Certain lights may show red when the pilot is too low on the glide slope or green when he is too high. The runway will be picked out generally by a double row of lights, and taxiway lights may assist the pilot to steer his aircraft to and from the runway.

LASERS

29. If light of a certain frequency is passed through a medium that has been activated by a source of energy, the energy of that particular frequency of light can be increased. If the light is passed to and fro through the activated medium, the power will build up and a beam of very pure light is produced which can be directed along an exact alignment.

30. The laser has been applied to navigation in two ways. First the ability to produce a very narrow beam of concentrated light has made the laser an ideal means of measuring distance for

the launching of military weapons. The beam of light can have a resolution comparable to the human eye so that it can be aligned visually on the exact target. The light can be transmitted in a series of bursts and the time taken for a burst of light to travel to the target and back again may be measured by means similar to those that will be described in Chapter XV.

31. The purity of light produced by a laser makes possible the measurement of doppler shifts using light waves. Very small frequency shifts can be detected and the sensitivity is such that, if light is passed in opposite directions round four mirrors arranged in a square, any rotation will be sensed as a shift of frequency between the light travelling round the square in one direction and that travelling round the square in the opposite direction. A gyroscopic device such as this is known as a ring laser. It has no moving parts to wear out and for certain applications the size might be acceptable.

4. INFRA-RED

1. Infra-red wavelengths are between 1 millimetre and 1 micron in length. They cannot penetrate far through fog and mist, and indeed, in very thick fog, light is probably equally penetrating. However, light depends on the reflection from illumination and, in fog and mist, the back scatter obscures these reflections. Infra-red, on the other hand, can depend on radiations emitted from the bodies themselves.

2. The longer infra-red waves may be detected by temperature sensors which act as integrators. Hence these can only detect a radiation stronger than the back scatter produced by the craft itself. Unless very large reflectors are used, the range tends to be limited. In the middle of the infra-red band, absorption by moisture is more serious. The shorter infra-red waves suffer from absorption by steam, oxygen and carbon dioxide but there are favourable frequencies. At these infra-red wavelengths, photoelectric cells may be used as detectors.

3. In addition to infra-red, all forms of thermal activity emit centimetric radio waves. These are extremely weak and the

noise in a normal receiver would drown them. However, recent developments in electronic oscillators and amplifiers make it possible that, eventually, receivers may be built that can receive these radiations effectively. This branch of science is known as radiometry.

4. The strength of the emissions of infra-red and also of micro-waves depends not only on the absolute temperature but also on the characteristics of the material concerned. Hence infra-red makes it possible to distinguish objects which appear identical to the human eye. Typical examples are animals and humans hidden in undergrowth, fish shoals and submarines at sea. This means that infra-red has a potentiality for identification which may be of great significance in military applications.

5. Unfortunately, infra-red systems suffer from interference. For example, an infra-red lock-follow equipment aimed at an aircraft may be distracted by the radiation from the Sun. As a result, infra-red tends to be used only when the target is simple and unmistakable and when the device can be aligned initially on to the target.

6. There will be three applications for infra-red equipments:

(a) Lock-follow homing systems for anti-aircraft missiles, generally small weapons launched from aircraft, often fitted with boosts to reach the necessary speed but without sustainer motors.

(b) Horizon sensors for space navigation, in particular for satellite stabilization. The planet will radiate according to its temperature even when the satellite is in the shadow.

(c) Military reconnaissance and identification systems.

5. TACTILE AIDS

1. Generally, the term contact navigation is used to describe navigation when contact has been established visually with the ground. However, there is one important aspect of navigation which involves the sense of touch. This is the business of feeling the bottom of the sea by means of a lead weight at the end of a line, known as a lead line.

2. The lead line has to be cast ahead of the moving craft so that the line will be vertical as the craft passes above it. Marks on the line give the depth in fathoms, a fathom originally meaning an embrace resulting from stretching out the arms to the fullest extent to 6 feet and then bringing the hands together ready to step out the next fathom along the rope.

3. A lead generally has a hollow underneath filled with tallow or some substance that can bring up from the sea-bed a sample of the type of bottom. This will enable the navigator to compare what he finds in his lead with what is marked on the chart. On the chart the texture and colour of the bottom may be indicated by self-evident abbreviations such as bl. for black and gty. for gritty, and this will provide an additional check on position.

6. SUMMARY

INFORMATION THEORY

Information is provided by means of waves:

(a) *Mechanical compression waves*
    (i) Sound waves, 100 c/s to 10 kc/s.
    (ii) Ultrasonic waves, 10 kc/s and higher frequencies.

(b) *Electro-magnetic waves*
    (i) Radio, 10 kc/s to 10^5 Mc/s (3 mm).
    (ii) Infra-red, 10^5 Mc/s to 10^8 Mc/s.
    (iii) Light, 10^8 Mc/s to 10^9 Mc/s.

The strength of a wave decreases as the square of the distance, and waves are also attenuated. Waves may be reflected or refracted. They will flow round obstacles, the longer the wavelength and the lower the frequency the less the effect of obstruction.

The accuracy of a navigation system depends on the band width.

Noise covers a wide band width and, hence, the more complex and accurate the information, the more susceptible it may be to noise. In order to pass a signal through noise, redundancy may be necessary and this increases the time taken to pass the signal.

The limit of range of a signal depends on the signal-to-noise ratio. The signal-to-noise ratio can be increased by:

(a) Increase of transmitted power.
(b) Beaming of signal.
(c) Coding, for example by the use of pulses.

Military systems tend to be self-contained within the craft in order to reduce jamming. The signals may have to be coded to prevent faking by the enemy.

LIGHT

Light bends down towards the horizon. The distance of the horizon in n. miles $= 1 \cdot 15 \sqrt{}$(height of observer in feet) provided that refraction is normal.

Abnormal refraction causes mirages and looming and makes measurement of dip inaccurate particularly at low heights.

High-quality optical systems use complex lenses and invert the image. The field of view will be reduced inversely as the magnification.

VISUAL NAVIGATION

The brain tends to interpret information from the eyes in accordance with what it expects to see. Hence visual identification must be achieved by combining unmistakable features and not by general impressions.

The marine chart is suitable for visual navigation at sea. The air chart can only contain a limited amount of visual navigation information and therefore visual navigation generally requires a topographical map, the features being selected according to significance when viewed from the air.

Identification is achieved with the help of the circle of uncertainty.

Coastal lights use simple codes. Aerial lights are more widely spaced and use Morse codes. Buoys are identified by shape, colour and sometimes by sound.

VISUAL POSITION FINDING

Positions are found by:

(a) Pinpoints.

(b) Bearings combined with the heading of the craft, which may be relatively inaccurate.

(c) Differences of bearings which generally give distances. Examples are:

    (i) Station pointer fixes.
    (ii) Transit or leading line.
    (iii) Dip compared to horizon.
    (iv) Rangefinder.

SPECIAL APPLICATIONS

Visual methods are valuable for collision avoidance because they assist the navigator to know what the target is likely to do:

(a) By enabling him to note the aspect of the target.
(b) By enabling him to see immediately if and when the target alters course.

Navigation lights are used at night which assist the navigator to judge the aspect of a target.

Visual methods are used for berthing a ship owing to the complexity of the factors involved.

Visual information may be used for landing and taking off aircraft. Special lighting systems are used to assist approach and landing at night.

LASERS

Lasers can be used for accurate rangefinding for aiming weapons and for doppler speed measurements of targets. The ring laser can act as a gyroscope.

INFRA-RED

Infra-red has potentiality for identification of military targets. Infra-red devices may be used for satellite stabilization.

TACTILE AIDS

The lead line measures the depth of the water and may also identify the type of sea bottom.

CHAPTER XII

Astro-Navigation

PRINCIPLES

1. The Sun, Moon and planets are generally known as astronomical 'bodies' and for convenience may be regarded as being on the celestial sphere, a hollow globe of great size within which the Earth rotates. The position of a particular body on the celestial sphere and the orientation of the Earth within it is tabulated for each instant of time in books of tables known as almanacs. It is therefore possible to find the point on the surface of the Earth above which is the particular body. Such a point is known as the sub-point of the body.

2. Astro-navigation provides techniques for finding position from sub-points. These positions are not found from bearings of the sub-points because the accuracy of bearing measurement will be limited by the heading reference. Positions are found from measurements of distances from sub-points, the distances being measured in minutes of arc.

3. If the craft is at the sub-point, the body will be directly overhead and at the navigator's 'zenith', so that the angle between the zenith and the body will be zero. If the craft is not at the sub-point, as shown in Fig. 187, the distance of the craft from the sub-point in minutes of arc will equal the angle between the body and the zenith. In practice, the angle between the body and the horizon may be measured more conveniently. This angle is known as the altitude. The possible confusion with the altimeter reading has been noted (page 74, para 30).

4. Position finding by astro-navigation may therefore be regarded as consisting of two basic processes:

   (a) *Sight taking* or 'shooting' the body, which is measuring the altitude and thus the angle between the craft and the sub-point.

(b) *Sight reduction.* Finding the position of the sub-point on the surface of the Earth and drawing a position line according to the distance of the craft from the sub-point.

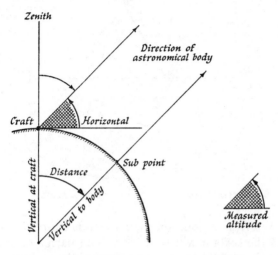

FIG. 187   Finding distance of sub-point

1. SIGHT TAKING

MARINE SEXTANT

1. The marine sextant consists basically of two mirrors, a moving mirror known as the index glass and a fixed mirror known as the horizon glass. The index glass is mounted on an arm so that it can rotate and the angle can be recorded on a scale as shown in Fig. 188. The light from the body strikes the index glass and is reflected on to the horizon glass which is partly silvered so that the horizon can be seen through it as well as the reflection of the body.

2. The observer measures the altitude of the body by rotating the index glass until the body appears to be exactly on the sea horizon. The reading of the index glass does not alter when the sextant is tilted fore and aft because two reflecting surfaces are used. However, if the sextant is tilted sideways, the altitude will

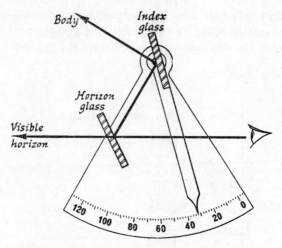

FIG. 188   Elements of marine sextant

be measured from a point on the horizon not directly below the
body and the sextant will over-read. The navigator avoids this
error by rolling the sextant to and fro sideways, making sure
that at no point does the body appear to go below the horizon
but that it just 'kisses' it.

3. A number of refinements may be fitted to the marine sextant.
Shades may be introduced between the index glass and the
horizon glass to reduce the light from a body such as the Sun.
Other shades may be introduced between the horizon glass and
the horizon to reduce glare. The arm that holds the index glass
and registers against the scale of altitude will be fitted either with
a vernier to enable more accurate readings to be taken or, more
commonly, with a micrometer. A telescopic eyepiece may be
fitted to improve the accuracy of observation and may include cross
wires to help to define the exact line along which the instrument
has been collimated or optically calibrated.

4. A tilt of the index mirror through 45° will alter the line from
the reflected body by 90°. Hence the index scale is graduated in
half-degree intervals calibrated as if they were degrees. The
graduations run down past 0° to a small negative value known as
the arc of excess. The index glass can swing through an angle of
60°, hence the name sextant or sixth of a complete circle, and

therefore the sextant can measure an object about 30° past the vertical. Certain instruments can only measure up to 90°, because the index mirror tilts only through 45°. These are correctly known as octants, but may be regarded as sextants.

MARINE SEXTANT ERRORS

5. In order to find the altitude of a body, the reading taken by the sextant has to be corrected in five different ways:

   (a) Index error.
   (b) Dip of horizon.
   (c) Refraction of line of sight to the body.
   (d) Semi-diameter of body.
   (e) Parallax of body.

6. *Index Error*. There are certain errors in a marine sextant for which adjustments have to be made:

   (a) *Index glass*. This must be perpendicular to the arm. This may be checked by viewing the scale by reflection and simultaneously viewing it directly.
   (b) *Horizon glass*. This must be perpendicular to the sextant frame. A star viewed through the horizon glass must be capable of coincidence with the image reflected from the index glass provided that the index glass is known to be perpendicular to the arm.
   (c) *Collimation error*. Two stars not less than 90° apart should retain coincidence when moved about the field of view.

7. In addition, there may be a constant index or zero error. This is found by viewing a star through the horizon mirror and moving the index glass to ensure coincidence. The sextant will then read the amount of index error. Alternatively, two observations of the Sun may be taken, one with the reflected Sun just touching the directly viewed Sun above, and the other observation just touching below. The average of the two readings will give the index error. Generally this error is allowed for arithmetically.

8. *Dip*. On page 399, para 3, the problems of calculation of dip were stressed. Tables are available but these are based on the

assumption that the temperature of the air is equal to that of the water. If this is not the case, the tabulated dip may be seriously in error and by an unknown amount. The situation is improved if sights are not taken close to the water, but the height must be known accurately. With a very high altitude, it may even be possible to take sights on opposite horizons. In any event, when dip is found, it is subtracted from the measured altitude as shown in Fig. 189.

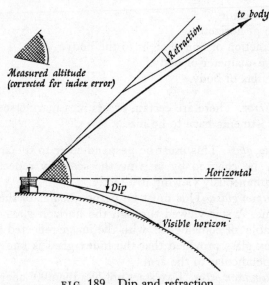

FIG. 189   Dip and refraction

9. *Refraction.* Fig. 189 also shows the effect of refraction which likewise has to be subtracted from the measured altitude. Again, refraction is based on assumptions as to temperatures and the tabulations will only be correct in so far as these assumptions hold good in practice. For a body nearly overhead, refraction may be ignored.

10. *Semi-diameter.* The Sun and the Moon have a finite size when viewed through a sextant and, therefore, when the body is made to kiss the horizon, an error will be introduced due to the radius of the disc. The radius of the Sun's disc represents about 16′ of arc, and this must be added to the measured altitude. The

radius of the Sun and the radius of the Moon, which is a little smaller and more variable, is tabulated in almanacs as semi-diameter. If the Moon, as shown in Fig. 190, is 'emptying itself out', it may be necessary to sit it below the horizon and subtract the semi-diameter.

11. *Parallax*. Fig. 190 also shows the parallax error that arises when the body is close to the Earth. The error will vary according to cos (altitude), that is according to the distance of the craft

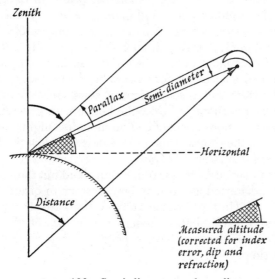

FIG. 190   Semi-diameter and parallax

from the sub-point so that, the less the altitude, the greater the parallax. The maximum parallax of the Moon is about 1°, for planets even at their closest it is only about $\frac{1}{2}'$, and for the Sun about $\frac{1}{8}'$. The actual values are tabulated in almanacs as 'parallax in altitude' (P. in A.).

12. *Overall Error*. It is difficult to assess the overall accuracy of measurement of altitude. It seems likely that the pattern of errors is exponential. It may be inferred from statistics that even a good observer is unlikely to achieve accuracies of 95 per cent within 1' of arc. The error is due largely to dip and tends to be greater on bodies of low altitude.

MARINE SEXTANT LIMITATIONS

13. A marine sextant can be used in rough weather and is unaffected by the accelerations of the craft, but observations should be taken near to the centre of gravity so that the height is as constant as possible. Much more serious will be fog, haze or mist since the horizon may be obscured, although it may be possible to obtain results from a low height from whence the horizon distance will be shortened.

14. Illumination of the horizon is another problem. Except for a couple of nights either side of full moon, the horizon may not be visible for long after the Sun has set nor for long before the Sun rises. On a moonless night, the horizon is generally not visible when the Sun is more than 9° below the horizon. On the other hand, darkness is necessary for stars to be visible and, apart from very bright stars and certain planets, stars are seldom visible unless the Sun is about 3° below the horizon. In general, therefore, star observations are confined on moonless nights to a short period around the time at which the Sun is 6° below the horizon (see page 458, para 27).

15. The Sun may be sighted through thin cloud but the shape and size may be distorted and it may be necessary to bisect the disc by the horizon. However, sextant observations are often prevented by cloud. This limitation, together with lack of visibility of the horizon, may deprive the navigator of observations for long periods of time.

BUBBLE SEXTANT

16. The bubble sextant carries its own bubble vertical instead of using the natural horizon and this is shown in the simplified drawing of Fig. 191(a). Nevertheless, to conform with the marine sextant, the scale is calibrated in terms of altitude. The star or other body has to be aligned within the bubble by tilting the index mirror until the body is level with the centre of the bubble and turning the sextant until the body is centred on the bubble. Provided that the bubble is between the two vertical lines, as shown in Fig. 191(b), the sextant will not be tilted sideways. As with all sextants, no error is introduced if the sextant is tilted fore and aft.

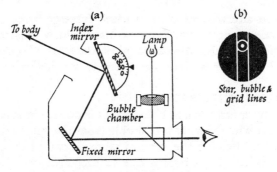

FIG. 191   Bubble sextant

17. At night, the bubble can be illuminated and the brightness varied to suit the brightness of the star, and, in particular, a red light may be used for weak stars. By day, shades will be needed to cut down the light from the sky so that the bubble can be seen and also to reduce the glare from the Sun. These shades will be introduced between the fixed mirror and the index mirror. Other shades, to reduce the amount of daylight illuminating the bubble, will be fitted above the bubble chamber. The bubble itself is made so that its size can be varied. This allows for the use of a small bubble which is less lively in bumpy conditions or for the use of a large sensitive bubble in steady conditions.

18. Early bubble sextants used an index glass that was only partly silvered. The bubble was reflected from it so that the observer could look straight at the star. This assists star identification, since a star is often identified by its position relative to the stars around it. Unfortunately, direct viewing is uncomfortable at high altitudes. Octants, on the other hand, have been designed to be used with the head bent forward and looking comfortably downwards. The loss of light in the complex optical system may necessitate the addition of a telescope which further reduces the field of view and makes star identification more difficult.

19. A well-supported human body, sighting through an open window or a sheet of optically flat glass, is probably the ideal sextant mounting. However, a bubble sextant is heavy and therefore a perspex dome known as an astrodome may be fitted in the craft and the sextant supported within it on a hook, a special allowance being made for dome refraction. Alternatively, in a

high-speed aircraft with a pressurized fuselage using a stressed skin, a periscopic sextant may be used which requires only a small hole. Inevitably the periscopic sextant has a limited field of view and therefore problems can arise in star identification.

BUBBLE SEXTANT ERRORS

20. The major error in a bubble sextant is due to the accelerations of the craft which deflect the bubble from the true vertical. The problems of defining the vertical were discussed on page 164, paras 2 and 5. Accelerations due to high-frequency vibrations can be eliminated by using a small bubble that tends to stick to the face of the bubble chamber. However, accelerations of longer periods will inevitably appear as errors in the vertical.

21. Fortunately, the errors due to accelerations tend to be periodic. Therefore, although the error of a single 'shot' may be 1° or 2°, the average of a number of shots taken over a period of 1 minute or 2 minutes may be ten times more accurate. Averaging can be arranged by fitting a 1-minute or a 2-minute averaging device on the sextant or, ideally, an integrator. Also, for a sight taken ahead or astern, it will be necessary to ensure that the forward speed of the craft is the same at the end of the run of shots as it was at the beginning. For a sight taken on the beam, it will be necessary to ensure that the course at the end of the run is the same as the course at the beginning of the run. Since it is often more difficult to ensure a steady course than a steady speed, bubble sextant sights tend to be more accurate on fore and aft bodies than on athwartships bodies.

22. Integration cannot remove errors due to sideways tilt. If a sextant tilts, it will over-read, particularly at high altitudes (page 419, para 2). Therefore, rough weather will introduce over-reading. Nor can integration remove errors due to the course that the craft is following. For example, a magnetic course will be curved by the convergency of the magnetic meridians and a gyro course will be curved according to the drift rate of the gyro. The error in minutes of arc from a cause such as this will be approximately:

speed (knots) × change of course (degrees a minute)/20

In addition, the vertical will be tilted by coriolis to the left in the northern hemisphere and to the right in the southern hemisphere. These errors are, however, generally dealt with as a final process in the finding of position.

23. The bubble sextant must be corrected for:

(a) Index error.
(b) Parallax in altitude.

Since the Sun or Moon is made to sit within the bubble, correction for semi-diameter is not required.

24. *Overall Error.* In a very steady slow-moving craft, a bubble sextant may be able to measure altitude with a 95 per cent accuracy of less than 2′ of arc. However, it is extremely difficult to follow the motion of a bubble in a seaway and, therefore, the bubble sextant is not commonly used at sea. On the other hand, it has to be used in an aircraft which, unless flying very low, will have no visible horizon. In aircraft, acceleration errors build up according to the speed, and the 95 per cent radial error in minutes of arc may approximate to around 5 per cent of the speed of the craft in knots. With great care at the beginning and the end of the sight, and using a steady aircraft flying under automatics, this error may be reduced, particularly on a fore and aft observation. In bumpy weather, on the other hand, the error may be much larger.

SEXTANT DEVELOPMENTS

25. *Marine Sextants.* Developments appear generally to be along two main lines:

(a) The use of higher-powered telescopes, which not only enable the accuracy of alignment of the body with the horizon to be increased but also make it increasingly possible to view stars when the sky is lighter and when the horizon is consequently clearer.
(b) The use of dip-meters, which compare the angle of the horizon in one direction with the angle of the horizon in the opposite direction. These devices can reduce the major error arising from failure to correct for dip accurately.

26. Nevertheless, the law of diminishing returns is operating against an increase in accuracy. An observation accurate to

within a fraction of a minute of arc means timing the observation to the nearest second, correcting the sextant by fractions of a minute of arc and increasing the precision and therefore the number of figures in the subsequent calculation of position. It seems likely, therefore, that for general navigation, the present standard of astro-navigation will be considered acceptable. It is worth remembering that although, in experienced hands, there is no more reliable method of navigation, its availability is dependent on the weather to an extent that would be quite unacceptable applied to radio equipment.

27. *Star Tracker*. The bubble sextant is best fitted close to the centre of gravity of an aircraft and where there is a good view of the sky. Taking a sight therefore generally means that the observer will have to leave his normal station. As speeds increase, time becomes more precious and, particularly in a military aircraft in which pressure suits may be worn, movement may be arduous. Hence automatic star trackers have been developed.

28. On page 375, para 20, lock-follow devices were described and optical lock-follow was used for purposes of illustration. Both types of lock-follow devices have been applied to star trackers. Alternatively, a device known as an iconoscope may be used. This is a form of cathode ray tube in which the screen gives off electrons when light falls upon it. These electrons modify a beam of electrons fired at the screen from an electron gun so that current is made to flow through a detector circuit. An iconoscope can find the direction of light from a body but unfortunately is relatively complex and fragile.

29. Although an automatic star tracker can lock on to a star with an accuracy of the order of a minute of arc, the accuracy of the altitude will depend on the accuracy of the vertical. It is unlikely that a vertical less complex than a Schüler-tuned inertial platform will be able to sense the vertical with an accuracy greater than that which can be achieved by a sextant in skilful hands. In practice, therefore, a star tracker used for finding position will be stabilized by an inertial platform.

30. It will be possible to transfer the alignment of the platform to the gimbals of a separate star tracker by optical means, locking the star tracker to the inertial platform by a beam of light. It will be simpler to build the star tracker as a part of the inertial

platform. The alignment of the tracker with the stars can maintain the alignment of the platform and combat long period gyro drift.
31. A combined star tracker and inertial platform may be known as an inertia-astro system. Accuracy of the order of 1 n. mile (95 per cent probability) may be achieved provided the intervals between star observations are not unduly long. If the observations can be continuous, a similar order of accuracy may be achieved with a relatively crude platform and the system is then known as auto-astro. Unfortunately, auto-astro will be little cheaper than inertia-astro and only applicable to aircraft flying above the weather. Either system will require a digital computer as described on page 449, para 22.

ALL-WEATHER ASTRO
32. Above the troposphere, the aircraft will be above the weather, and above 40,000 feet the sky becomes increasingly dark. Planets and bright stars become visible to the naked eye as height is increased, and star trackers become increasingly effective by day. The ability to use stars by day can be increased by the use of magnification, but this magnification reduces the field of view and consequently increases the time needed to search the sky to find a particular star.
33. As height is reduced, the chances of a clear sky will be lessened. At 10,000 feet, the chance of a clear sky is probably half that at 20,000 feet, and at the surface probably half that at 10,000 feet. In temperate regions in midwinter, the sky may be visible at the surface for less than 4 hours in 24 hours on a long-term average.
34. Even when the sky is clear, planets will seldom be seen by day and only the Moon may be visible in addition to the Sun. Three-quarters of the time, the Moon will either be below the horizon, too close to the horizon for accurate observation, or too close to the Sun to be visible. Even when it can be sighted, the direction may lead to a poor cut in combination with the Sun. Hence, by day, fixes may have to rely on successive Sun observations except at great heights.
35. Radio waves, unlike light waves, will penetrate cloud. There are in the universe a number of sources of radio waves known as radio stars. The positions of many of these radio stars have been

plotted. Unfortunately the signals are generally so weak that a very large aerial would be necessary in order to produce sufficient radio 'magnification' to read through the general background of radio noise.

36. The most powerful radiator of radio waves in the sky is the Sun. The next two are the Moon and a point in Cassiopeia. A parabolic reflector 2 feet or 3 feet in diameter and a radio lock-follow system is able to measure the direction of the Sun to within a couple of minutes of arc through rain, heavy cloud, snow and fog except when the Sun is close to the horizon and the radio waves have to penetrate a great thickness of water-laden atmosphere. The frequency used is extremely high and the waves may be only a couple of centimetres long. Better results, but with greater susceptibility to weather, can be achieved by working at a wavelength of between $8\frac{1}{2}$ and 9 millimetres, which happens to penetrate cloud better than slightly longer or shorter waves. Such a system can operate with an aerial only 1 foot in diameter. It will generally be known as a radio sextant.

2. THE CELESTIAL SPHERE

MAGNITUDE

1. Astronomical bodies are classified according to their brightness. It has been accepted that a star of the 1st magnitude is a hundred times as bright as a star of the 6th magnitude and that the distribution of magnitudes is logarithmic in terms of brightness. Thus each reduction in magnitude means an increase of brightness of about $2\frac{1}{2}$. A star of magnitude 0 is about $2\frac{1}{2}$ times as bright as a star of magnitude 1 and a star of magnitude -1 is about $2\frac{1}{2}$ times as bright as a star of magnitude 0. On this basis:

Body	Magnitude
Sun (Symbol ☉)	$-26\cdot7$
Full Moon (mean)	$-12\cdot5$
Venus (mean)	$-3\cdot4$
Jupiter (mean)	$-2\cdot2$
Sirius	$-1\cdot6$
Canopus	$-0\cdot9$
Mars (mean)	$-0\cdot2$
About ten stars	$0–1$
About twenty stars and Saturn	$1–2$

2. If the brightest star, Sirius, is taken as the standard, the Sun is ten thousand million times as bright, full moon twenty thousand times as bright, Venus five times as bright, Jupiter nearly twice as bright, Canopus half as bright and Mars a quarter as bright. In addition, certain stars and the planet Mars have a distinctive red colour, and this in conjunction with magnitude is helpful for identification. It is worth noting that the magnitude seen by a photo-electric cell may differ greatly from that seen by the human eye.

3. It is also worth noting that when the Sun has sunk 4° below the horizon, stars of magnitude +1 are generally visible, and that for each successive 1½° below the horizon, stars of the next magnitude generally become visible. This effect is not altered greatly by height up to 20,000 feet since, although the Sun will be at a smaller angle below the visible horizon, there will also be less reflection from the sky.

NIGHT SKY

4. In order to produce a fix, two or three stars in different directions may be observed so as to ensure a reasonable cut of position lines. To achieve this, it will generally be necessary to be able to choose from at least half a dozen stars which are well above the horizon. It follows that probably a couple of dozen stars in the northern and southern skies must be capable of being identified. These stars are generally known as navigational stars and are chosen for their distribution as well as for their brightness.

5. The navigational stars in the sky are identified by their positions in relation to certain features in the sky in the form of distinctive patterns known as constellations. The problem is closely analogous to the identification of a visual landmark. Indeed, difficulties in recognition can arise when there are a great number of stars visible in the sky. The brain can easily link up stars incorrectly for the same reason that it can link up the patterns of a vaguely seen landmark incorrectly. Hence only a few unmistakable constellations are used in navigation:

(a) Dipper or Plough.
(b) Chair or Cassiopeia.
(c) Sickle.
(d) Triangle of Vega.
(e) Orion.
(f) Pegasus.
(g) Southern Cross.
(h) Scorpion.

6. It will be noted that the constellation names do not tally very closely with those of the classical astronomer. The patterns of stars may hardly have changed since the constellations were originally named but the modern navigator may find it easier to relate the pattern of the stars to modern objects.

7. The eight constellations and twenty-four typical navigational stars distributed about the northern and the southern sky are shown in Fig. 192. It will be noticed that, of the eight constellations, only two are wholly in the southern sky, and of the twenty-four navigational stars, more than half are in the northern sky, although the two brightest, Canopus and Sirius, are southern stars.

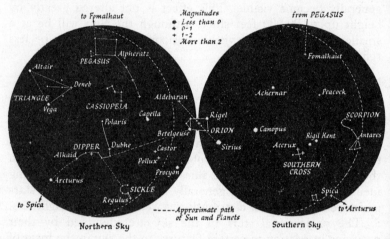

FIG. 192   Constellations and navigational stars

NAVIGATIONAL STARS

8. The Dipper or Plough, sometimes known as the Great Bear, or King Charles' Wain, has a pattern similar to the cross-section of a ladle or dipper with a long, curved handle, and is in an area generally free from bright stars. The side of the dipper away from the handle points towards the pole star, Polaris, the two stars in the Dipper being known as the pointers, the one nearer to Polaris being Dubhe. Polaris itself is about a degree of angle away from the celestial north pole, in a direction nearly opposite to that of the end star of the handle of the Dipper, a star named Alkaid or

Benetnasch. Another distinctive constellation, on the opposite side of Polaris to the Dipper, is the *W* shaped arrangement of stars known as the Chair or, more correctly, as Cassiopeia.

9. The side of the bowl of the Dipper next to the handle points in one direction towards a distinctive pattern of stars arranged in the form of a Sickle or a question-mark with the bright star Regulus at the further end. A line from the side of the Dipper next to the handle but in the opposite direction points to the large right-angled 'triangle' formed by the very bright star Vega at the right angle, the bright blue-white star Altair, which is the centre of three stars in a line, and Deneb, which combines with other stars to form a pattern sometimes known as the northern cross. The curve of the handle of the Dipper, if followed in a long sweep, passes through the bright yellow star Arcturus and on to the blue star Spica. It then comes on a small but distinctive constellation shaped like the mainsail of a gaff-rigged boat.

10. A line along the bottom of the Dipper running away from the handle points towards Orion, a constellation comprising four stars arranged in a quadrilateral, the two brightest being the red Betelgeuse nearest to the Dipper, and Rigel furthest from the Dipper. Three stars in a line in the centre of the quadrilateral run north-west and south-east and are known as the belt of Orion. To the north-west, the belt points roughly in the direction of Aldebaran, an orange star at one end of a narrow V of stars, and then on to an unmistakable flock of stars known as the Pleiades. The line of the belt, if followed in the opposite direction, points roughly towards Sirius.

11. The line from Orion through Aldebaran runs towards the great square of Pegasus, the star at the corner nearest to Orion being Alpheratz. Vega and Deneb also point to a corner of the square where there is a triangle of faint stars that represents the tail of the horse Pegasus. The line from this point to Alpheratz represents the back of the horse, and there is a long line of stars which may be regarded as the neck, which leads on towards the bright yellowish star Capella. The side of the square, which would represent the back legs, points towards Fomalhaut in the southern sky.

12. Three stars in the northern sky remain to be identified, white Castor and yellowish Pollux, known as the twins, and yellow-

white Procyon. These stars lie on a huge arc running from Capella and on to Sirius. Castor itself also lies on a line from Rigel through Betelgeuse; Procyon forms an equilateral triangle with Sirius and Betelgeuse.

13. The most famous of the southern constellations, the Southern Cross, is relatively insignificant and not close to the south celestial pole. It is perhaps best identified by its closeness to two very bright stars, the one further from the Southern Cross being known as Rigil Centaurus or Rigil Kent. The bright star at the end of the arm of the Southern Cross that points towards the south celestial pole is Acrux.

14. Between Sirius and the south celestial pole is the second brightest star in the sky, Canopus. A line from Canopus to the Southern Cross passes close to a constellation known as the False Cross, and this can cause confusion if the Southern Cross is not identified by its closeness to Rigil Centaurus. A line from Canopus to Fomalhaut passes through the bright star Achernar.

15. The most distinctive constellation in the southern sky is probably the Scorpion, which has a long, curved tail, and the red star Antares close to the head. The Scorpion is on a line from the Southern Cross through Rigil Centaurus, and forms a rough triangle with the Cross and Spica. From Antares, a line running down the body of the Scorpion passes close by the isolated star Peacock on the way to Fomalhaut.

16. The Sun, the Moon and the planets follow paths close to arcs in the northern and southern sky, shown dotted in Fig. 192, passing between Pegasus and Fomalhaut and close to Aldebaran, Pollux, Regulus, Spica and Antares. Of the planets, Venus can be identified as the morning or evening star, and may be by far the brightest object in the sky after the Moon, and Jupiter may be the next most bright. Mars and Saturn are generally relatively insignificant in appearance, although Mars, with its distinctive reddish tinge, can be bright.

17. The identification of stars, like the identification of landmarks, is greatly assisted by dead reckoning. It will be found in section 3 of this chapter, which deals with sight reduction, that the process involves calculating the altitude and direction of the body from the D.R. position. The same process can be used to estimate the likely altitude and direction of a star so that it may be identified,

even if only glimpsed through a gap in the clouds. Alternatively, this calculation may be necessary when a star has to be sighted through a telescope or other optical instrument that has a narrow field of view. When some form of automatic star tracker is being used, the computation will be performed by a digital computer (page 449, para 23).

POSITION ON THE CELESTIAL SPHERE

18. The celestial sphere has north and south celestial poles that lie on the extensions of the Earth's axis and a celestial equator that lies in the plane of the Earth's equator. Each half of a great circle on the celestial sphere that runs from one pole to another is known as a celestial meridian.

19. The position of a body on the celestial sphere is defined in terms of:

(a) *Declination* (*dec.*). The angle measured through 90° north or south of the celestial equator. Declination on the celestial sphere corresponds to latitude on the Earth.

(b) *Hour angle* (*H.A.*). The angle measured through 360° westwards from a reference meridian. H.A. on the celestial sphere would therefore correspond to longitude on the Earth if longitude were measured westwards all the way round the Earth. Occasionally, H.A. may be quoted in terms of 24 hours instead of 360°.

20. The prime meridian on the celestial sphere is the meridian that passes through the first point of Aries (Symbol ♈). This is the point on which the Sun is centred when it crosses the celestial equator on 21st March each year. Over the centuries, this point has drifted so that the meridian of Aries no longer passes through the constellation of Aries. The meridian of Aries runs from the north celestial pole close to Alpheratz and on to the south celestial pole. The constellation of Aries lies between this meridian and Aldebaran. The other half of the great circle which includes the meridian of Aries is known as the meridian of Libra.

HOUR ANGLE

21. Hour angle on the celestial sphere must refer to the Sun, Moon, planet, or star, and therefore the name of the appropriate

body is always written directly after the term H.A. The reference meridian from which hour angle is measured is always written immediately before the term H.A. There are four common variations of hour angle:

(a) *S.H.A. star.* The sidereal hour angle of a star is the angle of the star measured westwards through 360° from the first point of Aries.

(b) *G.H.A. body.* The Greenwich hour angle of a body is the angle of the body measured westwards through 360° from the Greenwich meridian.

(c) *G.H.A. ♈.* The Greenwich hour angle of Aries is the angle of the first point of Aries measured westwards through 360° from the Greenwich meridian.

(d) *L.H.A. body.* The local hour angle of a body is the angle of the body measured westwards through 360° from the local meridian, the meridian that passes through the craft. This corresponds to the difference of longitude between the body and the craft measured westwards from the craft through 360°.

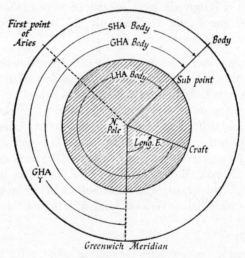

FIG. 193   The Earth within the celestial sphere

22. Fig. 193 illustrates these various forms of hour angle. It also shows that:

(a) G.H.A. ♈   (angle of Aries westwards from Greenwich)
   + S.H.A. body (angle of body westwards from Aries)
   = G.H.A. body (angle of body westwards from Greenwich)

(b) G.H.A. body   (angle of body westwards from Greenwich)
   − Longitude   of craft (measured westwards from Greenwich. If longitude should be east, it will be necessary to subtract it from 360° to convert it to west.)
   = L.H.A. body (angle of body westwards from craft).

Example. A star whose S.H.A. is 240° is observed from a craft at longitude 60° E. The G.H.A. ♈ for the time is 320°.

S.H.A. star	240°	
G.H.A. ♈	+ 320°	
G.H.A. star	= 560°	(could be expressed as 200°)
Long. W	− 300°	(360° − 60° E.)
L.H.A. star	= 260°	

TABULATION IN THE ALMANAC

23. The stars move relatively slowly over the celestial sphere. Much of this movement is due to the pull of the Sun and the Moon on the Earth's equatorial bulge. This pull causes the axis of the Earth to precess at right angles and the resulting change of tilt of the equator causes the first point of Aries to travel eastwards at about 0″.8 per year. This movement is known as the precession of the equinoxes. In addition, the Earth wobbles or nutates slightly on its axis. Furthermore, the planets tend to shift the orbit of the Earth and to change the axis of rotation.

24. As a result of the disturbances to the Earth's axis, the hour angles of the stars will slowly change and their declinations will also change but much more slowly. In addition, the stars themselves are generally moving about in space, albeit relatively slowly in terms of angles. Finally, the direction of a body measured at right angles to the line along which the Earth is travelling on its orbit will be shifted by about ⅓′ because the

speed of the Earth is about one ten-thousandth of the speed of light, and therefore the direction is distorted by 60°/10,000 approximately (page 22, para 19).

25. The cumulative changes in declination and in hour angle are generally small so that the position of a star on the celestial sphere rarely changes by 1′ per year and nearly all of this change is in S.H.A. Hence stars can be tabulated in terms of S.H.A. at three- or six-monthly intervals if the accuracy requirement is 1′, but correspondingly more frequently if the accuracy requirement is 0′.1.

26. In order to find the geographical position of the sub-point of a star, S.H.A. has to be converted to G.H.A. by the addition of G.H.A. ♈. Since G.H.A. ♈ moves at a steady rate of 360° every 23 hours 56 minutes, the tabulation of G.H.A. ♈ can be on almost any basis. The longer the intervals between tabulations, the larger the interpolation table necessary. Generally, the interval of tabulation is determined by the interval chosen for G.H.A. of the Sun, Moon and planets.

27. The Earth travels round the Sun in an orbit inclined to the equator by $23\frac{1}{2}°$. Hence the Sun will appear to move over the celestial sphere along a great circle known as the ecliptic which is inclined at $23\frac{1}{2}°$ to the celestial equator. This is shown as a dotted line in Fig 192. Owing to the tilt of the ecliptic, the Sun will change declination throughout the year and, although this change will be regular, it will be necessary to tabulate it approximately once an hour if the errors are not to exceed 1′, and more frequently if the errors are not to exceed 0′.1.

28. Since the Sun travels round the ecliptic once a year, S.H.A. Sun increases roughly at 1° per day. For this reason, it is as simple to tabulate in G.H.A. as in S.H.A. It would also be possible to tabulate the hour angle of the Sun by comparing it with an imaginary Sun that would cross the Greenwich meridian every day at exactly 1200 G.M.T. The difference between the ideal Sun and the actual Sun may be expressed as a time ahead or behind the ideal Sun and tabulated as the equation of time.

29. It is the general practice to tabulate G.H.A. Sun in the same intervals as the declination. An interpolation table for the exact seconds of time between the intervals can be of a permanent nature since the rate of change of G.H.A. Sun over a period of an

hour is negligible. In an exactly similar fashion, the declinations and G.H.A.s of the planets may be tabulated. Since these, like the Sun, travel across the celestial sphere at speeds largely determined by the movement of the Earth along its orbit, the interpolation table for G.H.A. planet can be the same as the interpolation table for G.H.A. Sun.

30. The Moon presents a special problem. In a 10-minute period, the Sun and planets will only change declination by a fraction of a minute of arc but the Moon may change by as much as $2\frac{1}{2}'$. Hence some form of interpolation will be necessary. If accuracy to within $1'$ will suffice, then a mental estimate may be possible. However, if accuracy of $0.'1$ is required, the interpolation table may have to be such that it can be adapted to the rate at which declination is changing at the particular time. For example, if the declination is tabulated every hour, the change of declination can be tabulated and entered into a table together with the time in minutes to find the additional declination to account for the intervening minutes of time.

31. The orbit of the Moon is roughly in the same plane as the ecliptic but, because the Moon travels round the Earth, it moves backwards over the celestial sphere at about $13°$ per day so that G.H.A. Moon increases at about $14\frac{1}{2}°$ per hour instead of the $15°$ common to Sun, Moon and planets. In addition its speed, like its declination, changes rapidly and may vary by anything up to $3'$ in 10 minutes. Hence the tabulation for G.H.A. Moon has to be as frequent as the tabulation for declination Moon and, unless $1'$ accuracy is ample, the interpolation table will itself have to include a correction to allow for the particular rate of change of G.H.A. Moon at the particular time.

32. In order to make the calculation of declination and G.H.A. as standard as possible, almanacs generally tabulate the following elements in the same intervals of time, an hour being common for nautical almanacs and ten minutes for air almanacs:

  (a) G.H.A. ♈.
  (b) G.H.A. Sun and declination Sun.
  (c) G.H.A. planets and declination planets (generally Mars, Jupiter and Saturn or, when available, Venus).
  (d) G.H.A. Moon and declination Moon.

33. The intervening minutes of time are allowed for by interpolation tables either:

(a) Every minute and second of time for
    (i) G.H.A. ♈.
    (ii) G.H.A. Sun and planets.
    (iii) G.H.A. Moon and declination Moon.
    This is common in nautical almanacs and may allow for
    G.H.A. body and declination body to be extracted within
    0′.1.
(b) Every 4 seconds for
    (i) G.H.A. ♈, Sun and planets.
    (ii) G.H.A. Moon.
    This is common in air almanacs and will generally allow
    for G.H.A. and declination to be extracted within ½′ with
    generally an accuracy of around 1′ for the Moon.

3. SIGHT REDUCTION

STAR CURVES

1. If the navigator could identify that part of the sky that was
directly overhead at any instant, for example by taking a vertical
photograph and developing it by a rapid reproduction process, he
could find the point in the celestial sphere directly above the craft.
He could define this point in terms of declination and S.H.A. and,
by adding G.H.A. ♈ to the latter, could express the position of
his craft at the sub-point in terms of latitude and longitude west
of Greenwich. The latter could if necessary be converted into
longitude east by subtraction from 360°.

2. It would be an extraordinary stroke of luck if one of the
navigational stars were exactly overhead. It would be possible to
identify the overhead point by a bearing and distance from the
nearest navigational star but this would introduce heading errors.
The navigator therefore defines the overhead point by distances
from two or more navigational stars and uses his sextant to
measure the altitudes in minutes of arc, subtracting these
altitudes from 90° to find the distances in minutes of arc. A
natural development will be to choose a number of bright stars

on the celestial sphere and to draw range circles tabulated in altitudes around each star, as shown in Fig. 194.

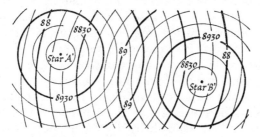

FIG. 194.   Equal altitude circles

3. Any sideways sextant tilt will greatly increase the error in altitude when observing a star close to overhead. Therefore, star circles may be drawn of large radii and the resulting pattern will be a lattice of intersecting curves as is suggested in Fig. 195.

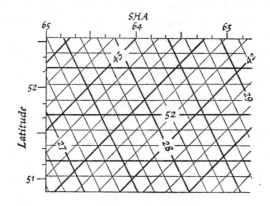

FIG. 195   Star lattice

Plotting will be a matter of drawing the altitudes observed in the appropriate positions according to the star curves. The position of a fix on the celestial sphere can then be transferred to the chart by relating declination to latitude and correcting S.H.A. by G.H.A. ♈ to find longitude.

4. *Weems Star Curves*. Weems star curves are drawn with L.H.A. ♈ increasing from the reader's right towards his left. A watch that

reads time in terms of the passage of Aries rather than the passage of the mean Sun will give G.H.A. ♈ directly in hours, minutes and seconds, and this form of time is known as sidereal time. The figure on the star curves for L.H.A. ♈, which is given also in time will, when subtracted from sidereal time, give the longitude of the position west of Greenwich in terms of time. This can then be converted at 15° per hour into chart longitude.

5. *Astrograph.* In the original form of astrograph, star curves printed on a film were projected on to a mercator plotting chart from above. The movement of the star curves westwards with time was controlled manually by aligning a time scale with a mark on the chart, the mark being chosen to allow for the correct minutes and seconds for the particular night. To allow for the correct hours, a simple conversion table was used for the particular night in question. The original astrograph provided the fastest of all known methods of sight reduction apart from automatic reduction of inputs by a computer.

6. Star curves and early versions of the astrograph could only be applied to a few stars, a normal limit being three. Below broken cloud or with high cirrus and a strong Moon, one or more stars might be blotted out. The stars change their positions slightly owing to precession and therefore curves have to be reprinted every five years unless a system of corrections is to be applied. There are also difficulties in the applications to Sun, Moon and planets. Nevertheless, these devices illustrate vividly the basis on which position is measured by astronomical means.

MARCQ ST. HILAIRE

7. The method normally used for sight reduction is named after the originator, Admiral Marcq St. Hilaire. It has already been described in general terms on page 364, para 15. The distance and bearing to the sub-point are calculated from an assumed position, either the D.R. position or a convenient point near to it. The distance is calculated as a zenith distance (Z.D.), or angle between the zenith and the body, and subtracted from 90° to give the calculated altitude of the body (H_c).

8. The intercept (page 364, para 14) will be the difference between the calculated altitude and the corrected sextant reading or observed altitude (H_0). This is stepped off along the bearing

to the sub-point from the assumed position, either away from the body, if the body is lower in the sky than has been calculated, or towards the body, if it is higher in the sky than has been calculated. The intercept should be in minutes of arc but is generally measured in minutes of latitude. This is a reasonable approximation although, on the equator, page 16, para 4, suggests that, by this means, the E.–W. intercept will be plotted $\frac{1}{2}$ per cent too short.

9. *PZX triangle.* The altitude of the body is traditionally calculated from the PZX triangle shown in Fig. 196. The elements of the triangle are:

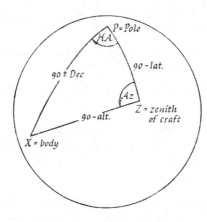

FIG. 196   PZX triangle

(a) Z represents the assumed zenith of the craft.
(b) X represents the body or its sub-point.
(c) P represents the pole nearer to the assumed position of the craft. It is known as the elevated pole because it is elevated in the sky.
(d) ZX will be the zenith distance or (90° – altitude).
(e) ZP will be (90° – latitude).
(f) XP will be (90° – declination) or, if X is in the opposite hemisphere to P and Z, it will be (90° + declination).
(g) ZPX is the local hour angle. In practice, it may be measured eastwards as well as westwards and may be tabulated as hour angle.

(h) PXZ is the parallactic angle. It is not in fact used in sight reduction.

(j) PZX is the azimuth.

10. *Azimuth.* The azimuth (Az.) of a body is its direction from the assumed position measured in the horizontal plane through 180° either eastwards or westwards from the line to the elevated pole. The use of azimuth for tabulations makes possible the application of one set of figures for bearings in both north and south hemispheres and for bodies approaching or receding from the zenith. The conversion of azimuth to true bearing will be:

$$\text{Bearing (T)} = \left. \begin{array}{l} \text{azimuth E. or} \\ 360° - \text{azimuth W.} \end{array} \right\} \text{ in northern hemisphere}$$

$$= \left. \begin{array}{l} 180° - \text{azimuth E. or} \\ 180° + \text{azimuth W.} \end{array} \right\} \text{ in southern hemisphere}$$

11. The calculated altitude of a body is found in one of three ways:

(a) Calculation from the D.R. position.

(b) Precomputed altitude and azimuth tables using an assumed position.

(c) 'Short' tables.

To reduce tabulation, declination may be known as 'same name' if it is in the same hemisphere as the assumed position and 'opposite name' if it is in the hemisphere opposite to the assumed position.

CALCULATION OF ALTITUDE

12. The cosine-haversine formula has already been described on page 334, para 12. The same formula can be used to calculate the zenith distance:

$$\text{hav (Z.D.)} = \cos \text{(lat.)} \times \cos \text{(dec.)} \times \text{hav (L.H.A.)} \\ + \text{hav (lat.} \sim \text{dec.)}$$

The zenith distance is subtracted from 90° to find the altitude. In the formula, if lat. and dec. are of opposite names, hav (lat. ~ dec.) becomes hav (lat. + dec.).

13. Calculation of altitude from the cosine-haversine formula can give an accuracy of better than 1′. The accuracy is due to:

(a) Working from the D.R. position, the errors due to the craft being at a distance from the assumed position are reduced to a minimum.

(b) The tabulations of haversines and cosines in books of nautical tables permit great accuracy.

The objection to the method is the time that it consumes. It is probably the slowest of all accepted methods of sight reduction. Also it is necessary to calculate azimuth separately.

PRECOMPUTED TABLES

14. The difficulty of achieving 1′ accuracy in observation has already been stressed in section 1 of this chapter. If the 95 per cent accuracy is a few minutes of arc, and this will be common at sea, precomputed altitude and azimuth (Alt.—Az.) tables may be used. These tables are generally in two parts:

(a) *Star tables.* The pages may be arranged according to latitude so that, if arranged in volumes, the navigator need only carry those that cover the latitudes in which he will be operating. On each page, entries of L.H.A. ♈ and half a dozen or more convenient stars enable altitude and azimuth to be extracted directly. Owing to precession and nutation such tables have a limited life of, say, 5 to 10 years if accuracy is to be achieved without sophisticated correction tables.

(b) *Sun, Moon and planet tables.* The pages will again be arranged according to latitude. On each page, entries of L.H.A. body and declination enable altitude and azimuth to be extracted directly. The life of these tables is not limited. The range of declination is normally just under 30°.

15. Variations of this standard pattern may be used. The star tables may be tabulated for L.H.A. star, in which event three calculations of hour angle will be needed for three star position lines instead of only one L.H.A. ♈ calculation. The star tables may alternatively be tabulated in 'time to go before the Aries

meridian is overhead', so that if this time is added to watch time, the tabulation will be in terms of the passage of the Aries meridian across the chart and this passage can be marked before the observations are begun. Alternatively, the star tables can be combined with the Sun, Moon and planet tables by extending the declinations of the latter up to much higher figures to cover all the useful stars. This makes the tables slower to use but removes the disadvantage of the limited number of stars and also the need to correct according to the passage of the years.

16. Precomputed tables are usually tabulated for whole numbers of degrees of latitude and hour angle. In order to use the latter, an assumed longitude near to the D.R. position is chosen such that, when added to G.H.A. ♈ or G.H.A. (body), the total is a whole number of degrees. Even with these simplifications, the pages may run into hundreds. One result of this simplification is that the assumed position may be 30′ of latitude and 30′ of longitude away from the D.R. position. This introduces errors of the type described on page 364, para 15. Hence, quite apart from the fact that the tables only record altitudes to the nearest 1′, additional errors of 1′ can readily arise. Thus the tables probably have a 95 per cent error of rather more than 1′.

SHORT TABLES

17. The major objection to precomputed tables is bulk and cost. Short tables generally provide the solution of the PZX triangle by splitting it into two right-angled triangles. In order to reduce tabulations, a number of rules and conventions, similar to those mentioned in paras 10 and 11 but peculiar to the individual tables, have to be introduced. These rules may be complex and, in certain instances, ambiguity is not readily resolved. However, the resulting compression can be impressive. Compact examples are Ageton's, Aquino's, Dreisonstok's, Hughes', Myerscough and Hamilton's, Ogura's and Yonemura's, the last named being built round the cosine-haversine formula.

18. Short tables generally work in whole degrees of latitude and L.H.A. (body) and therefore the assumed position may differ considerably from the D.R. position. However, by interpolation, many of the tables may be used to calculate altitude from the D.R. position although, when used in this way, they may not be

much faster than the haversine formula. When used in the quicker way, they will be midway between the cosine-haversine formula and precomputed tables for speed.

19. Most of the short tables are arranged so that azimuths can be calculated, Ageton's being particularly well designed in this respect. Alternatively, a number of special tables tabulated in whole numbers of declination as well as latitude and L.H.A. may be used to calculate azimuth independently. Examples such as ABC tables may generally be found in books of nautical tables or separately in Davis' or Burdwood's tables.

AZIMUTH DIAGRAMS

20. The cosine-haversine formula and certain short tables do not provide azimuths except with difficulty. Azimuths are only required for plotting the intercept and drawing the position line, and even if the azimuth is 1° in error and the assumed position is 60 n. miles from the correct position, the error resulting is most unlikely to be as much as 1' of arc. Hence special simple tables already mentioned in para 19 may be used to find azimuths. Alternatively, azimuth diagrams may provide quick and sufficiently accurate answers.

21. Azimuth diagrams are generally one of two types:

(a) *Distorted charts.* Fig. 197 illustrates Weir's diagram. The chart is symmetrical about the equator and declination is

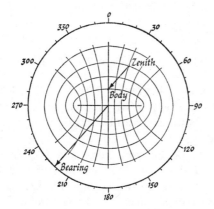

FIG. 197 Sketch of Weir's diagram

plotted on the central meridian. Parallels of latitude are distorted into ellipses and lines of constant L.H.A. into hyperbolae. On such a chart, a line between the plotted position of the body and the plotted position of the craft or its zenith will represent the true direction of the body measured from the craft.

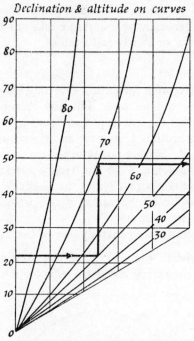

Declination & altitude on curves

FIG. 198   Sketch of Rust's diagram

(b) *Graphs.* Rust's diagram is illustrated Fig. 198. Declination and altitude curves are plotted on a rectangular grid which has hour angles and azimuths as vertical graduations. From the appropriate hour angle, a line is drawn horizontally to the declination curve and then vertically to the altitude curve. From this second point, a line is drawn horizontally to the azimuth scale. The system is simple and elegant but altitude has to be known before azimuth can be found.

COMPUTERS

22. The earliest type of computer was a model of the spherical triangle with microscopes working along meridians and parallels. These have developed into very finely engraved charts using microscopes to provide accuracy, typical examples being the German wartime ARG1 and the Batori astro computer which has an accuracy of the order of 2 minutes of arc. An analogue computer capable of solving the PZX triangle has already been described on page 336, para 18. A digital computer, however, is able not only to calculate positions but also to store information regarding the positions of bodies on the celestial sphere.

23. A digital computer with an accurate timing control is able to calculate, from the D.R. position, the altitude and azimuth of a suitable star and to direct the star tracker in the required direction. The star tracker can then lock on to the star and correct the D.R. position according to the observed altitude. If cloud should cover the star, or the star should sink below the horizon, the computer can programme a search for another star. Such a computer will be used in inertia-astro systems (page 429, para 31).

STAR IDENTIFICATION

24. In the absence of a computer, the navigator may use altitude and azimuth calculations to help him identify a body, particularly when sighting through a telescope with a limited field of view. By such means, it may be possible to observe bright stars by day provided there is sufficient optical magnification and very clear skies.

25. *Planisphere.* A planisphere is a star chart with a transparency that moves across it to represent the craft. By setting the transparency according to the latitude and the L.H.A. of the craft, the position of its zenith on the star map may be established. The star map will then show the relative distribution of the bright stars and, by marking on the transparency a grid of lines of the appropriate pattern, altitude and azimuth may be measured within approximately 5°. Star globes with adjustable declination and hour angle circles may also be used.

30—P.N.

26. *Star Diagram.* The navigator may construct a star diagram to assist in identifying a particular star as shown in Fig. 199. A circle is first drawn with a convenient radius, say 2¼ inches, to represent the horizon with the centre representing the craft or its zenith. Two points are marked each end of a diameter to represent east and west. At right angles to this diameter, a distance is stepped off to represent the latitude. A circle is drawn through this point and the east and west points to represent the celestial equator. The elevated pole is then marked at a distance from the equator equal to the radius of the original circle.

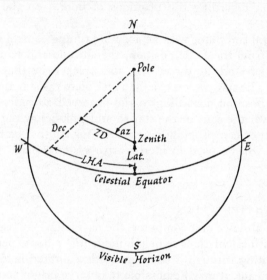

FIG. 199   Star diagram

27. The star can be plotted on the star diagram in terms of azimuth and zenith distance, zenith distance being measured in the same scale as latitude. A line from the pole through the position of the star will cut the celestial equator at a point which, according to the proportion of the arc from the centre point to the east or west point, will represent the L.H.A. of the star. The distance of the star up this line as a proportion of the total distance to the pole will represent the declination of the star. The method is only very approximate and fails with a star of high declination.

4. SPECIAL PROCEDURES

HEADING REFERENCE

1. The difficulties which arise with magnetic compasses and gyro compasses in high latitudes have been emphasized in Chapter V. Astro can, however, provide a general heading reference to realign a directional gyro at regular intervals. Astro heading checks can also be used in lower latitudes to ensure that an error has not developed in a magnetic compass or a gyro compass.

2. The accuracy of an astro heading reference depends mainly on two factors:

(a) The tilt of the sight at right angles to the azimuth of the body. This will cause an azimuth error equal to:

tilt × tan (altitude)   (page 40, para 18)

Thus a tilt of $\frac{1}{4}°$ can cause an azimuth error of $1\frac{1}{4}°$ if the altitude of the body is 80°.

(b) The error in the position of the craft, which leads to an error in the calculation of azimuth. The error can be regarded as a form of sideways tilting error and, indeed, an error of 1° of arc at right angles to the line to the body will cause an error of 1° × tan (altitude). Thus an assumed position 20 n. miles away from the true position can cause an error of nearly 2° if the altitude of the body is 80°.

3. These two factors illustrate the importance of taking an azimuth on a body low in the sky. They also illustrate that, if the tilt of the sight is due to the tilt in the vertical measuring the position of the craft, the azimuth error will cancel out.

4. *Astro-compass*. The astro-compass is a model of the celestial sphere based on an equatorial drum which is tilted according to latitude so that it lies in the plane of the equator as shown in Fig. 200. On the equatorial drum is a sight that can be rotated according to L.H.A. (body) and tilted according to declination (body). If the astro-compass is level and the latitude and longitude of the craft is known with reasonable accuracy, the body will be in line with the sight provided that the compass card on which the equatorial drum has been mounted is correctly oriented. By

rotating the whole astro-compass until the body is in line with the sight, any misalignment of the compass card with the true direction can be measured.

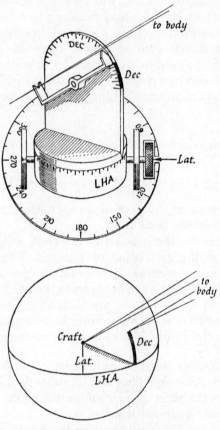

FIG. 200   Astro-compass

5. A simple astro-compass should be accurate on 95 per cent of occasions to 1 or 2 degrees, provided that the body is low on the horizon. A 95 per cent accuracy of $\frac{1}{4}$ degree can be obtained with care from a sight that can be levelled more accurately, such as a periscopic sextant, the normal astro-compass having only a spirit level and manual adjustment. In a marine craft, a bearing plate may be used to check heading, azimuth being calculated by one of

the methods dealt with in the previous chapter. In an aircraft a periscopic sextant or a star tracker stabilized by a bubble system may be used possibly with an azimuth drive so that rate of change of azimuth can be fed into the sight and coincidence with the body maintained over a short period.

6. *Sun Compass.* When the Sun is used to check heading, G.H.A. may be found with sufficient accuracy by adding 12 hours and the equation of time to G.M.T. and converting to degrees at 15° per hour. The declination (Sun) will change by less than $\frac{1}{2}$° a day even around the equinoxes, so that one setting will generally do for the day. So useful is the Sun for checking heading that a Sun compass has been devised for use in polar regions. It consists of an automatic tracker mounted in a fashion similar to an astro-compass but with the L.H.A. drum driven by clockwork so that, once the equation of time or some value of L.H.A. (Sun) has been set in, the sight will follow the Sun provided latitude is not changed too greatly.

7. The Pfund Sun compass is a development which measures the direction of the polarization of the light from the Sun caused by its passage through the atmosphere. By this means, it is possible to measure the direction of the Sun when the sky is overcast or the Sun is just below the horizon. A 95 per cent accuracy of measurement of the order of 1° is possible.

LATITUDE OBSERVATIONS

8. *Meridian Passage.* If altitude is measured when a body is exactly north or south of the craft, the body will be crossing the meridian and the sight is known as a meridian passage (mer. pass.). Latitude can be found from declination (body) and from zenith distance as follows:

(a) Lat. = dec. − Z.D., if body is between pole and craft (see Fig. 201(a)).

(b) Lat. = dec. + Z.D., if body is between equator and craft (see Fig. 201(b)).

(c) Lat. = Z.D. − dec., if body is of opposite name (see Fig. 201(c)).

(d) Lat. = 180° − dec. − Z.D., if body is on the side of the pole opposite to the craft (see Fig. 201(d)).

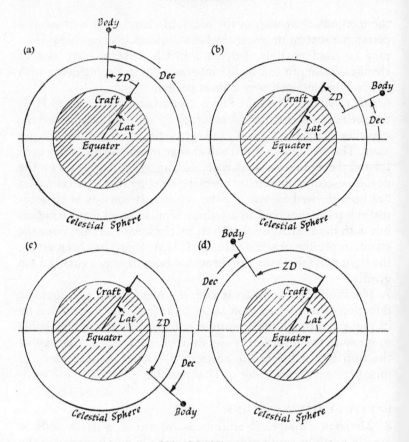

FIG. 201   Meridian passage

9. The time of meridian passage can be calculated by finding when the L.H.A. is zero. Alternatively, it may be possible to take a series of observations and choose the maximum altitude. At this altitude, the sub-point must be at its closest to the craft and therefore the body must be on the meridian provided that there is no northerly or southerly velocity of the craft with respect to the body. For example, at declination 60°, a sub-point is travelling westwards at 450 knots, and if the craft is travelling northwards at 45 knots, a drawing of the relative velocity triangle will show that the nearest approach distance may be several degrees from the

meridian. A similar error can occur when observing the Moon due to change in declination.

10. Although the position found by meridian passage may be recorded as a latitude, it will be a circle centred on the sub-point. The errors described on page 364, para 15, which arise when a craft is to one side of the line from the sub-point to the assumed position, will therefore arise if the body is not exactly on the meridian of the craft.

11. *Noon sight.* It is common marine practice to try to obtain a latitude from the Sun at midday. If the vessel is moving slowly or is travelling along a parallel of latitude, the maximum altitude can be used to find latitude provided the Sun can be continuously observed. The procedure of the noon sight is so general that ex-meridian tables have been developed so that a latitude can be obtained even when the Sun happens to be obscured by cloud at the time of meridian passage.

12. *Ex-meridian Tables.* Ex-meridian tables correct the latitude by a reduction to the zenith distance to account for the body not being on the meridian. The amount of hour angle that the body can be away from the meridian will be roughly twice the square root of the zenith distance so that for a body of altitude 65°, or zenith distance 25°, the maximum L.H.A. will be $\pm 10°$ approximately. The tables may be in two parts, each entered with latitude and declination with different tables according to whether declination is the same or the opposite 'name'.

13. *Pole Star Sight.* If there were a star at the celestial pole, its declination would be 90° and, from para 8(a):

$$\text{Latitude} = 90° - \text{Z.D.}$$
$$= \text{altitude (body)}$$

There is no bright star close to the southern celestial pole but Polaris is about 1° of arc from the north celestial pole in a direction roughly opposite to Alkaid (page 432, para 8), the end star in the handle of the Dipper. Hence, when the handle is below the pole star, latitude will equal altitude $- 1°$ approximately and when the handle of the Dipper is above the pole star, latitude will equal altitude $+ 1°$ approximately.

14. In practice, the correction to be applied to altitude to find latitude from the pole star is tabulated in special pole star tables,

sometimes known as Q correction tables. If the assumed position of the craft is to one side of the actual position, an error will arise as was shown on page 364, para 15. A similar error will arise when Polaris is at the extreme eastern or western end of its travel around the pole. For this reason, pole star tables for high accuracies include a table for a correction according to latitude.

15. The pole star can be used to check the heading of the craft provided an allowance is made for the rotation of the star about the celestial pole. This allowance can be estimated from the position of Alkaid, the end star in the handle of the Dipper. When Alkaid is due east or west of Polaris, the correction is about 1°. sec (latitude) and is correspondingly less in-between.

16. The errors that arise in a pole star observation due to errors in timing are very small. Since the pole star travels round the pole on a circle of about 1° radius, the Q correction cannot change by more than 1′ in any 4 minutes of time and the direction, even at a latitude as high as 60° N., by only about $\frac{1}{4}$° in 40 minutes. Indeed, it is a feature of all latitude methods that the observations are relatively insensitive to errors in time of observation.

LONGITUDE METHOD

17. If latitude is known, an altitude taken on a body roughly east or west can be used to find longitude. The value may be calculated exactly from latitude, declination and altitude, using for example the cosine-haversine formula or 'short' tables such as Martellis. However, although measurement of latitude is not sensitive to time, measurement of longitude depends absolutely on time. An error of 4 seconds of time means an error of 1′ of longitude. Also, if the body is less than 30° in azimuth or greater than 150°, the cut will be poor compared to latitude and the timing errors will be more than doubled. It is perhaps interesting to note that the first astro position line was found from a series of longitude calculations for various latitudes, the line through the points being known as a Sumner line after its originator.

POLAR NAVIGATION

18. The importance of astro-heading measurements in polar navigation has already been stressed. When navigating close to the pole, the navigator uses a polar stereographic chart with grid

steering, directions being measured clockwise through 360° from the Greenwich meridian. At the pole, the direction of a body measured clockwise through 360° will be the G.H.A. and therefore G.H.A. can be used close to the pole as a measure of grid direction.

19. At the pole, the altitude of a body will equal its declination. Hence it will be convenient to use the pole as the assumed position. Since the position of the craft may be many hundreds of miles from the pole, the position lines will have to be plotted as curves. Fortunately, on a polar stereographic chart, range circles will appear as arcs of circles. The position lines can therefore be plotted using the pole as the assumed position but plotting by means of a template with arcs drawn on it according to the altitude of the body.

20. In polar regions, it is often necessary to use bodies low on the horizon, particularly the Sun and the Moon. With a low body, the refraction changes rapidly with altitude. If the navigator is using precomputed tables which include a correction for refraction that applies to the assumed position, this refraction may be incorrect for the actual position if the altitude is very different.

PRECOMPUTED OBSERVATIONS

21. If a route is planned to a time schedule, it will be possible to prepare beforehand the altitudes and azimuths of certain stars for points along the route according to the times and positions. These can be graphed so that an observation can be taken at any time and the difference between the observed altitude and the graphed altitude will show how far the craft is from the position that it should have reached and in what direction the error must be. This system has been used most successfully in pioneer air operations.

22. For marine work the Mjchell Astro-plot takes account of the triangle of velocities formed by the motion of the body on the celestial sphere and the motion of the craft over the surface of the Earth. This makes it possible to plot directly in time after having made an initial calculation of L.H.A. ♈. Plotting is subsequently nothing more than a matter of noting subsequent time intervals and entering the same column of the tables provided

that the tables are of the precomputed type with stars tabulated in L.H.A. ♈. A number of position lines can thus be found from various stars extremely quickly and, to make plotting even faster, a form of template is used for setting in the various parameters.

RISING AND SETTING

23. The times of sunrise and sunset are of interest to the navigator as they may determine when he should take his observations on the stars. It is also possible to obtain an approximate longitude by noting the time of rising or setting of the Sun or the Moon. Furthermore, he can check the heading of his craft by the azimuth of the Sun or Moon as it rises or sets.

24. *Amplitudes.* At the equinoxes, when the Sun's declination will be 0°, the Sun will rise due east 6 hours before midday and set 6 hours after midday in the west. At other times of the year, the timing will differ from 6 hours according to declination and latitude, and is tabulated in time amplitude tables. Also the direction will vary from due east and due west and is similarly tabulated in bearing amplitude tables. These tables can also be used with the Moon.

25. Owing to refraction and semi-diameter, the Sun or the Moon appear to be on the horizon when about 1° below. The necessary correction is generally given in tables. However, the height of the observer will also affect the amplitudes and from an aircraft will cause an unacceptable error at high latitudes and declinations.

26. *Rise and Set Tables.* To reduce complications of this nature, rise and set tables are provided in almanacs with times in G.M.T. as if the craft were on the Greenwich meridian. To the G.M.T. must be applied the following corrections:

(a) For longitude of craft, 4 minutes must be added for every 1° west and subtracted for every 1° east.
(b) Height must be corrected by a special table.
(c) In the instance of the Moon, a special additional correction for longitudes other than Greenwich must be added.

27. In addition, almanacs may tabulate twilight. The times are little affected by height because, although at height the angle of

the Sun below the horizon is less, there is also less reflection off the sky above. Twilight is of three standards:

(a) *Civil twilight*: Sun 6° below the horizon. Barely enough light to read.
(b) *Nautical twilight*: Sun 12° below the horizon. Lights are needed and the horizon is no longer generally visible.
(c) *Astronomical twilight*. Sun 18° below the horizon. Pitch dark unless there is a Moon.

SPECIAL SYSTEMS

28. Position can be found by comparison of star azimuths, one star being used to ensure alignment and the other two to measure the two azimuths precisely. The system has the advantage that there will be no errors due to atmospheric refraction. However, the 'protractor' against which the azimuths are measured must be absolutely level. If the vertical controlling this 'protractor' is in error by 5' of arc, then position will be in error by 5' of arc. This will apply however the angles to the stars are measured, because astro observations depend on the measurement of the vertical for their identification of position on the Earth.

29. The only exception to this rule applies to satellites. If the alignment of a satellite can be compared with the stars around it, position can be found according to the amount by which it is displaced from its location among the stars when viewed from its sub-point. This is, of course, the reverse of the method used to correct the Moon for parallax. The Moon itself is so far away that 1' of parallactic shift will represent more than 1° or 60 n. miles of distance even when the Moon is overhead, and when the Moon is low, 1' may represent 600 n. miles. However, if a satellite were placed, say, 10,000 n. miles from the surface of the Earth, at which height it would orbit once every 5 or 6 hours, it would be possible to find position by parallax to within a mile or so. Unfortunately, the calculations would be extremely laborious.

30. Calculations would be simpler if a satellite could be at 19,300 n. miles above the equator since it would then in theory be stationary. Owing to the increased height, the error in position would be twice as great. However, in practice, the sub-point would drift and oscillate (page 605, para 9(b)).

5. SUMMARY

SEXTANT

General. Errors are due to:

(a) Sideways tilt, particularly on high altitudes.
(b) Refraction of line of sight to body at low altitude.
(c) Index error (correctable).
(d) Semi-diameter (tabulated in almanacs).
(e) Parallax of Moon (tabulated in almanacs).

Limitations.
(a) Sky visible on less than 50 per cent of occasions on the Earth's surface in certain areas.
(b) Only one body may be visible by day except at heights of over 40,000 feet.

Marine Sextant. Major limitation is that the horizon and stars may be visible only during twilight. Errors arise owing to refraction of line of sight to horizon, which cannot be measured precisely even with a dip-meter, and to errors in height of observer. Accuracy 95 per cent less than 2′ and less than 1′ only in skilled hands.

Bubble Sextant. Suffers seriously from acceleration errors including coriolis and curvature of course. 95 per cent error probably 5 per cent of the speed in knots. Sight-taking in astro-dome or by periscopic sextant is inconvenient and tiring if pressure suits are worn.

Radio Sextant. Probably limited to Sun.

STAR IDENTIFICATION

The 24 navigational stars are identified by:

(a) Position in sky compared to constellations. Only possible if wide view of sky is available.
(b) Position in sky according to altitude and azimuth calculated from assumed position or plotted on planisphere on star diagram.
(c) Magnitude and colour.

Planets are identified by extreme brightness or by position in the sky where no bright star is known to be.

CELESTIAL SPHERE

Position on the celestial sphere is defined by:

(a) Declination north or south.
(b) Hour angle, generally sidereal hour angle.

The celestial sphere has poles and equator that correspond to the Earth's poles and equator. The standard meridian is the first point of Aries.

Stars move very slowly over the celestial sphere chiefly due to the precession of the Earth's axis of rotation.

The Sun and planets move round the celestial sphere, the Sun following the ecliptic and the planets generally not more than 5° from it.

The Moon moves round the celestial sphere once a month following the ecliptic within 5°.

ALMANACS

(a) Stars are tabulated in S.H.A. (star) and declination (star) at intervals of days.
(b) Sun, Moon and planets are tabulated in G.H.A. (body) and declination (body) at hourly intervals or more frequently, with interpolation table for minutes of time. The Moon has special interpolation tables.
(c) Aries and pole star correction tables are tabulated in G.H.A. ♈.
(d) Parallax of Moon is tabulated according to altitude.
(e) Sunrise and sunset may be tabulated in G.M.T. with a correction table.

SIGHT REDUCTION

Star curves. Weems Star curves and the astrograph are extremely fast, but only three stars are generally available, life is limited to few years, and accuracy to several minutes of arc.

Marcq St. Hilaire. Intercept calculated by:

(a) Cosine-haversine formula with tables or diagrams for azimuth. Works from a D.R. position.
(b) Short tables. These are very compact, but operate with many conventions. Shorter generally than cosine-haversine formula but usually work from assumed position.

(c) Precomputed altitude-azimuth tables. Very fast. Star tables have limited life and generally cover about 7 stars. Extremely bulky. Work from assumed position.

(d) Precomputed graphs. Extensions of above methods speed up sight reduction under specific circumstances.

Latitude Methods:

(a) Meridian passage.
(b) Ex-meridian sight.
(c) Pole star correction tables.

Polar Astro. Pole used as assumed position and position lines plotted by means of template. This gives:

(a) Declination = altitude.
(b) G.H.A. = Greenwich grid azimuth.

HEADING CHECKS

Heading checks may be by:

(a) Astro-compass.
(b) Sun compass by day.
(c) Bearing plate using computed azimuths.
(d) Star tracker using bubble level.

SPECIAL SYSTEMS:

(a) Inertia-astro gives fixing and heading to 1′ (95 per cent).
(b) Parallax on artificial satellites is not practicable.

BIBLIOGRAPHY: BASIC AIDS

The techniques of position finding and of visual or astro-navigation are invariably described in general books which are listed on page 613 according to the various types of craft. In addition, there are certain books and papers written on specialized aspects of position finding and astro-navigation.

POSITION FINDING AND GENERAL OR VISUAL AIDS

Ashby, W. R., *Introduction to cybernetics*, Reinhold Publishing, New York.

Bell, D. A., *Information theory*, Pitman, London.

Brillouin, L., *Science and information theory*, Columbia University, U.S.A.

Guilband, C. M. T., *What is cybernetics?* Blackwell, Oxford, England.

Heavens, O. S., *Optical masers*, Methuens, London.

Jessell, A. H., see Trow, G. H., and A. H. Jessell.

Oudet, L., The characteristic phases of marine lights, *J. Inst. Navig.*, **14**, 466.

Parker, J. B., Determining the most probable position, *J. Inst. Navig.*, **6**, 44.

Parker, J. B., The treatment of simultaneous position data in the air, *J. Inst. Navig.*, **5**, 235.

Reza, F. M., *Introduction to information theory*, McGraw-Hill, New York.

Schawlow, A. L., *Optical masers*, Freeman, London.

Trow, G. H., and A. H. Jessell, The presentation of fixing accuracy of navigation systems, *J. Inst. Navig.*, **1**, 313.

Wiener, N., *Cybernetics*, Wiley, New York.

Woodward, P. M., *Probability and information theory with applications to radar*, Pergamon Press, London.

ASTRONOMICAL NAVIGATION

Blewitt, M., *Celestial navigation for yachtsmen*, Iliffe, London.

Burton, S. M., *The art of astronomical navigation*, Brown, Son & Ferguson, Glasgow.

Chichester, F., *Observer's Book on Astro-Navigation*, Allen & Unwin, London.

Clegg, J. A., see Lovell, B., and J. A. Clegg.

Dutton, B., *Navigation and nautical astronomy*, U.S. Naval Institute, Annapolis.

Eaton, E. P., Star trackers, *Navigation (U.S.A.)* **6**, 24.

Fell, J. I., *Star recognition*, Pitman, London.

Fletcher, A. Astronomical refraction at low altitudes in marine navigation, *J. Inst. Navig.*, **5**, 307.

Freiesleben, H. C., Investigations into the dip of the horizon, *J. Inst. Navig.*, **3**, 270.

Graham Smith, F., *Radio astronomy*, Penguin Books, London.

Kooman, M. J., see Tousey, R., and M. J. Kooman.

Lovell, B., and J. A. Clegg, *Radio astronomy*, Chapman & Hall, London.

Marner, Gene R., Automatic radio-celestial navigation, *J. Inst. Navig.*, **12**, 249.

Michell, R. B., Navigation at sea with a star lattice, *J. Inst. Navig.*, **6**, 63.

Millman, P. R., The visibility of stars during twilight, *J. Inst. Navig.*, **10**, 11.

Sadler, D. H., Altitude corrections for coriolis and other accelerations, *J. Inst. Navig.*, **1**, 22.

Sadler, D. H., Astronomy and navigation, *Occ. Notes. R. astro. Soc.*, No. 13, 1949.

Sadler, D. H., An improved astrograph, *J. Inst. Navig.*, **6**, 373.

Sadler, D. H., Continuous plotting of astronomical position lines, *J. Inst. Navig.*, **7**, 111.

Sadler, D. H., A modern view of astronomical navigation, *J. Inst. Navig.*, **12**, 54.

Sadler, D. H., The place of navigation in astronomy (Presidential Address), *J. Inst. Navig.*, **9**, 1.

Sadler, D. H., The precision of the Air Almanac and A.P. 3270, *J. Inst. Navig.*, **7**, 49.

Sadler, D. H., The provision for astronomical navigation at sea, *J. Inst. Navig.*, **1**, 290.

Sadler, D. H., Tables for astronomical polar navigation, *J. Inst. Navig.* **2**, 9.

Sadler, D. H., and others, The accuracy of astronomical navigation at sea (working party report), *J. Inst. Navig.*, **10**, 223.

Shufeldt, H. H., Precision celestial navigation experiments, *J. Inst. Navig.*, **15**, 301.

Tousey, R., and M. J. Kooman, The visibility of stars and planets during twilight, *J. Optical Soc. of America*, 1946.

Vandervord, R. K., *ABC of practical astro navigation*, Pitman, London.

PART FIVE

ELECTRONIC AIDS

CHAPTER XIII. RADIO AND RADIO BEARINGS. The first two parts of the chapter summarize the principles of radio in general and in particular the propagation characteristics of the various radio frequencies, the different types of aerial and their polar diagrams, and the elements of transmitters, receivers and cathode ray tubes. Direction finding then follows and is dealt with sufficiently completely for errors, such as quadrantal errors and night effect, to be explained. The various ground D.F. systems are then described, followed by shipborne D.F. and automatic D.F. The plotting of radio bearings has already been covered in section 2 of Chapter X. Finally, descriptions are given of radio guides which can be coupled into the control system of a craft, typical examples being VOR and ILS. The problems of coupling have already been dealt with in section 2 of Chapter X.

CHAPTER XIV. RADIO DISTANCE MEASUREMENT. The first two sections are concerned with distance measurement by pulse systems and by continuous waves. Pulse systems make possible the use of transponders. CW systems can be applied to long-range navigation and are used for radio altimeters. However, the large section subsequently devoted to difference of distance or hyperbolic systems emphasizes how widely these are used as en-route aids. Since these systems were not described in Chapter X, the ways in which position lines may be plotted are explained and also the coverage diagrams of the various arrangements of stations. Pulsed hyperbolic systems are then dealt with in broad outline, with Loran as the main example, followed by CW hyperbolic systems with Decca explained in some detail. Finally, Consol illustrates collapsed hyperbolic systems.

CHAPTER XV. RADAR AND SONAR. The basic principles of radar are first described including scanners and the various cathode ray tube presentations. The picture shown on the radar screen is examined in terms of the appearance of different objects, of the clarity of definition, and of the reduction of unwanted clutter. The next section deals with marine radar and emphasizes the importance of stabilized displays

31—P.N.

and the difficulty of accurate measurement of target velocity. The use of bearings and distances as a means of avoiding collision has already been tackled in section 2 of Chapter IV. The section on marine radar is followed by a section on aircraft radar, which is seen to comprise mainly ground equipments, airborne equipments being confined to weather radar and to military aids. The use of radar to guide missiles is included in this section. Next is a brief section on doppler radar, the principles having already been covered in section 2 of Chapter V. The applications of doppler to transit satellites, to airborne doppler, to moving target indicators and to doppler VOR are briefly explained. Finally, there is a section on sonar which is seen to have close resemblances to radar. It is used particularly for depth measurement and underwater detection.

CONTENTS

CHAPTER XIII

Radio and Radio Bearings

1. PROPAGATION

SPECTRUM

1. The radio spectrum is generally split into the following frequency bands:

	Frequency	Wavelength
(a) VLF (very low frequency)	10–30 kc/s	30–10 km
(b) LF (low frequency)	30–300 kc/s	10–1 km
(c) MF (medium frequency)	300–3000 kc/s	1 km–100 m
(d) HF (high frequency)	3–30 Mc/s	100–10 m
(e) VHF (very high frequency)	30–300 Mc/s	10–1m
(f) UHF (ultra high frequency)	300–3000 Mc/s	1 m–10cm
(g) Centimetric wave band	3–30 kMc/s	10–1 cm
(h) Millimetric wave band	30–300 kMc/s	10–1 mm

2. The UHF band is sometimes known as the decimetric or the *L* band. The centimetric and millimetric bands are also known as SHF (super high frequency) and commonly divided into:

(a) *S* Band, around 10 cm.

(b) *X* Band, around 3 cm.

(c) *K* Band, around 1 cm.

The decimetric, centimetric and millimetric bands are also known as microwaves.

3. The propagation of radio waves is modified by the Earth and its atmosphere in four main ways:

(a) *Atmospheric attenuation.*

(b) *Atmospheric refraction.*

(c) *Ionospheric reflection.*

(d) *Ground effects.*

ATMOSPHERIC ATTENUATION

4. From VLF to VHF frequencies, very little signal strength is absorbed by the atmosphere. At the shorter UHF wavelengths some absorption appears and the effect is accelerated through the centimetric band to the millimetric band. The centimetric absorption is due to water vapour and there is a temporary peak effect at $1\frac{1}{4}$ cm. In the millimetric band, oxygen absorption also appears with an early peak at 5 mm. Therefore, wavelengths less than 3 cm are seldom transmitted and wavelengths less than 1 cm, apart from a favourable band between 8 and 9 mm, are hardly used at all.

5. The pattern of interference by rain is similar to that of water vapour. Not until the centimetric band is approached will the size of a water droplet be significant compared to the wavelength. At 10 cm, the very large drops in a tropical downpour will begin to take effect. By 3 cm, the effect will be greatly magnified and extended to smaller raindrops such as are found in moderate rain. At 1 cm, even fine drizzle will weaken signals and heavy rain will blot out transmissions. Hail has less effect except in the millimetric band, and snow has less effect than hail.

ATMOSPHERIC REFRACTION

6. When a radio wave is transmitted from the ground at an angle, it passes through layers of air of decreasing density, temperature and humidity. As a result of the slightly increased speed, radio waves will be refracted or bent downward towards the Earth's surface. The radio engineer may use a special graphical representation, as in Fig. 202, known as 'curved Earth paper' which shows the way in which waves would be propagated if the atmosphere were to follow a normal pattern. As a result of this refraction, the distance at which a direct radio signal can be received from a ground station does not vary with the square root of the height by the same ratio as a visual line of sight. The radio relationship is closer to:

$$\text{distance n. miles} = 1 \cdot 22\sqrt{\text{height (feet)}}$$

7. In warm air mass conditions, the lower lapse rate and greater change of humidity with height tends to increase refraction and leads to super-refraction. In the limit, a strong inversion, such as

can occur low over a calm sea, may form a radio duct along which waves may be funnelled. In such circumstances, signal strength will no longer be according to the area of an expanding sphere but according to the area of an expanding strip of air, that is, proportional to the distance rather than to the square of the distance. Exceptional distances can be covered by this 'anomalous propagation'. However, as the duct height is generally considerably lower than 100 feet and the wavelength has to be a very small fraction of the duct height, the effect is seldom dramatic except at UHF and shorter wavelengths.

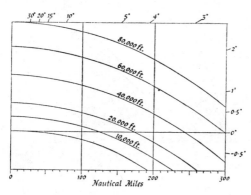

FIG. 202   'Curved Earth' paper

IONOSPHERIC REFLECTION

8. On page 71, para 27, the ionosphere was described as a series of belts of electrons. These are caused mainly by ultra-violet light from the Sun acting on the gases in the atmosphere. During the night, the electrons tend to recombine with the gases and, since the gases closer to the Earth are denser, the lower layers of electrons tend to weaken or disappear. The ionosphere becomes higher and since only the belts of denser electrons persist, more radio waves are reflected and fewer are diffused.

9. The ionospheric belts of interest to the navigator are:

(a) D *layer*. A rather tenuous belt a few tens of miles high which only appears by day.

(b) E *layer*. Sometimes known as the Kennelly–Heaviside layer. A fairly stable layer generally not much more than 50 n. miles high and rather lower by day than by night.

(c) F *layer*. Sometimes known as the Appleton layer. It appears at night at around 150 or 200 n. miles up. By day it splits into:

    (i) F₁ *layer*. Generally between 100 and 150 n. miles up.
    (ii) F₂ *layer*. Generally approaching 200 n. miles up.

10. When a radio signal strikes an ionospheric belt at an angle, it will be deflected as shown in Fig. 203. However, as the angle

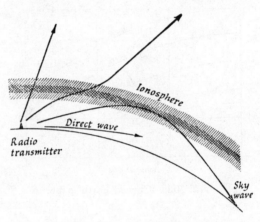

FIG. 203 Formation of sky waves

becomes finer, the radio signal will be returned to the surface of the Earth and may be known as a 'sky wave'. The reflection depends on the frequency of the waves and on the density of the electrons in the layer as well as on the angle at which the radio waves strike the ionosphere. The higher the frequency, the finer the angle at which the radio waves must strike before reflection occurs. The higher the electron density, the coarser the angle.

11. In practice, the electron density of the ionosphere is insufficient to reflect waves of a length shorter than VHF and will only reflect HF or longer waves regularly. The reflection increases until, at LF or VLF, the ionosphere acts as a barrier so

that the radio signals are channelled between it and the Earth below.

12. MF and HF waves, being the borderline of waves affected by the ionosphere, are affected according to whether it is day or night. The lower tenuous layers by day tend to absorb MF waves, and sky waves are much stronger at night when the ionosphere is higher but less diffuse. Similiar effects apply to HF waves except that these normally penetrate the lower layers of the day ionosphere. At night, they will penetrate the upper ionosphere unless they strike it at a sufficiently fine angle.

13. A signal that arrives at a point after being reflected from the ionosphere will have travelled further than if it had been radiated directly. The extra distance will be significant in distance measuring systems. Also, waves that strike at the limiting angle for reflection, tend to be reflected at angles. These first reflections which strike the ground closest to the transmitter, can appear to come from a direction differing from the direction of the transmitter.

14. Sky waves may be re-reflected off the ground and thence back to the ionosphere and to the ground again. Waves that have travelled in this way are known as second hop sky waves to distinguish them from first hop sky waves that have only been reflected once. Second hop sky waves will naturally travel even further than first hop sky waves.

GROUND EFFECTS

15. As a radio wave travels over the Earth, some of the energy penetrates the surface. The penetration depends on the wavelength. VLF waves penetrate many yards, MF waves penetrate several feet and very short waves several inches. In the process of penetration, speed is slightly reduced. A radio wave may travel 0·015 per cent slower through water and nearly 0·2 per cent slower through dry Earth. This reduction of speed retards the lower edges of the wave front and deflects it downwards to follow the curvature of the Earth. The result is a 'ground wave' which is strong at VLF and LF frequencies where the penetration is deep but is weak at HF frequencies and almost non-existent at VHF frequencies.

16. The difference in speed of radio waves in water as compared to earth can change the direction of a wave by several degrees as it crosses a coast line, the change in direction naturally being towards the land. This is known as 'coastal refraction'. A similar but weaker 'mountain effect' can occur in mountainous regions.

17. VLF, LF and MF waves travel round obstacles freely. Short waves, however, tend to be obstructed so that 'shadows' are thrown. Short waves are readily reflected and, in particular, may be reflected from the ground. As the original wave and the reflected waves travel along together they will interact. If the difference in the path lengths is a multiple of the wavelength, the waves will add to each other. If the difference is half a wavelength, they will cancel each other out. As a result, a propagation pattern can occur as shown in Fig. 204, but naturally with a much greater number of interference patterns. The areas of optimum propagation are known as 'lobes'.

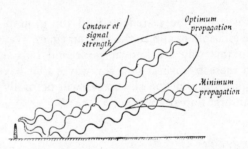

FIG. 204   Interference from reflections

PROPAGATION CHARACTERISTICS

18. Fig. 205 summarizes the characteristics of the various wave bands under four headings:

(a) *VLF and LF*. The ground wave is assisted by the funnelling of the signals between the ionosphere and the Earth and consequently the transmissions can cover long ranges. VLF waves penetrate sea water for short distances and also pack-ice so that reception by submerged submarines is possible.

(b) *MF.* By day the ground wave predominates, but at night the sky waves become stronger after several hundred miles. In the intervening distance, ground waves and sky waves may interfere, and at dawn or dusk, when the ionosphere is changing, reception at a few hundred miles may be particularly unreliable. This distance is known as the critical distance.

(c) *HF.* The ground waves will die away rapidly and there will be an interval called the skip distance or dead space before the first sky waves strike the ground. The higher the frequency, the finer the angle for reflection and the longer the skip distance. Bearings are unreliable on the edges of the skip distance.

(d) *VHF and shorter waves.* The ground wave may be only $1\frac{1}{2}$ times the normal range at VHF frequencies, shortening to about $1\frac{1}{4}$ times the visual range at centimetric wavelengths. Ionospheric reflections are unreliable at VHF frequencies and sky waves do not appear at shorter wavelengths. As wavelengths are shortened below 3 cm, rain absorption and then absorption by atmospheric gases reduces the range so that at millimetric wavelengths only short distances can be covered.

NOISE

19. Although long waves are not affected by rain, they are seriously affected by static electricity caused by storms. Rain can cause precipitation static, and a rainfall map of the world will indicate areas likely to be troubled by this interference. In particular, the background of noise can be a serious nuisance in the tropics by day and can blot out signals at night. In addition, aircraft reception can be seriously interfered with by snow static. This noise is known generally as atmospherics.

20. The strength of atmospheric noise decreases with frequency, being less than the noise generated within the equipment at VHF. Even at HF the problem is seldom serious except in the tropics, but interference increases greatly at MF and still further within the LF wave band.

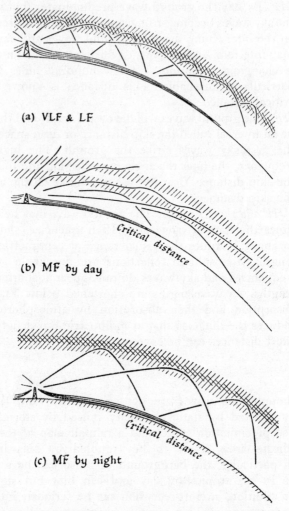

(a) VLF & LF

Critical distance

(b) MF by day

Critical distance

(c) MF by night

FIG. 205 (i) Propagation of radio waves

POLARIZATION

21. A vertical wire aerial produces waves that vibrate vertically and are said to be vertically polarized. A horizontal wire aerial will produce horizontally polarized waves. The polarization is subsequently changed by reflection so that sky waves will be

polarized differently from ground waves. Hence, on arrival at the receiver, the polarization of a transmission may be confused. 22. If a radio wave be transmitted by means of a helical coil of wire, the polarization will be circular. Circular polarization may also be achieved within the transmitting equipment and will normally lead to circular polarization of the reflections. However, the reflections from circular rain drops reverse the polarization so that the waves will be detected much less readily by the same aerial and this characteristic is used in certain radar equipments to reduce reflections from rain.

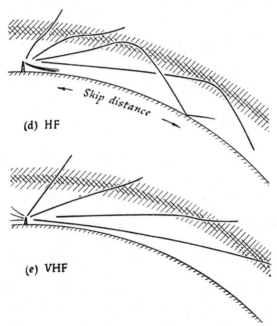

FIG. 205 (ii) Propagation of radio waves

2. RADIO EQUIPMENT

AERIALS

1. It will be convenient first to consider transmitting aerials. These may consist of a simple rod fed at the centre by the transmitter. Such an aerial is known as a dipole. If the length of

the aerial is half the wavelength, it is known as a half wave dipole.

2. Fig. 206 (a) shows the way in which the radio energy radiated from a half wave vertical dipole is projected in plan. A diagram of this nature is known as a polar diagram. Fig. 206(b) shows a polar diagram for a vertical half wave dipole in elevation. There is naturally an element of directivity in this plane.

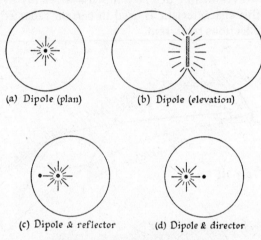

(a) Dipole (plan)   (b) Dipole (elevation)

(c) Dipole & reflector   (d) Dipole & director

FIG. 206   Polar diagrams of dipoles

3. If another suitably designed dipole not connected to the radio transmitter be placed alongside the transmitting dipole at a distance of between one-eighth and one-quarter of a wavelength, it will act either as a reflector or as a director according to its characteristics and will modify the transmission of the vertical dipole in plan as shown in Fig. 206 (c) and (d). Such an aerial is the familiar H aerial used for television reception. If the aerial has a reflector and a director or a reflector and a series of directors, the transmissions may be 'beamed' as is shown in Fig. 207,

FIG. 207   Polar diagram, parasitic array

although spurious directional characteristics known as side lobes appear which complicate the original simple polar diagram. Such an aerial may be known as a Yagi. Aerials with reflectors or directors are known generally as end fire or parasitic arrays.

4. An alternative type of aerial has all the dipoles in the array connected to the radio transmitter. As a result, interference patterns will be developed for the same reason that interference patterns are caused by reflection (see page 474, Fig. 204). If a large number of dipoles are used, the radio energy will be channelled into two narrow beams producing a polar diagram as shown in Fig. 208. An array of aerials of this type is known as a

FIG. 208   Polar diagram, driven array

broadside or driven array. If a reflecting screen is placed behind the array, the radio waves will be mostly directed in one direction but a weak 'back beam' will often appear in the opposite direction.

5. The transmitting power may be led to aerials along wires at VLF, LF and HF frequencies, normally two wires being used. The energy lost by transmission lines increases with frequency and, in the VHF band, it becomes excessive. A coaxial feeder line is therefore used in which the energy is guided along the space between a central wire and a sheath outside the wire, the space between being filled with insulation. With this arrangement, the energy cannot be dissipated but the resistance of the wires and of the insulating material becomes too great at centimetric wavelengths.

6. At centimetric wavelengths, the wave guide is used which consists of a hollow tube made of metal down which the radio signal travels. The way that a radio signal travels down a radio duct is comparable to anomalous propagation (page 470, para 7). In order to transmit the power, a simple horn could be used as an aerial but, generally, this horn is arranged to project the centimetric waves on to a parabolic reflector which produces a parallel beam.

7. The beam width of a radio transmission is defined as the distance from the centre line at which the signal strength drops to half the signal strength at the centre line. At centimetric waves:

beam width° = 2 × (wavelength (cm))/(reflector diameter (ft))

Example. A 4 ft reflector is used with 3 cm waves

$$\text{beam width} = (2 \times 3/4)° = 1\tfrac{1}{2}°$$

At longer wavelengths this rule of thumb is less accurate and the beam width will be wider than the formula suggests.

8. The size of a transmitting aerial depends on the wavelength. If the half wave dipole is used as an example, it would have to be tens of feet long at HF and hundreds of feet long at MF. Indeed, at MF and LF frequencies, aerials of another type will be used. However, it follows that, as a general rule, VLF transmitting aerials are too large to be fitted to craft, MF transmitting aerials can only be fitted to large craft such as ships, and HF transmitters are generally the maximum for normal craft. Small craft use VHF transmitters.

9. If the radio transmission has to be in the form of a narrow beam, para 7 shows that the aerial will have to be large. As a result, narrow beams transmitted from ground stations generally use VHF or higher frequencies. Narrow beams transmitted by craft will be on centimetric waves.

10. Unlike transmitting aerials, receiving aerials may pose no serious problems of size. The more efficient a receiving aerial, the greater the amount of atmospheric noise it will receive as well as the wanted signal. Hence a relatively inefficient aerial will satisfy the crucial signal to noise requirement, though a directional aerial will generally improve the signal-to-noise ratio.

11. Excrescences are undesirable in high-speed craft. Aerials may therefore be designed as part of the structure and may be built into the hull often as slots in the skin. A broadside array may be provided by a line of slots. Alternatively, parts of the craft may be made to radiate. If a parabolic reflector has to be fitted, it may be mounted in a perspex fairing known as a radome. The same aerial will generally be used for transmission as for reception, a special quick acting transmit–receive switch (T.R.

switch) or an electronic cut-out being used to protect the receiver from the transmissions.

TRANSMITTER

12. A transmitter (Tx) has two basic elements:

    (a) Oscillator which produces the raw radio waves.

    (b) Modulator which applies signals to the radio waves.

13. *Oscillator.* The earliest oscillators were copies of nature's oscillators, flashes of lightning. The invention of the thermionic valve, which could produce radio oscillations and amplify them, made possible the development of transmitters on medium and long waves. However, at the shorter wavelengths, the stability of the oscillations produced by such a complex device was hardly sufficient and this led to the introduction of the crystal oscillator. Also the size of the thermionic valve became too large in comparison with the wavelength, and any attempt to miniaturize failed owing to the impossibility of leading the heat generated by the transmission away from a miniature thermionic valve.

14. Although it is more difficult to produce high powers at short wavelengths, the need for high powers is also less, due mainly to the reduced noise. In addition, at HF frequencies, waves will travel long distances at low powers by being reflected off the ionosphere.

15. At UHF, centimetric and millimetric wavelengths, cavity resonators have been developed which can produce high powers and yet can be readily cooled. A typical example is the magnetron which consists of a copper block with specially machined cavities in which electrons revolve at high rates constrained by a very powerful magnetic field. The spinning electrons form radio waves that can be fed into a wave guide and the copper block can be cooled by a high-speed fan.

MODULATOR

16. As explained on page 395, para 13, waves may be amplitude modulated, frequency modulated or pulse modulated. In the latter event, the signals that control the transmission of pulses are produced in a pulse generator and the rate at which the pulses are produced is known as the pulse recurrence or repetition

frequency (P.R.F.) or pulse repetition rate (P.R.R.). Amplitude and frequency modulated transmitters are known as CW (continuous wave) transmitters in contradistinction to pulse transmitters.

RECEIVER

17. Both amplitude modulated and pulse systems transmit information by varying the strength of the signal. In the receiver (Rx) the radio oscillations may be rectified or detected so that the strength of the signal appears as a voltage. The amplitude modulation will then appear as a varying voltage or the pulse modulation as a stepped voltage.

18. Frequency modulations are measured in several ways. Typical methods include:

(a) The frequency received is compared with a frequency generated within the receiver and the difference is made to operate a drive to the tuning control so that the receiver frequency is set to the incoming frequency. The tuning control can then be graduated in terms of frequency. A phantastron, which is a device that can be arranged so that the frequency generated is proportional to an input voltage, may be used to generate the frequency.

(b) The signal may be fed to a number of filters each of which will only allow a certain frequency to pass through. The outputs from these filters can be arranged to indicate the frequency of the incoming signal. The system only gives limited accuracy.

(c) A counting circuit may give an output corresponding to the number of waves arriving. The system is accurate but will tend to break down if there is a temporary loss of signal.

19. In order to do useful work when detected, radio waves have to be amplified. This amplification is generally one of three types:

(a) RF (radio frequency). Amplification of the original radio waves. The whole amplifier has to be tuned.

(b) IF (intermediate frequency). An oscillator is tuned which generates a frequency close to that which is being received and the two are mixed to produce a beat frequency or heterodyne which is of a constant lower frequency and easily amplified. Unfortunately, the oscillator tends to introduce additional noise. A receiver using an IF stage or stages is known as a super-heterodyne (super-het).

(c) LF (low frequency). After the signal has been detected, it may have to be amplified to produce a power output. Power amplifiers are known as audio amplifiers if the final output is aural or as video amplifiers if the final output is visual.

20. *Displays.* The final output of a radio receiver may be made to control an automatic equipment or, more generally, will be presented to the navigator in one of three forms:

(a) Aurally by head-phones or loudspeaker.
(b) By instruments such as dials or meters.
(c) On a cathode ray tube.

21. *Cathode Ray Tube* (*C.R.T.*). A cathode ray tube consists of an electron gun operated by a very high voltage and firing a stream of electrons on to a fluorescent glass screen as shown in Fig. 209 (a) so that a spot of light appears on the fluorescent backing. The fluorescence may be given a degree of persistence if it is desirable that the mark made by the spot of light shall not die away too quickly. The stream of electrons on its way to the screen passes through a tube known as a grid. When a negative voltage is applied to the grid, the electrons, being also negative, are repelled and the strength of the stream reduced as shown in Fig. 209(b). Thus the brightness of the spot can be varied or the spot may be blacked out.

22. The electron stream also passes between two pairs of deflector plates at right angles known as the X and Y plates. Fig. 209(c) shows the vertical Y plates. If a positive voltage is applied to one plate and a negative voltage to the other, the stream will be attracted to one plate and repelled from the other. Thus the spot may be moved over the face of the screen in any direction. In place of plates, the spot may be moved by electromagnetic coils and this is known as electro-magnetic deflection.

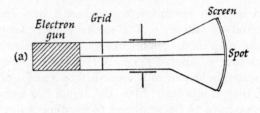

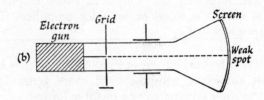

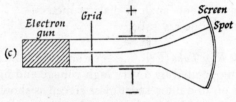

FIG. 209 Cathode ray tube

COMMUNICATIONS EQUIPMENT

23. It can be argued that, provided a craft be navigated with precision and with certainty, there is little need for communications. However, in practice, communications play a part in navigation as follows:

(a) Transmission of distress signals. This is evidently of extreme importance.
(b) Transmission of weather information. This can vary from the simple reception of meteorological forecasts from broadcasting stations to the use of receivers which can reproduce facsimiles of the meteorological chart. Facsimile recorders are of particular use for weather routing.
(c) Transmissions of information regarding position or other navigational information such as the course to steer.

The communications may be aural or by Morse code or by a data link system that transmits signals automatically when interrogated by radio.

24. It is worth noting that communications can be so important to the small boat that it has been suggested that the provision of radio-telephony (R.T.) equipment is the key navigational aid. It can likewise be said that R.T. is the key equipment for the light aircraft and indeed for all aircraft since the operations of air-traffic control are dependent on R.T.

25. Fig. 210 shows the arrangement of a typical R.T. communications equipment. It comprises a common aerial for transmission

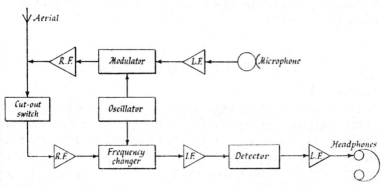

FIG. 210   Elements of communications equipment

and reception with a cut-out switch. The oscillator not only controls the frequency of the transmitter but also the heterodyne frequency of the receiver. Automatic data link equipment will be of a similar type except that an interrogating signal from the station will set off a chain of signals according to the information produced by various sensors. In this connection, it is widely held that the navigator in the craft ought to be able to monitor these automatic data link signals.

EQUIPMENT DESIGN

26. The detailed design of radio equipment is continually developing towards miniaturization, which tends towards robustness, increased efficiency in terms of transmitter output

and receiver power consumption, and improved reliability. Ground radio equipment in particular may be provided with its own monitoring units including monitors of the radiation of ground transmitters. In the event of malfunction, the monitor may operate a warning or, in certain equipment, may connect a stand-by automatically.

27. There is an increasing tendency to design units of specific dimensions to fit into standard racks in craft. In civil aviation, standard sizes are accepted known as ATR (air transport radio) racks. Similar standardization is extended to instruments. These developments allow the constructor of a craft to make allowance in his design for the installation of the navigational equipment, but may tend to inhibit the development of new conceptions if followed too rigidly.

3. D.F. (DIRECTION FINDING)

THEORY

1. If a loop of wire is at right angles to the direction from which radio waves are coming, the wave front will strike each side of the loop simultaneously. There will be no difference signal but the two will cancel each other out. If the loop is aligned in the direction of the radio waves, the two sides will be met by the waves at slightly different instants of time and a difference signal will appear. This difference signal will be gradually reduced to a null as the angle from which the radio waves are coming changes from being in line to being at right angles to the loop. The polar diagram will therefore be as shown in Fig. 211.

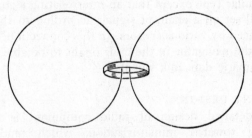

FIG. 211   Polar diagram of loop aerial

2. It will be noted that the polar diagram of a loop is a symmetrical figure of eight and therefore the measurement of direction will be ambiguous. However, because the loop is measuring a difference signal, it is 90° out of phase with the actual signal (page 21, para 16). Hence if a normal aerial is placed a quarter of a wavelength away from the loop aerial, it will receive a signal either in phase with the loop or in opposition to the loop. The polar diagram will therefore be as shown in Fig. 212. In practice,

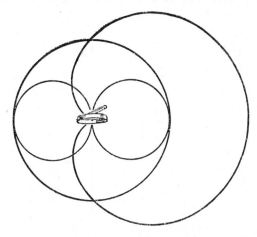

FIG. 212   Polar diagram of loop and sense aerials

the normal aerial is located with the loop aerial and the signal is delayed electrically by a quarter of a wavelength. An aerial used in this way is known as a sense aerial.

3. The operation of an elementary loop receiver is now seen to involve two stages:

(a) The loop is rotated until a null is received from the radio signals. It is much easier to distinguish a null, which Fig. 211 shows to be sharp, than to distinguish a maximum which is a flat part of the curve.

(b) The loop is then rotated through 90° and the sense aerial switched in. According to whether the signals are increased or decreased, the radio transmissions must be coming from one side or other of the line established by the null.

4. In place of the rotating loop, two fixed loops at right angles may be used, the signals from each loop being passed to two field coils at right angles so that the signals are reproduced on a small scale. Within these two coils, a small gonio coil or goniometer is made to rotate, the gonio picking up signals from the two field coils and finding the null in exactly the same way as the rotating loop finds a null. This is illustrated in Fig. 213.

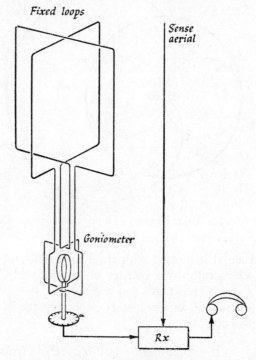

FIG. 213   D.F. with gonio

5. Any D.F. system will be subject to:

   (a) *Systematic errors* due to loop aerials.
   (b) *Random errors* due to radio propagation.

SYSTEMATIC ERRORS

6. The systematic errors in a loop aerial are similar to the systematic errors in a compass. The errors can be measured by 'swinging' the craft and will generally be one of three types:

(a) Constant error due to misalignment of loop or the gonio coil (Fig. 214(a)).
(b) Single sine wave siting error due to poor siting of the aerial in the craft (Fig. 214 (b)).
(c) Quadrantal error due to the craft affecting the signal (Fig. 214(c)).

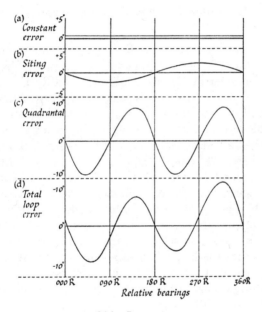

FIG. 214   Loop errors

7. Quadrantal error is the most important systematic error. The craft itself will tend to act as a loop as shown in Fig. 215. The effect will generally be to deflect the D.F. loop towards the fore and aft line of the craft. The error will consequently be nil when the loop is aligned fore and aft or when the loop is aligned abeam but a maximum on the quadrantal points. The error is

close to a double sine wave but the peaks are theoretically around 040R, 140R, 220R and 320R.

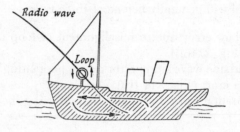

FIG. 215   Cause of quadrantal error

8. It may happen that the radio waves are not constrained to follow the line of the craft but at an angle to it. This will shift the quadrantal error. If the angle was 010R, the quadrantal peaks would be at 050R, 150R, 230R and 330R. Alternatively a loop formed by the forestay, mast and hull of Fig. 215 will reduce the fore and aft signal strength. In an aircraft, a loop mounted just above the main spar of the wings could well have a quadrantal error 90° out of alignment with the fore and aft line.

9. If a gonio coil is fitted, quadrantal error may be compensated by introducing a corrector field coil that will have an effect opposite to that of the craft. This method is used on ships. Alternatively, quadrantal error may be corrected by a mechanical cam or by a correction card similar to that used with a magnetic compass. Since the loop effect of a ship is generally close to the fore and aft line, a set of synthetic curves may be prepared and the appropriate curve chosen by recording one error at 040R, 140R, 220R or 320R.

10. The constant error is eliminated by adjusting the alignment of the loop or the gonio coil, and the single sine error by correcting the siting of the loop within the craft. In addition a small octantal error can arise due to gonio coupling. All these errors will apply to ground stations as well as to craft. In a craft, however, the quadrantal error may be changed by the cargo and may vary according to the attitude in a ship; the deeper the hull the less the quadrantal error.

11. *Tilting Error.* A bearing taken from a craft may be in error if the craft is rolling or pitching, due to tilting of the plane in which the bearing is being measured. This effect can be more serious with sky waves than with ground waves (page 40, para 18).

PROPAGATION ERRORS

12. Major errors in D.F. systems arise from sky wave reflections. Since sky wave reflections are stronger at night, the phenomena are generally known as night effects. Sky and ground waves may interfere with each other, causing fading and making it difficult to find the null. The sky waves arriving at an angle will produce a difference signal on a loop at right angles unless it is tilted backwards. Hence sky waves may cause erratic signals and a blurred minimum.

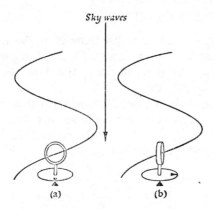

FIG. 216   Effect of sky waves (it is assumed that radio transmissions are coming from the direction of the reader)

13. The effects of polarization may be more dramatic. Fig. 216 (a) shows a loop aerial which is assumed to be receiving signals coming from the direction of the reader but an an angle from slightly above. The loop is at right angles to the direction of the reader and therefore ought to register a null. However, if the wave coming from above is polarized horizontally it will pick up a signal. It will indeed only fail to pick up this signal if it be

turned through 90° as shown in Fig. 216 (b), in which position
the signal would normally be a maximum.

14. Radio transmissions that are not beamed are generally
vertically polarized, but transmissions from sky waves may be
horizontally polarized. Hence it is possible for a null to be found
90° in error. Generally the polarization is mixed and there is a
ground wave as well as a sky wave. However, the combination
will often cause a steady error of tens of degrees. An additional
error, fortunately slight except sometimes at dawn or dusk, may
arise due to reflections from the ionosphere being warped through
an angle.

15. Summarizing, night effect can cause:

(a) Major errors in bearings.
(b) Blurring of the minimum signal.
(c) Weakening of the signal.

These effects are most unpredictable at dawn and at dusk
when the ionosphere is changing. In polar regions, where the
Sun may travel round the horizon, the dawn and dusk effects
may last for long periods.

16. An Adcock aerial consists of four vertical aerials and a fifth
central sense aerial, the connections between the opposite
vertical aerials being shielded as shown in Fig. 217. Since the
loops are replaced by two U-shaped aerials with the horizontal

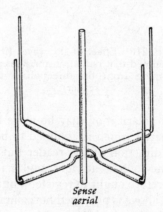

*Sense
aerial*

FIG. 217   Fixed Adcock aerial

members shielded, the elements of sky waves that cause night effects will be largely eliminated. In certain instances, a rotating Adcock aerial consisting of one U aerial may be used in place of the two fixed Adcock aerials.

17. Adcock aerials cannot eliminate errors due to the radio waves being reflected from the ionosphere at an angle nor errors due to coastal refraction or mountain effect (page 474, para 16). Nor can they reduce the interference between ground and sky waves, but they can reduce the blurring of the minumum. Unfortunately, Adcock aerials are basically less efficient than normal loop aerials and therefore are not generally used in high-speed craft where miniaturization is important.

GROUND BASED D.F.

18. *Cathode Ray D.F.* A ground station may need to take D.F. bearings on a number of craft or on an individual craft in distress. The use of a rotating goniometer would take time and therefore the two loops may be oriented north–south and east–west and made to pass signals to the X and Y plates of a cathode ray tube as shown in Fig. 218. The two receivers

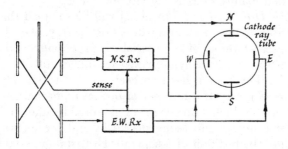

FIG. 218   C.R.D.F.

amplify the incoming signal in such a way that the spot of light at the centre of the tube is drawn out into a radial line towards the circumference of the tube, 50 times per second being a common rate. The tube has a fixed compass card round the outside so that a bearing can be read immediately.

19. A system of this type is known as a cathode ray D.F. (C.R.D.F.) or Watson–Watt direction finder. It is commonly

used in ground VHF and HF D.F. stations, the cathode ray D.F. receiver acting also as a communications receiver so that a bearing is automatically provided on any craft which is sending a message. The system can also detect thunderstorms.

20. *HF D.F. Systems.* In the instance of HF ground stations, the angle at which the sky wave is reflected will be fine and, even from the F layer, will only strike the ground at an angle of a few degrees at distances measured in thousands of miles. A ground station with careful siting and a well-built Adcock system can therefore be expected to measure long-range bearings with errors of a few degrees. Even at 500 miles, where the sky waves may come in at angles of over 30°, the errors may not be unduly large, but as the skip distance is approached they will increase greatly. HF D.F. is therefore used for long range rather than short range D.F.

21. *VHF D.F. Systems.* VHF does not produce sky waves and therefore operates only on direct waves. Provided the site is good and there are no serious reflections, a VHF D.F. system can be very accurate and a 95 per cent error of 1–2° is achievable. Since the range is not much greater than visual range, VHF D.F. is confined mainly to assisting aircraft.

22. *UHF D.F. Systems.* The aerial will be so small that it may be possible to use a rotating directional array. An alternative system uses a number of fixed aerials, 12 is common, and arranges the rotation electrically, giving accuracies of 95 per cent within 1°. The system has also been applied to HF D.F.

23. *Fixer Systems.* If a number of optical units that can project pencils of light in any direction are mounted behind a large-scale map, each optical unit being placed behind the map so that it represents the position of a separate D.F. station, simultaneous bearings taken from several D.F. stations may be projected as bearings on the map, the intersection showing the position of the craft.

24. A similar system may be used on a cathode ray tube, the signals from each station being made to move the point of light sequentially, the persistence of the screen giving an appearance of simultaneous position lines. Such systems operate mainly at HF, VHF or UHF and have been used by rescue organizations to fix the positions of craft in distress.

D.F. SYSTEMS IN CRAFT

25. *Marine D.F.* In 1948, the International Convention on Safety of Life at Sea specified that D.F. equipment must be carried by any vessel of more than 1600 tons. Today many yachts carry D.F. generally of the aural null type which, in the hands of an experienced operator, can give good results and warnings of sky wave errors. In larger ships the C.R. D.F. receiver may be fitted. A compass card round the cathode ray tube may be slaved to true North by the gyro compass so that the bearing given is true.

26. Marine D.F. equipments take bearings on the special radio beacons installed along the coast and on light vessels. The beacons operate at around 1000 metre wavelengths and so have the characteristics partly of MF and partly of LF. They transmit a steady note, on which the bearing is taken, and a Morse signal for identification. Some beacons only transmit in fog. D.F. bearings can also be taken on broadcasting stations or on other ships. The accuracy is generally better than 95 per cent within 5°.

27. *ADF (Automatic direction finding).* In an aircraft, a small rotating ferrite cored loop may be fitted into a shallow recess in the skin of the fuselage or two fixed loops may be used with a miniature gonio. The signals are compared with the signals from a sense aerial and amplified so that the relative bearing is measured. Originally this relative bearing was combined with a relative compass dial and known as a radio compass. Today it is generally combined with a signal from the gyro-magnetic compass and presented as a magnetic bearing on an instrument known as a radio magnetic indicator (RMI). The accuracy is generally 95 per cent within 5°.

28. Aircraft radio beacons are known as NDB's (non-directional beacons) to distinguish them from the directional beacons described in the next section. The wavelengths are similar to those used for coastal beacons, but the beacons are sited along airways at turning points and close to airfields. An aircraft may be instructed by air-traffic control to use an NDB close to an airfield to fly a holding pattern (page 351, para 7) while waiting turn to land.

29. *Performance.* The range of a radio beacon depends on power, siting, aerial size, atmospheric conditions, and whether the waves

are travelling over sea or over land. Over land, the range may be only a hundred miles when bearings are taken by a surface craft, but will be much greater when the waves travel over the water or when the bearings are taken from an aircraft.

30. The accuracy of a ship-borne or airborne D.F. will depend on the correct allowance being made for quadrantal correction and, unless an Adcock aerial is used, on ionospheric conditions. Since an Adcock aerial is seldom used on a craft, errors at night will increase greatly at distances of over 100 miles. The overall accuracy of radio bearings taken from craft can be gauged by the definitions used to qualify a D.F. bearing:

(a) *First class.* The operator will trust it within 2°.
(b) *Second class.* The operator can trust it within 5°.
(c) *Third class.* The operator cannot trust it within 5°.

4. RADIO GUIDES

1. A radio guide is a ground transmitter that defines a position line on the surface of the Earth. Generally a craft will travel along a radio guide. Accordingly, in aviation, a radio guide is known as a track guide. There are three main types:

(a) *Radio ranges* that define four position lines radiating from a central point.
(b) *Omnidirectional beacons* that provide position lines in all directions.
(c) *Radio beams* that define single position lines. A beam may define a line in the vertical plane as well as in the horizontal plane.

RADIO RANGE

2. A radio range or four-course beacon is a ground transmitter comprising two loops at right angles. The transmissions are switched from one loop to the other so that one loop transmits dots and dashes (*A*'s) and the other transmits dashes and dots (*N*'s). The overlapping of the two polar diagrams produces four equisignal zones. The merging of the signals is, of course, not

abrupt as suggested in Fig. 219. Along the centre line of the equisignal zone, the *A*'s and *N*'s will merge into a steady note. Any deviation from this line will cause the *A* or the *N* signal to obtrude. By listening to the signals a pilot may fly his aircraft down one side of the equisignal line to the radio station. The signals do not radiate upwards so that, on arrival at the station, the aircraft will enter a 'cone' of silence.

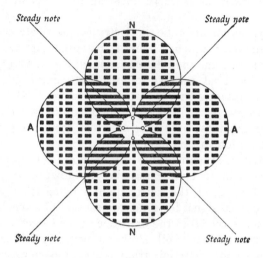

FIG. 219   Polar diagram of radio range (two
loops at right angles)

3. Radio ranges may be sited along airways at crossings and at turning points. The pattern of two equisignal lines at right angles may be modified symmetrically by altering the angle between the loops and unsymmetrically by introducing an additional aerial. Using radio ranges, an aircraft fitted with a simple receiver may navigate along airways with an accuracy which may be 95 per cent within 5°. Unfortunately, the frequency used for radio ranges is MF and the signals may be blotted out by the very weather conditions in which radio aids are most necessary. Also, instead of separating aircraft, radio ranges tend to canalize traffic. Hence, omnidirectional beacons have been developed.

33—P.N.

OMNIDIRECTIONAL BEACONS

4. Omnidirectional beacons are sometimes known as omnirange beacons (ORB). The earliest beacons comprised a loop rotating once a minute and transmitting an aural signal and a north–south signal. The signals were received in the craft and the navigator listened on his headphones, stop-watch in hand. By timing the interval between receipt of the north–south signal and the null signal, he could measure the bearing to an accuracy of a few degrees.

5. Today, aerials are rotated electrically at a rate according to the modulation frequency being transmitted. At the same time, a signal of the same modulation frequency is transmitted from a non-rotating aerial, the two modulations being exactly in phase when the rotating transmission is facing north. Thus, by comparing the phase of the two modulations in a receiver, and displaying the phase difference on a dial, the bearing of the craft from the station can be indicated.

6. This type of system has been applied on LF frequencies using three aerials in an equilateral triangle radiating in pairs every quarter of a second, the fourth quarter being taken up with an omnidirectional signal for synchronization. The synchronization signal when received in the craft operates a switch connected to three electro-magnetic coils so that a magnetic field is produced according to the direction from the station compared to true north. The system was known as Navaglobe. The errors were probably 95 per cent greater than 2° and often as much as 5°. This inaccuracy combined with technical difficulties inhibited development.

7. *VOR* (*VHF OmniRange*). VOR is the standard airways navigational aid. The transmitter is effectively an aerial rotating 30 times per second and transmitting a signal amplitude modulated at 30 c/s. The fixed aerial transmits a frequency modulated signal at 30 c/s and the two modulations are synchronized so that they are in phase when the rotating aerial is looking towards magnetic north. The two signals are received by the craft, and the frequency modulation representing the fixed aerial is filtered out from the amplitude modulation representing the rotating aerial. The difference of the phase of the two modulations can be presented on a radio magnetic indicator as the

magnetic direction of the craft from the VOR station as suggested in Fig. 220. In addition, a Morse identification signal is transmitted.

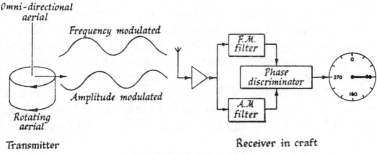

FIG. 220   VOR system

8. VOR transmitters use horizontally polarized aerials which tend to suffer less from random ground reflections. Unfortunately, the fitting of an omnidirectional horizontal aerial in the craft is not easy. The VOR transmitter does not transmit upwards so that, above the station, there is a gap known as the 'cone of confusion'.

9. The position line radiated by a VOR transmitter is known as a radial. Being a position line, it has no direction but is named according to its magnetic direction from the VOR station. By means of an omnibearing selector (OBS) it is possible to select a radial. Any angular deviation from the selected radial can be made to appear as a left–right indication on a separate left–right meter, or fed as left–right signals into the automatic control system. However, the orientation of left or right will vary according to whether the aircraft wishes to fly inbound along the radial towards the VOR station or outbound along the radial away from the VOR station. This may be varied by means of a 'to–from' switch.

10. The accuracy of VOR is generally 95 per cent within 3° and is seldom worse than 5°. The range depends on height but should cover at least 100 miles. In addition a very low power terminal VOR (TVOR) station may be installed to guide aircraft on to the correct approach path to an airfield. A more accurate VOR known as PVOR (precision VOR) transmits a coarse and a fine

pattern similar to that described in the next paragraph and has an accuracy probably 95 per cent within $1\frac{1}{2}°$.

11. *Tacan.* A type of VOR working in the UHF band is used to provide the bearing element of a bearing and distance system known as Tacan (Tactical Air Navigation) which has particular military applications. The aerial radiates a simple coarse pattern by methods similar to VOR and also a fine pattern which has nine peaks of ambiguity within the 360° rotation. Hence the receiver automatically chooses the correct 40° sector by the coarse pattern and the correct part of the 40° sector by the fine pattern. The 95 per cent error is probably around 1°. An identifying Morse signal is transmitted every half minute.

BEAM SYSTEMS

12. Radio beams generally consist of two directional transmissions in place of the four shown in Fig. 219. If the signals are to be transmitted aurally to the navigator, one transmission may signal dots or *A*'s and the other dashes or *N*'s, the equisignal line between giving a steady note. The side lobes may introduce false equisignals or spurious beams. In addition a strong back beam may appear.

13. *Marine aural beams.* Short-wave beams have been used coded aurally so that, by means of a very simple receiver operating a small loudspeaker, the marine navigator can tell to which side of a line leading into port his craft is running. The range is short but the accuracy is generally high and the simplicity of operation makes such systems attractive for guiding small vessels into narrow harbours.

14. *ILS (Instrument Landing System).* ILS is a VHF system working on a frequency of a little above 100 Mc/s. It has three components:

   (a) Localizer beam that guides the aircraft in plan.
   (b) Glide-slope beam that guides the aircraft in elevation generally at an angle of 2° or 3°.
   (c) Marker beacons, which are vertical beams that tell the pilot how far it is to land. Normally there is an outer marker at 4 miles, a middle marker at half a mile and sometimes an inner boundary marker.

15. The localizer comprises two overlapping modulation lobes superimposed on the main radiation lobe so arranged that a line of zero difference of modulation defines the centre line of the runway. Any deviation from the centre line appears as a difference in depth of modulation (DDM) which is filtered in the airborne receiver and displayed as an angular deviation from the centre line. The localizer pattern is shown in Fig. 221. The right-hand side as seen from the approaching aircraft is known as the blue sector and the left-hand side as the yellow sector. The glide

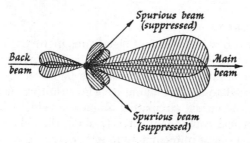

FIG. 221   Typical beam polar diagram

slope operates in a similar fashion and can be regarded as a localizer placed on its side but with the beam width reduced by a factor of approximately four. Hence, while a localizer may guide an aircraft within $1°$, a glide path may guide it within $\frac{1}{4}°$.

16. Signals from ILS can be affected by reflections from objects near by and, in particular, the glide slope can be distorted by reflections off the ground. Errors can also be introduced when other aircraft are flying overhead. These errors can be reduced by improvements in aerial design and by care in siting. However, owing to the difficulties, ILS systems are divided into three categories:

   (a) Category I. Suitable only for approach down to 200 feet.
   (b) Category II. Suitable for guidance down to 50 feet.
   (c) Category III. Suitable for landing.

17. *Flarescan.* In place of a fixed beam with fixed patterns of modulation, a moving beam can be used and the modulation may be changed as the beam moves so that the craft can measure how far it is from the correct line. Flarescan uses two such beams,

one swinging from side to side in azimuth and the other nodding in elevation. Each beam is coded so that, according to the signals received, the aircraft can measure position relative to the glide path. The accuracy and constancy of the system is high and the aircraft can choose its own glide-slope angle but the airborne equipment is complex compared to the ILS airborne equipment. (See also page 566, para 12.) A similar system known as REGAL (Range and Elevation Guidance for Automatic Landing) operates only in elevation.

LEADER CABLES

18. Leader cables are a form of electro-magnetic track guide and, although not radio, are alternatives to radio for azimuth guidance. In the simplest system, a cable is laid and an alternating current passed to and fro along it. The resulting magnetic flux which is, so to speak, circulating about the cable will obviously have no vertical component directly along the cable but a large vertical component immediately to either side. Two coils placed one each side of the craft can guide the craft towards the leader cable, and the sharp null at the leader cable can provide fine guidance. The range depends on the current, but about half a nautical mile would be a reasonable distance.

19. Single leader cables laid on the bottom have been used to guide ships through narrow channels. Twin leader cables, one either side of the runway, have been used to guide aircraft down the centre of the runway during the last phase of an automatic landing. The leader cable is accurate, cheap and reliable but, unfortunately, practical difficulties in laying leader cables beyond the thresholds of runways for a sufficient distance has militated against general acceptance for automatic landing.

5. SUMMARY

PROPAGATION

Radio waves can be divided into four groups:

(a) LF and VLF. Propagation mainly by ground waves supported by sky waves.

(b) MF. Propagation mainly by ground waves by day with an increase of sky waves at night and consequent increase of range.

(c) HF. Propagation mainly by sky waves with generally a skip distance between the ground waves and the first sky waves.

(d) VHF, UHF centimetric and millimetric waves. Propagation mainly by direct line of sight.

Absorption. S. band waves are affected by rain, *X*. band by rain and water vapour, and *K*. band by rain, water vapour, hail, snow and oxygen absorption.

Interference. Atmospheric noise is greatest at long wavelengths and negligible at VHF wavelengths. At sea it is worst in the tropics. In the air, it is worst in snow.

Polarization. Polarization may be changed by reflection. Circular polarization is reversed by reflection from water droplets and this effect can be used to reduce rain clutter.

RADIO EQUIPMENT

Aerials. The length of a transmitting aerial depends on the wavelength. The efficiency of a receiving aerial is less important because the key factor is the signal-to-atmospheric-noise ratio.

Polar Diagrams.

(a) A dipole has a circular polar diagram when viewed end on.

(b) A dipole viewed from the side or a loop aerial viewed end on has a figure-of-eight polar diagram.

(c) A row of driven aerials produces two beams in opposite directions at right angles to the aerials. One of the two beams can be reduced by shielding.

(d) A dipole with a parasitic array produces a beam in one direction only.

(e) All beams have spurious 'side lobes'.

Beam Width. At very high frequencies:

$$\text{beam width}° = 2 \times (\text{wavelength (cm)})/(\text{reflector diameter (ft)})$$

D.F.

Loop systems. The loop may be rotated or a gonio may be used. Alternatively the presentation may be made directly on a cathode ray tube. A sense aerial is needed to reduce 180° ambiguity.

Errors. The main errors in a loop system are:

(a) Quadrantal error, which may be compensated.
(b) Polarization errors. In ground stations, these errors can be reduced by Adcock aerials.

D.F. systems in craft. Marine craft obtain D.F. bearings from MF coastal beacons. Aircraft use ADF on MF beacons sited along airways. Accuracy greater by day but generally about 95 per cent within 5°.

Ground based systems.

(a) HF D.F. is used for aircraft distress signals at ranges of over 500 n. miles. Marine craft transmit on MF or LF. Accuracy 95 per cent within 2° under good conditions.
(b) VHF D.F. is used for line of sight distances with a rotating aerial that may be rotated electronically. Accuracy 95 per cent within 2°.
(c) UHF D.F. Similar to VHF but accuracy is 95 per cent within 1°.
(d) Fixer systems may be provided by combining D.F. stations.

TRACK GUIDES

Radio Range. MF with aural signals and a simple receiver. Accuracy 95 per cent within about 5°.

Navaglobe. 2000 n. mile LF transmitter with aerial rotated electronically. Accuracy 95 per cent within about 3°.

VOR. Short-range VHF system with aerial rotated electronically. Can be made to provide signals for display on an RMI or on a flight compass. Accuracy of radials, 95 per cent within about 3° or about $1\frac{1}{2}°$ with PVOR.

Tacan. Has a radial element on UHF similar to VOR but more refined. Accuracy of radials, 95 per cent within about 1°.

Aural Beams. Have been used at sea and over the land generally for short distances.

ILS. Localizer and glide-path beams produce glide-path information on pilot's instruments or control the aircraft. 95 per cent accuracy should be within 1° of localizer centre-line and $\frac{1}{4}$° of glide path centre-line.

Leader cables. Produce electro-magnetic signals for control of craft along precise tracks at very short ranges. High accuracy and reliability.

CHAPTER XIV

Radio Distance Measurement

Radio waves travel at about 160,000 n. miles per second, which is rather more than 300 yards in a microsecond. In order to measure how long a radio wave took to travel from one point to another, it would be necessary to know exactly the instant at which the wave was transmitted. In practice, therefore, distance is measured by the time that a radio wave takes to travel out and back, so that the timing process can be started by the outgoing transmission. For the measurement of distance to be accurate, the time interval between transmission and reception has to be accurate, and also an allowance may have to be made for the time taken for the signal to pass through the various transmitting and receiving circuits.

A radio distance measuring system therefore depends on a precise clock, generally a crystal oscillator. The signal used to measure distance may be either:

(a) *Pulse.*
(b) *Continuous waves.*

1. PULSE DISTANCE MEASUREMENT

ELEMENTS

1. Fig. 222 shows a simplified block diagram of a pulse distance measuring system. The crystal oscillator controls a pulse generator which converts the sine waves into rectangular pulses. These are passed to the modulator which controls the transmitter so that the transmissions appear in the form of small discrete packets of radio waves.

2. Simultaneously with the pulse generator, the oscillator operates a saw-tooth generator which is linked to the cathode

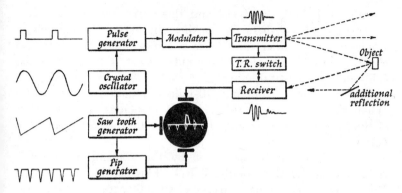

F I G. 222   Pulse distance measurement

ray tube so that the spot of light is made to travel steadily across the tube and then to flick back to the start again. During this fly-back period, the spot is made to black-out, so that the result is a line or trace drawn at a certain speed across the face of the tube and starting always at the exact instant that the pulse is transmitted.

3. The pulse sent out from the transmitter is echoed from an object and received back at the receiver a few tens of microseconds later. The resulting signal is passed to the other plates of the cathode ray tube so that the spot of light is made to flick upwards causing a kick or blip to appear on the trace. If the spot were travelling at the rate of $\frac{1}{4}$ inch for each 120 microseconds and the blip appeared $\frac{1}{2}$ inch from the start of the trace, the pulse must have been travelling for 240 microseconds or about 40 miles, so that the object must be about 20 miles away. Hence by means of a scale on the trace, the distance of the object may be measured. It will be noted that distance is measured according to the moment when the pulse first returns. that is, by the leading edge of the blip. This type of display is known as an A scope.

4. In place of a graduated scale, the oscillator may be made to generate blips known as calibration pips every 120 microseconds, and these can appear on the trace itself as shown in Fig. 222. Since signals will take 120 microseconds to travel 10 miles to an object and 10 miles back, these pips will represent

a scale of 10-mile intervals, and this scale will be accurate irrespective of any distortion in the tube itself. Alternatively, a single pip or marker, known as a strobe, may be controlled electronically by a knob with a pointer registering against a dial calibrated in nautical miles. For each 120 microseconds, the strobe will move from one 10-mile graduation to the next. When the strobe is moved so that it coincides with the start of the blip, the distance may be read off on the dial against the pointer.

5. The original pulse sent out by the transmitter has not appeared on the trace of the C.R.T. This can be arranged by means of a T.R. (transmit–receive) switch (page 480, para 11). Thus the receiver will be able to operate on the same aerial as the transmitter without being damaged by the energy from the pulses.

SYSTEM CHARACTERISTICS

6. The accuracy with which distance can be measured will depend on the sharpness of the leading edge of the blip. It will be impossible to measure exactly where a blip starts if its leading edge is sloped. If the wavelength used were a large fraction of a mile, a sharp pulse would naturally be impossible. The wavelength must therefore be not longer than a few metres and, preferably, only a few centimetres. A short wavelength will will also make it more easy to accommodate the band width necessary to create a sharp pulse (page 394, para 12).

7. If the direct echo from an object is accompanied by echoes that have been re-reflected from other objects, these later returns will have travelled by longer paths and will therefore appear behind the main blip as suggested in Fig. 222. Distance is measured from the leading edge of the blip and therefore these returns will not affect the measurement of distance. Hence distance measurement does not suffer from reflections as does measurement of bearing.

8. The pulse repetition frequency is limited by the range of the equipment. If the receiver is capable of picking up an echo from an object 100 n. miles away, the interval between transmission of pulses must be at least 1200 microseconds even if the time

taken for the spot to fly back is negligible. Hence the P.R.F. will have to be not more than 800. In general terms:

maximum P.R.F. (pulse per second) = 80,000/range (n.m.)

9. P.R.F. introduces an element of coding which enables the radar receiver to identify the pulses that it is transmitting. If two transmitters were working on a similar wavelength, the wide band width would mean that each would receive the pulses from the other. However, if one transmitter receiver were working on a P.R.F. differing by only 1 per second from the other, the blip from the other transmitter would appear somewhere along the trace flashing backwards or forwards once a second. Only a remarkably small difference in P.R.F. would produce a 'walking' blip. On an equipment with a range of about 100 miles, a difference of P.R.F. of as little as a thousandth of 1 per cent would cause a walking blip to travel at the rate of about a mile a second across the trace.

10. The continuous appearance of a blip at the same point in the trace enables the operator to distinguish the signal in which he is interested from a background of noise. Noise appears as a very fast succession of blips of all shapes and sizes that will produce an effect known as grass. Against this grass, a continually repeated blip may be distinctive. The ability to read through noise is particularly important to the military navigator since it means that a distance-measuring equipment using pulses will not be easy to jam. If the equipment can be devised to transmit not one pulse but a series of pulses at certain intervals, and if each pulse returning back to the receiver may be made to open the gate for the next pulse, the system of coded pulses will be very difficult to mislead.

11. To discriminate between two objects very close together, a short pulse will be necessary. A pulse of 1 microsecond cannot separate two objects less than about 160 yards apart. The echoing pulse from the further will arrive before the blip from the nearer has been completed. The pulse length also limits the minimum range of the equipment. With a 1 microsecond pulse an object less than 160 yards away would produce a return echo while the T.R. switch was still set to transmit. The time taken by the T.R. switch to work will add a small addi-

tional distance to the minimum range, but generally only a few yards.

PULSE RADIO ALTIMETER

12. The pulse radio altimeter or radar altimeter is a typical distance-measuring system that records the vertical distance between the aircraft and the ground. The system is similar to that shown in Fig. 222 except that the trace will be radial, the transmitted pulse will appear, and the distance will be registered against a fixed scale so that the presentation will be as suggested in Fig. 223. By means of a switch that operates dividers, the equipment may be made to record ground clearance in terms of 1000-foot or 10,000-foot intervals.

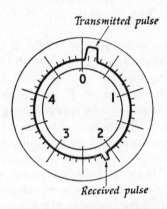

FIG. 223   Radio (pulse) altimeter, reading 2100 ft

13. The accuracy with which the system can be read is quite high and the errors in the equipment are such that a 95 per cent error of less than 200 foot is to be expected at low heights. Unfortunately, the transmitted pulse represents a band of perhaps 200 feet even with a quarter microsecond pulse. Hence the minimum height is limited and the equipment cannot be used for landing aircraft. It may, however, be used to measure drift, as explained on page 260, para 26(c).

MAXIMUM RANGE

14. With a P.R.F. of 1000 per second and a pulse lasting 1 microsecond, the transmitter will only be transmitting for one-thousandth of its time. This enables extremely high power to be packed into a pulse, the heat developed being dissipated during the intervals. The magnetron (page 481, para 15) can develop extremely high power for short intervals of time.

15. The power of a radio signal decreases as the square of the distance from the transmitter (page 392, para 6). If the whole of the wave front were reflected, the returning wave would also decrease in signal strength according to the square of the distance, and this is approximately true in the instance of a radio altimeter. However, the area of a reflecting object will generally be limited. Therefore, the further it is away from the transmitter the smaller the area of the wave front that it will reflect, the area diminishing as the square of the distance. Hence the strength of an echoing signal will generally vary as the fourth power of the distance to the object.

Example. A distance measuring equipment has a maximum range of 100 n. miles. The power is increased by a factor of 10. By how much is the range increased?

$$\text{new maximum range} = 100 \times \sqrt[4]{10} \text{ n. miles}$$
$$= 178 \text{ n. miles approximately}$$

Therefore increase of distance is less than 80 per cent for 1000 per cent increase of power.

16. The range of a distance-measuring equipment is affected considerably by the aerial. The aerial may be designed to concentrate the radio waves into a narrow beam. The concentration may be defined as the signal strength in the direction of the beam compared to the average signal strength in all directions, and this ratio is known as the gain of the aerial. By doubling the aerial gain, the power transmitted along the beam and the power received along the beam will both be doubled. Hence the basic formula will be:

Signal strength from echo is according to
$$(\text{aerial gain})^2/(\text{distance})^4$$

17. The range of distance-measuring equipment is also influenced by the shape, size and type of surface of the reflecting object. This may differ greatly from one aspect to another. For example, a change of aspect of an aircraft by only a fraction of a degree can reduce the reflection by more than one order.

TRANSPONDERS

18. In order to increase the range of a system measuring distance to an object without a disproportionate increase in transmitter power, a radio transmitter may be fitted on the object which will produce an answering pulse when it receives the original interrogating pulse. Responding equipments are known as transponders or responders, and systems of transponders are sometimes known as Racons (RAnge beaCONS).

19. The transponder will need a finite time to receive the interrogating pulse and to transmit an answering pulse and, for accurate distance measurement, a small allowance may have to be made. If the interrogating pulse is short, it will be unlikely that two pulses from two interrogating transmitters will arrive simultaneously, and even more unlikely that the P.R.F.s of the two transmitters will be close enough for the interference to be more than transitory. However, the transponder receiver must not be too sensitive or it will pick up noise and re-radiate all the time. Also it will usually transmit on a wavelength differing from that of the interrogating pulse, so that it cannot pick up reflections from its own transmissions and trigger itself off continuously.

20. The number of transmitters that can interrogate a transponder is limited by the power of the transponder transmitter. In general, after transmitting a pulse, a transponder will take an appreciable time to recover, and 100 microseconds is not an uncommon figure. Hence, if the interrogating pulses arrive more frequently, there will be a diminution of signal strength. For this reason, systems that are likely to involve a large number of interrogating pulses generally use a low P.R.F. for interrogation. Theoretically, a P.R.F. of 25 per second will allow for 400 interrogating transmitters if the recovery time is 100 microseconds.

In practice, owing to overlap, efficiency may tend to fall off soon after the hundred mark is reached.

21. For long-range bombing systems, a special type of transponder known as a repeater has been used. The repeater is fitted in an aircraft flying between the ground station and the transponder in the bomber aircraft. The pulse is received by the repeater, passed to the transponder in the bomber, sent back to the repeater and so back to the ground station.

DISTANCE MEASUREMENT SYSTEMS

22. One of the earliest transponder systems used a portable beacon known as Eureka which could be carried by ground troops or dropped from aircraft. This beacon was interrogated by an airborne equipment known as Rebecca. In the earlier equipments, the trace was vertical and the Eureka responses were picked up by two aerials one each side of the aircraft. The left-hand aerial produced a blip to the left and the right-hand aerial a blip to the right on alternate traces. The relative size of the blips showed which way to turn to head at the Eureka beacon and the distance of the blip from the bottom of the trace showed the distance to go. The equipment worked on VHF and had a 95 per cent slant accuracy of the order of 2 per cent of distance. Later equipments used direct heading indications and counters for distance measurement. By using a beamed beacon known as BABS (Blind Approach Beam System), the Rebecca equipment could provide an elementary form of guidance for approach to an airfield.

23. *DME.* In high air-traffic density areas, DME (distance-measuring equipment) has been introduced. The DME beacon operates on VHF and may be sited with a VOR station, thus giving distance and bearing from one point. The resulting system is known as VOR/DME or, when combined with doppler-VOR (page 576, para 16), as Vordac. The accuracy of the distance measurement is 95 per cent within less than 1 per cent.

24. *Tacan.* DME has been developed at UHF frequencies, particularly for military use, and is known as DMET (distance measurement equipment Tacan). It has an accuracy which is 95 per cent within a fraction of 1 per cent. It is generally sited with the UHF Tacan radial transmitter (page 500, para 11) to

form a Tacan station. Alternatively, it may be sited with a VOR beacon, in which event the system is known as Vortac or VOR/ DMET.

25. DME systems measure slant distances so consistently that they can record the speed of a craft by differentiation. Evidently, the noise will be such that the measurement of speed cannot be instantaneous. Nevertheless, over a period of seconds the accuracy of the speed thus measured can be reasonably high.

26. *Rho–Theta*. VOR/DME, Tacan and Vortac are known as rho–theta systems, rho being the symbol for distance and theta the symbol for bearing. The pattern of radials and distance circles has also led to the term spider's web. Such a system can be provided with a simple computer that can show the distance that the craft will pass by the ground station by means of the calculation:

$$\text{closest distance} = \text{rho} \times \sin(\text{course} - \text{theta})$$

A required track can be defined in terms of a required closest distance to a rho–theta station and a required course. A simple computer consisting of two subtractors and a resolver can then generate an error signal as follows:

$$\text{error signal} = \text{required closest distance}$$
$$- \text{rho} \times \sin(\text{required course} - \text{theta})$$

27. *Rho–Rho*. In addition to rho–theta systems used in terminal areas, rho–rho systems have been used for bombing. Oboe comprised two ground transmitters with responders in the aircraft. One transmitter directed the aircraft along an arc over the target and the other sent bomb release information to the pilot. The range was naturally limited to the line of sight but could be extended by means of repeaters as described in para 23. The accuracy was extremely high and, since the aircraft was being tracked by a ground station, the performance of the pilot under fire could be monitored.

28. A similar device but with the transmitter in the aircraft was known as Shoran. Naturally, Shoran beacons could operate numbers of aircraft whereas Oboe could only operate one at a time unless the ground transmitters were duplicated. The systems were developed to give automatic bomb release and

would have been capable of accuracies of 200 yards had the bomb trajectories been sufficiently consistent. So accurate were the systems that the linking together of surveys of adjacent countries was necessary before the potentiality of the devices could be realized.

29. Long distance measurement by ground stations using satellites as repeaters and the craft as responders can be devised. Such systems will concentrate complexity into the ground stations which will have to know repeater satellite positions continuously in addition to computing the individual craft positions on request.

2. CW DISTANCE MEASUREMENT

CHARACTERISTICS

1. A chain of waves may be transmitted and compared with the chain of waves echoed back from an object. If the two are in phase, the crests will coincide and the waves must have travelled an exact number of wavelengths. If not in phase, a phase discriminator can measure the phase difference. A phase difference of 90° means that the waves must have travelled a distance of a quarter of a wavelength, to which must be added an unknown whole number of wavelengths.

2. The ambiguity of a CW system may be resolved by:

(a) Ensuring that the wavelength is longer than the distance.

(b) Noting the phase of the received waves when the distance is known by other means. Any change of phase subsequently can be translated into a change of distance and applied to the original known distance.

(c) Applying a modulation temporarily or permanently to the continuous waves so as to mark them in some way. For example, an additional frequency could be transmitted for a short period.

3. A CW system has certain disadvantages compared to a pulse system:

(a) Re-reflections cannot be separated from direct reflections. This may limit accurate distance measurement by CW to objects that are simple and uncluttered.

(b) The system is less effectively coded than a pulse system and therefore is less attractive militarily.

(c) A transponder cannot be used effectively since it would be impossible to arrange time sharing.

4. On the other hand, a CW system has certain advantages compared to a pulse system:

(a) The range measured may be as short as is desired.

(b) Owing to the absence of a pulse, the band width may be narrow. If a modulation has to be applied to reduce ambiguity, the band width will be increased but may still be much less than a pulse system.

RADIO ALTIMETER

5. The ground below an aircraft is an unmistakable target. For landing it is essential to be able to measure height right down to the ground. The radio altimeter used for landing is therefore generally a CW equipment. In order that all reflections from the ground below shall return to the aircraft at approximately the same time, it is necessary for the transmissions to be beamed vertically downwards. In order to achieve this beaming, the radio altimeter has to operate in the UHF waveband.

6. It would be impossible to measure ground clearance with ambiguities of only 10 cm or so, and therefore the VHF signals are frequency modulated, the frequency being varied about the mean either in a sine wave or in a saw-tooth pattern.

7. The difference between the transmitted and the received modulation frequencies will vary continuously. If the transmitted frequency is just passing the end of a swing whereas the received frequency is just approaching it, the frequency difference will be nil. A quarter of a modulation later, the frequency difference will be a maximum, this maximum depending on the height of the aircraft above the ground. However, the mean difference between the frequencies of the transmitted and the received waves can be found by a process of integration, the integrated frequency differences being calibrated to represent ground clearance.

8. Since continuous waves are used, the transmitter and the receiver must have separate aerials. To link the transmitted and received waves together, the waves from the transmitter aerial

may be allowed to diffuse into the receiver aerial or, alternatively, transmitter and receiver may be connected.

9. Unfortunately, the waves echoed from the ground will come not only from directly beneath but also from an angle. These waves will cover a longer path than the vertical waves and will produce a mixture of frequencies, the average tending to cause the radio altimeter to over-read. An allowance can be made for this effect but the inevitable result is a loss of accuracy. With a well-designed aerial, the error is of the order of 1 or 2 per cent on 95 per cent of occasions. Hence above a few thousand feet, the pulse radio altimeter is more accurate. Also, errors will arise if the aircraft changes its attitude. In addition, unless well shielded, the radio altimeter may pick up spurious reflections from parts of the aircraft such as flaps and undercarriage doors.

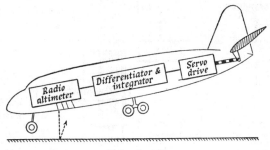

FIG. 224   Autoflare

10. The signal produced by the radio altimeter is suitable for automatic control of an aircraft and is used for automatic landing. When the approaching aircraft is less than 50 feet up, the radio altimeter signal, with the necessary rate and integration terms added, may be made to pitch the nose of the aircraft up progressively so that the aircraft is flared automatically as suggested in Fig. 224. In certain equipments, this system of autoflare is combined with visual alignment of the aircraft with the runway. In other equipments it forms part of the autolanding system with a localizer coupled to control the aircraft in azimuth. This is the basis of the BLEU (Blind Landing Experimental Unit) system.

11. *Capacity Altimeter.* For very low heights, generally limited to less than the length of the aircraft, an altimeter can be used that

measures the electrical capacity between the aircraft and the ground. The accuracy of height measurement is remarkably independent of the type of surface, but the signals are liable to be affected by changes in the configuration of the aircraft due, for example, to the lowering of flaps.

VLF DISTANCE MEASUREMENT

12. In pulse systems such as DME, the craft and the ground both transmit. A corresponding technique exists that uses CW but, to achieve long ranges, the signals have to be LF or VLF. Transmitting equipment would be too big to install in small craft, but such systems have been used for survey vessels.

13. VLF distance measurement systems have been devised, as shown in Fig. 225, that do not require a transmitter in the craft

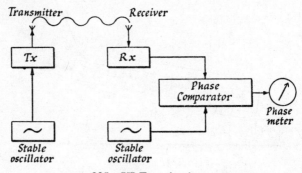

FIG. 225   VLF navigation system

but measure change of distance since the start of a run. The ground station sends out signals of an exact frequency and a stable oscillator in the craft operates at exactly the same frequency. The phase of the received signal and the oscillator are compared and displayed on a phasemeter.

14. If the craft is stationary or travelling in a circle about the station, the phasemeter will not move. As the craft travels a distance equal to a wavelength towards or away from the station, the phasemeter will rotate once. The total number of rotations may be clocked up on counters and the phasemeter will show the interval between rotations. Thus the phasemeter and the counters will show the distance that the craft has moved towards

or away from the station in terms of wavelengths. With two such transmitters, a craft starting at a known point may be able continually to record its change of position and therefore its position.

15. The system depends on the maintenance of an exact frequency in the craft. Also the system must not suffer a break or the sequence of distance changes will be interrupted. This danger may be averted by using more than two stations and providing redundancy of receivers. The alternative will be to modulate the transmissions in some way, but this will involve additional frequencies that may travel to the craft along slightly different paths. This solution is therefore not generally favoured.

16. The accuracy of position finding depends on the constancy of the oscillator and on the constancy of the speed of radio waves. The latter may vary so that errors of upwards of 10 n. miles can occur at long ranges, but the errors may be reduced by corrections. The distances will be in n. miles and not minutes of arc so that positions will have to allow for the shape of the Earth.

17. VLF systems for world-wide coverage have been proposed that would use only a dozen high-power transmitters already operating for other purposes, their frequencies being controlled by atomic clocks. Alternatively, precisely controlled transmitters may be sited at long-range Navaglobe beacons (page 498, para 6), the rho–theta combination being known as Navarho.

18. Unfortunately, VLF systems introduce special problems. In marine craft, the length of a journey may be so long in time that atomic clocks may have to be used to achieve the necessary precision. In aircraft, it is extremely difficult to design a system that will control a craft automatically in the same way that VOR will control a craft. Without automatic control the demands on the time of the crew might be too great.

3. HYPERBOLIC SYSTEMS

ELEMENTS

1. For a single hyperbolic position line (page 365, para 18) there must be two transmitters operating in synchronism. This is effected by making one transmitter the master station and

arranging for the transmissions from this master to control the transmissions of the second station, known as the slave.

2. One advantage of a hyperbolic system is that the accurate oscillator in the craft becomes unimportant. Provided that the receiver is adjusted either to the P.R.F. of the master station or to the wavelength of the modulation frequency of the master station, there will be a stable reference against which to measure the difference of distance. For example, if the system displays pulses on a cathode ray tube, and if the P.R.F. is adjusted until the blips from the master station are stationary, then the P.R.F. of the receiver will be geared to that of the master station.

3. Unfortunately, pulses or continuous waves from two ground transmitters will travel to the craft along two different paths which may have different ionospheric conditions. Hence, for long-range pulse systems depending on sky waves, the accuracy will be limited by ionospheric constancy over the area. This difficulty will not occur at higher frequencies but, since the master station will have to trigger off the slave by direct pulse transmissions, the distance between the two will have to be limited and the short base line will reduce the accuracy.

COVERAGE DIAGRAMS

4. For a fix, two position lines are needed. Hence a hyperbolic fix requires two time differences and these may be obtained from:

(a) Two master–slave pairs which may be either in line or at an angle to each other.
(b) 1 master and 2 slaves which may be either in line or forming an angle with the master in the centre. Such a configuration is known as a chain.

5. The accuracy of two–master-slave pairs in line is indicated by Fig. 226 and the accuracy of two master–slave pairs at an angle is indicated by Fig. 227. In the instance of one master and two slaves chain, the coverage diagrams are very similar. In practice, a hyperbolic chain will often consist of one master and three slaves symmetrically disposed to form what is known as a star

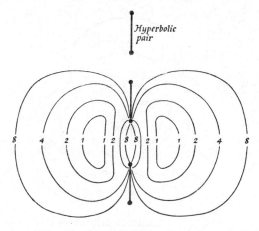

FIG. 226   Accuracy diagram of two hyperbolic
pairs in line

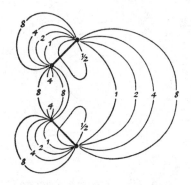

FIG. 227   Accuracy diagram of
two hyperbolic pairs angled

chain with a coverage diagram suggested by Fig. 228. Alternatively, the chain may comprise four stations in a square giving
great accuracy within the square as shown in Fig. 229
6. It will be noticed that, at long range, the lobes of all these
hyperbolic diagrams have two features in common:

(a) Accuracy decreases approximately logarithmically with
distance. Thus the interval between radical error contours

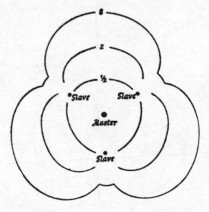

FIG. 228 Accuracy diagram of star
chain

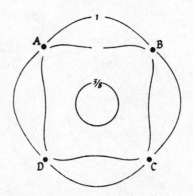

FIG. 229 Accuracy diagram of
square chain

of 1 and 2 approximately equals the interval between
radial error contours of 2 and 4.

(b) The contours approximate to arcs of circles passing
through the two extreme stations.

PLOTTING

7. A hyperbolic fixing system consists of an equipment for
measuring two or more sets of time differences which can be
applied directly to a chart on which are printed two or more sets

of hyperbolae annotated according to the time differences as shown in Fig. 230.

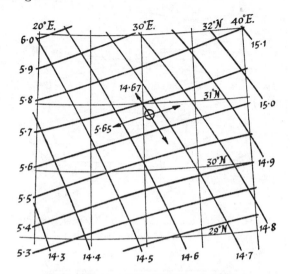

FIG. 230   Plotting a fix (14.67 and 5.65) on a
hyperbolic lattice

8. In order to avoid clutter on the chart, the hyperbolae are generally overprinted in colour, either red, green or purple, and the slaves of a star chain may be known as the red, green and purple slaves. In Fig. 231 the craft is shown at a point well away from the centre of the chain so that the hyperbolae cut at a fine angle. It is not easy to interpolate between the lines and, therefore, interpolation dots may be printed to increase the accuracy.

9. The pattern produced by sheafs of hyperbolae is known as a lattice. It would be possible to distort the hyperbolae until they became straight in which event the lines of latitude and longitude would become curved. This is known as an inverted lattice and is shown in Fig. 232. The main advantage of the inverted lattice appears if the hyperbolic chart is used only for finding positions in latitude and longitude, positions being subsequently transferred to the plotting chart. In that event, the exact point can be plotted easily and consistently. However, the inverted lattice

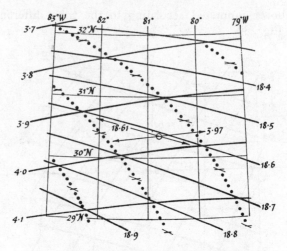

FIG. 231 Plotting a fix (18.61 and 3.97) at the edge
of a hyperbolic lattice

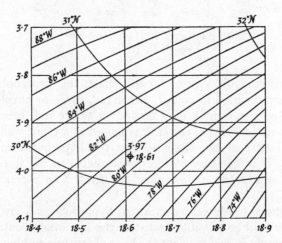

FIG. 232 Plotting a fix (18.61 and 3.97) on an
inverted lattice

distorts directions and shapes and may give false ideas of distances.
10. A hyperbolic system may be used to control a craft. The
time differences can be made to operate a left–right meter that
will control a craft to follow a certain hyperbola. Likewise, the

distance to destination may be measured in time differences and the rate of change can be converted to an E.T.A. However, it will often be inconvenient to follow a hyperbolic path over the surface of the Earth.

11. As a rule, the centre of a hyperbolic chain will be at a focal area towards which craft converge. Craft therefore tend to travel along the diagonals of hyperbolic lattices. The system can be made to read in terms of diagonals by subtracting the time differences of the two lattices and, by adding the time differences, a cross-track lattice may be generated. This may simplify the application of automatics to hyperbolic systems.

12. A chain comprising four stations, one in each corner of a square, has already been mentioned. If the hyperbolic pairs are arranged so that they comprise the opposite points of the square, the lattice produced is as shown in Fig. 233(a). However, by

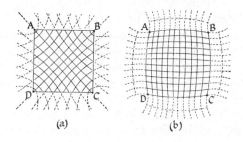

(a)　　　(b)

FIG. 233 'Square' hyperbolic lattices

adding and subtracting the time differences, a diagonal lattice can be derived. This diagonal lattice will give the convenient pattern shown in Fig. 233(b), which is almost rectangular.

13. A digital computer can convert hyperbolic time differences into latitudes and longitudes and thence into distances and bearings from known points. In the latter event, a hyperbolic system can be used to guide a craft along a chosen line, or to any point chosen as the destination. By this means hyperbolic systems, which are known generally as 'area' systems, can operate as flexible 'point' systems, the name generally given to rho–theta aids.

TYPES OF SYSTEM

14. As with distance measuring systems, hyperbolic radio aids are basically one of two types:

(a) *Pulse systems.*
(b) *CW systems.* The latter suffer from ambiguities which can be resolved by integrating the changes of time differences or by generating frequencies which are lower than the basic CW frequencies by factors so that a coarse pattern as well as a fine pattern of hyperbolae is produced.

It will transpire that, in practice, pulse systems may use methods similar to those of CW systems and CW systems may develop what are virtually pulses.

LORAN

15. Probably the most widely used pulse hyperbolic system is Loran. The original Loran (LOng RAnge Navigation) system, known as Standard Loran or Loran A, is an MF system, the frequency being chosen to take advantage of the height stability of the E layer. The chain comprises a number of master and slave pairs, each pair on a separate P.R.F. The receiver in the craft displays the pulses as blips on two horizontal traces of a cathode ray tube and, by a coarse adjustment of the equipment P.R.F., the blips of the selected pair may be made to stand relatively still, while blips from other pairs run to and fro. By a fine P.R.F. adjustment, the selected blips can be walked along the two traces until the master blip stands on its step on the left-hand edge of the upper trace. The step on the lower trace is then moved until the slave blip stands upon it as shown in Fig. 234(a).

16. The spot is sweeping across the face of the tube relatively slowly and the picture is said to be on slow sweep. To increase the accuracy of the measurement of time interval, the sections of the two traces represented by the steps can be taken out and stretched across the tube by causing the spot to move faster. The slave blip can then be shifted until it is below the master blip and the two blips walked across the screen until they are both at the left-hand edge of the medium fast sweep as shown in Fig. 234(b).

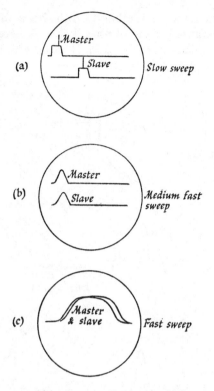

FIG. 234   Loran, alignment of blips

17. The accuracy can further be increased by switching in a fast sweep which not only stretches out the first parts of the two traces but also superimposes them as shown in Fig. 234(c). The slave blip is then moved until the leading edge fits the leading edge of the master. Calibration pips are switched in so that, on the fast sweep, 10-microsecond intervals can be measured, on the medium fast sweep, 50-microsecond intervals and on the slow sweep, 500-microsecond intervals. Thus the time interval can be measured in units, tens and hundreds of microseconds and a position line plotted on the appropriate lattice of the Loran chart.

18. The shapes of the blips are seldom as simple as suggested in Fig. 234. The long wavelength makes a sharp pulse impossible

owing to the extremely large band width that would be needed. Also, the appearances of the blips will change between daytime and darkness as shown in Fig. 235. The reflection from the *E*

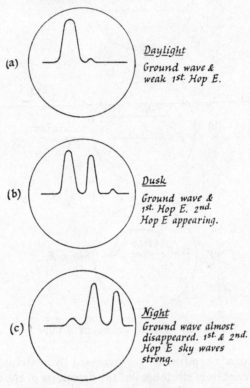

(a)   <u>Daylight</u>
Ground wave & weak 1st. Hop E.

(b)   <u>Dusk</u>
Ground wave & 1st. Hop E. 2nd. Hop E appearing.

(c)   <u>Night</u>
Ground wave almost disappeared. 1st. & 2nd. Hop E sky waves strong.

FIG. 235   Appearance of Loran blips

layer will grow stronger as darkness falls. To the normal reflection of the *E* layer, known as the first hop sky wave, will be added a second reflection caused by a double reflection off the *E* layer and a single reflection off the ground, known as a second hop sky wave. Also, waves reflected back from other layers in the ionosphere may appear.

19. The average range of the ground wave will be rather over 500 n. miles over the water but much less over the land. The ground waves will also be effective at longer ranges in arctic

regions than in equatorial regions where the noise level is high. When working on the ground wave, the fixing accuracy from a Loran chain may be 95 per cent within $\frac{1}{2}$ n. mile or $\frac{1}{4}$ n. mile for each 100 n. miles of distance of the craft from the centre of the baseline of the chain, the accuracy falling off as the line of shoot is left as suggested in Figs. 226–7 on page 521. The accuracy is dependent very much on the skill of the operator except at short ranges.

20. Outside the ground wave, reflections from the first E hop can be used and corrections may be provided on the lattice charts. Inevitably the accuracy falls off and will be 95 per cent between 1 per cent and $\frac{1}{2}$ per cent of the distance of the craft from the centre of the base line with even greater errors as the line of shoot is left. The increased error is due not only to the errors in corrections but also to difficulties in alignment of blips. Also, in the critical range of 500–700 n. miles, sky waves and ground waves may be confused and errors increased.

LORAN C

21. Loran C is an LF development of Standard Loran. The use of LF in place of MF allows for greater range on the reliable ground wave and for separation of the master and slave stations by around 800 n. miles instead of about 300 n. miles. The pulse shape is inevitably poor, but the sweeps are arranged so that the matching is accomplished not only by the overall shapes but also by the waves within these shapes.

22. Loran C receivers are arranged so that phase comparison between the actual waves is automatic. In addition, the phase of the waves may itself be switched according to a code and, by comparing with a generator within the receiver, it is possible to remove to a large extent the sky wave errors due to multiple reflections. The process is complicated because it takes perhaps 75 microseconds for the pulse to build up fully and the sky wave pulses will be coming in 30 microseconds after the initial pulse has started. Owing to the system of matching, automatic time difference measurement is possible so that the appropriate figures can be displayed on counters.

23. The range of Loran C is about 1500 n. miles by night and rather less by day. The accuracy, as a result of the matching

of the individual waves, can be extremely high, and under favourable conditions may be 95 per cent within a few n. miles along the line of shoot at 1000 n. miles from the base line. It is interesting to note that Loran C is half-way between the pulse and the CW hyperbolic systems.

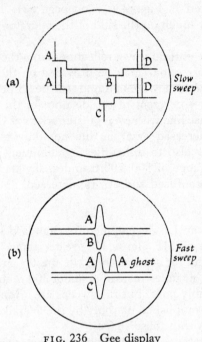

FIG. 236   Gee display

GEE

24. Gee was the first operational hyperbolic system. The system transmits on VHF with a master or *A* station and generally three slaves, *B*, *C* and *D* stations. The master station transmits alternatively a single and a double pulse, the single pulse triggering off the *B* slave and the double pulse the *C* slave while both pulses trigger off the *D* slave which itself uses a double pulse. The blips are walked along the two horizontal traces until the *A* pulse is settled on the step at the left-hand end with the single pulse on the upper trace. The steps are then moved to enclose the pulses which are then automatically turned upside down as shown in Fig. 236(a).

25. The fast sweep stretches out the pulses and arranges them so that the B and C (or D) pulses are below the A pulses as shown in Fig. 236(b). The pulses are then lined up and the calibration pips switched in. The distance between the A and B and the A and C blips is measured on a fine scale on the fast sweep and on a coarse scale on the slow sweep.

26. Gee can be used conveniently not only for finding position but also for homing. The calibration pips are set up according to the destination and the A blips settled on their steps. The craft is then manœuvred so that the B and C blips gradually converge on the A blip. When two of the blips coincide, the craft is steered to maintain this coincidence until the other two blips also coincide and destination is reached.

27. Gee is particularly suited to aircraft because it is not affected by sky waves and therefore fixing is simple, needs little skill and may only take a fraction of a minute. Later developments provide for automatic display of time differences so that the switching of calibration pips is not necessary. The range is short at sea-level, averaging a little over 150 n. miles depending on the siting, but at 20,000 feet it is generally over 300 n. miles. The separation of the stations has to be considerably less than 100 n. miles, and this limits the accuracy at long range. The 95 per cent error of a Gee fix may, however, be as little as $\frac{1}{4}$ n. mile close to the centre of the star chain and, at 300 n. miles, the accuracy on a 95 per cent basis is probably between 2 and 3 per cent of the distance. The reduced range at sea-level makes it essentially an aircraft aid, and the stations tend to be arranged to provide area coverage over land rather than maximum shoot over the sea.

DECCA

28. Decca is a CW system operating in the LF wave band. A master and red, green and purple slaves transmit different multiples of a 'basic' frequency. The Decca receiver has multipliers that convert these into three lowest common multiple 'comparison' frequencies as shown in Fig. 237, and the phase differences are displayed on phasemeters known as decometers. The red, green and purple decometer readings can be plotted directly on to coloured hyperbolae overprinted on a plotting chart.

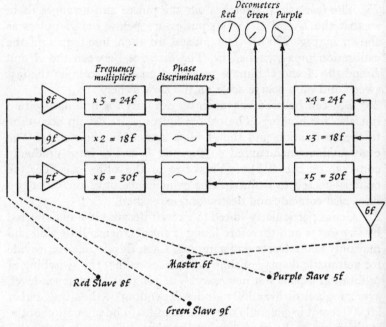

FIG. 237   Decca system (f = 'basic' frequency)

29. The main hyperbolae on the chart represent whole revolutions of the decometers and are separated by about $\frac{1}{4}$ mile along the base line between master and slave, spreading out as suggested in Fig. 163 on page 366. These hyperbolae are known as lanes, and the decometers therefore indicate intervals between lanes. A decometer can indicate a hundredth part of a lane so that the potential accuracy is extremely high. However, since a simple decometer can only measure position in a narrow lane, the ambiguity is also high.

30. In practice, the inner decometer pointer is geared to an outer 'lane pointer', as shown in Fig. 238(a), and the outer lane pointer is further geared to a 'zone' indicator which appears in a window and represents blocks of lanes. Zones and lanes will be marked on the chart. However, a craft could be unaware of its position within a lane on entering Decca coverage, or a temporary loss of signal could cause a lane to be skipped.

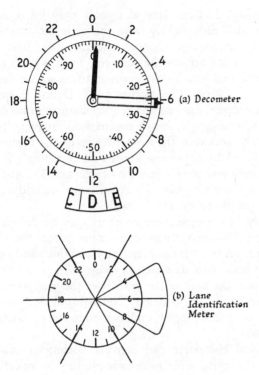

(a) Decometer

(b) Lane
Identification
Meter

FIG. 238   Decca presentation, red decometer
illustrated

31. *Lane identification.* Identification of the lane is provided by special frequency transmissions lasting $\frac{1}{2}$ second, the red lane identification occurring at the exact minute, and the green and purple lane identifications at 15-second intervals subsequently. Just prior to these transmissions, a frequency change from the master station switches the Decca receiver so that the special frequencies from the master and the particular slave can be compared and displayed by a lane identification meter. A six-armed pointer indicates the lane and a sector pointer reduces the ambiguity as shown in Fig. 238(b).

32. *Zone Identification.* At a basic frequency of 10 kc/s, a zone will be about 3 n. miles along a base line spreading out at long range (Fig. 163, page 366). If it is considered necessary to reduce

ambiguity still further, special signals may be transmitted at frequencies differing slightly from the main frequencies, so that comparison frequencies of only a fraction of the basic frequency may be generated within the receiver. By this means the zones may be parcelled into blocks and identified within the blocks.

33. *Airborne Decca*. The accuracy of Decca is higher than needed in aircraft, whereas the requirement to reduce ambiguity is greater. Accordingly, lower comparison frequencies are used which involves dividing the master frequency by 6, the ambiguity being removed by a process known as 'notching'. This widens the red, green and purple lanes by factors of 3, 2 and 6 so that, whereas on a marine chart the green lanes are widest, on an air chart the purple lanes will be widest.

34. *Display*. An inverted lattice chart may be driven on rollers and a pen simultaneously made to move across the chart either by signals from two decometers or by additions and subtractions of signals from two decometers (page 525, para 11). Thus the pen will trace the path of the craft over the ground although the map will naturally be distorted. This equipment as used at sea is known as the Track Plotter, and as used in the air is known as the Flight Log.

35. A digital computer can convert decometer readings into latitude and longitude for automatic plotting on an orthomorphic chart. Alternatively, the computer may provide distance and bearing from any selected point and also permit coupling to automatics. It is also worth noting that Decca chains have been developed to use a form of pulse technique to reduce sky-wave errors, an interesting example of the tendencies of CW and pulse systems to converge.

36. *Accuracy*. Close to the base line, the accuracy may be as high as 95 per cent within 100 yards. At 100 n. miles from the centre of a chain, the accuracy is probably 95 per cent less than 1 n. mile and less than $\frac{1}{2}$ n. mile along the line of shoot. The errors roughly double every additional 50 miles. At long range errors may be multiplied by 4 during twilight, by 8 at night or even by 12 during winter nights, and by day the errors may increase by a factor of 4 over broken terrain. A form of coastal refraction can also arise but corrections may be given on marine charts.

DECTRA

37. Dectra operates on a waveband similar to Decca and uses common units. It consists of two pairs of stations, one at each end of a route, each pair providing alternative tracking information. The master and slave of each pair transmit the same frequency but one is suppressed while the other is transmitting and the Dectra receiver is made to switch in synchronism. The waves from the master station control an oscillator in the receiver which remembers the master frequency and enables it to be compared with the frequency subsequently received from the slave. For along track information, the waves from each master station are compared on a phase discriminator and, in the event of the craft being unable to receive the far master station, a very stable oscillator may be used to remember it. The system is shown in Fig. 239.

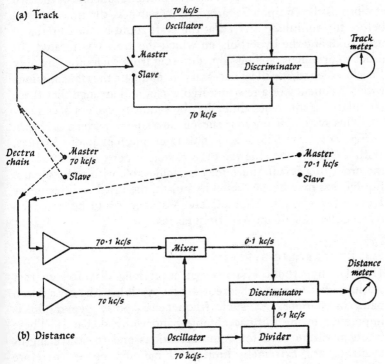

FIG. 239 Dectra system (frequency 70 and 70·1 used for illustration)

38. The accuracy of Dectra is naturally concentrated along the route between the two pairs of transmitters and the 95 per cent accuracy of a fix along a 2000-mile route should be of the order of 10 n. miles within 500 miles either side. Errors, particularly in ranging, can occur due to sky waves but can normally be detected by the inconsistency of the information compared to the dead-reckoning system of the craft.

RADIO-MESH

39. By selection of frequencies, it is possible to generate a moving pattern of hyperbolae. For example, if from a master and a slave, transmissions were radiated differing by 1 cycle a second, the coincidence of the crests of the waves, known as the equiphase, would shift completely across the sheaf of hyperbolae once a second. If a time signal were also transmitted from one of the two stations as the equiphase started on its journey, the time interval before the equiphase arrived at the craft could be measured and used to define the hyperbola on which the craft was located. In order to produce transmissions differing from each other by only 1 cycle a second, it will be necessary to modulate the transmissions with a frequency of a few hundred cycles and arrange that these modulated frequencies differ by the requisite cycle a second.

40. This system, using four stations in a square pattern as shown in Fig. 233, page 525, is known as radio-mesh or Radio-Mailles. With a 600-n. mile side for the square, 95 per cent accuracy of the order of a few n. miles may be achievable within the square. Equiphases may be generated by pulses, the P.R.F.s differing by 1 cycle per second. Alternatively, a system could be based on rectangular signals on MF frequencies.

VLF HYPERBOLIC SYSTEMS

41. VLF hyperbolic systems can cover long distances so that world-wide cover may theoretically be possible with only a dozen pairs of stations. At such frequencies, pulse generation is impossible owing to unacceptable band width demands. These frequencies are used for communications and the wavelengths available are extremely limited. Time sharing is therefore adopted.

42. A master may transmit a frequency which an oscillator in the craft remembers. The slave then transmits the same frequency which is compared with the frequency that the oscillator has remembered. The phase difference is used to generate a hyperbolic position line. The second master then transmits and is followed by the second slave and then by a third master and slave. The sequence of pairs is distinguished either by the transmissions being of different durations or by a special separate synchronizing transmission. The ambiguity arising from simple phase comparison is resolved by the master and slave pairs transmitting other frequencies in sequence.

43. *Omega*. Omega operates on a basic frequency of 10·2 kc/s and, as the phase meter completes 1 revolution for 180° of phase change, the interval between lanes on the 5000 n. mile base line is about 8 n. miles. Ambiguity is reduced by a second frequency on 13·6 kc/s. The 3·4 kc/s difference introduces coarse patterns separated by about 24 n. miles on the base line.

44. *Delrac*. Delrac uses three frequencies in the same waveband as Omega, each master transmitting three frequencies in succession followed by each slave, the differences in frequency between each successive frequency being in a constant proportion. This enables coarse patterns to be generated in two stages, the coarsest pattern being far coarser than the coarse Omega pattern. The arrangement permits the system to use some items of Decca equipment.

45. *Accuracy*. The accuracy of a VLF hyperbolic system is likely to be limited by propagation characteristics. On a worldwide basis, a 95 per cent accuracy of the order of 10 n. miles is unlikely to be achieved. It is worth noting that the use of VLF stations for distance measurement implies their use also for difference of distance measurement.

4. COLLAPSED HYPERBOLIC SYSTEMS

1. A hyperbolic chain could consist of a master and two slaves equally disposed along a straight line with the master as the central station. If the chain were to transmit waves in phase, the signals would be a minimum along the hyperbolae where

the differences in distance between the master and the slaves was half a wavelength and a maximum where the differences in distance was equal to a wavelength. It would, however, be necessary for the master to transmit waves as powerful as both the slaves. If the three stations were sited very close together, the pattern would be a collapsed hyperbolic system as shown in Fig. 164 on page 366.

CONSOL AND CONSOLAN

2. Consol is the international name for the German Sonne system. Each Consol 'beacon' consists of a collapsed hyperbolic system of three aerials sited in line. The aerials are separated by about three wavelengths, the frequency being at the MF end of the LF waveband. The three aerials of the beacon thus form a collapsed hyperbolic system with a polar diagram as shown in Fig. 240.

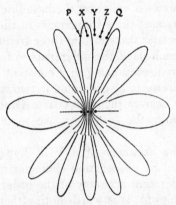

FIG. 240   Polar diagram of Consol

3. Suppose that the phases of the two outer slaves were switched by 180°. The maxima and minima would be interchanged. In a Consol beacon, this switch operates for $\frac{1}{8}$ second every $\frac{1}{2}$ second. Thus a craft at X would hear dashes of $\frac{3}{8}$ second followed by gaps of $\frac{1}{8}$ second, whereas a craft at Z would hear gaps of $\frac{3}{8}$ second and dots of $\frac{1}{8}$ second. A craft at Y would hear both signals equally as a steady note and would therefore be on an equisignal line.

4. In addition to the switching to achieve the dots and the dashes, the whole pattern of Fig. 240 is swung from one maximum to the next maximum by altering the phases of the outer slave transmissions at a rate of 180° in 30 seconds. Thus the point Y in the equidistant line would hear a total of 60 dashes as the pattern rotated. The point Z would hear a total of 30 dots gradually merging to the equidistant signal and then 30 dashes. The point X would hear the 30 dashes gradually merging to an equisignal and then to dots as the dots sector to the left swung across. The point P would, like Y, be on an equisignal line and would hear a total of 60 dots and so also would the point Q. Thus, by means of a simple aural radio receiver, the navigator can locate his bearing from the Consol beacon as being somewhere within a sector PQ, or in an adjacent sector.

5. In order to determine the sector, the navigator may need to take a D.F. bearing on the Consol station. To permit this, the slaves are shut down for 10 seconds at the end of the 30-second period, and the master transmits a steady note with a call sign for identification. The plotting of Consol bearings may be assisted by tables or special gnomonic Consol charts which have the sectors marked and the patterns of dots and dashes indicated.

6. Consol is particularly useful over the sea and the range is about 1000 miles. By day the range is less because only the ground wave is available, but by night the range is greater. In the tropics, the effective range is greatly reduced by noise, particularly at night. This reduction results from the difficulty in counting a pattern of dots and dashes against a background of atmospheric noise.

7. The accuracy of Consol depends on the direction of the craft compared to the line of sight, as suggested on page 369, para. 25, and as evident from the spacing of the zones in Fig. 240. Generally, the 95 per cent error may be less than 1° along the line of shoot, increasing to nearly 2° at the edges of the cover. At night, systematic errors occur due to the additional distances covered by the sky waves. These are at a maximum at the critical distance of about 400 n. miles from the beacon due to the mixture of ground wave and first hop sky waves. The distortion may be as much as 4° at 60° to the line of shoot, but will be much less along the line of shoot. The systematic errors drop to a fraction

of this maximum value at 200 n. miles and at 1200 n. miles. Random errors of a similar scale accompany these systematic errors.

8. Consol has great practical advantages. No equipment other than a normal radio receiver is required in the craft though a loop aerial may be necessary to discriminate between sectors. The main disadvantages are the masking of the signal by atmospheric noise and the relative inaccuracy at night away from the line of shoot.

9. *Consolan.* Consolan is a form of Consol that operates with only two aerials instead of three. The operation is similar to Consol but certain practical difficulties arise in the transmissions.

RADIO INTERFEROMETER

10. Fig. 241 shows a special type of collapsed hyperbolic system in which there are four aerials sited on a landing pad.

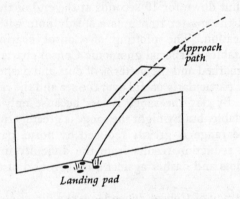

FIG. 241   Radio interferometer

The two nearer and the two further aerials may transmit together so that a centre line is established in the form of a plane of equisignals. The left-hand and right-hand aerials transmit with a time difference so that a hyperbolic surface is established at right angles to the azimuth plane. The aircraft may be guided down the intersection of the plane and the surface until very close to the ground, at which point the surface will become vertical. Such systems are suitable for landing and take-off guidance of VTOL aircraft such as helicopters.

5. SUMMARY

GENERAL

Radio reflections depend on shape and nature of objects and may vary very greatly with aspect.

Range varies as the fourth root of the power and the square root of the aerial gain for a simple echoing system.

PULSE DISTANCE MEASUREMENT

Characteristics:

(a) Short wavelengths are necessary to achieve a sharp pulse for accurate measurements of distance.

(b) Reflected returns not coming directly from objects arrive after the leading edges of the pulses and do not affect accuracy.

(c) Pulses can be coded for military security.

(d) Transponders may be used.

Limitations:

(a) Maximum range limited by P.R.F.

(b) Minimum range and discrimination between objects limited by pulse length.

Systems:

(a) UHF or centimetric radio pulse altimeter. Minimum ground clearance about 200 feet. Accuracy about 95 per cent within 400 feet.

(b) VHF Rebecca in aircraft with Eureka on ground. Used by military. Slant-range accuracy about 95 per cent within 2 per cent of distance.

(c) VHF-DME may be combined with VOR to form rho–theta system. Slant-range accuracy about 95 per cent within 1 per cent of distance.

(d) UHF-DMET may be combined with VOR to form rho-theta system (Vortac) or may form part of the UHF TACAN system. Slant-range accuracy 95 per cent within less than 1 per cent of distance.

(e) Oboe and Shoran long-range bombing systems. Accuracy 95 per cent within a few hundred yards where the cut is good.

CW DISTANCE MEASUREMENT

Characteristics:

   (a) Narrow band width.
   (b) Ambiguity. This may be resolved by:
      (i) Long wavelength or low frequency modulation.
      (ii) Modulation patterns superimposed on waves.
      (iii) Integration according to change of distance from a known starting distance.

Limitations:

   (a) No minimum range limitations.
   (b) Re-reflections cannot be separated out.
   (c) Transponder cannot be used.

Systems:

   (a) Radio altimeter. Accuracy 95 per cent within 2 per cent of height. Used for automatic landing.
   (b) VLF and Navarho distance measurement. Accuracy better than 10 n. miles on a 95 per cent basis for world-wide coverage. Technical difficulties exist.

HYPERBOLIC SYSTEMS

Characteristics: Similar to distance measurement systems but:

   (a) Requirement for accurate timing in craft is greatly reduced.
   (b) Errors arise due to signals travelling over different paths.

Coverage:

   (a) Two hyperbolic pairs or 1 master and 2 slaves in line produce a figure-of-eight coverage with lines of shoot at right angles to base line.
   (b) Two hyperbolic pairs or 1 master and 2 slaves arranged in a V produce a main circular lobe facing outwards from the mouth of the V.
   (c) A star chain produces lobes based on pairs of slaves.
   (d) A square chain produces an approximately rectangular lattice within the square.

HYPERBOLIC SYSTEMS, PULSE:

(a) Gee (VHF). Fixes up to 300 n. miles at height but only 100 n. miles at surface. Accuracy 95 per cent within a few n. miles at 100 n. miles.

(b) Standard Loran (MF). Position lines at about 500 n. miles. Accuracy depends on operator skill. Probably 95 per cent within a few n. miles at 500 n. miles along the line of shoot.

(c) Loran C (LF). Position lines at about 1000 n. miles. Accuracy in good conditions probably 95 per cent within a few n. miles at 1000 n. miles along the line of shoot.

HYPERBOLIC SYSTEMS, CW:

(a) Decca (MF). Very accurate fixing close to chain. Range several hundred miles. Accuracy lower at night but probably 95 per cent within 2 n. miles at 200 n. miles along the line of shoot.

(b) Dectra (MF). Two pairs of stations at ends of route of 2000 miles. Accuracy probably 95 per cent within 10 n. miles along the route.

(c) Omega and Delrac (LF). Range 1000 n. miles. Accuracy 95 per cent within about 10 n. miles.

(d) Radio-mesh. Accuracy 95 per cent within a few n. miles within a 600-n. mile square.

COLLAPSED HYPERBOLIC SYSTEMS

Consol and Consolan (MF). A collapsed hyperbolic system. Range about 1000 n. miles. Bearing accuracy 95 per cent within a few degrees.

CHAPTER XV

Radar and Sonar

1. RADAR PRINCIPLES

BASIC EQUIPMENT

1. The class of equipments covered by the word radar (RAdio, Direction And Range) has never been clearly defined. To the navigator the term generally implies a form of radio that measures distance and bearing simultaneously by means of a beamed transmission. The target may be a craft or an object on the land or on the water. If the equipment operates by means of echoes from a passive target, it may be known as primary radar. If the target cooperates by means of a transponder, the system may be known as secondary radar.

2. Fig. 242 shows the elements of a typical radar equipment. The oscillator controls the transmission of pulse signals to the magnetron, which generates the pulses and passes them to the

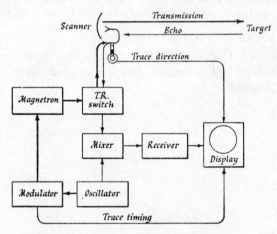

FIG. 242   Elements of radar equipment

transmit–receive switch and thence through a special joint to the rotating aerial, known sometimes as a scanner. The scanner may comprise a horn and a parabolic reflector or a device known as a slotted waveguide, both systems producing a narrow beam of waves.

3. The echoes from the target or the answering pulses from the transponder are received by the same aerial and pass through the joint to the T.R. switch. When the pulse has been transmitted, the switch will be set to receive, and the signals will pass to a mixer where they will be mixed with signals from an oscillator and fed through IF amplifiers and a detector to video amplifiers and hence to the display. At the same time, a signal from a synchro or similar device on the rotating aerial is passed to the display for directional information and a pulse signal from the modulator is also passed to the display in order to synchronize it with the pulse transmissions.

SCANNER

4. *Single-Plane Scanners.* A scanner may search in one of the following ways:

(a) *Horizon scan.* The beam sweeps round the horizon continuously at a scanning rate that may vary from several times a minute to less than 1 second.

(b) *Sector scan.* The beam sweeps to and fro across a sector of the horizon.

(c) *Elevation scan.* The beam sweeps up and down through an angle of elevation. This type of sector scan is sometimes called a nodding scan.

5. A scanner that rotates in one plane will be wide in that plane but may be narrow in the plane at right angles. The result will be a beam in the form of a narrow wedge as suggested in Fig. 243. The polar diagram will in practice be complicated and the narrow beam in one plane will be accompanied by side-lobes as shown in Fig. 244(a). The wide beam in the other plane will have similar side-lobes and, if it is propagated over the land, reflections will occur that will cause a complicated pattern of lobes as shown in Fig. 244(b).

36—P.N.

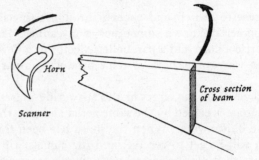

FIG. 243 Main beam of scanner

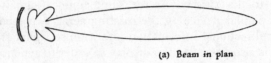

(a) Beam in plan

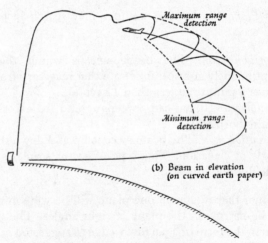

(b) Beam in elevation
(on curved earth paper)

FIG. 244 Polar diagrams of scanner

6. In Fig. 244(b), an aircraft is shown flying through the beam and it is evident that, at long range, it may only be detected intermittently. It happens that the number of lobes can be increased and dead spots reduced by shortening the wavelength

and increasing the height of the aerial. It will be noted that the minimum angle of the first lobe is quite considerable. This angle in degrees is roughly equal to:

$$(\text{wavelength (cm)})/(2 \times \text{scanner height (ft)})$$

Hence, a 50-cm scanner at 25 feet will have a minimum angle of elevation of 1° at long range.

7. *Two-plane Scanner.* A scanner may search an area rather than a line and may rotate in two planes simultaneously. For example:

(a) The scanner may move slowly over a sector and nod quickly so as to cover a volume of space and measure the direction of a target in elevation and in azimuth.

(b) The scanner may travel in a spiral pattern, starting at the centre of its field of view and working outwards. This is sometimes known as a conical scan.

8. A scanner that searches in two planes will generally be circular in shape and is popularly known as a dish. The dish will be mounted on gimbals with motors arranged to turn the dish and to nod it so that it follows the required pattern of search.

9. *Stabilization.* If a scanner is rotated on a mounting fixed to a craft, errors of two types will arise when the craft tilts:

(a) *Loss of target.* The failure of the beam to follow the correct path may cause it to miss a target unless the depth of the beam is sufficient.

(b) *Tilting error.* A tilting error will arise when directions are measured on an axis that is not vertical (page 41, para 19). For example, with a horizon scanner, a pitch or a roll of 20° will cause a 2° error in measurement of bearings at 45° to the fore and aft axis of the craft. If the scanner has to be tilted in elevation or dipped, the errors will be far greater.

10. A scanner on a craft can be stabilized in one of three ways:

(a) The axis of rotation can be mounted on a stabilized platform. This will remove all tilting errors and maintain a target in the beam. If the pitch of the craft is small, the scanner may be stabilized in roll only.

(b) The scanner may have a gimbal on the rotating axis to tilt the beam up or down so that it will always point in the correct direction. However, if the craft should tilt at right angles to the line of sight, the beam may move out of alignment if it is elevated or depressed. This can be avoided by adding another gimbal to correct the sideways or cross tilt. Nevertheless, because the axis of rotation itself is not stabilized, but follows the tilt of the craft, tilting errors in the measurement of bearings will persist even though the beam may be correctly aligned.

(c) If the scanner is intended to lock itself on to an individual target, it may be stabilized by a line of sight gyroscope which is aligned with its axis along the line of sight.

DISPLAY

11. Generally, a radar display consists of a cathode ray tube, the trace being driven according to the direction in which the scanner is 'looking'. As the pulse is transmitted, the trace starts to move along an appropriate line according to the direction of the scanner. Any echo received from a target is applied to the grid of the cathode ray tube so that a bright spot appears on the trace. At the end of its travel, the trace is blacked out and flies back to start the next trace when the next pulse is transmitted and to draw this new trace according to the new direction in which the scanner is now looking. The complete cycle or picture produced on the display is known as a 'paint'.

12. The screen is provided with 'afterglow' so that the trace and its signals persist for several paints though initially they die away quickly. In certain special cathode ray tubes known as storage tubes, it is possible to regulate the persistence of the afterglow by means of a wire mesh placed between the electron stream and the screen.

13. The traces generally follow one of five patterns:

(a) *P.P.I.* (Plan Position Indicator). The horizon scanner will be reproduced by traces, as shown in Fig. 245(a), so that presentation is in terms of distance and bearing. The centre of the traces need not be at the centre of the screen but may be offset.

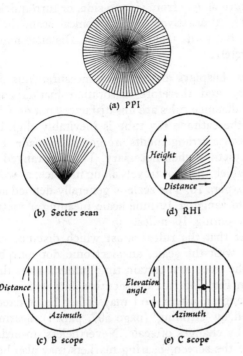

FIG. 245 Radar displays

(b) *Sector P.P.I.* The sector scan will be reproduced as shown in Fig. 245(b).

(c) B *Scope.* This is a sector P.P.I. with the origin stretched out into a horizontal line and all the traces running upwards. As a result, the horizontal scale is in azimuth and the vertical scale is in distance, as shown in Fig. 245 (c).

(d) *R.H.I.* (Range and Height Indicator). The nodding scan is reproduced by a sector in elevation. The horizontal scale is in distance but the vertical scale is invariably distorted to exaggerate height as shown in Fig. 245(d).

(e) C *Scope.* Direction in the horizontal plane is displayed horizontally and direction in the vertical plane vertically as shown in Fig. 245(e), thus providing a view as seen looking forwards. The aerial may nod up and down quickly and turn slowly from side to side, or turn quickly and nod slowly. Alternatively, with a conical scan, the trace may spiral outwards from the centre. Distance may be shown separately.

14. *Markers.* Displays are used for measurements of distances and bearings and therefore calibration markers are needed. Mechanical distance rules are unsatisfactory not only because the picture on the cathode ray tube is inevitably slightly distorted but also because arrangements are generally made to adjust the scale of the picture when necessary. This is arranged by altering the rate at which the spot travels along its trace, as was explained on page 526, para 16. The scale is generally defined according to its maximum range, a 10-mile scale meaning a picture with a radius representing 10 miles.

15. In order that the rule against which distance is measured can expand with the scale, an electronic dot may be made to appear on the trace at a certain time interval after the start. As suggested in Fig. 245, the consecutive dots will appear as lines known as range markers, and may either be at fixed distances or controlled by 'strobing' (page 507, para 4). Bearings will not be affected by changes of scale. Nevertheless, in order to avoid distortion of the screen, bearing markers may also be produced electronically.

P.P.I.

16. *Orientation.* The sector scan, R.H.I., *B* and *C* scopes will be oriented as shown in Fig. 245. A ground radar P.P.I. can be oriented in any convenient way. However, a P.P.I. in a craft may be oriented and driven in one of three ways:

(a) *Head upwards.* The relative orientation will show target directions as seen from the craft looking forwards. When heading is changed, the targets will move along arcs in the opposite direction.

(b) *Stabilized.* The directions of targets will not change if the craft changes heading. The motions of the targets will be relative and therefore stationary objects will appear to move backwards. Generally, the orientation will be north upwards or true.

(c) *True motion.* By applying signals according to the course and the speed to the deflecting system of the cathode ray tube, the centre of the traces may be made to move over the face of the P.P.I. as the craft moves over the surface of the Earth. Stationary objects will appear stationary and moving objects, including the craft itself, will appear to move with true motion.

17. The three types of P.P.I. display have important effects on afterglow. If an object is moving over the screen, previous paints will persist with an intensity that dies away according to time. These dying paints will appear as a tail to the object on the screen. The motion of the object will be indicated by the direction and the length of the tail.

The effect of tails on the three types of display will be as followers:

(a) *Head upwards.* If the craft alters heading or yaws, all the objects on the screen will travel in arcs which will persist and cause confusion. Long afterglow is not convenient with this orientation.

(b) *Stabilized.* The tails will show relative motion. This will give immediate warning of a target on a collision course. However, stationary objects will have tails astern and also the astern edges of large targets will be blurred by afterglow.

(c) *True motion.* The tails will show true motion and this will distinguish between the moving and the stationary object. A tail will also appear on the centre of the traces. The tails of moving craft will indicate the aspect of the craft but only very approximately and provided the craft is not altering heading at the time.

18. A compromise is a stabilized display with the course upwards instead of north upwards. If course or speed be altered, the display will behave as if it were centred on a ghost craft that is maintaining the original course and speed. This is mentioned on page 272, para 37, as the Calvert plot. Another suggestion is to use a true-motion display to show aspect but to orient it head upwards to give relative directions of targets. This will imply short afterglow (para 17(a)) unless the whole C.R.T. is rotated.

SPECIAL DISPLAYS

19. It is possible, by means of a rapid photographic process and a projector, to throw each paint on to a screen a few seconds after it has been completed. This allows for daylight viewing by a number of individuals and avoids the distraction of the moving trace and the complication of the initially rapid fade of the afterglow. The system also provides a permanent record. Each paint may be projected or, alternatively, the integrated picture may be projected from a few successive paints.

20. For certain applications, a craft may be fitted with a sideways-looking fixed beam, and the display may be in the form of a recorder printing on a strip of paper which travels on rollers according to the speed of the craft. The resulting picture will be permanent but will only show the area past which the craft has travelled and, if the craft alters course, the picture will become distorted, unless some form of stabilization is introduced.

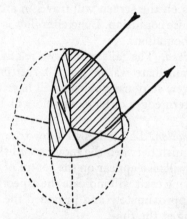

FIG. 246   Corner reflector

RETURNS

21. Radar echoes are produced by diffuse or scattered reflections from rough surfaces or by specular or direct reflections from smooth surfaces at appropriate angles. The corner reflector illustrated in Fig. 246 is an extreme example of specular reflection, and if the three planes are extended as suggested by the dotted lines, specular reflections will result irrespective of the direction

from which the radar waves are coming. Corner reflectors may be fitted to buoys and to small craft to ensure detection by marine radars.

22. The returns from various types of surface will vary as suggested in Fig. 247. From water there will be little diffuse

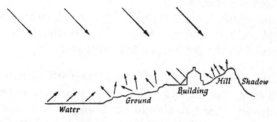

FIG. 247 Radar returns

reflection unless the sea is very rough and little specular reflection except at certain angles to waves. As a result, water will appear dark on the radar screen. There will, however, be diffuse reflections from land, which will therefore appear light, with perhaps some specular reflection from woods which may appear as lighter patches. Specular reflection will also occur from cliffs, and there will be shadows cast on the far sides of hills. Vertical walls and flat roads will produce strong specular reflections so that towns will appear as bright patches. The over-all effects are shown in Fig. 248, which is a photograph of a radar presentation in an aircraft.

23. At sea, ships and even buoys will show up as bright spots, and these may be seen in Fig. 249, which is a photograph of harbour radar. Icebergs will appear unless awash. Shore lines and cliffs will show up at long ranges, although low sand banks may be invisible.

24. There may also be returns on the radar screen which are difficult to identify. For example, parked vehicles are able to give exceptionally strong specular returns. In addition, storm clouds will appear as fuzzy patches, as shown in Fig. 250, the brightness depending on the size of the water droplets and therefore on the violence of the up-currents. However, clouds will only show well on the shorter centimetric wavelength.

DEFINITION
25. The sharpness and discrimination presented on the radar screen depends on two factors:

   (a) *Pulse length.* This determines the length along each trace for which brightness will persist when representing a point source of reflection.
   (b) *Beam width.* This determines the length of the arc that a single echo will form. If a beam is 1° wide, it may produce an echo in the form of an arc subtending 2°.

26. Although pulse length will not vary with distance, beam width will cause the arc of a single echo to increase linearly with distance. Ideally, the two should be arranged to be comparable at the normal operating range. However, beam width cannot be reduced beyond a certain point depending on range and scanner speed. For example, at 300 n. miles range, the time taken for a pulse to travel out and back is about 0·04 second. With a beam width of $\pm 0°1$, the scanning rate cannot be greater than $0°1/0·04$ sec. $= 25°$ a second without there being a danger of missing a target.

27. To achieve very narrow beam widths with small aerials and short pulse lengths, centimetric waves have to be used. The shorter the wavelength the greater the effect of rain and water absorption. The shorter the pulse, the wider the band width and therefore the more noise will be received and the worse the signal-to-noise ratio will become.

28. It is evident that discrimination, aerial size and range introduce conflicting requirements. The solutions to these requirements lie in the hands of the radio engineer, but it is important that the navigator should appreciate that an improvement in one aspect can lead to a degradation of performance in another direction.

CLUTTER
29. Near to a radar, even a small object will produce a return. The multiplicity of echoes at the centre of a P.P.I. causes a confusion known as clutter. This is particularly evident at sea where the reflections from the water will be a maximum at zero

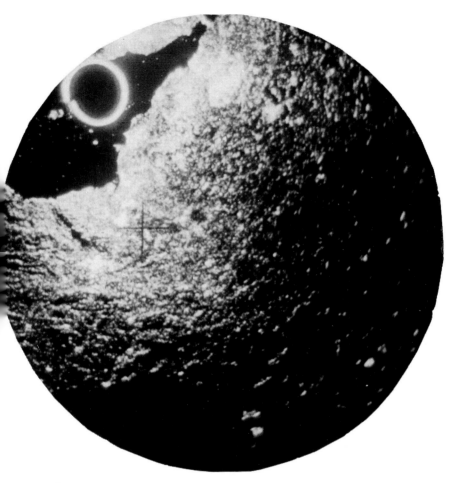

FIG. 248   Airborne radar photograph. PPI with centre offset showing
Bristol Channel. *Acknowledgments to A. & E.E., Boscombe Down*

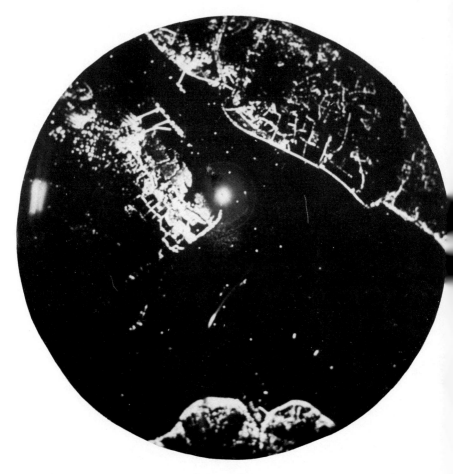

FIG. 249   Harbour radar photograph, showing the Queen Mary rounding
the West Bramble Buoy. *Acknowledgments to A.S.W.E. Portsdown*

range gradually diminishing outwards. A normal P.P.I. is probably fully brightened by a signal not many times stronger than the general noise background and, once this brightness is reached, no signal, even if many times as strong as the clutter, can appear.
30. The problem is tackled by arranging for the amplification or gain of the receiver to be very low as the trace starts and to increase as the trace moves towards the edge of the screen. This is known as swept gain or sensitivity time control. The rate at which the gain is increased is generally logarithmic and the facility may then be known as logarithmic gain control.
31. Clutter is also reduced by shortening the pulse. This will reduce the extent to which an unwanted echo will spread lengthwise along a trace. In addition, it may be possible to reduce clutter by discriminating between moving and stationary objects by means of a moving target indicator (page 574, para 8). Rain clutter may be reduced by circular polarization (page 477, para 22). Clutter from other radars is, however, not a problem. Differences of P.R.F. will cause echoes from other radars to travel up and down the traces and appear as sporadic spirals of dots.

SECONDARY RADAR

32. A radar transponder introduces certain problems. Unless the transponder transmits on a separate frequency, it must always appear on the P.P.I. whether it is wanted or not. Since the transponder may have to reply to many radars all on slightly differing frequencies, the transponder will have to sweep through the frequency band so that it will only appear on the P.P.I. at intervals. Since it may respond to reflections from the interrogating radar or to interrogations from other radars, a number of responses may be received when the aerial is not 'looking' directly towards the station. However, in practice, the bright direct echo can be distinguished.
33. If the transponder works on a separate frequency, it need only be switched in when needed and therefore the responses need not clutter up the P.P.I. when they are not wanted. This ability to switch to the transponder frequency means a complication in the receiver, and hence a radar system in a craft may not have this facility.

34. Radar transponders are generally one of two types:

(a) *Ramarks*. These produce a signal that appears as a line on the P.P.I. from the centre to the circumference and displays bearings unmistakably. It tends to clutter the centre of the screen in an area where immediate detection of a target may be important. This is not a serious objection when the Ramark operates on a separate frequency.

(b) *Racons*. These measure distances as well as bearings. They may be of several types:

(i) A short pulse transmitted as an echo to appear as a bright spot on the P.P.I.

(ii) A long pulse transmitted as an echo to appear on the P.P.I. as a line running outwards from the Racon.

(iii) A complete bearing line with a gap starting at the Racon. This causes clutter at the centre but can be used for Racons operating on a separate frequency.

35. The Racon cannot transmit a pulse instantaneously with the arrival of the radar interrogation. There must always be a time delay. This may have to be allowed for in measuring distances by Racons.

MULTIPLEXING

36. Radar equipments can be developed for time sharing. For example, the radar transmissions may carry messages either superimposed on the pulses or in the form of patterns of pulses or, alternatively, signals may be transmitted while the radar elements are quiescent. In particular, this form of time sharing may be developed by craft that carry responders, the transponders transmitting data such as identity, course and speed and, in the instance of aircraft, height.

37. The spot on the cathode ray tube will have an idle period after it has drawn a trace and returned to the origin ready for the next trace. During this period, it may be used to draw patterns on the screen such as centre lines of channels or airways. The spot may be made to form a ring round a certain target and even to follow this target by keeping the target central, thus recording

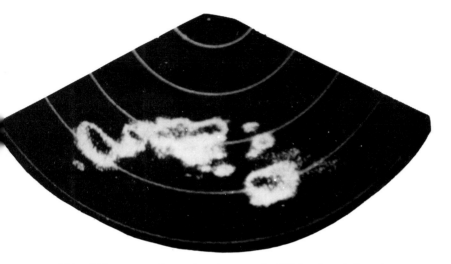

FIG. 250 Airborne weather radar photograph. *With acknowledgments to E. K. Cole Ltd*

the position of the ringed target continuously. Techniques which use the spot during idle time are known as interscan techniques.

2. RADAR AT SEA

MARINE RADAR

1. Marine radar is generally taken to mean radar fitted to merchant marine vessels. Horizon scanners are mounted to give an all-round view clear of obstructions. On 3 cm, a 6-foot-wide scanner gives a 1° beam width, the depth producing a 20° beam. Marine scanners are not stabilized and it is usual to allow for a roll of 20° without losing a target.

2. A 3-cm radar is generally used, which allows for a 0·1-microsecond pulse, and swept gain adjustment may be fitted to reduce clutter close to the centre of the traces. For reducing rain clutter, circular polarization may be used. A 10-cm radar will need a wider aerial for the same beam width but generally will be less affected by rain.

3. The P.P.I. will often be less than 1 foot in diameter, though larger screens may be used. The trace is generally bright enough to be seen in daylight, but the afterglow may decay too quickly unless a visor is fitted to cut out the daylight. With a visor, only one viewer at a time is practicable. Arrangements are made so that the speed of the sweep can be doubled or halved several times. By this means, the outer edge of the picture may be set to a scale of $\frac{3}{4}$, $1\frac{1}{2}$, 3, 6, 12, 24 or 48 n. miles or similar multiples of a basic range scale.

4. The inconveniences of a heading upwards display have been stressed in the previous section. The stabilized P.P.I. will maintain targets steady and will make it possible to take a bearing without simultaneously taking a reading of the compass. In many equipments, true motion can be switched in when required. Afterglow will indicate the velocity of a target and, on a medium-range scale, a tail may be distinguished when the target is moving at only a few knots, provided the craft is steady. If the speed of a target approaches 10 knots, the tail should indicate the direction of motion of the target. Special storage tubes may be used so that the persistence of the afterglow may be varied or the after-

glow from past paints may be switched in. However, only on very large ships close at hand can aspect be judged.

BEARING AND DISTANCE

5. Bearing may be measured by a rotating transparent protractor on the face of the screen which can register against a bearing scale fitted round the outside of the P.P.I. Such a device can introduce parallax, particularly on an object close to the centre of the tube. Also, on a true-motion display, alignment may be difficult even if the protractor is gridded. Therefore, an electronic marker may be fitted which may be set on to the target, the setting registering on a scale or on counters.

6. The errors of a radar measurement of bearing using a north upwards presentation on a steady craft will depend mainly on:

(a) The measurement of bearing on the P.P.I. This should have a 95 per cent error of much less than a degree.

(b) Instantaneous compass reading. Over a short period, the gyro compass may be accurate within 1°. However, an instantaneous reading may be in error by a greater amount and on 95 per cent of occasions may be between 1° and 2°.

(c) Synchronization of aerial with trace. The 95 per cent error should be well within 1°.

7. From these figures, it appears that the order of error of a radar bearing will be 95 per cent within 1° or 2° assuming a stabilized presentation and a reasonably steady craft. In rough weather, since the major errors in level are likely to be in roll, errors in bearings are likely to be most noticeable where the target is at 45° to the fore and aft line of the craft.

8. Unlike bearings, distance measurements are unaffected by the level of the craft or the type of presentation. Distance may be measured by means of fixed-range circles, but estimates of target distances may be considerably in error not only due to the finite width of the range circles but also because it will be difficult to maintain a mental estimate of the centre of an echo when a tail is present. Accuracy can be considerably increased by a variable range marker that can be set exactly on to the target and the distance read from a scale or from counters.

9. With a variable range marker, the main sources of error will be the sharpness of the echo, the experience of the operator in interpretation and the precision in timing of the radar equipment. In practice, the 95 per cent error is probably of the order of 2 per cent of distance. This is comparable to the bearing error and suggests that, on a target that can be identified, the 95 per cent radial error should be of the order of 3 per cent of the distance.

MEASUREMENT OF TARGET VELOCITIES

10. When successive bearings and distances are taken on a target to establish its velocity, the errors will be less than might be expected because certain compass and range errors will be semi-systematic. Probably over a 6-minute period, the error in change of range between two successive ranges will be of the order of $1\frac{1}{2}$ per cent and the error in change of bearing less than 1°. This represents an error in knots of about 15 per cent of the target range, both in terms of the along-track and across-track measurement of the target velocity. The error will be proportionally greater when taken over an interval of time shorter than 6 minutes.

Example. Two measurements of distance and bearing are taken at 6-minute intervals on a target at about 14 miles. The speed of the target is found to be 12 knots and its course 045T.

Error in target speed or course over 6 minutes is 15 per cent of 14 n. miles = 2 knots

$$\therefore \text{ speed of target } = 12 \pm 2 \text{ knots} = 10 - 14 \text{ knots}$$
$$\therefore \text{ course of target} = 045\text{T} \pm 60° \times 2 \text{ knots}/12 \text{ knots}$$
$$= 045\text{T} \pm 10°$$
$$= 035\text{T} - 055\text{T}$$

11. The figures derived from the previous paragraph will vary according to the steadiness of the craft and will be less accurate if the radar equipment consists only of a protractor with a heading upwards display and fixed-range circles. However, the figures show the difficulty in establishing on radar the exact course and speed of a target except at very close range. It also shows the uselessness of a small alteration of course as a means of indicating to another ship's radar that action has been taken.

PLOTTING

12. It was shown in Chapter VII that collision avoidance is a variation of the general navigational problem of choosing a course. The navigator will, therefore, wish to plot the progress of a target that may introduce a danger of collision. Plotting can be achieved by the transfer of distances and bearings to a chart, and this may be practicable where only one target is involved. However, when a number of targets are involved, it will be far quicker to plot on the display itself.

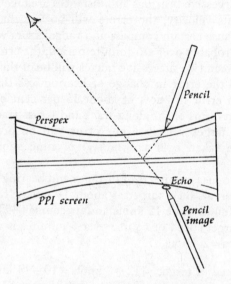

FIG. 251   Reflection plotter

13. The reflection plotter consists of a transparent perspex plate superimposed on the P.P.I. so that the navigator can plot directly from the echo by means of a suitable pencil. The transparent plate is made slightly concave to match the convexity of the face of the P.P.I., and a glass plate with the outer surface of a texture that will reflect about a fifth of the light is placed between as shown in Fig. 251. As a result, the point of the pencil can be made to appear to coincide with the echo on the P.P.I., and the position of a target can thus be plotted without any parallax error. By this means, the progress of a number of targets may be followed.

14. The rapid photographic process which enables the P.P.I. to be projected on to a screen is particularly convenient for plotting. The display has the advantage that several individuals can work together and, by exposing past portions of the film, automatic plotting is available.

15. Although marine radar is used essentially for collision avoidance, it is also a valuable position-finding aid. As with visual aids, there is a large amount of information that should assist positive identification but, unfortunately, the eye is apt to see what it expects. In this respect, a radar picture is even more deceptive than a visual picture since it is always necessary to interpret what is seen and there is no support in the form of colour.

16. To assist with identification, the navigator may use a Racon or a Ramark and these can also help with position finding. In their absence, the D.R. position will be the main support. Chart comparison units make it possible to superimpose the radar picture optically on the chart so that the position can be verified, but these are rarely provided. In any event, once position has been established with certainty, it should be possible to identify each new feature as it appears and so to 'thumb a way' along a coast line to destination.

17. It has been suggested that marine radar should be used with transponders on each craft so that each target would automatically pass course and speed signals and, possibly, identification signals. The advantages of such a system are manifest, but the difficulties in introduction are equally obvious. A craft fitting a responder confers little advantage on itself unless other craft are commonly fitted to take advantage of the transponder. A craft without a transponder suffers little disadvantage at any stage. Such a system would only be truly effective if signals could be exchanged between craft and, apart from the language difficulties, unilateral agreement on action between two craft could cause confusion in a crowded situation.

NAVAL RADAR

18. Everything that has been discussed in the context of marine radar applies to some degree to naval radar. However, radar used on a naval craft may have to detect not only targets on the surface but also aircraft. Hence the scanner may have to operate

in elevation and, unless stabilized, the bearing errors will be considerable.

19. The scanner may be stabilized by having the axis of rotation mounted on a stabilized platform, or it may use a rotating axis fixed to the craft with a means of elevating the beam and tilting the scanner in the event of rolling or pitching. In the latter event, a very simple device can be used to correct the bearing error, for example a universal joint. Although a universal joint may not be used as such, it does illustrate the relative simplicity of the correcting computer (see also missile radar, page 569, para 24).

HARBOUR RADAR

20. A harbour radar display is shown in Fig. 249. Harbour radar is used mainly for three purposes:

(a) To warn the harbour authority of the arrival of vessels at the entrance to the harbour.

(b) To supervise the flow of traffic and the movements of vessels within the confines of the harbour.

(c) To give navigational assistance to craft.

21. A harbour radar may be a modified marine radar on 3 cm or a specialized radar on 10 cm. Indeed, harbour radars vary greatly in characteristics. The siting should be high and not too close to the water so that the clutter close in can be avoided. To this end, the best site is probably inside a bend, since vessels will probably travel round the outside of the bend and the ground round the radar scanner will generally be fairly low.

22. It may be possible for one scanner to watch the whole harbour. Alternatively, in a large port, several radars may be required. The P.P.I. pictures from these radars may need to be transmitted to a central position where the pictures can all be displayed together. The central display may be scanned by television and the picture transmitted to receivers carried by the harbour pilots, so that each will have a picture of the area around his craft which is sharp and free from clutter.

23. The picture provided by the harbour radar and transmitted to the pilots may use interscan techniques for producing, on the P.P.I., lines to mark channels, leading lines, depth contours or

other information. Long afterglow may be useful since it will emphasize the moving vessels without any blurring of the permanent echoes.

24. A responder may be provided on a ship, to be switched on when demanded by the harbour radar. This will assist in the identification of a ship entering a busy port. The need for identification by a harbour authority is evident, since the authority will be concerned with the over-all pattern of the flow of traffic. It may, therefore, be necessary to issue advice to ships to follow courses that, as individual ships, they would not generally take.

25. When it is difficult to put a pilot on board a ship owing to the weather and yet the entrance to the harbour is sufficiently wide for the relative poorness of discrimination of the radar to be no serious disadvantage, it may be possible to assist a ship remotely by radar. This remote pilot system may give position reports to the master of a ship and advise him of special signals that he should make at certain points or of local regulations that can affect his actions.

3. RADAR AND AIRCRAFT

AIRWAYS RADAR

1. Long-range radar which will detect an aircraft at 200 miles may be used by air-traffic controllers. The wavelength may be 50 cm, partly to reduce rain clutter and also because, at the longer wavelengths, the maintenance of a steady frequency is easier. This is important for the reduction of ground echoes by means of a moving target indicator (M.T.I.) (page 574, para 8).

2. At 50 cm, the aerials may be 50 feet long and half as deep, giving a beam of perhaps 2° in azimuth and 5° in elevation. The rotation rate can be slow, since the radar will be used for intermittent position finding rather than for continuous control. The pulse length may be several microseconds, but this will not matter since aircraft will need to be kept well separated. The picture will be displayed on a P.P.I. with interscan markers and possibly with facilities for C.R.D.F.

3. For height finding, the requirement for accuracy will be

much greater. A 40-foot-high nodding scanner may give a beam width of $\frac{1}{2}°$ at 10 cm, the width of the scanner allowing for a reasonably wide azimuth spread of perhaps 4°. The display will be R.H.I. (page 549, para 13 (d)) and the equipment will be used to find the height of specific aircraft generally on request from the controllers, who will be watching the aircraft in plan on their P.P.I.s.

4. The accuracy of long-range radars may be increased by the use of multiple beams. The signal strength of a target is compared by two beams that bracket it in bearing or in elevation. By this means, it may be possible to measure directions to within one-tenth of the beam width. With an accuracy of this order, it may be possible to collect together the echoes from the multiple beams according to their elevation and range, so that aircraft within specific height bands may be separated out and displayed on separate P.P.I.s.

5. Airways radars are used for two purposes. Firstly, they provide information to the air-traffic controller that enables him to plan the orderly flow of air-traffic so as to maintain a safe separation. Secondly, they enable the air-traffic controller to provide navigational assistance on demand to aircraft who are uncertain of their position. In order to perform either of these functions, it is necessary for the radar to be able to identify each target as it appears on the P.P.I. at extreme range. This may be managed by a message passed from a previous radar or by means of the C.R.D.F. facility working on the aircraft transmitter. Otherwise, it may be necessary to request the aircraft to alter course temporarily in order that it may be identified.

6. As traffic increases, R.T. congestion increases and the need for secondary radar with transponders on aircraft increases. A transponder may be coded to give identity. It may also be coded to give course and speed automatically from the aircraft instruments and altitude from the pressure altimeter. This will be a more useful measure of height than true height found by radar (page 74, para 31).

7. Special arrangements may be made to provide long-range radar displays with automatic target-following facilities (page 556, para 41). These facilities may be used to track the individual aircraft and to feed this tracking information into the air-traffic

control system. Radar thus becomes the basic tool of the air-
traffic controller, which enables him to up-date the flight plans
previously provided by the aircraft at take-off.

AIRFIELD RADAR

8. An airfield radar assists in the control of aircraft taking off or
landing and also monitors the progress of overflying aircraft.
The radar will probably be 10 cm to provide the necessary
discrimination, and the presentation will be P.P.I. possibly with
interscan markers. The first task of the controller will be to
identify the individual targets. The information may be passed
to him by an airways radar. If not, he will have to identify targets
by C.R.D.F. or by requesting a manœuvre. The controller will
then arrange for the aircraft to orbit in a pre-arranged pattern
if it has to wait before landing. When the aircraft is free to land,
the controller will direct it to leave the orbit and may follow it
down towards the runway.

9. An airfield radar may be part of a GCA (ground control
approach) system. In this event, the task of the controller will be
to feed the aircraft into the field of view of the precision approach
radar (PAR) that will follow the aircraft during the approach to
land. An airfield radar used in this way is known as the surveillance radar element (SRE) of the GCA system.

10. The precision approach radar generally operates on 3 cm
and consists of a fast sector scan to follow the aircraft in plan and
a fast nodding scan to follow the aircraft in elevation. A common
radar transmitter and receiver will be used and switched from one
scanner to the other in quick succession, so that the target is
displayed simultaneously on a sector scan P.P.I. and on an R.H.I.
with interscan markings to show the centre line of the path down
to the end of the runway. The precision approach radar will be
extremely accurate with a beam width of the order of $\frac{1}{2}°$. However,
the delay inevitable in the transmission of verbal messages to the
pilot makes the system only suitable for guiding the aircraft down
to the point at which the pilot can see the runway and can land
visually.

11. The Bell system is an automatic lock-follow ground radar
which follows the aircraft down the approach path and computes
the action that it should take to maintain the correct glide path.

This information is signalled to the aircraft control system. Unfortunately, such systems cannot measure the aspect of the aircraft and, therefore, cannot direct the action of kicking off the drift or decrab.

12. *Flarescan.* Flarescan has already been mentioned (page 501, para 17) as a landing aid. It is in fact a combined landing aid and approach radar. Each scanner transmits for one-third of the time, and that is chosen to coincide with the centre of the swing from side to side or up and down. When a scanner is travelling in one direction, the system acts as a precision approach radar and when travelling in the other direction, the pulses are coded so that it acts as a landing aid. The remaining third of the time may be used for data transmission or DME. By means of DME, allowance can be made for the increasing sensitivity of the approach information as the aircraft closes with the ground transmitter.

13. For control of the aircraft on the ground, even finer definition is required than is needed for precision approach radar. Accordingly ASMI (airfield surface movement indicator) radar uses an 8-mm wavelength which, with a 6-foot scanner, can give a beam width of about $\frac{1}{3}°$ and, with a 0·05 microsecond pulse width, a discrimination of 10 yards in terms of distance. The picture will be displayed on a P.P.I. and normally will scan an area of about 1 mile radius. Such an equipment can detect vehicles and even men, except in heavy rain, when aircraft alone may be visible.

14. A radar may be devised to fulfil to some extent the four functions of surveillance, height-finding, precision approach and airfield surface movement, and a composite equipment of this type has been known as a quadradar. The equipment will inevitably be a compromise and may work on 3 cm with probably a half microsecond pulse. A simple P.P.I. presentation with a horizon scanner may be used. The distance of the aircraft from touchdown can be noted on a reflection plotter which can include a scale that enables this distance to be translated into a barometric height which should agree with the height on the pilot's altimeter provided he is on the correct glide path and his altimeter sub-scale setting is set to zero at the airfield itself.

WEATHER RADAR

15. Although any radar of less than 10 cm will detect rain clouds, special ground radars may be used for meteorological purposes. The frequency depends on the weather to be detected. Ten-centimetre radar will cut through light or medium rain to detect cyclones. Six-centimetre radar will cut through light rain to detect heavy rain and turbulence. Three-centimetre radar will detect light rain.

16. Weather radars may produce a plan of a storm system on a P.P.I. using a horizon scanner and may be provided with a height-finding scanner and an R.H.I. to show the storm pattern in elevation. An important feature of a weather radar is the ability to vary the gain of the receiver in discrete steps so that the regions of very heavy rain can be distinguished from the lighter rain. This ability to measure 'contours' may be assisted by an iso-echo presentation by which, when the strength from an echo exceeds a certain limit, the echo is inhibited. Thus a cloud with heavy rain in the centre will appear as a light patch on the screen with a dark centre, the width of the light surround being a measure of the gradualness of the build-up from light to heavy rain, and this is shown in Fig. 250.

17. The strength of an echoing signal will vary according to the fourth power of the distance. An object twice as far away will have only one-sixteenth of the signal strength. However, in the instance of weather radar, a storm cloud may be so large that it fills the whole of the radar beam. In that event, the strength of the signal received will vary according to the square of the distance.

18. *Airborne Weather Radar.* Many civil aircraft carry airborne weather radar. In order to be able to see a way through a gap between clouds, a 3-cm wavelength is desirable but, to penetrate light rain to see turbulent clouds ahead, a 5-cm wavelength is to be preferred. The scanner will take the form of a dish giving a beam narrow in elevation as well as in bearing so as to prevent the lower edges of the beam striking the ground too close to the aircraft and reducing the range at which clouds can be detected. For the same reason, it is important that the scanner be stabilized (page 561, para 19). Iso-echo presentations are used on the sector scan P.P.I. together with range scales as shown in Fig. 250.

19. The scanner may be tilted to look up at cloud tops or down on to the ground ahead. The beam may be given a downwards tilt so that at a certain range it will just detect a cloud top which is below the aircraft by a fixed amount considered by the operator of the aircraft to be the safe clearance. Any cloud appearing on the screen outside the chosen range circle will therefore be a possible source of danger but, unless it appears within the chosen circle as distance closes, it need not be avoided.

MILITARY AIRBORNE RADAR

20. Airborne radar is not fitted to civil aircraft for position-finding. Over the land, airways aids are available and, over the sea, position cannot be found. Airborne radar for 'looking' at the ground is therefore mainly a military equipment used for striking at a target through cloud or for detecting a craft on the surface of the sea.

21. Military mapping radar works in the centimetric band with a horizon scanner fitted in a radome generally under the fuselage sufficiently far aft to be in an area where the airflow is already disturbed. The scanner will be wide to give a beam narrow in plan and shallow to give a beam wide in elevation. The presentation will be a north upwards P.P.I., generally with true motion so that, by linking the motion of the P.P.I. with the motion of echoes from the ground, the course and ground speed may be measured directly. The equipment may be used as a bomb sight by setting electronic cursors on to the target and maintaining coincidence until the point is reached at which the weapon is released. Equipments of this type used for attack on land may be known as H_2S, or if used for maritime strike and reconnaissance, as A.S.V. (air-to-surface vessel). Fig. 248 shows a typical high-altitude radar picture.

22. Fighter aircraft may use an airborne interception (AI) radar with a dish fitted in the nose and a conical or a combined nod and turn scanner. The equipment may present the target on a C scope so that the fighter can be directed into the attack. A separate cathode ray tube may be used for distance measurement or the target may be made to sprout wings as the distance lessens.

23. Military airborne radar systems have used an aerial fitted in the leading edges of the wing which can be electrically

rotated through an angle and will produce an extremely narrow beam. Alternatively, a very narrow beam has been arranged by a sideways-looking radar with aerials in the sides of the craft, the echoes being recorded as explained on page 552, para 20.

MISSILE RADAR

24. Radar is used to guide defensive missiles. There are four main types of guidance:

   (a) *Command.* A radar follows the target and instructions are passed by a computer to the missile, as shown in Fig. 252(a). This is known as a passive system because the missile takes no action.

   (b) *Beam rider.* A radar follows the target and the beam is arranged so that a missile may be guided up it automatically, as shown in Fig. 252(b). This is also known as a passive system.

   (c) *Active.* The missile carries its own radar and homes itself on to its target, as shown in Fig. 252(c).

   (d) *Semi-active.* The target is floodlighted by a radar and the missile homes by means of a radar receiver, as shown in Fig. 252(d).

25. *Command Guidance.* A command system allows for the minimum complexity in the expendable missile and the maximum complexity in the ground, shipborne or airborne system. The main weakness is the number of frequencies involved and the danger of jamming or interference. Nevertheless, the command system has been used for guided bombs and for anti-ballistic-missile missiles (ABM) in which discrimination of the war-head against a background of decays may demand complex sensing devices and sophisticated computing.

26. *Beam Rider.* To guide the missile, up-down and left-right beams may be used so that the missile will be steered in Cartesian co-ordinates. Alternatively, the beam may rotate so that, if the missile is not centred, a signal will be received which will steer it in polar co-ordinates according to the phase. The beam will need to be narrow in two planes and is therefore known as a pencil beam. Just after launch, the missile error will be greatest

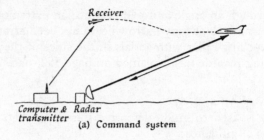

(a) Command system

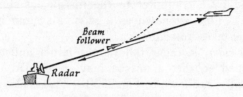

(b) Beam rider

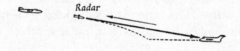

(c) Active system

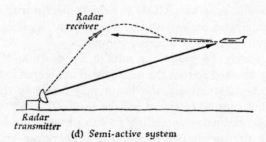

(d) Semi-active system

FIG. 252 Defensive missile guidance

while the beam will be narrowest. Hence, a wider gathering beam will also be needed to shepherd the beam rider into the narrow pencil beam.

27. The beam rider is a complex vehicle whose precision is reduced as the target is approached. When aimed from the surface at an attacking aircraft, it will start at a low trajectory and gradually increase its rate of climb, thus spending an undue time at a low height where the fuel consumption will be much higher. The beam rider has, however, two great advantages. First, because it is controlled from aft, it may be relatively unresponsive to enemy jamming from ahead. Secondly, it can, like the command missile, work close to the surface of the sea. For these two reasons, it is suitable as a naval defensive weapon. Airborne beam riders have also been used as air-to-air weapons.

28. *Active Guidance.* Active systems use lock and follow dishes (page 547, para 8). A line of sight gyro is used to stabilize the dish and is precessed to follow the dish. The rate at which it is precessed will be the rate of change of the line of sight to the target. By proportional navigation (page 256, para 17) the rate of change of line of sight is made to alter the line of flight of the missile.

29. The active missile needs considerable power for radar transmission and the transmitter is heavy and costly. Hence, the active missile is only used for very short ranges, for example for air-to-air missiles.

30. *Semi-active Guidance.* The semi-active missile can be used for much longer ranges as it can use a remote transmitter and needs only a receiver in the missile. The method of homing will be identical to that of the active missile. The missile will also receive the original radar transmissions so that it can be locked to the correct P.R.F. and can also be given some measure of the distance to the target.

31. *Offensive Missiles.* Radar has also been used to guide unmanned aircraft, the system being provided in the form of automatic map matching equipment which compares the radar picture with a photograph. Generally, inertial techniques are used for launching ballistic missiles, but when a launcher is used for space craft or satellites, and will not be subject to interference, it will be guided by radio and radar techniques.

4. DOPPLER

1. The principles of doppler were explained on page 220, para 1. In terms of radio, the basic doppler formula becomes:

doppler shift frequency (c/s)
= radio frequency (kc/s) × speed (knots)/160

As a result of this radio shift, the band width of a radio system that has to work with a moving craft must be increased by approximately:

(speed (knots)/3000) per cent of the radio frequency

2. It has already been explained that a doppler system works on reflections because it is impossible otherwise for the receiver to know the exact frequency that is being transmitted. For example, a space craft may have its frequency locked to a transmitter on the Earth and its transmissions may be received and compared with the original transmissions. This will enable the speed of the space craft relative to the particular station on the Earth to be measured. Since the speed of the space craft from the Earth and the speed of the Earth from the space craft are being measured simultaneously, a factor of two is introduced and the formula of para 1 becomes:

speed (knots)
= doppler shift frequency (c/s) × 80/radio frequency (kc/s)

DOPPLER RADAR

3. Possibly because all doppler systems that measure speed instantaneously have to use beamed transmissions, they are generally known as doppler 'radars'. It is obviously necessary to separate the received from the transmitted frequencies and, since the latter may leak into the receiver, the two will be separated either by transmitting a modulation of a certain frequency or by pulse transmissions. In the former instance, the received modulation signal will be of a phase differing from the transmitted signal according to the time interval taken for the signal to travel to the target and back. In the latter instance, a T.R. switch will disconnect the receiver while the transmitter is operating.

4. Both modulation frequency and pulse systems suffer from 'holes'. In the instance of a CW system, the receiver will not detect an echo when the time delay is an exact multiple of a whole cycle of the modulation frequency since there will then be no way in which to distinguish transmitted from received signals. Similarly, a pulse system cannot detect an echo received while the receiver is cut off for the transmission of a pulse. These holes will be particularly serious if the transmissions are fine pencil beams on small objects. They may be reduced by varying the frequency of the modulation or the P.R.F., for example by locking it to the doppler shift frequency.

5. The doppler shift may be measured by methods similar to those described on page 482, para 18. Alternatively, a device known as a phonic wheel may be used. This is a wheel with a number of teeth which are rotated to synchronize with the doppler shift frequency, any difference being fed to a motor that speeds up or slows down the phonic wheel. The wheel thus counts the doppler shifts and can be connected to a counter to display the integrated distance gone instead of the instantaneous speed. Phonic wheels may be used in airborne doppler equipments.

6. *Airborne Doppler*. The principles of airborne doppler have already been described (page 222, para 8). The equipment generally operates on 3-cm or $2\frac{1}{4}$-cm wavelength. The signals must be beamed and the amount of beaming depends on whether the aerials are rotated mechanically or not. If the aerials are fixed and the resultant doppler shifts are compared electronically, the beams will need to be relatively narrow, otherwise there may be an appreciable change of frequency from one side of the beam compared to the other. As a result, fixed aerials will need to be relatively large. However, in the instance of rotating aerials, the frequencies either side of the main line of the aerials are nulled one against the other so that the changes of frequency either side which may be caused by a wide beam will be cancelled out. Consequently the aerials may be smaller but, since they must be able to rotate, may take up considerable space. ACV doppler generally uses fixed aerials as explained on page 224, para 14.

7. Airborne doppler was first discovered by the manual rotation of a wide radar beam. The beam was sufficiently wide for a doppler beat frequency to develop unless it was pointed along

the course of the aircraft. The doppler beat frequency in such instances is perhaps best displayed on a cathode ray tube using an *A* scope.

8. *Moving Target Indicator*. It is possible by doppler to eliminate either moving objects picked up by the radar receiver or stationary objects. The latter are eliminated by the moving target indicator (MTI) which increases the returns from objects which have a doppler shift but reduces the returns of stationary objects with no doppler shift. By this means, it is possible to reduce the clutter from nearby ground objects and to emphasise moving objects such as aircraft.

NAVIGATION SATELLITES

9. It is impossible to measure instantaneous speed by doppler without beaming the transmissions, but it is possible to measure the speed and to find the closest approach distance by doppler readings over a period of time. The greater the change of note as a vehicle passes by, the faster the vehicle must be travelling. The more abrupt the change of note, the closer it must be passing by. The method has been used to measure satellite orbits. The main requirement for the system is an extremely stable oscillator within the radar so that the frequency will not shift over the period of observation.

10. *Transit*. Transit uses a converse system to that just mentioned. Four satellites circle the Earth at a height of about 600 miles transmitting very precisely controlled VHF or UHF C.W. The height chosen is outside serious deceleration by the Earth's atmosphere, but is low in order that the satellite shall travel fast. A fast travelling satellite will change its note faster and the requirement for stability of oscillators will thereby be reduced. At this height, an orbit will take 110 minutes, so that any craft on the surface will be on a line of sight to a satellite once every 110 minutes. However, if the satellite passes close overhead, a small error in distance will introduce a large error at right angles to the satellite path and, in the limit, may cause ambiguity. The craft may need to wait a further 110 minutes before it can obtain useful information.

11. The receiver in the craft measures the doppler frequency change by mixing the signal from the satellite with the signal

from a stable oscillator. The necessary order of stability can fortunately be achieved by a temperature controlled crystal. In practice, the crystal frequency is offset from the satellite frequency so that a continuous difference in frequency is registered as the satellite passes by and not a difference in frequency that becomes nil and then increases, which could introduce ambiguity.

12. The beat notes produced by comparing the satellite frequency and the oscillator frequency are counted and automatically printed every 2 minutes. At the same time, orbital information is printed which is transmitted by the satellite. The information is obtained from a memory within the satellite which is up-dated every 12 hours when the satellite passes over a transmitter on the the Earth known as an injection station. This injection station feeds new orbital information into the satellite as a result of doppler measurements from the ground.

13. The real problem then becomes apparent, the reduction of the information into a position. The process is extremely complex and, if only a simple mechanical calculator is available to the navigator it will take him upwards of an hour and more if he is not in practice. The reduction time can be reduced to negligible dimensions by the use of a sufficiently sophisticated computer. Unfortunately, this will hardly be available in small commercial vessels.

14. The accuracy of the Transit system will be affected by errors due to refraction of the ionosphere. It happens that this refraction depends on the frequency. Accordingly, each satellite transmits on two frequencies simultaneously and, if two receivers are fitted, they can record the differences, measure the refraction error and use this information to correct the signals. The same stable oscillator will serve both receivers but the mixing of the two signals will involve additional complexity.

15. With an oscillator stable to about 1 in 10^9 and using two frequencies to find the ionospheric refraction, a craft may be able to find its position on 95 per cent of occasions to within about 1 n. mile. Working on one frequency only, the error will probably be doubled. However, these accuracies can only be obtained if the speed of the craft is known precisely, the error depending on the speed error in knots. In a slow marine craft, it may be possible to measure speed accurately to within a

fraction of a knot, but with an aircraft this order of accuracy will be impossible. In any event, for air navigation the fixing interval of 100 minutes will be impracticably long.

DOPPLER POSITION LINES

16. *Doppler VOR*. If a transmitting dipole at a ground station be mounted on the end of an arm and be driven round in a circle, a doppler shift will occur when the aerial is moving towards or away from a craft. If the craft is north of the aerial, its receiver will pick up a sine wave pattern as shown in the upper part of Fig. 253. If the craft were east, the receiver would pick up a sine

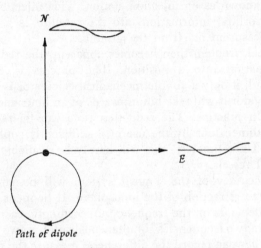

FIG. 253   Doppler VOR

wave pattern as shown in the right-hand side of Fig. 253. Thus the aerial travelling in a circle will set up an oscillation of doppler shift, the phase of the oscillation depending on the direction of the craft from the aerial.

17. The bearing recorded by the VOR receiver described in page 498, para 7, was measured according to the phase difference between a 30 c/s frequency modulation and a 30 c/s amplitude modulation, the latter coming from a fixed aerial. If the aerial travelling in a circle can be made to rotate at 30 revs per second,

the doppler shift will produce a 30 c/s frequency modulation, and if a fixed aerial is added to transmit a 30 c/s amplitude modulation, the station will act as a normal VOR and will give bearing information on a normal VOR receiver. However, it has been found that the use of an aerial travelling in a circle reduces siting errors by a large factor as compared to a normal VOR station.

18. In practice, the aerial will be driven in a circle electrically and not mechanically. In a typical installation fifty dipoles about 16 inches apart arranged in a large circle are fed sequentially in order to produce the equivalent of a single dipole travelling in a circle.

19. *Difference of Doppler Shifts.* Doppler shifts from aerials travelling in a circle can be applied in other ways. In particular, two such aerials can be used and the two doppler phase shifts compared. It is possible, by selecting the correct phase between the two aerials, to generate patterns along which the phase differences are constant and, in particular, to generate track guides along which there are no phase differences. These equiphases can be arranged so that divergences from the track guide appear not as expanding sheafs of lines, as with all bearing systems, but as parallel strips of lines, so that control of the craft is irrespective of distance from the stations, except close to the stations.

5. SONAR

1. Sound waves may be used to measure bearings and distances. Animals can distinguish the direction from which sound is coming by differences in reception in each ear. Similar lock-follow systems have been used for sound location of aircraft. Distances are measured by bats that squeak and sense the time for an echo to return. In marine navigation, an echo from a cliff has been used to measure distance in n. miles by timing with a stopwatch and dividing the number of seconds by 11. In the first world war, enemy gun positions were located by the time differences of sounds of firing picked up at listening posts and plotted as hyperbolae on charts. These are all examples of acoustic systems.

PRINCIPLES

2. The main use of sound waves is for underwater sound navigation and ranging, known as sonar. The problems are closely analogous to those of radar. The wavelengths used may be 3 cm, but the frequency will be around 50 kc/s since the speed of sound in water is about 5000 ft/s. The speed is slightly affected by density and salinity, but mainly by the temperature. Thermal gradients cause sound waves to be reflected and refracted and, below several thousand feet, sound ducts, comparable to radio ducts, cause anomalous propagation.

3. The range of sonar systems in theory varies inversely as the square of the distance except in a duct, and the echoes from a small target vary inversely as the fourth power of the distance. In practice, attenuation is a major limiting factor. In addition, the reception depends on the signal-to-noise ratio. The noise is from two sources:

(a) Thermal noise which increases with frequency and is serious above 100 kc/s.

(b) Wave noise depending on the height of the waves, which becomes increasingly serious below 10 kc/s.

4. *Transducers.* The essential element in a sonar system is the transducer which may transmit and detect sound waves. A transducer used only for detection is commonly known as a hydrophone. The power that a transducer can transmit in water is limited by cavitation (page 113, para 15(b)). Transducers are of four main types:

(a) Simple electro-magnetic devices similar to loudspeakers. These are only efficient at low frequencies, and at these frequencies wave noise is troublesome.

(b) Magneto-strictive devices which consist of magnetic cores, generally nickel, whose dimensions change in an electro-magnetic field. Below 10 kc/s, they tend to be heavy and, above 100 kc/s, eddy losses are great.

(c) Piezo-electric (quartz) crystals are generally more efficient than magneto-strictive devices and can handle comparable power.

(d) Electro-strictive devices are insulators, commonly ceramic, which are distorted when made to act as the dielectric material of a capacitor. The efficiency is generally less than that of a piezo-electric crystal, but ceramic transducers can operate over a wide frequency range.

5. *Passive Sonar*. A passive sonar device that listens to sound signals in water may be a complicated and subtle equipment. It may provide bearing information from a directional hydrophone. It may link up with other passive equipments to measure the time difference of the origin of underwater sounds. A chain of passive sonar devices may thus locate a source of underwater sound or movement. In particular, sonar devices suspended below floating buoys and known as sonobuoys are used to locate moving submarines.

6. *Active Sonar*. Active sonar systems are generally used primarily for measurement of distance and secondarily for measurement of bearing. There are two important classes of active systems:

(a) Echo sounders that measure the clearance of the hull of a craft above the sea bottom.

(b) Asdic that measures the direction and distance of an underwater target which may be a whale, a shoal of fish or a submarine.

ECHO SOUNDERS

7. An echo sounder or depth sounder is analogous to a radar pulse altimeter. The frequency may be between 10 and 50 kc/s using a magneto-strictive or piezo-electric transducer. The pulse may be as short as 1 millisecond, giving discrimination in water of a few feet. The transmissions may be beamed at an angle of 20° either side of the vertical in order that a moderate roll shall not cause the echo from directly below to be lost. A very wide beam can cause false readings if the bottom is shelving steeply.

8. The received pulse is displayed on a sheet of moving paper by means of a stylus which prints like the trace of a cathode ray tube but moves much more slowly and generally in an arc as shown in Fig. 254. The use of moving paper allows each trace to be correlated with the previous traces so that the depth of the water

may be read through noise. The record thus provided is also used to find positional information from the sea bottom and can give long-term longitude information from latitude found by marine inertial navigation systems.

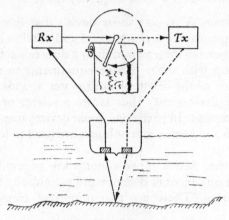

FIG. 254   Simple echo sounder

ASDIC

9. Early forms of Asdic were operated by a human observer who controlled a rotatable transducer which could 'look' in various directions. The pulses were produced in the form of an audible 'ping' and the operator listened to the echoes and, by rotating the hydrophones, identified the direction from which the echoes were coming. He could also assess speed from the doppler effect, and distance according to the time interval between the original 'ping' and the echo. He could use the hydrophones to listen to the noises of the propellers of another craft and so measure its direction. This discrimination of types of noise can be so subtle that a human operator may always be able to provide something that an automatic system can only produce with great difficulty.

10. It is possible to arrange for the received sonar pulses to be discriminated by means of a directional 'aerial' operated electronically to sweep very quickly from one angle to another. A series of hydrophones may be mounted in a line. An echo from directly below the craft would strike all hydrophones simultaneously and be made to record a target on the centre line of a B scope. An

echo to one side would strike the hydrophones with a successive delay and would record a series of signals not in phase. and this would appear as a trace to one side of the central line of the *B* scope.

11. An Asdic system may be aligned horizontally in order to detect fish, whales or submarines in any direction from the craft. In this way, the location of shore lines and of breakwaters can also be plotted. An Asdic system may be suspended below a floating buoy to detect submarines and may be known as an active sonobuoy.

SPECIAL APPLICATIONS

12. As with a radar system, sonar can be used to measure velocity by doppler. The system is similar to that of airborne doppler and will introduce identical problems. However, the attainment of high accuracy is more difficult owing to scattering and refraction. The system has been used in submarines as a velocity damper for inertial systems.

13. Hydrophones which are directional can also be used as lock-follow devices to track the sound of a target underwater. The system has been applied to acoustic homing torpedoes.

14. Underwater sonar beacons may be provided for navigational purposes and laid on the sea-bed to direct marine craft, as radio beacons on the surface of the Earth direct aircraft.

6. SUMMARY

RADAR EQUIPMENTS

Scanners. Scanners may rotate in plan to traverse the horizon or a sector of the horizon, or they may rotate in elevation. For target acquisition in two dimensions, they may rotate in plan and in elevation or may follow a spiral pattern.

A scanner may be stabilized in pitch and roll or in roll only. Alternatively, the scanner may be stabilized in elevation with cross tilt stabilization added if necessary. In a missile, a scanner may be stabilized by a line of sight gyro.

Clutter. Sea or ground clutter may be reduced by shortening the pulse, by swept gain control, and by a moving target indicator.

Rain clutter may be reduced by a longer wavelength or by circular polarization.

Displays. The radar picture may be presented in plan on a P.P.I. or a *B* scope. In elevation, an R.H.I. may be used or, for bearing and elevation, a *C* scope.

Distances and bearings may be measured by electronic distance and bearing markers. Additional information may be displayed by interscan techniques.

The P.P.I. in a craft may present information in various forms:

- (a) *Relative:* so that the craft appears at the centre. This will show relative motion and may be oriented:

    - (i) *Head upwards.* Targets will move as heading changes or craft yaws.
    - (ii) *Stabilized.* Targets will not move as heading changes or craft yaws. The presentation may be north upwards (or course upwards).

- (b) *True motion:* distinguishes stationary from moving targets by means of tails caused by afterglow.

TARGETS

In addition to simple targets such as ships and aircraft, radar will 'see' the following:

- (a) Towns as bright patches.
- (b) Ground as a light background with brighter patches for slopes facing the radar and with shadows behind. Woods may show up more brightly than level ground.
- (c) Water as dark areas except close to the radar and when there are waves of appreciable size.
- (d) Icebergs except when awash.
- (e) Rain clouds on short wavelengths unless circularly polarized.

The returns from targets can be intensified by:

- (a) Reflectors.
- (b) Transducers. Racons give ranges and bearings. Ramarks give bearings only.

MARINE RADAR

Ships use 3-cm unstabilized scanners with P.P.I. displays and afterglow. A reflection plotter or a rapid photographic process assists plotting.

Measurement of target velocity, even if electronic distance and bearing measurement is provided, is relatively inaccurate so that great care has to be taken in making assumptions regarding the course and speed of a target ship.

Harbour Radar. Harbour radar may supervise the flow of traffic and give navigational assistance generally in the form of positions and advice regarding local conditions. The picture may be televised and transmitted to pilots. Remote pilotage will generally be reserved for emergency when the ship has plenty of sea room.

AIRWAYS RADAR

The complete system may include:

(a) Airways radar on 50 cm with 10-cm height-finding radar. Used for long-range identification and control. Targets will be passed to:

(b) Surveillance element of a GCA at an airfield working on 10 cm. Targets will be followed and if necessary controlled until they have settled on the approach. They may then be passed to:

(c) Precision approach radar on 3 cm, which will follow each aircraft in plan and in elevation down towards the landing point and may give guidance instructions. After landing, the aircraft may be passed to:

(d) ASMI working on 8 mm for control of airfield including airfield vehicles.

WEATHER RADAR

Ground radar or airborne weather radar may be used to provide warning against storms. Iso-echo presentations show intensity contours. Airborne weather radar will be stabilized.

MILITARY RADAR

Naval shipborne radar may be stabilized and may direct beam rider missiles. Military ground radars on land can command missiles or provide floodlighting of targets for semi-active homing missiles. Military aircraft may carry radar for strike, reconnaissance, map reading and homing on to enemy aircraft.

DOPPLER

Doppler may be used for:

(a) Airborne speed measurement (and ACV speed measurement).
(b) Missile and space craft speed measurement from the ground.
(c) Position measurement from Transit.
(d) Moving target indicator to remove ground clutter.
(e) Doppler/VOR systems.

SONAR

Echo sounders measure the clearance of the hull above the bottom. Asdic measures the direction and distance of an underwater target.

The main limitations in sonar are noise and attenuation. Transmitted power is limited by cavitation.

BIBLIOGRAPHY:
ELECTRONIC AIDS

GENERAL

Attwood, S. S., see Burrows, C. R., and S. S. Attwood.

Bauss, W. (Editor), *Radio systems for aviation and maritime use*, Agardograph, 1963, Pergamon Press, London.

Burrows, C. R., and S. S. Attwood, *Radio wave propagation*, Academic Press, New York.

Clarricoats, J., *Radio Simplified*, Pitman, London.

Glazier, E. V. D., and H. R. L. Lamont, *The services text book of radio*, Vol. V, H.M.S.O.

Grover, J. H. H., *Radio aids to air navigation*, Heywood, London.

Hansford, R. F. (Editor), *Radio aids to civil aviation*, Heywood, London.

International Hydrographic Bureau, *Radio aids to maritime navigation and hydrography*, Monaco.

Lamont, H. R. L., see Glazier, E. V. D., and H. R. L. Lamont.

Sturley, K. R., *Radio receiver design*, Wiley, New York.

Terman, F. E., *Electronic and radio engineering*, McGraw-Hill, New York.

Thorne, T. G. (Editor), *Navigation systems for aircraft and space vehicles*, Agardograph, 1964, Pergamon Press, London.

DOPPLER

Beck, G. E., Airborne doppler equipment, *J. Inst. Navig.*, **11**, 117.

Clegg, J. E., and T. G. Thorne, Doppler navigation, *Proc. Instn Elect. Engrs*, 1958.

Clegg, J. E., Doppler navigation, *Navigation*, **1**, 5, Australian Inst. of Nav., Sydney.

Durst, C. S., The sea surface and doppler, *J. Inst. Navig.*, **11**, 143.

Grocott, D. F. H., Doppler correction for surface movement, *J. Inst. Navig.*, **15**, 220.

Kershner, R. B., and R. R. Newton, The transit system, *J. Inst. Navig.*, **15**, 129.

Newton, R. R., see Kershner, R. B., and R. R. Newton.

Thorne, T. G., see Clegg, J. E., and T. G. Thorne.

BEARING SYSTEMS

Anon., *Consol, an aid to navigation*, H.M.S.O.

Caporale, P., Present accuracy of VOR system, *Proceedings of the*

International Meeting of the Institutes of Navigation, Auschuss für Funkortung, Düsseldorf, May, 1961.

Cotter, C. H., *The principles and practice of radio D.F.*, Pitman, London.

Hauteville, T. V., *TACAN, TACAN-data-link and VORTAC*, Sonderbücherei der Funkortung, Düsseldorf.

Keen, R., *Wireless direction finding*, Iliffe & Sons, London.

Stansfield, R. G., Statistical theory of D.F. fixing, *J. Instn Elect. Engrs*, 1947.

HYPERBOLIC SYSTEMS

Dippy, R. J., Gee, a radio navigation aid, *J. Instn Elect. Engrs*, 1946.

Gaudillère, P., Un système de base pour la navigation aèrienne, Radio-Mailles, *Aéro-Electronique*, Dunod, Paris, 1955.

Hasegawa, K., Loran accuracy diagrams, *J. Inst. Navig.*, **12**, 153.

Hendrickson, H. T., *Loran-C system, accuracy and effective range*, Diskussionssitzung, Munich.

McKenzie, A. A., see Pierce, J. A.

O'Brien, W. J., Radio navigational aids, *J. Brit. Instn Rad. Engrs*, 1947.

Pierce, J. A., A. A. McKenzie, and R. H. Woodward, *Loran*, McGraw-Hill, New York.

Powell, C., Air and sea tests of the Dectra radio-navigation system, *J. Inst. Navig.*, **12**, 289.

Powell, C., The Decca navigation system for ship and aircraft use, *Proc. Instn Elect. Engrs*, 1958.

Powell, C., The use of VLF transmission for navigation, *J. Inst. Navig.*, **15**, 277.

Woodward, R. H., see Pierce, J. A.

RADAR

Alabaster, R. C., see Stride, P. L., and R. C. Alabaster.

Baker, C. H., *Man and radar displays*, Pergamon Press, London.

Burger, W., *Radar observers' handbook for Merchant Navy officers*, Brown, Son & Ferguson, Glasgow.

Hallows, R. W., *Radar simply explained*, Chapman & Hall, London.

Hugon, P., *Le Radar de navigation*, Société d'éditions Géographiques, Maritimes et Coloniales, Paris.

Institute of Navigation working group, Radar and the collision regulations, *J. Inst. Navig.*, **12**, 221.

Lang, D. G., *Marine Radar*, Pitman, London.

Le Page, L. S., and A. L. P. Milwright, Radar and ice, *J. Inst. Navig.*, **6**, 113.

Milwright, A. P. L., see Le Page, L. S., and A. P. L. Milwright.

M. I. T. Radar School Staff, *Principles of radar*, McGraw-Hill, New York.

Moorcroft, G. J., Precision approach radar, *Proc. Instn Elect. Engrs*, 1958.

Povejsil, D. J., R. S. Raven, and P. J. Waterman, *Airborne radar*, Van Nostrand, New York.

Radiophysics Laboratory staff, C.S.I.R.O. Australia (Ed. E. G. Bossen), *A text-book of radar*, Cambridge University Press.

Raven, R. S., see Povejsil, D. J.

Ridenour, L. N., *Radar system engineering*, McGraw-Hill, New York.

Robb, E. M., *The application of radar to seamanship and marine navigation*, Birchall, London.

Roberts, A. (Editor), *Radar beacons*, McGraw-Hill, New York.

Skolnik, M. I., *Introduction to radar systems*, McGraw-Hill, New York.

Sonnenburg, G. J., *Radar and electronic navigation*, Newnes, London.

Stride, P. L., and R. C. Alabaster, Airborne Weather Radar, *J. Inst. Navig.*, **15**, 415.

U.S. Hydrographic Office, *Radar plotting manual*, H.O.

Van Valkenburg, Nooger and Neville, *Basic radar*, Brolet Press, New York.

Waterman, P. J., see Povejsil, D. J.

Woodward, P. M., *Probability and information theory with applications to radar*, Pergamon Press, London.

Wylie, F. J., Fifteen years of marine radar, *J. Inst. Navig.*, **13**, 419.

Wylie, F. J., Marine radars for large ships, *J. Inst. Navig.*, **14**, 402.

Wylie, F. J., Radar and sea sense, *J. Inst. Navig.*, **8**, 45.

Wylie, F. J. (Editor), *The use of radar at sea*, Hollis and Carter, London.

SONAR

Dunn, J. R., see Howson, E. A., and J. R. Dunn.

Galway, H., *Echo sounding at sea*, Pitman, London.

Horton, J. W., *Fundamentals of Sonar*, U.S. Naval Institute, Annapolis, Maryland.

Howson, E. A., and J. R. Dunn, Directional echo sounding, *J. Inst. Navig.*, **14**, 348.

Rand, G., Sonar and the fourth dimension, *Navigation, U.S.A.*, **6**, 203.

Sonnenburg, G. J., *Radar and electronic navigation*, Newnes, London.

PART SIX

CONCLUSION

CHAPTER XVI. MAN AND MACHINE. The chapter deals with the relationship of the navigator to the equipment that is used for navigating. From an examination of the various stages of automation, the case for human captaincy of the craft emerges, except in special instances in which the craft has no human cargo or the conditions are such that action is beyond human capability. In the course of the chapter, there are brief descriptions of the lines of development of automatic equipment in the marine field, in aircraft and in air-traffic control organizations. The bibliography includes a general navigational bibliography.

SUMMARIES. The summaries consist of lists of equipments and of techniques used by certain types of craft and typical navigational installations. All the information is indexed so that the various items can be traced in the previous parts of the book.

INDEX. The index is planned to act also as a glossary by the inclusion of as many navigational terms as possible. Specific items which appear in several chapters are linked together. The index is preceded by a list of contractions and abbreviations and a few common symbols which are used in the book and may appear in navigational publications generally.

CONTENTS

CHAPTER XVI

Man and Machine

A craft may be controlled in three ways:

(a) *Direct control* by a man within the craft who is present in space and time.

(b) *Remote control* by a man controlling the craft from a distance so that he is present in time but not in space.

(c) *Automatic control* by engineers who may design the equipment many years previously and may work far from the operational area of the craft and in a very different environment. The engineers will be present neither in space nor in time.

1. DIRECT CONTROL

THE MAN

1. Man is at his best when his tasks demand judgment, integrated thought and adaptability. To make these demands meaningful, it is essential that he be given a considerable degree of responsibility. It is inevitable that direct control of a craft may have to be relinquished temporarily. The master or captain may have to follow the instructions of a remote controller better able to assess the over-all situation; he may recognize that his automatics give his craft a potentiality beyond his capabilities. Nevertheless, although the master or captain of a craft will fail at his peril to take full advantage of his equipment, he must retain final authority if his sense of responsibility is not to be impaired.

2. Although man is remarkably reliable, he does make mistakes and these mistakes tend to be quite unpredictable, so that a second man will tend to detect them, and even the originator

will generally recognize the mistake when it is brought to his attention. The support of the human by a second human is therefore a recognized practice in all civil carriers both marine and air except for very short journeys.

3. The use of two men implies a measure of democracy. Accidents have occurred because the master of a ship or the captain of an aircraft has been unwilling to recognize an error pointed out by the mate or the co-pilot. Perhaps the ideal system is for the second-in-command to take the maximum of executive action and for the captain to monitor him. This system will at least train future captains.

4. Unfortunately, man tends to be a poor monitor. To monitor, it is necessary to have a parallel source of information. The accumulation of information against the unlikely chance of it being needed is unrewarding. Furthermore, if the main source of action should break down, the man who is monitoring may be out of practice just when skill of the highest order is needed to enable him to take over.

5. In performing a control task, a man tends to act like a self-adaptive system, sampling his actions and correcting them extremely quickly and accurately. This extraordinary adaptability means that he can cope under extraordinary conditions. However, it also means that he tends to be relatively inconsistent when the action demands extreme nicety of control.

6. *Training*. When controlling a craft, a man may act contrary to the senses that serve him well when walking about the Earth. Accelerations produce deceptive signals in his semicircular canals and the world glimpsed through a small window may not react to his control as he expects. In addition there are problems of co-ordination, problems which can be overcome by practice on simulators as an alternative to more expensive practice on the craft itself. As a result of these problems, the period of training needed to control a craft may be long, and constant practice may be essential if the standard of control is to be maintained.

7. The problems of training in position-finding are different. The senses used in walking are not applied. The navigator acts consecutively; he takes a fix, he looks at his watch, he notes the time. Hence positional navigation can be taught piecemeal without expensive simulation, and the main value of practical

experience is to give confidence. Once positional navigation has been learnt, only a small amount of familiarization will be necessary for a navigator who is out of practice to continue at the standard at which he left off. It also seems likely that there is a correlation between the ability to navigate and the intelligence quotient. Certainly, individuals show considerable ability even during the early stages of training.

8. The navigation of the craft is generally undertaken in three areas, though in many craft two or more of these areas may be combined:

(a) Navigator's station provides positional and steering information.
(b) Radar operator's station provides information for the avoidance of collision.
(c) Helmsman's and pilot's instrumentation is used for steering control.

NAVIGATOR'S STATION

9. It is general for the man engaged in the business of finding the way to be known as the navigator even though he may not be the captain of the craft and therefore not responsible for the navigation as a whole. In a ship, he will be stationed either at a console on the bridge or in a separate compartment with ready access to the bridge. In a military aircraft of sufficient size, a station will be provided for him on the flight deck generally close to the captain, but in a civil aircraft operating along airways, a navigator's station is seldom provided since aircraft operate on track guides.

10. The navigator's instruments are generally mounted on an upright panel at the back of the chart table or plotting table. The displays may be at eye-level with controls below and switches above. To achieve this convenient arrangement, it is necessary to sacrifice a good view outside. Indeed it is common for the navigator's station to have no provision for look-out apart from a small window for psychological reasons.

11. The navigator's displays will include position-finding equipment and instruments that give information in the vertical plane. Heading and speed will be required for dead reckoning.

Dead reckoning itself may be assisted by automatic plotters or read-outs of position, particularly in military craft that may have to manœuvre continuously. The only aid that may not be operated from the navigator's station is astro. On a ship, there will not be an adequate view of the sky and the horizon. In the air, the navigator's seat is seldom sufficiently close to the skin at the top of the fuselage for him to be able to take an observation without moving.

12. A number of documents and books, such as astro-navigation tables, will be needed by the navigator, and these will have to be stowed handy. In large ships, weather facsimile charts may be reproduced automatically to assist navigation and will generally be sited close to the navigator's chart table.

RADAR OPERATOR'S STATION

13. The radar operator's station will vary according to the type of equipment provided. If the radar has a normal type of screen, it may be necessary for the operator to work in a special light. On the other hand, if a visor is acceptable or a rapid photographic process is provided, the radar display can be alongside the navigator's chart table.

14. At sea, the radar operator may be provided with two radar displays, one display being north upwards with the craft at the centre so that relative motions of targets may be displayed by tails, and the other display being true motion so that true motion will be displayed by tails, and stationary objects such as buoys may be more easily distinguished. In civil airways operations, the collision avoidance radar operator is part of the air-traffic control organization. In large aircraft, weather radar may be fitted between the two pilots' positions for avoidance of bad weather. Military aircraft, however, may have a full-time radar operator's station.

HELMSMAN'S INSTRUMENTATION

15. The helmsman on the bridge may be provided with any or all of the following:

(a) Compass or compass repeater, generally supported by a stand-by magnetic compass. Some means of setting the course that it is desired to steer may also be provided.

(b) Rudder angle indicator, which will show the amount of helm carried on a steady heading.

(c) Rate of turn indicator, that will indicate the start of a yaw and is also useful in river navigation where a steady known rate of turn may be necessary to negotiate a bend.

(d) Speed indications, to assist the helmsman to judge how his craft will answer to the helm. A log repeater or an engine revolution meter or both may be fitted.

(e) Failure warning. An off-course warning may be provided, particularly when an automatic helmsman is engaged.

(f) Autohelmsman switches.

(g) Means of intercommunication with other parts of the craft. This is particularly important when the helmsman's position is being used for berthing.

16. The instruments need to be mounted without obstructing a clear view ahead and to each side. The instruments may be mounted on a binnacle or fitted close to the roof, since the requirement for the helmsman will be a clear view of the horizon.

FLIGHT CONTROL SYSTEM

17. The flight control system of an aircraft includes the basic flight instruments and the autopilot with autostabilizers and auto-throttle added if required to assist the pilot. The flight instruments will be used not only to enable the pilot to fly the aircraft but also to monitor the autopilot. To achieve this, a considerable measure of duplication of inputs is implied.

18. Many aircraft carry two pilots. There must therefore be duplication of flight instruments. This duplication is generally supported by duplication of navigation receivers, of compasses, of sensors such as vertical references, and of power supplies, much of the duplication being mandatory for carriers operating along airways. The autopilot can be fitted into this system in several ways, of which two are common:

(a) *Split cockpit*. The two sides of the cockpit are completely independent and the autopilot is operated from the co-pilot's side so that the captain can monitor the operation and can take over if the co-pilot's instruments fail.

(b) *Integrated flight system.* The autopilot is given a degree of independence of the flight instruments. Commonly the two attitude directors are operated in parallel so that the captain can monitor the co-pilot's flying as well as the autopilot. However, he cannot use his own instruments if the co-pilot's instruments fail.

19. In all flight-control systems, there is a conflict between flexibility and simplicity. A simple system suffers because any breakdown must lead to a considerable loss of facilities. A flexible system with switching can mitigate the effects of a breakdown but the switching complicates the pilot's panels and introduces additional possibilities of human error, although systems of interlocks may inhibit certain switching blunders.

20. Flight-control systems are provided with various warning devices. There may be a central warning panel and, in addition, individual instruments will have their own warning flags, which are small labels made to appear on the faces of the instruments. As in all warning systems, even the most elaborate system may be ignored during intense concentration. Indeed, pilots have landed aircraft with wheels up in spite of the blowing of warning horns. In addition stand-by instruments will be provided which can also act as umpires if there is a gross disagreement between the main instruments.

21. *Flight Instrument System.* The attitude director is the basic pilot's instrument and is mounted in the centre of the instrument panel just below the coaming with the flight compass below (see Fig 169, page 373). To the left of the attitude director, and also just under the coaming, the air-speed indicator will be installed, and to the right just under the coaming the altimeter. These four instruments are thus arranged in a T which is known as the basic T. Often a machmeter in high-speed aircraft or an RMI in low-speed aircraft will be mounted below the air-speed indicator and a vertical-speed indicator below the altimeter.

22. The engine instruments are generally sited on the panel between the two pilots. The autopilot controls and other switches are often mounted on a pedestal between the two pilot's seats. In the roof above the pilots, radio switches and tuning controls are commonly arranged.

23. In general, the left-hand seat will be occupied by the captain of the aircraft with the co-pilot in the right-hand seat. The co-pilot is sometimes known as a second pilot and sometimes as a first officer, but confusion can arise if either of these terms has a special meaning in any particular airline. The exception to the rule of the captain in the left-hand seat is to be found in helicopters which are normally operated from the right-hand seat. The helicopter is basically unstable and often requires the simultaneous operation of two separate controls so that the crucial attitude control is exercised by the right hand and the less crucial common throttle control by the left hand.

2. REMOTE CONTROL

1. Remote control by a human agency depends on communications. For accuracy, communications must either cover a wide band width or be transmitted slowly. For control purposes, information has to be immediate and therefore the limitations of the radio spectrum make it necessary to restrict remote control by the human operator to positional or steering information. Control will be exercised either automatically or by a human helmsman or pilot.

2. The exception to this rule is the field-of-battle wire-guided missile in which the signals are channelled down wire. In other missiles, positional information is provided by a radio beam but the missile steers and control itself. More generally, the positional information is not provided by a human agency but is automatic so that the complete system can best be regarded as a fully automatic equipment. Space navigation systems are automatically controlled in this way and so are anti-ballistic-missile missiles.

3. The problems of handling a ship have already been described (page 125, para 1). It is evident that the number of interacting parameters is so large that not even steering information can be passed remotely. All that can be managed is positional information which has to be interpreted by the navigator of the ship into steering instructions for the helmsman. The aircraft, on the

other hand, because it is operating in one medium only, may be given steering instructions as well as positional information.

4. In military aircraft, remote control has been used for the operations of fighter aircraft. Ground-controlled interception (GCI) systems have been devised to control aircraft to the point at which they may aim their weapons or make contact with the target by means of their short-range AI radar. However, the most outstanding example of the use of remote control is to be found in air-traffic control systems.

AIR-TRAFFIC CONTROL

5. Air traffic is generally one of three types:

(a) Air transport or air carriers that transport passengers and freight from one airport to another and generally travel along airways.

(b) General aviation or private flying which is mainly confined to local flying around small airfields.

(c) Military flying which includes local sorties and long-range sorties not connected with airways and sometimes at low levels.

6. Inevitably these classes are not clearly separated. However, general aviation aircraft may not be equipped to operate in accordance with air-traffic control instructions. Fortunately, most of these aircraft fly below 8000 feet, and those that fly above can be expected to be adequately equipped. Subsonic transports generally operate between 8000 and 20,000 feet if fitted with piston engines, or from 30,000 to 45,000 feet with jet engines. Supersonic aircraft will cruise 30,000 feet above the subsonic jets. Above 25,000 feet, aircraft will be well equipped and, as height is increased, so it will be increasingly possible for an aircraft to choose its own route without interfering with other craft. An exception to this rule may be the supersonic aircraft operating on important trunk routes. In order to operate the maximum number of daily schedules at times when the noise is acceptable, it may be necessary to concentrate traffic into certain limited periods during the day.

7. If the pilot can see another aircraft at 5 miles and keep well away from cloud, he may operate without the assistance of air-

traffic control if below a certain height. In these circumstances, an aircraft is said to be operating under VFR (visual flight rules). If these conditions are not present, the aircraft will operate under IFR (instrument flight rules). In practice, operations under IFR are common even when VFR conditions prevail.

8. Fig. 255 shows an elementary form of air-traffic control. The airman navigates his craft with the assistance of his aids and on

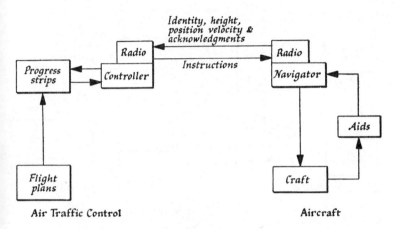

FIG. 255   Elementary A.T.C. system

request passes his identity and position to the controller by means of his radio communications equipment. The controller has a copy of the flight plan of the aircraft and prepares flight progress strips (page 314, para 9) which he updates according to the position reports that he receives. He compares these flight progress strips with the flight progress strips of other aircraft and, if he judges that separation is not adequate, he may instruct the aircraft to alter heading. To assist the controller in his decisions, simple rules generally define safe separation standards. For example, on an airway 10 miles wide, aircraft not separated by more than 1000 feet in height may be considered to be dangerously close if within 5 minutes' flying time of each other.

9. The simple system is entirely dependent on the accuracy of position transmitted by each aircraft and only operates if every aircraft is able and willing to co-operate. The next step will be to

use radar to provide the controller with a check on the position of aircraft that are co-operating and information regarding those that are not. The resulting system is shown in Fig. 256. The radar can be made to measure height as well as position. However, as aircraft operate on height as measured by pressure altimeter, this height finding cannot do more than indicate the height separation between aircraft.

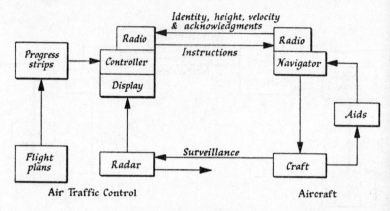

FIG. 256   A.T.C. with radar control

10. The main weakness in this or indeed in any system of traffic control arises from the problem of workload. The directing of any particular craft has to take into consideration reactions on all the other craft in the vicinity so that the workload demanded for control increases as the square of the number of craft rather than linearly with the number of craft. If a number of controllers are employed to handle the traffic density, an additional workload builds up due to the need for each controller to co-ordinate his efforts with others. As a result, the overall work load of a traffic-control system bears a relationship to:

$$(\text{number of craft})^2 \quad \text{and} \quad (\text{number of controllers})^2$$

It follows that the workload on an individual controller bears a relationship to:

$$(\text{number of craft})^2/(\text{number of controllers})$$
$$\text{and to (number of controllers)}$$

Since the workload on the individual controller increases with the number of controllers, there will come a point at which increasing the number of controllers to handle increased traffic can only increase the workload on the individual controller. The system will then be saturated.

11. *Data Link.* The workload can be lightened by eliminating the voice communication of position reports between the craft and the controller by means of an automatic data link. When interrogated by the controller, a transmitter in the aircraft will pass the identity, height, heading and air speed and the radar will find the position. The transmission of pressure height by the aircraft will provide information which is more relevant than that given by height-finding radar and also more accurate. The information transmitted by the aircraft will probably need to be monitored by the captain. However, the data link will leave radio voice-communication channels free for non-routine messages such as instructions by the controller and acknowledgments or requests by aircraft.

12. *Data Processing.* The improved communications provided by a data link system will demand that the increased flow of information be handled more expeditiously. The information from the data link may be fed together with the flight-plan information into a computer which will act as a data processer. This data processer can be made to operate an equipment that will up-date flight plans automatically. The basis of the complete system is shown in Fig. 257.

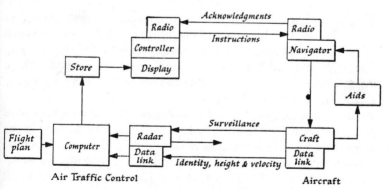

FIG. 257   A.T.C. with data link and computer

13. *ATC Computer*. The final step will be to use the computer to assist the controller in the making of decisions (see also page 32, para 26). The computer may be arranged to warn the controller when the minimum safe separation standard is likely to be violated. The controller may then be able to feed his suggested solution to the conflict into the computer so that the results in terms of other conflicts can be played back to him. The computer may eventually be developed so that it can suggest action, not only immediate routine action but also action in the form of long-term planning to relieve congestion. Nevertheless, because the computer can only take into account certain circumstances which its designers have foreseen, there will remain a need for the supervision of the human controller.

14. When this stage in the use of a computer is reached, the distinction between the strategic avoidance of collision by routing and the tactical avoidance of collision by subsequent alterations of heading or height may no longer apply. Strategic separation is necessary to simplify the task of the controller when many craft are involved. A computer can work so quickly and can handle so many craft apparently simultaneously that it may be practicable to handle traffic tactically instead of strategically. This could allow the individual aircraft full freedom of routing consistent with the achievement of sufficient separation.

3. AUTOMATIC CONTROL

1. The digital computer is able to remember instructions, to make choices, to solve extremely complex problems at great speed when those problems have been exactly stated and even to learn, once the area of learning has been precisely defined. These capabilities are so impressive that the limitations of an automatic system are apt to be obscured.

2. An automatic system can achieve only what its designers have foreseen it will need to achieve. It cannot possess flexibility in the sense that its human creator possesses flexibility. It cannot be provided with human discrimination. It relies on designers working in a different environment several years before the event and these designers cannot be expected to exercise clairvoyance.

Hence an automatic system can never be more than a genius who has been asleep for a period.

3. The use of automatic systems to assist the crew of a craft introduces special problems. When an operation has become the task of an automatic system, the man may lose the skill necessary to replace it in an emergency. If an automatic control system is available, the designer of a craft may take advantage of this to improve performance to a point where only automatics can exercise full control. Thus, once started down the road to automatics, there may be no turning back.

4. Nevertheless, it must be recognized that an automatic system is able to compress the months of effort of a team of designers working without immediate pressure into seconds of time in a critical situation. Furthermore, given the same situation, the automatics can be made to react consistently and, in this respect, the system may be superhuman. All that is required is that the conditions under which the system is to work can be exactly defined. It is because of this final requirement that the human supervisor may always be an essential element in the system and the craft will remain under the control of a master or a captain. Furthermore, the human passenger will not wish to trust his life to an equipment that does not fear death.

5. Automatic systems may be used for:

    (a) Missiles.
    (b) Space navigation.
    (c) Marine navigation.
    (d) Critical phases of air operations.

MISSILES

6. The three facets of missile automatic systems have been described independently as follows:

    (a) *Control mechanisms* (Chapter III). Generally fins mounted fore or aft, or movable wings in ram-jet missiles. Exceptions are long-range ballistic missiles and small field of battle weapons which may be steered by altering the direction of thrust.

    (b) *Control systems* (Chapter IV). Generally hydraulic but, in small missiles, may be pneumatic or even electric.

(c) *Guidance.* Normally by radio, either by command signals from a ground radar and computer, or by homing on to reflections from a directing radar (page 569, para 24). However, the ballistic missile may use inertial guidance (page 235, para 31, and page 302, para 12), the field of battle weapons may use visual guidance with signals sent along wires to the missile (page 411, para 25), the small anti-aircraft missile may use infra-red (page 414, para 6(a)), and homing torpedoes may use sonar (page 581, para 13).

SPACE NAVIGATION

7. There are three main types of space vehicle:

(a) Satellites that orbit the Earth in steady orbits.
(b) Satellites whose orbits can be varied.
(c) Space craft that operate out from the Earth into areas where the major gravitational pull originates from bodies other than the Earth.

8. *Uncontrolled satellites.* Uncontrolled satellites may be used for scientific experiments, for reconnaissance or for surveillance. However, the purely navigational applications will be:

(a) *Navigation.* Position information on the surface of the Earth may be provided. Transit (page 574, para 10) and repeater satellites (page 515, para 29) are examples.
(b) *Communications.* Satellites may act as repeaters or as transponders. In the latter event, they may store messages to be retransmitted when passing over a chosen area.
(c) *Weather mapping.* Satellites may photograph cloud formations. This may be combined with military reconnaissance.

9. The orbits of uncontrolled satellites in terms of the celestial sphere will generally be one of three types:

(a) *Polar.* A polar orbit will follow a celestial meridian. As a result, the coverage will be concentrated as shown in Fig. 258(a), and this will be uneconomic except possibly for weather mapping of polar source regions.

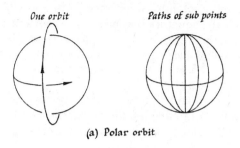

One orbit   *Paths of sub points*

(a) Polar orbit

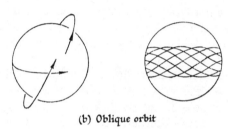

(b) Oblique orbit

FIG. 258   Satellite orbits

(b) *Equatorial.* The orbit will be planned to follow the celestial equator so that coverage will be limited to low latitudes unless the satellite is at a considerable height. Such orbits may be used by communications satellites or repeater satellites. If the orbit is at a height of about 19,300 n. miles, the satellite can in theory be made to remain stationary over a point on the equator. In practice, errors in height of the orbit will cause the satellite to drift round the Earth, ellipticity of orbit will cause it to oscillate in longitude, and the angular inclination of the orbit will cause it to oscillate in latitude.

(c) *Oblique or inclined orbit.* This can be arranged to give the optimum cover. For example, two satellites on orbits inclined at an angle of $67\frac{1}{2}°$ to the equator will provide coverage from 45° latitude to the poles, and two more satellites inclined at $22\frac{1}{2}°$ to the equator will provide coverage at latitudes below 45°. Oblique orbits will precess because the satellite, at extreme latitudes, will be attracted towards the equatorial bulge of the Earth and the orbit will accordingly precess at right angles as shown in Fig. 258(b). Navigational satellites may be expected to use oblique orbits.

10. The problem of launching a satellite into its orbit differs from that involved in launching a ballistic missile. A satellite may be launched initially along a similar path but, as the apex of the path is approached, the satellite will have to be accelerated, otherwise it will fall back to the Earth. Indeed, thrust will have to be available until the craft has finally been settled into its orbit. As a result, the period of guidance will be much longer than that required for a ballistic missile. However, radio guidance may be used since there will generally be no need to take precautions against counter measures.

11. The acceleration of a satellite into its orbit will require that its alignment be known precisely in all three axes. Stabilization of a satellite can be achieved by lock-follow devices locked on to the Sun and the stars. Alternatively, alignment in two of the axes may be by a horizon seeker working in the infra-red frequency band.

12. Once settled into orbit, precise stabilization may be relatively unimportant. The alignment of solar cells to within 10° of the direction of the Sun may be adequate for power, and several degrees will suffice for a directional aerial. Also it may be possible to allow the satellite to spin about one axis, thus reducing the requirement for alignment to only two axes.

13. *Controlled Satellites.* Controlled satellites may be used for military purposes, in particular for orbital bomb release and for anti-satellite operations. For operations in peace, controlled satellites will be used to assemble vehicles in space and to supply or refurbish satellites. The problem will therefore be one of interception.

14. It will be extremely difficult to place a satellite into an orbit similar to that of another satellite without the assistance of a large and complex computer supported by doppler to monitor the orbits of both satellites. Even with the assistance of the computer, the launch guidance is unlikely to be sufficiently precise

to place the two satellites very close together. It will therefore generally be necessary to compute a correction to the orbit of the intercepting satellite. For example, should the intercepting satellite be on a similar orbit to the target satellite but somewhat behind it, mere acceleration towards the target will not achieve interception but will simply cause the intercepting satellite to change its orbit. Therefore, a complex allowance has to be made and, subsequently, a contrary acceleration has to be applied when the intercepting satellite is close to the target.

15. The final stage in the interception will be the joining of the two satellites together. It is likely that this docking stage will be most readily achieved by a human pilot within the satellite since he will be able to use visual guidance that will increase in precision as contact is approached. He may be assisted by range measurement and doppler.

16. *Space Craft.* In operations to the Moon or to other planets, it seems certain that there will be three phases of control:

(a) *Launch.* The craft may first be launched into an orbit around the Earth and then accelerated out of this parking orbit into its space trajectory. To reach a planet whose orbit is outside the Earth's it may be necessary to wait until the craft on its orbit round the Earth is travelling in the same direction as the Earth in its orbit round the Sun. Hence the launch may be in two distinct phases and will be longer and more complex than the launch of a satellite.

(b) *Cruise.* For most of the cruise, the craft will continue on its trajectory undisturbed. However, it is likely that the original trajectory will need correction by bursts of thrust calculated perhaps with the assistance of astronomical observations taken from the satellite but resolved by a computer on the Earth. The process is known generally as mid-course guidance.

(c) *Terminal.* The first stage will be to reduce the trajectory to an orbit around the Moon or planet by decelerating with the aid of thrust. The final stage will be to reduce speed still further and to add thrust to offset gravity. For a return to the Earth, the satellite may be made to decelerate by making passes through the atmosphere. In the event of a landing on the Earth, the re-entry stage into the atmosphere will be followed by the final descent of the capsule by glide or by parachute.

MARINE AUTOMATIC SYSTEMS

17. It is only to be expected that, with the passage of years, the navigation of the ship will be increasingly supported by automatic equipment. There will, however, be a long step between the ship navigated partly automatically but with the master in control and the ship that carries no crew from the time that the outward bound pilot is dropped to the time that the inward bound pilot is picked up. The step to complete automation without any human intervention may never be worth taking at sea.

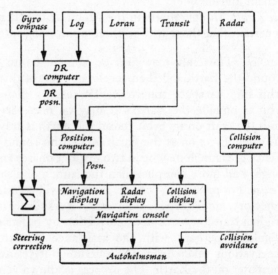

FIG. 259 Automatic ship system

18. Fig. 259 suggests the outline of a system that may operate under supervision. The compass and the log may feed information into a D.R. computer to be up-dated by Loran and Transit in a position computer. The corrected position may pass to the navigation display on the navigation console. Heading to steer

may be compared with actual heading and the error signal passed to the autohelmsman.

19. Radar information may be displayed in its raw form on the navigation console and fed directly into a collision computer. The collision computer may be programmed to ask a series of questions and to calculate the answers. Is the relative track of the target dangerous? Is it the duty of the ship to give way? What course should be followed? These and other questions (see page 273, para 41) can be answered extremely quickly by the computer, but the accuracy depends on the quality of the information provided. The problems of providing the information are very great. For example, it is difficult to determine how the ship could distinguish between a sailing boat and a powered craft.

20. The collision computer will have to feed over-riding instructions to the autohelmsman. In order that this may be monitored, the situation will have to be displayed on the navigation console. In addition, the navigation console will have to be fitted with controls so that the human supervisor can cancel the automatic instructions and pass his own orders directly to the autohelmsman.

AIRCRAFT AUTOMATICS

21. Automatic systems have been used for specific phases of air operations that demand speed of reaction and consistency of performance. Typical examples are automatic control of military aircraft during strike and of aircraft generally for landing.

22. The BLEU landing system has already been outlined (page 517, para 10). Other automatic systems are based on Flarescan, Regal or the Bell systems. Except when used for aircraft-carrier landings, it is important that the touchdown should be consistent so that decrab can be operated automatically at the correct instant before contact is made with the runway (page 126, para 8).

23. Automatic landing equipment has to be able to provide a guarantee of safety since the pilot will not be able to take over at the last moment. With such a high degree of safety, it will be necessary to discourage the pilot from last-minute action based on a lesser degree of reliability. For example, it will be dangerous for him to monitor the automatics on instruments with a lower

degree of redundancy since, unfortunately, instruments can be very compelling.

24. Although the pilot may not intervene with an equipment that is working within its designed limits, he must be available to intervene when it is evident that some element not allowed for in the design has been introduced. For example, the automatics cannot take account of a vehicle blocking the runway.

25. In addition to autolanding, an aircraft may be fitted with automatics to assist the pilot in other critical phases. Typical examples are:

(a) *Auto-overshoot*. An overshoot is the breaking off from landing, generally at the last moment, and the subsequent climb away.

(b) *Taxiway guidance*. May be used to control the roll out after touchdown and the subsequent taxying to the apron.

(c) *Auto-take-off*. This may include the monitoring of the ground run to make sure either that thrust is sufficient to ensure lift-off or that the take-off is abandoned in time. A system may also control the rotation of the aircraft to the flying attitude, the lift-off and the subsequent climb away.

4. SUMMARY

Systems may be based on:

(a) Direct control, particularly applicable to passenger craft.
(b) Remote control, used mainly for traffic organization.
(c) Automatic control used for tasks demanding extreme speed, accuracy and repeatability within an envelope of conditions which can be exactly defined.

DIRECT CONTROL SYSTEMS

Direct control systems may include a navigator's station which may not be able to provide a good view outside the craft.

Marine and aircraft instrument systems include handling instruments, heading displays, automatic switches and controls, and failure warnings. Instrument systems may monitor automatics or replace them.

REMOTE CONTROL SYSTEMS

Remote control is used for field of battle missiles, control of fighter aircraft, occasionally for marine terminal operations and, in particular, for air-traffic control.

Air-traffic Control. Control is exercised in IFR conditions, or in VFR conditions in congested areas, along airways and around airfields.

Flight strips may be up-dated by:

(a) Pilots' position reports.
(b) Radar, including height finding.
(c) Data links giving aircraft identity, height, heading and speed.

Information may be data processed and flight plans up-dated automatically.

Air-traffic control computers can warn the controller of conflicts, can be made to warn the controller of conflicts resulting from his intended actions, and can suggest actions not only to solve immediate conflicts but also to promote an orderly traffic flow.

AUTOMATIC SYSTEMS

Missiles. Apart from small field of battle missiles which are remotely controlled, missiles are generally controlled automatically.

Space Craft. Controlled automatically in launch and in acquisition of orbit or trajectory outside the Earth's gravitational field. They may be controlled directly for the final stages of contact between satellites or if the automatics fail.

Automatic control of satellites demands stabilization generally by lock-follow systems working on the Earth or on Sun, Moon or stars.

Satellite orbits may be:

(a) Polar for weather satellites.
(b) Equatorial for communications and repeater satellites.
(c) Oblique for navigational satellites.

Marine Automatics. May provide automatic navigation if continuously monitored by a human operator.

Aircraft Automatics. May provide automatic landing, taxiway guidance, and overshoot.

BIBLIOGRAPHY:

AUTOMATION AND GENERAL

This bibliography includes not only automation but also covers books and papers which deal with the navigating of ships or of aeroplanes or of some other class of craft.

AIR CUSHION VEHICLES
Hovercraft navigation, *J. Inst. Navig.*, **15**, 359.

AIR NAVIGATION
Anderson, E. W., *The principles of air navigation*, Methuen, London.
Bennett, D. C. T., *Complete air navigator*, Pitman, London.
Branch, W. J. V., see Williams, E. B., and W. J. V. Branch.
Dohm, J., *An airline navigation manual*, Pan American Navigation Service, New York.
Redpath, P. H., and J. B. Coburn, *Air transport navigation*, Pitman, London.
Weems, P. V. H., *Air navigation*, Van Nostrand, New York.
Williams, E. B., and W. J. V. Branch, *Air navigation, theory and practice*, Pitman, London.

AIR-TRAFFIC CONTROL
Colchester, C. D., *Air-traffic control*, Marconi W. T. Co., London.
Hunt, V. A. M., The long-term plan for air-traffic control, *J. Inst. Navig.*, **14**, 270.

ANIMAL NAVIGATION
Matthews, G. V. T., *Bird navigation*, Cambridge University Press.

AUTOMATION
Automation and remote control (translated from Russian), Consultants Bureau, Enterprises Inc., New York.
Clayton, C. T., *Merchant ship automation study*, U.S. Department of Commerce Maritime Administration, Washington, D.C.
Fearnside, K., Instrumental and automatic control for approach and landing, *J. Inst. Navig.*, **12**, 66.
Goode, H. H., and R. E. Machol, *System engineering*, McGraw-Hill, New York.

Lees, S. (Editor), *Airspace and instruments*, McGraw-Hill, New York.

Machol, R. E., see Goode, H. H., and R. E. Machol.

Majendie, A. M. A., *Automatic landing, the role of the human pilot*, Inst. of Aerospace Sciences national meeting, Seattle, 1962.

Pyke, M. *Automation, its purpose and future*, Hutchinson, London.

Richardson, D. W., *Jets, digital computers and mach 3*, International Air Transport Association meeting, Lucerne, 1960.

Roberson, R. E., Attitude control of a satellite vehicle, *International Astronautical Congress*, New York, 1957.

Wepster, A., The arrangement of navigational equipment in modern cargo vessels. *J. Inst. Navig.*, **15**, 241.

Wylie, Automation in marine navigation (Presidential Address), *J. Inst. Navig.*, **12, 1.**

GENERAL

Moody, A. B., *Navigation dictionary*, H. O. 220.

GLIDING

Irving, F. G., see Welch, A. and L., and F. G. Irving.

Kukuski, J., *Theory and technique of soaring*, Pitman, London.

Welch, A. and L., and F. G. Irving, *Gliding*, John Murray, London.

GUIDED AIRCRAFT

Ross, J. M., *Navigation guidance and control system for drone aircraft*, U.S. Army Signal Research and Development Laboratory, Fort Monmouth, New Jersey.

LAND NAVIGATION

Bagnold, R. A., Navigating ashore, *J. Inst. Navig.*, **6**, 184.

Gatty, H., *Nature is your guide*, Collins, London.

MARINE NAVIGATION

Admiralty manual of navigation, H.M.S.O.

Bowditch, N., *American practical navigator*, H.O. 9.

Cobb, G. (Editor), *Lecky's wrinkles in practical navigation*, Philip and Son, London.

Dutton, B., *Dutton's navigation and nautical astronomy*, U.S. Naval Inst., Annapolis.

Freiesleben, H. C., *Navigation*, Matthieson-Verlag, Hamburg.

Lee, C. V., see Weems, P. V. H., and C. V. Lee.

McClench, D., see Mixter, G. W., and D. McClench.

Mixter, G. W., and D. McClench, *Primer of navigation*, Van Nostrand, New York.

Noel, J. V., *Knight's modern seamanship*, Van Nostrand, New York.
Weems, P. V. H., and C. V. Lee, *Marine navigation*, Van Nostrand, New York.

MISSILE NAVIGATION

Ley, W., *Rockets, missiles, and space travel*, Viking Press, New York.
Locke, A. S., *Principles of guided missile design—guidance*, Hutchinson, London.
Puckett, A. E., and S. Ramo, *Guided missile engineering*, McGraw-Hill, New York.
Ramo, S., see Puckett, A. E., and S. Ramo.

SPACE NAVIGATION

Advances in astronautical sciences, Plenum Press, New York.
Adams, C. C., *Space flight*, McGraw-Hill, New York.
Angle, E. E., Attitude control techniques, *Navigation, U.S.A.*, 6, 66.
Baker, R. M. L., Navigational requirements for the return trip from a space voyage, *Navigation (Los Angeles)*, 1958.
Carter, L. J. (Editor), *Communications satellites*, Academic Press, London.
Carter, L. J. (Editor), *Realities of space travel*, McGraw-Hill, New York.
Farrier, J. S., see Robertson, E. E., and J. S. Farrier.
Kurnosova, L. V. (Editor), *Artificial earth satellites*, Plenum Press, New York.
Leondes, C. T. (Editor), *Guidance and control of aerospace vehicles*, McGraw-Hill, New York.
Robertson, E. E., and J. S. Farrier, *Guidance and control*, American Rocket Society Symposium, 1961, Stanford University Press, Stanford.
Technical Staff of Research Division Radiation Inc., *Space trajectories*. American Astronautical Society Symposium, 1960, Academic Press, London.

YACHTING

Olson, L. B., *Olson's small boat seamanship*, Van Nostrand, New York.
Rantzen, M. J., *Little ship navigation*, Herbert Jenkins, London.

Summaries

1. EQUIPMENTS
(Alphabetical Arrangement)

1. CONTROL SENSORS
Accelerometer (page 161, para 31; page 224, para 1; page 239, para 44).
Aerodynamic sensor (page 163, para 36).
Pendulum (page 165, para 6).
Position gyroscope (page 157, para 15).
Precision gyroscope (page 186, para 10; page 227, para 10).
Rate gyroscope (page 156, para 13).

2. DEAD-RECKONING EQUIPMENT
Air position indicator (page 289, para 32).
Doppler (page 220, para 1; page 299, para 2; page 572, para 1).
Drift sight (page 259, para 26(a)).
Ground position indicator (page 289, para 33).
Inertial navigation (page 224, para 1; page 302, para 10; page 397, para 24).
Plotting table (page 283, para 19).

3. HEADING REFERENCES
Astro-compass (page 451, para 4).
Auto-astro (page 429, para 31; page 449, para 22).
Directional gyroscope (page 184, para 3).
Gyro compass (page 176, para 3;   page 294 para 7;   page 318, para 1).
Gyro heading reference (page 186, para 9; page 238, para 40).
Magnetic compass (page 193, para 10; page 294, para 6).
Sun compass (page 453, para 6).

4. HEIGHT AND DEPTH
Altimeter, barometric (page 73, para 29).
Echo sounder (page 579, para 7).

Lead line (page 414, para 1).
Radio altimeter (page 516, para 5).
Radio pulse altimeter (page 510, para 12).
Vertical-speed indicator (page 217, para 19; page 239, para 43).

5. MEASURED SPEED
Air-data computer (page 218, para 20).
Air-mileage unit (page 214, para 8).
Air-speed indicator (page 101, para 8; page 215, para 12).
Log (page 214, para 7).
Machmeter (page 103, para 12(b)).
Pitot pressure (page 215, para 11).

6. NON-RADIO NAVIGATIONAL AIDS
Asdic (page 580, para 9).
Auto-astro (page 429, para 31; page 449, para 22).
Bearing compass (page 406, para 13(b)).
Bearing plate (page 406, para 13(a); page 452, para 5).
Inertia-astro (page 429, para 31; page 449, para 23).
Sextant and tables (page 419, para 1; page 437, para 23; page 453, para 8).
Sonobuoy (page 579, para 5; page 581, para 11).

7. RADIO NAVIGATIONAL AIDS (NAVAIDS)
  (a) *Bearings*
      ADF (page 495, para 27).
      Consol (page 538, para 2).
      Consolan (page 540, para 9).
      D.F. loop (page 486, para 1).
      HF D.F. Fixer (page 494, paras 20 and 22).
      UHF D.F. homer (page 494, para 22).
      VHF D.F. homer (page 494, para 21).
  (b) *Directions and Distances* (also see radar)
      Rebecca-Eureka (page 513, para 22).
  (c) *Distances* (radio altimeters in, page 516, para 5)
      DME (page 513, para 23).
      DMET (page 513, para 24).
      Oboe (page 514, para 27).
      Shoran (page 514, para 28).
      VLF distance measurement (page 518, para 12).

(d) *Glidepath*
ILS (page 500, para 14).
Interferometer (page 540, para 10).
(e) *Glidepath and position*
Bell system (page 565, para 11).
Flarescan (page 501, para 17; page 566, para 12).
GCA (page 565, para 9).
(f) *Glideslope*
Regal (page 501, para 17).
(g) *Hyperbolic Lattices*
Decca (page 531, para 28).
Dectra (page 535, para 37).
Delrac (page 537, para 44).
Gee (page 530, para 24).
Loran A (page 526, para 15).
Loran C (page 529, para 21).
Omega (page 537, paras 43 and 45).
Radio-mailles (page 536, para 39).
(h) *Positions*
Fixer (page 494, para 23).
Pin-point (page 377, para 2).
(j) *Radar*
AI (page 568, para 22).
Airways radar (page 563, para 1).
ASMI (page 566, para 13).
ASV (page 568, para 21).
GCA (page 565, para 9).
GCI (page 598, para 4).
H2S (page 568, para 21).
Harbour radar (page 562, para 20).
Height-finding radar (page 563, para 3).
Marine radar (page 557, para 1; page 594, para 13).
Naval radar (page 561, para 18; page 571, para 27).
Quadradar (page 566, para 14).
Weather radar (page 567, para 15; page 594, para 14).
(k) *Rho–Theta*
Navarho (page 519, para 17).
Tacan (page 500, para 11; page 513, para 24).
Vordac (page 513, para 23).

VOR–DME (page 513, para 23).
Vortac (page 513, para 24).
(l) *Track guides*
Aural beam (page 500, para 13).
Four-course beacon (page 496, para 2).
Navaglobe (page 498, para 6).
PVOR (page 499, para 10).
TVOR (page 499, para 10).
VOR (page 498, para 7).
VOR-doppler (page 576, para 16).

8. SATELLITES
Repeater satellites (page 515, para 29).
Transit (page 574, para 10; page 605, paras 8(a) and (9c)).

2. CRAFT

1. *Aircraft.* General references are too numerous. Special references to the following:

General aviation (page 598, paras 5(b) and 6).
Gliders (page 109, para 2; page 163, para 37; page 217, para 19).
Helicopters (page 107, para 24; page 108, para 28; page 115, para 21; page 123, para 22; page 540, para 10; page 597, para 23).
Private flying (page 598, paras 5(b) and 6).
STOL aircraft (page 102, para 11).
Supersonic aircraft (page 69, para 20; page 103, para 12(b); page 108, para 26; page 110, para 4; page 115, para 20; page 216, para 16; page 239, para 44; page 308, para 11; page 349, para 40; page 598, para 6).
VTOL aircraft (page 107, para 24; page 115, para 21; page 122, para 21; page 169, para 20; page 540, para 10).

2. *Land Vehicles* (page 15, para 2(a); page 106, para 17; page 113, paras 15(a) and 16; page 117, para 3; page 119, para 10; page 199, para 32; page 212, para 2; page 213, para 5; page 251, para 3; page 272, para 38; page 290, para 36; page 295, para 11; page 309, para 18; page 346, para 27).

3. *Marine Craft*. General references are too numerous. Special references to the following:

Acoustic homing torpedoes (page 581, para 13).

Air-cushion vehicles (page 98, para 3; page 103, para 12(a); page 105, para 14; page 110, para 6; page 119, para 9; page 122, para 20, page 219, para 26; page 224, para 14; page 573, para 6).

Ground-effect machines, see air-cushion vehicles, above.

Hydrofoil and planing craft (page 103, para 12(a); page 105, para 14; page 119, para 9).

Sailing craft (page 106, para 17; page 109, para 1; page 125, para 6; page 163, para 36; page 209, para 14; page 255, para 13; page 266, para 20; page 345, para 24; page 485, para 24; page 495, para 25; page 552, para 21).

Sidewall air-cushion vehicles (page 98, para 3; page 122, para 20; page 219, para 25).

Submarines (page 83, para 26; page 105, para 14; page 106, para 17; page 110, para 4; page 114, para 18; page 222, para 7; page 233, para 25(b); page 238, para 39; page 474, para 18(a); page 579, paras 5 and 6(b); page 580, para 9; page 581, para 12).

4. *Missiles* (page 26, para 2; page 110, para 5; page 114, para 18; page 119, para 10; page 123, para 23; page 158, para 19; page 161, para 32; page 222, para 8; page 257, para 20; page 375, para 20; page 410, para 23; page 414, para 6(a); page 569, para 24; page 603, para 6). Also the following are specially referred to:

Anti-ballistic-missile missiles (page 569, para 25).

Ballistic missiles (page 108, para 27; page 123, para 23; page 227, para 8; page 234, para 30; page 302, para 12; page 305, para 21; page 338, para 24; page 596, para 25).

Field of battle missiles (page 123, para 24; page 154, para 7; page 411, para 25; page 597, para 2).

Guided bomb (page 411, para 25; and page 569, para 25).

5. *Space Craft* (page 25, para 26; page 105, para 15; page 108, para 27; page 110, paras 4 and 5; page 114, para 19; page 116, para 24; page 123, paras 23 and 26; page 171, para 24; page 319,

para 4; page 338, para 24; page 375, para 20; page 414, para 6(b); page 571, para 31; page 572, para 2; page 574, para 9; page 604, para 7). Also there are special notes on:

Satellites (page 459, para 29; page 574, para 10; page 604, para 8).

3. TYPICAL INSTALLATIONS

1. The following are examples of systems in craft navigated by captains:

TABLE XV. TYPICAL SYSTEMS IN CRAFT

	Large ships	Sailing boats	Air-cushion vehicles	Passenger aircraft
Automatic control	Auto-stabilizer Auto-helmsman	(Automatic steering)	—	Auto-pilot (Auto-stabilizers)
Heading	Gyro compass	Magnetic compass	Gyro-magnetic compass	Gyro-magnetic compass (or gyro)
Speed	Log or engine speed	Log or pitot head	(Doppler)	Pitot head (Doppler)
Technique	D.R. plot	D.R. plot	(Moving maps)	Track guides (Doppler)
Position finding	Loran Astro Decca (Transit)	D/F Consol or Consolan Astro	(Decca)	VOR/DME ADF Loran (Doppler) (Decca)
Vertical navigation	Echo sounder	Lead line	—	Altimeter (and radio altimeter)
Anti-collision	Radar	Radar reflector	(Radar)	Air-traffic control

2. The following are examples of guided missile systems:

TABLE XVI.   TYPICAL MISSILE SYSTEMS

	Field of battle missiles	Anti-aircraft missiles		Ballistic missiles
		Ground launched	Air launched	
Control mechanism	Vanes in jet efflux	Fins (or wings in ram jets)	Fins	Gimballed motors
Guidance	Visual, wire transmission	Ground radar, homer in missile	Infra-red homer	Inertial platform and computer

3. The following are examples of space systems:

TABLE XVII.   TYPICAL SPACE SYSTEMS

	Launchers	Space craft
Control mechanism	Gimballed motors	Wheels and thrust
Guidance	Radar, doppler and ground computer	Astro in craft, doppler and ground computer

Index

1. CONTRACTIONS AND ABBREVIATIONS

Contractions and abbreviations in the book are listed below, but not symbols that are not contractions (i.e. A correction of compass). Convention dictates the placing of full points after each initial and after an abbreviation that does not finish with the end letter of a word. However, it is common practice to omit points at the ends of mathematical and meteorological abbreviations. Also period marks are omitted generally in air navigation, and therefore the normal convention has been discarded in the instances of aeronautical terms not used at sea. In addition, periods have been left out from contractions used for radio frequencies or radio modulations.

In case the reader may wish to refer to pages in the book by means of contractions or abbreviations, page and paragraph numbers are appended, but additional references are available in the Subject Index where mentioned.

2. SYMBOLS

The following symbols appear in the book and, with the exception of the symbols for gyroscopes, are in common use.

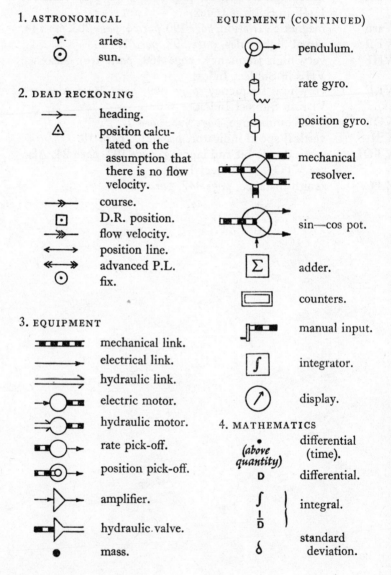

1. ASTRONOMICAL

♈.	aries.
☉	sun.

2. DEAD RECKONING

→	heading.
△	position calculated on the assumption that there is no flow velocity.
→»	course.
⊡	D.R. position.
→»»	flow velocity.
←→	position line.
«←→»	advanced P.L.
☉	fix.

3. EQUIPMENT

	mechanical link.
→	electrical link.
⇒	hydraulic link.
	electric motor.
	hydraulic motor.
	rate pick-off.
	position pick-off.
	amplifier.
	hydraulic valve.
●	mass.

EQUIPMENT (CONTINUED)

	pendulum.
	rate gyro.
	position gyro.
	mechanical resolver.
	sin—cos pot.
Σ	adder.
	counters.
	manual input.
∫	integrator.
↗	display.

4. MATHEMATICS

(above quantity)	differential (time).
D	differential.
∫ 1/D	integral.
δ	standard deviation.

5. RADIO

aerial.

microphone.

headphone.

6. WEATHER MAP

cold front.

warm front.

occlusion.

3. SUBJECT

(Paragraph numbers are referred to in italic figs.)